# ANARCHISM

# IN

# NORTH EAST ENGLAND

# 1882 — 1992

TYNESIDE ANARCHIST ARCHIVE

*Published by Active Distribution, May 2021. Printed in Croatia*

www.activedistribution.org

Layout by VoW

*ISBN 978 1 909798 90 8*

This work is dedicated to the memory

of Ewan Brown (1991—2019)

*A full obituary, and links to ongoing memorials is available at the following website: tynesideanarchistarchive.wordpress.com/for-ewan/*

**Contents**

**Contents**

Contents

# INTRODUCTION

'It is not the task of the historian to respect myth: but it is the task of the historian to confront defamation, misrepresentation and insult when they pass themselves off as historical narrative.'[1]

Before Albert Meltzer's death in 1996, I informed him of this proposed writing, for him to respond that the material I then had was 'only the tip of the iceberg'. Sadly a lot of this historical information was lost with the passing away of Albert. I hope that what I have uncovered and researched since that time does his memory justice.

A full and comprehensive study of anarchism in North East England is such an immensely large task that numerous difficulties arise. The majority of material recording the activities and general history of anarchism in the region is either, as I hope to show, blatantly ignored, irretrievable, lost, or predominantly unrecorded. This is especially true in the case of, for example, Tom Browns memoirs which written by hand whilst retired in his Gateshead home "a university student offered to type them if she could use parts for her thesis, but he died before she finished and his widow wasn't interested in their return. If they could be found they would be worth a ton of that passed off by the political research industry."[2]

The majority of 'down to earth' accounts of group activities, the histories of the lives of 'lesser personalities' within the movement, the lifetimes of activism despite, at times, prevailing odds, rarely, or do not appear in any of the 'official' histories of anarchism[3]. Even when they are available, the many accounts of grassroots working class anarchism and syndicalism are all too often completely ignored or misinterpreted by academic historians such as George Woodcock, who states "English anarchism has never been anything else than a chorus of voices crying in the wilderness, though some of the voices have been remarkable. At no time did the anarchists have even a remote chance of controlling the British labour movement. They have always been a small sect, hardly existent outside London and Glasgow, and in adapting themselves to their situation without admitting it, they have concentrated more than libertarians in many other countries on the graces of art and intellect."[4] This statement of ignorance, as I hope to prove, is undoubtedly untrue and nothing but mere assumption. Against this backdrop of biased information and 'official' histories on behalf of the academics and others riding their intellectual high horses of self esteemed importance, I have endeavoured to use as much source material that could be found from those directly involved and not pertaining to be a part of any limelight. Thus a voice is hopefully given to those historically, and traditionally ignored. Individual personalities go unexplored, priority given to what was being said, not the speaker. Vanity has no place here. It is common knowledge within the region that anarchists spoke at places like Newcastle's Bigg Market, and the Sandgate area of Newcastle Quayside, but I believe, for the first time, this history records what they were actually speaking about at open air meetings, what they were saying during lectures, and what they were actually writing about at the time, hence long sections of this book are given over to them. The ultimate aim here is not to glorify any personalities who at times purposely put themselves on pedestals, and there have been a few that have endeavoured to do so amongst local anarchists throughout the decades, but to give a voice to the voiceless, so to speak.

In highlighting our history we also draw attention to various aspects of anarchist belief, the ideal that sustains and drives our struggle, our ultimate aim. Errico Malatesta wrote "The word 'anarchy' comes from the Greek and its literal meaning is 'without government'; the condition of a people who live without a constituted authority, without government."[5] Government and the state exist in order to maintain and protect property and capital with no or little regard for human welfare or environmental destruction. In order to retain this position of dominance and authority, governments and states freely exploit in many ways with a view of keeping their equilibrium of control. "The anarchists are therefore justified in assuming that anarchism – the absence of government – will insure the widest and greatest scope for unhampered human development, the cornerstone of true social progress and harmony."[6]

Anarchism advocates a philosophy and workable practical examples of a new social system based on liberty and freedom for all, unrestricted by government, states, and their laws of domination, their perpetuation of competition not co- operation. Anarchists believe in a social system based upon mutual aid and voluntary co-existence where a share in the prosperity of un-exploited labour produce is shared equally by all. A system that breaks down all barriers of social control and separation such as racial, sexual, religious, and national divisions that are enforced upon us from birth. Anarchism is a society where the state, capitalism, and the ethos of wage slavery are abolished and replaced by self-managed production for everybody's need, not a minority's profit.

Anarchism, as a social theory, is concluded by Peter Kropotkin as "The name given to a principle or theory of life and conduct under which society is conceived without government – harmony in such a society being obtained, not by submission to law, or by obedience to any authority, but by free agreements concluded between the various groups, territorial and professional, freely constituted for the sake of production and consumption, as also for the satisfaction of the infinite variety of needs and aspirations of a civilised being."[7]

Part One of this history (1882-1920) charts the growth of anarchist groups in the region, the rise of the philosophy and its disassociation from parliamentary socialism, quite often explained in their frequent lectures and public street meetings, where every opportunity was seized for the tireless spreading of propaganda. The numerous visits of Peter Kropotkin and the advocating of basic anarchist communism, which when put into practice by local anarchists, resulted in the world renowned commune at Clousden Hill. The explosion of Syndicalism and its encouragement of direct action taken up with relish in the region, none more so than the Chopwell Anarchists and their agitation throughout local pits. The anarchist conference in Newcastle that was instrumental in drawing national interest and coverage. The outbreak of World War 1 and its horrific consequences for whole swathes of anarchist and syndicalist areas of the country, and the minor local resistance it perpetuated.

From 1920—1950, there is little evidence of specific anarchist activity in the North East, and what little there was is swallowed up in or accredited to, the authoritarian dominance of the Communist Party. Nevertheless in Part Two we look at the build up and events during the 1926 general strike, with eye witness accounts described by Tom Brown being of particular interest. The 1930s rise of local fascism and the unique local battles in its eventual defeat. The role of the North East during the 1936 Spanish Revolution through to World War Two and the industrial agitation throughout.

In Part Three (1950—1980) we again chart the rise of local anarchist groups from the gradual build up of the 1950s to the numerous groups and activities of the 1960s. The perception of the Sixties being a time of 'flower power' and 'peace & love' bares little resemblance to actual events of the period where industrial struggle and workplace militancy was at the forefront of activity, and again it is the words of Tom Brown that give us a narrative to many of the decades events.

The 1970s, after a slow beginning, bring specific anarchist agitation and activities to the fore with, for the first time, the production of local literature, the public squats highlighting the regions homelessness, and the rise of the local punk movement running alongside events. Anti royal and anti nuclear events also feature in prominence, whilst the joining together with other groups in the North of England and the creation of the North Eastern Anarchist Federation would encourage the cooperation for further shared activity.

Part Four (1980-1992) encompasses the majority of this study. The period gradually builds momentum to an eventual explosion of anarchist events and a rollercoaster ride of protest activity. Too much to mention so... read on, jump in, and enjoy the tumultuous journey.

What exactly can we conclude from this story? Well, we learn from our mistakes and we also learn from our history. The parallels are apparent throughout this study. Today a new local group, the North East Anarchist Group, with their regular anarchist history discussion meetings bare resemblance to the Newcastle anarchists of 1907 who hosted similar events. The lessons learned of the anarchists at the Clousden Hill Colony in Newcastle during the late 1890's are implemented by today's co-operatives, social centres, and communes / squats etc. The creation of group anarchist libraries for self, as opposed to state education, was happening with anarchists in 1907,with the Tyneside Anarchist Federation of the late 1960's early 1970's, with the Newcastle Anarchist Group in the early 1980's, and Tyneside Class War in the late 1980's and early 1990's, this is carried on today with Newcastle's Canny Little Library. The account of the Chopwell Anarchists and their laying of anarchist literature for sale on the grass at the annual Durham Miners Gala in 1913 brings back vivid personal memories from the late 1980's. This is our history, and this is the purpose of our history, this is our culture, a culture of resistance to the state and its enforced fallacies of indoctrination, control and coercion. And hopefully, this is our future, for the sake of our children or our children's children, who we may hope can live a life without the destructive nature of capitalism, and a planet recovered from its devastating ravages.

On a personal note, I work full time for little money, I am a single parent for half of the week, I don't have the time or finances to visit many libraries for research, and I am no academic with university funding or access to specialist literature collections. More time could have been spent interviewing past friends & accomplices, but instead between 30-40 letters, emails and repeated wider movement pleas were sent to local anarchists past and present, which elicited hardly a response. Therefore any factual errors, especially in particular dates of events, or any missed group or activity, couldn't be helped. And of course, some activities and events have deliberately been left out for security purposes.

Initially, and in my self-professed naivety with such things, the original manuscript of this book was filled with photos, pictures, press clippings, images of the covers of literature etc throughout the text. For the purposes of editing, space, copyright, printing and publishing (and saving the trees!) 99% of these have been removed.

It was during the editing of this book that the sad news reached us of the death of Stuart Christie (10 July 1946 — 15 August 2020). Stuart features a few times in this book and eagerly awaited its publication, and who also unsuccessfully searched for an actual picture of Tom Brown on our behalf, alas... I give thanks to the few who have helped, and, or contributed. I also apologise for the repeated use of the words 'man', 'mankind', 'men' etc within quotes. These were just a sign of the times. I have read works where (sic) is inserted after every mention of, for instance 'men', I haven't here as this annoyingly disrupts the text.

Nothing in this work is 'copyrighted'. I only ask if you use anything, quote or review, that you please send a copy to;

tynesideanarchistarchive@riseup.net

To see many of the original images that were to be included here, and to further read most of the published literature mentioned within, and much more please visit our website;

https://tynesideanarchistarchive.wordpress.com/

# PART ONE 1882—1920

## 1.1 THE FIRST VISITS OF PETER KROPOTKIN

Joseph Cowen, Jr., (9 July 1829 – 18 February 1900) The North East's 'radical' MP and owner of the Newcastle Daily Chronicle turned the newspaper into one of the most "freedom-supporting newspaper of the time. He also provided active support for movements of freedom in every country – Irish, Polish, Hungarian, Italian, Spanish, American, and Caribbean. His was a voice that consistently defended everyone's freedom"[8] Under Cowan's editorship, the Chronicle opened its pages to Russian anarchist Peter Kropotkin, inviting him to write a series of articles on life under Tsarist rule during 1881-1882. Cowen and Robert Spence – Watson (founder of The Friends of Russian Freedom[9]) then invited Kropotkin, who was eager to put the case of Russian freedom to an English audience, to a series of lectures.

Previously Kropotkin and his comrade Chaikovsky organised a series of lectures in London working men's clubs in which audiences were tiny but still prevailed in their description of the then situation in Russia as well as combining discussions on anarchism within the lectures.[10] Nevertheless, Kropotkin in his unwavering devotion to the cause of freedom prevailed through the small audiences, and we can imagine his surprise and delight when on the 1st July 1882 he "spoke in broken English before the Durham miners at their annual gathering"[11] to an estimated audience of between 40,000 to 50,000 people.[12]

The 1st Durham miners gala was in August 1871, which "From its inception the demonstration was a show of solidarity, unity and strength to show the powers that be at the time – the coal owners –that the miners were organised."[13] The gala was host to many speakers, but "Perhaps the strangest choice of speakersduring this period was that of Prince Kropotkin, the Russian anarchist, who addressed the gathering in 1882 and spoke about the conditions of the Russian peasantry and the

Tsar's police methods."[14] As well as Czarist oppression Kropotkin also spoke against coercion in Ireland noting "that in the English dominions people are also imprisoned without being judged"[15]. The Chronicle claimed his speech was the highlight of the day for the assembled masses, especially when "His account of the condition and resistance of miners in Russia and their willingness to follow the tactics employed by the Durham miners proved most popular"[16]

Kropotkin, three days after the Gala, was to "deliver an extremely interesting lecture last night, in Newcastle, on the "present state of Russia". There was a large audience, and at the conclusion of the lecture, a resolution was passed condemning the treatment of the Russian people by the Government of that country."[17] The following Monday evening Kropotkin spoke at the Nelson St lecture rooms, Westgate Rd to another crowded audience where "he was received with enthusiasm, a crowd of workers giving hearty cheers"[18]. In his lecture he condemned "the English press for its constant portrayal of the resistance to Tsarism as bloodthirsty nihilists"[19].

Buoyed by his receiving of enthusiastic audiences and support Kropotkin also declared "It is in Newcastle that a Russian revolutionary writer has, for the first time, found the means of disclosing in an English daily paper, the true state of Russia; and it is, again, in Newcastle that I have found for the first time the honour of addressing a large English audience, to relate, in plain words, the true state of Russia."[20]

Later in Durham, during a smaller meeting, Kropotkin, accompanied by Joseph Cowen was 'cordially received' and "addressed briefly upon the conditions of the Russian peasantry, who he stated were literally starving for the benefit of the rich aristocrats of the Empire. The resolutions were carried unanimously amid cheers, and cordial votes of thanks closed the proceedings"[21]

"Kropotkin also chaired a series of smaller meetings in the Haymarket pub in Newcastle, as well as street meetings. It was from the North–East that Kropotkin drew some small encouragement before he gave up on

England"[22]

Kropotkin then went on to lecture in Glasgow and Edinburgh. It was at the Newcastle and Scottish meetings that Kropotkin and Chaikovsky "according to the Russian police spies, collected small sums of money for 'the Red Cross of the Peoples Will'"[23] In Autumn Kropotkin, tired of his time in London, returned to France eager to join the apparent three thousand anarchists 'in Lyons alone'. After a spell in a French prison, the Kropotkin's wouldn't return to the North East for a further four years.

## 1.2 1886 NEWCASTLE AND SUNDERLAND LECTURES

After a concerted campaign and his eventual release from the French Clairvaux prison, Kroptkin again visited Newcastle as a guest of Cowan and Spence – Watson. His following lecture at the Tyne Theatre[24], Westgate Hill in late October was said to be to an audience of over 4000. Freedom paper at the time, over enthusiastically and wrongly reports (as it wasn't his first visit) "Encouraging tidings reach us from the North, where our comrade P.Kropotkin is explaining Anarchism before large and sympathetic audiences. His lecture on the 31st of October in the theatre at Newcastle-the first public exposition of our ideas in that part of England-was attended by over 4000 persons, and many hundreds were unable to obtain admittance."[25]

Socialist society's throughout the country had laid the foundations and encouraged public interest "in social reconstruction, and the novelty of anarchist communism".[26] This coupled with the 'prospect' of hearing an anarchist Russian real life Prince, ensured large and varied audiences.

The next day's unsympathetic press report of the lecture states;

> "Last evening Prince Peter Kropotkin opened the session of the Tyneside Sunday Lecture Society by a discourse on Socialism and Anarchy. It is probable that after this experience the Society will not again risk its future by engaging lecturers who treat on

such combustible topics as these. A poorer lecture, probably, was never delivered under circumstances so well calculated to give it an importance to which it had no natural claim. Mr R.S. Watson, the Chairman, said there was much to think about in what Prince Kropotkin had said; and, in a restricted sense, that is quite true, but those who trouble themselves with speculations on the subject will think much less about the views expressed than about the more curious problem of how a cultivated, and no doubt in some respects,able man, came to acquire them. If prince Kropotkin were not a Russian noble, if his name were not associated with great misfortunes, if he had not proved his sincerity by suffering, few of those who heard the lecture last night, or who have read the reports of it, would hesitate to characterise the whole of the discourse as so much maundering nonsense. It is at once amazing and mournful that a man who is evidently of fine character, who is capable of great and high enthusiasm, and who possesses that rarest of all human qualities – perfect willingness to endure martyrdom for an idea – should have wrecked his life, and faced exile, imprisonment, misery and deprivation, for such futile reasons as those which he explained to his audience at Newcastle last night. It will be admitted by even the most determined opponent of Socialism that the subject is at least arguable. It cannot be pooh-poohed into significance. It has a great deal to say for itself in various ways, and it must be met by argument rather than a contemptuous wave of the hand. Whilst, however, this may be said of Socialism in general, it has no application to Prince Kropotkin's lecture, which is less an argument than a loose statement of discontent, and which concluded by setting forth a system which would be utterly destructive of the ideas set forth at the commencement. It is evident, indeed, that Prince Kropotkin feels very strongly, but scarcely reasons at all. His argument is that of the hungry man who feels that he is being persecuted by the community because there is bread in a shop around the corner. That he has a very genuine pity for the poor we do not doubt; that he has thought out an effective way of helping them his lecture peremptorily forbids us to hope."[27]

The press report continues in a similar vein, with the authors biased and pre- conceived notions against Kropotkin's lecture, whilst not actually letting us know, in an impartial manner, what Kropotkin was actually saying during the lecture.

Wednesday, November 10th, 1886, and Kropotkin also "addressed a meeting of Socialists in the Temperance Hall, Gallowgate, Newcastle, on the nationalisation of land"[28] Whilst a few days later The Sunderland Daily Echo gives a more reasonable account of his lecture at the towns Assembly Hall on November 14th 1886, which I quote in full for elements of posterity.

> "Last night Prince Kropotkin lectured in the Assembly Hall on the principles of Socialism. Mr G. O. Wight occupied the chair, and there was a numerous attendance. In the course of his address Prince Kropotkin said that the propagation of Socialism was not now the work of a few agitators, but was becoming a power in Europe. Socialist ideas were at the bottom of the Chartist movement in England, and also behind the Republican movement in France in 1848, and they still, notwithstanding all attempts at suppression, existed in France, Spain, and Germany. So strong were they in the later country that they had no less than 22 Socialist representatives in the German parliament. What was this Socialism, the principles of which so many were ready to sacrifice liberty, life, fortune, and everything to promote? Socialism said that each man in the country should have a proper share of everything he produced, but ten people in this country were producing what 45 people were squandering, and wealth was getting into the hands of the few. It was said that if a man spent a thousand pounds over a luxury he didgood, inasmuch as he provided work, but that was not the question. The thousand pounds would be of more value to the State it spent over, say, improved wellbeing's for the working classes. There was a good deal of talk just now about

over-production, but did it mean that everyone had too much clothing and food, and fuel? No. It meant that the purchasing power of the working men of England had so much decreased that they could not produce for themselves, and that the capital which should be used for producing the necessaries of life for them was locked up in other hands. It had gone in loans to the Russian Government, loans on Turkish railways, and in supporting the Khedive of Egypt, who was squandering it in vice and luxury. It was said that after the workman got his wages the balance went to those who managed the industry, but were there nottoo many managers? (Hear, hear.) He contended that the workmen employed in the making of the Atlantic cable and in the digging of the Suez Canal were as much entitled to the results of their labours as M. De Lesseps and the capitalists. While he admitted that the position of the workman was better than it was formerly, it could not be denied that the richer portion of the community had increased their riches in a much greater portion, and pauperism had developed more and more. They wanted the hours of labour limiting, so that the benefits of general, technical, and scientific education might be more widely diffused. He contended that if everyone worked, and was a producer, four hours labour per day was quite sufficient, though it had been calculated that even an hour and a half per day would suffice to place every man in the position of those now enjoying an income of £300 a year. In order to bring about this great change, Socialism said that it was necessary for the community to be common proprietors of land, machinery, and everything necessary for production. The idea of nationalisation of land had made great progress during the last four years, and that implied also the nationalisation of capital and machinery. There were two systems of Socialism – State Socialism, by which the people would elect representatives to manage the common property, and Anarchy. He was an Anarchist, and would do without a Government. A great portion of our life was now carried on without Government interference, and why not all of it? It might be asked who would put the thieves in prison? But they would do without prisons, which were but universities of crime. The best way to do without prisons was to prevent crime by seeing that children were properly educated and not abandoned to the streets by vicious parents; to place them in conditions under which they would become more moral. Under such conditions surely humanity would grow to be much better and require less Government. (Applause.) Mr W.M. Brockie, in moving a vote of thanks to the lecturer, said he doubted whether a better sermon had been preached in Sunderland that night. (Hear, hear.) The subject of the lecture was one on which they should all think deeply and earnestly. – The motion was seconded by Mr J. Crown, and carried unanimously."[29]

Kropotkin, later reflecting on the period tells us that "As I had, as a rule, accepted the first invitation I received to stay the night after the lecture, it consequently happened that I stayed one night in a rich man's mansion, and the next night in the narrow abode of a working class family. Every night I saw considerable numbers of people of all classes; and whether it was in the workers small parlour or in the reception rooms of the wealthy, the most animated discussions went on about socialism and anarchism till a late hour of the night – with hope in the workman's home, with apprehension in the mansion, but everywhere with the same earnestness."[30] This wouldn't be the last visit of Kropotkin.

## 1.3 THE NEWCASTLE SOCIALISTS AND CHICAGO ANARCHISTS

The execution of the Haymarket martyrs was an important event in the historyof anarchism internationally, and Newcastle was no exception. In the spring of 1886 workers struck at the McCormick Harvesting Machine Company in Chicago demanding an eight hour day. On May 1, 1886, a large May Day parade was held in Chicago, and two days later, a protest outside the McCormick plant resulted in a demonstrator being killed. A mass meeting was called to take place on May 4, to protest what was seen as brutality by the police. The location for the meeting was to be Haymarket Square in Chicago. At the May 4th meeting a number of radical and anarchist speakers addressed a crowd of 1,500 people. The meeting was peaceful, but the mood became confrontational when the police tried to disperse the crowd. As scuffles broke out, a bomb was thrown, seven policemen were killed, and it's likely that most of them died from police bullets fired in the chaos, not from the bomb itself. Four protestors were also killed. More than 100 people were injured. In the following public outcry newspapers throughout the US denounced "anarchists," and advocated hanging those responsible for the Haymarket Riot. Looking for scapegoats, a number of arrests were made, and charges were brought against eight men.

> "After a time August Spies, Albert R. Parsons, Louis Lingg, Michael Schwab, Samuel Fielden, George Engel, Adolph Fischer, and Oscar Neebe were indicted for the murder of Mathias Degan. The prosecution could not discover who had thrown the bomb and could not bring the really guilty man to justice, and as some of the men indicted were not at the Haymarket meeting and had nothing to do with it, the prosecution was forced to proceed on the theory that the men indicted were guilty of murder, because it was claimed they had, at various times in the past, uttered and printed incendiary and seditious language, practically advising the killing of policemen".[31]

One of the condemned men killed himself (Louis Lingg) in prison, and four others were hanged on November 11, 1887 (August Spies, Albert R. Parsons, George Engel, & Adolph Fischer) The three remaining men had their death sentences commuted to life in prison, they served 6 years before their eventual pardon. This state sanctioned murder sparked worldwide protests, including Newcastle.

During a strike in the Northumberland coal field the Social Democratic Federation asked Tom Mann "to go to Newcastle-on-Tyne, and to report as to whether the prospect was favourable for educational work". "I commenced operations, and remained in Northumberland and Durham all that year. Every Sunday evening I addressed large audiences at the Cattle Market, Newcastle; every Wednesday I also had a meeting in Newcastle. On Sunday mornings I addressed meetings at the Quayside and on other days of the week in some mining town or village in Northumberland or Durham."[32] Although not an anarchist himself, Mann, along with the rest of the entire labour movement worldwide was obviously angered at the events in Chicago.

Sunday morning 13th November a large meeting took place on the Newcastle Quayside, which then proceeded to march to Newcastle cathedral (where the archbishop of York was to preach) behind red flags. The protest against poverty and the churches role in denying it attracted about 200 people. On Sunday afternoon, a mass meeting was held in the Bigg Market, Newcastle to upwards of 1000 people;

> "Mr Mann, in the course of an energetic speech, said he cared no more for being taken by the neck of the police than did the anarchists in America. He called on those present who believed that the executed anarchists had done their duty and had become martyrs to let their voices go up in cheers. (Three cheers of great heartiness were then given.) That was not bad for Newcastle, they were getting on, and had done what three months ago they would not dared to have done. There were not four more noble men than those who were hung in America, and it was their conduct he asked them to imitate. They had

> spoken the truth in saying that those who were revelling in luxury were doing so at the expense of those who were crushed in the gutter. The amount of wealth produced every year in the country was four times as much as the working classes took. Who took the rest?" and that "The socialists hated and abhorred robbery, and they meant to put a stop to legalised robbery in the quickest way they could".[33]

The annual May Day march through Newcastle has been a regular event for generations of anarchists ever since. An account of some of these will follow later.

## 1.4 1887—1888

November 29th 1887 see's the next mention of anarchism in Newcastle, with a local press report on the visit and lecture of Auberon Herbert. This we haven't given much space as Auberon Herbert was not an anarchist as the Northern Daily Mail wrongly reported in a usual case of the misconception of anarchism.[34]

Auberon Herbert (1838—1906) was a 19th-century British political philosopher and Member of Parliament, who recognized that each individual has inalienable rights to direct his own mind and body, and to keep and use the product of his own effort. In defence of these rights, Herbert advocated a strictly limited, voluntarily funded, rights-protecting government. This social system, which Herbert called "voluntarism," is what is known today as laissez- faire capitalism, or 'Anarcho-Capitalism'!

1888, and Kropotkin is again appearing in local media, where in an interview covered by the The Shields Daily Gazette, conducted at his Harrow home, Kropotkin would remark, whilst speaking of his two years spent at the 'terrible fortress of St Peter and Paul prison';

*"My longing to hear the human voice became more and more intense. At last, at the end of 18 months, I for the first time heard someone speak. First there came the high tones of a woman's voice, and then the low gruff tones of a soldier's. This woman was a fellow prisoner, and had not only broken the rule about talking herself, but had actually drawn the warder and the soldier into conversation. Ah,* women are born anarchists. They can upset discipline anywhere," said the Prince, with a happy twinkle in the eye."[35]

## 1.5 THE PRINCE ON THE PROBLEMS OF THE CENTURY

Sunday December 2nd 1889 saw the visit of Kropotkin again to Newcastle and his lecture at the Tyne Theatre. Kropotkin, living in Harrow and suffering from ill health, would regularly lecture throughout the country on everything from anarchism to his prison experiences, whilst "He turned his provincial tours to good purpose, for, with the habit of observation gained in his youth, he neglected no opportunity to inspect factories, workshops and coal mines in the towns he visited, while he always kept an acute eye on the state of agriculture".[36] These observations were collected together as a series of articles and later collated together as the book *Fields, factories and WorkshopsTomorrow* .1899. The book, coupled with *The Conquest of Bread*, would be instrumental in their influence of the Clousden Hill Free Communist & Co-operative Colony (1894-1902) in Newcastle (more on which later).

During the lecture 'problems of the century', Kropotkin firstly thanked the Newcastle audience for their repeated appreciative kindness he always received on his visits, before showing that the current and chief problems ofthe century were due to the social question.

"He would try to show that other problems were merging into

the great problem, and rendering its solution the more necessary and the more unavoidable. If they cast a broad glance upon history they at once discovered that the great feature of history – that the very essence of history – from olden times was the continuous struggle between the masses who were endeavouring to realise a life of liberty and equality and the small minority which was struggling on the contrary to introduce a life of inequality and submission of the masses. They could go as far back as they liked in the history of humanity, and everywhere they would find the same struggle."[37]

Examples were given including the first strikes of Egyptian workers during the construction of the pyramids, to early Buddhist movements striving to highlight the great differences between the possessors or wealth and those who created the wealth, and the need for the abolishment of this divide, to early 'Christian' movements against the inequalities of the expanding Roman empire, to the French revolution. Kropotkin also stressed that preceding philosophies (of educated peoples) had only tried to excuse "what had already existed, to explain what existed, and to perpetuate what existed"[38]. "in his opinion, the point in the philosophy of the 18th century which made its most important to the 19th century was that it had shown that man was not a wicked person, that humanity was not necessarily imbued with all possible vices, but that on the contrary humanity, if it had the opportunity of developing freely, would develop better qualities than it had until now."[39] Kropotkin's lecture not only highlighted his perception of what constituted the 'problems of the century', but also practical solutions to the aforementioned problems, including mentions of soil/ land cultivation in order to produce more for the benefit of the community, and society in general, not the enrichment of the owners of capital.

The lecture concluded with;

"It was one of the greatest problems of our times to organise in such a way that while maintaining the complete liberty of the individual they might combine efforts so as to organise production for the benefit of society. We had made immense advances towards socialism. What had prevented socialism from being introduced? It had always been said we were not good enough for it. He thought, however, that the great reason why no serious attempt had been made in centuries past was because our production was so infinitely small. Now it had immensely increased. At the same time the forces of organisation had immensely grown. The workers all over Europe had shown that they had a formidable power of organisation. The future before them was smiling. Among the workers the philosophy of pessimism had not many adherents. It was because the work was one of hope and of a change in conditions. They had to look upon that matter, not simply as one affecting their own personal conditions, but as one affecting a general improvement for the greatmass of humanity. There was plenty of scope for their activity before they reached the emancipation of humanity and attained the goal of liberty and equality."[40]

## 1.6 1890 - KROPOTKINS DARLINGTON LECTURE

Kropotkin once again visited the North – East during 1890, as *Freedom* reports "On 9th March Kropotkin spoke before the Sunday Lecture Society at Darlington, upon "The Problems of our Century." 'Taking the historical development of society as his text, the lecturer pointed out the necessity of Socialism. The lecture was extremely well received and in the discussion which followed the audience admitted the perfect reasonableness of the arguments put before them."[41]

Pre-empting his visit, the local paper would advertise the event as well as givea lengthy expose of Kropotkin's life, and noted;

"The standpoint from which Kropotkin approaches these problems is not that of the average Englishman. Though he is familiar with our language, and with our public life, and is by no means unknown on North Country platforms – Prince Kropotkin approaches our social problems from the extreme Continental rather than the English point of view. He is, like many other advocates of extreme opinion, an earnest and even mild and gentle man in social life. His lecture cannot fail to be of extreme interest, and he himself is a picturesque figure."[42]

The press report that later covered the lecture, I quote in full, again for historical posterity and interest.

"Under the auspices of the Darlington Sunday Lecture Society, Prince Kropotkin delivered an address in the Central Hall, last night, on "The Problems of Our Century." The lecturer speaks with a pronounced foreign accent, so much that it required quite a mental effort to follow him last night in a building not remarkable for its good acoustic properties. The intellectual countenance of the Russian exile, while "sickled o'er with the pale cast of thought" shows unmistakable traces of the physical sufferings he has undergone in the cause of liberty. At the outset, he referred to the demonstration in London that night, taken part in by all political parties, to denounce the atrocities which had been committed in Siberia – the flogging of women and other political exiles. This formed one of the episodes, he said, of the great and immense struggle which had been going on for centuries. On the one side were the masses, struggling to obtain freedom and equality, caring for nothing else but the possibility of working and enjoying the fruits of their labour and having a certain liberty of movement and of life. On the other side were the minorities, which always tried to subdue the masses, to compel them to more labour than was necessary for their own maintenance, and to enforce upon them conditions of authority and misgovernment. It was often said that equality was not possible upon men; but the longer he lived the more he came into contact with persons of all nationalities and positions in society, the more he was brought to the firm conviction that men did not enter life with irregularities as immense as those which were created by artificial conditions of life. (Applause.) There was not naturally an immense inequality between intellects, but there was an immense variety of capacity. The tendency of the century, and the first great problem to be solved was to give everyone an equal chance for starting in life. (Applause.) Great results had been achieved in this direction already, but much more remained to be done. Society was divided into two classes – the brain worker and the manual worker. We heard so much now a days about technical education that we must come to the conclusion there was something wrong in this division. Neither brain work nor manual work was the better for the division. Watt, with all his intelligence, could have not made a practical engine out of his invention without the assistance of skilled labour; and he saw that the chief engineer of the Forth Bridge made a similar admission the other day with regard to that latest marvel of engineering skill. The inventions of the steam engine, the telephone, etc, did not emanate from professional men of science but from men who were accustomed to work in the workshops, just as our great Newton was able to make his own telescope and ground the glasses for his instrument. We need not send expeditions to Africa to find customers for our produce. The natural customers for that produce were the inhabitants of these islands. (NOTE – *the followingsentence can be taken out of context and be deemed as racist in its implication, but bear in mind this was written by a reporter in 1890 as to what they perceived were the words Kropotkin spoke.*) Every babe born in this country was a better consumer of produce than a dozen Zulu chiefs. (Laughter and applause.) The whole of our production was made not for what was wanted but that it might give some benefit to those people who were in possession of the instruments of labour. To write a "Utopia" was not a solution of the social problem, which, however, could be brought about by the combined efforts of everyone who was willing to contribute his own share towards the improvement of the condition of his country, and without

> those great disturbances which the obstinacy of the ruling class rendered unavoidable in the last century in the great French Revolution. (Applause.)"[43]

"Kropotkin never regarded his anarchism as utopian, and always contended that it represented a method of social organisation which could be put into practice at any given moment."[44] These progressive and illuminating ideas of anarchist – communism espoused by Kropotkin would have far reaching effects and aspects of influence, aspiration and above all hope amongst the existing anarchists throughout the North East during the following decade.

## 1.7 THE 1890s

Franz Kapir was born 1858 in the Bohemian town of Slany, 25km North West of Prague. Inspired by Johann Most[45], in 1882 Kapir declared himself a revolutionary anarchist. "When his activism attracted the unwelcome attention of the authorities Kapir opted for exile."[46] Renaming himself Frank Kapper. Arriving in London around 1887, Kapper secured work as a tailor, and in his spare time was a (founding?) member of the Autonomie Club. As worked soondried up in London, Kapper headed north seeking employment. "Settling in Newcastle, in November 1890[47] he founded the towns first 'Anarchist-Communist Group'. By the middle of the following month he was confident enough to advertise weekly meetings at Lockhart's Cafe, Bigg Market."[48] "When Tyneside libertarians founded Newcastle Anarchist Communist Group, it was 'comrade Andrew Hall – the socialist navvy of Chesterfield' who they chose to headline their first public event on Sunday 28 December 1890 who 'addressed a large workmen's meeting on the Quay, and in the evening spoke against parliamentary action."[49] An accomplished linguist, Kapper wasted no time in teaching students and fellow comrades within the group French, "His French class was apparently popular and was certainly different: language teachers usually relied on French literary classics as teaching materials, whereas

Kapper translated books and pamphlets on Anarchism."[50] And in particular those of Kropotkin, which showed Kapper's gradual move from revolutionary anarchism preached by the likes of Johann Most, to a firmer conviction of anarchist-communism.

> "In those halcyon days before 'Labourism' suffocated activism, NACG wasted no opportunity in steering the local labour movement away from the illusory appeal of electoral politics. In the New Year (1891) NACG hosted a series of public debates where anarchist speakers opposed the statist program of the Social Democratic Federation (SDF). In March the libertarians explained their positive alternative with a talk on, 'Organisation under Anarchism'."[51]

On the 18th March, 1891, an international gathering of anarchists in London was held to commemorate the events of the Paris Commune where Malatesta, Louise Michel, Kropotkin, Yanovsky, John Turner etc all gave passionate speeches. *Freedom* then publicised reports from groups, unable to attend, on events in their area to commemorate the event, including "NEWCASTLE-ON- TYNE.-March 22nd, Comrade Kapper opened a discussion on the Paris Commune. The opening was a very interesting review of the Commune and the events which led up to it. Great interest was evinced by the asking of many questions afterwards."[52]

It is a false notion that anarchism only became established throughout the North East with the arrival of Kapper, especially in Sunderland[53]. Highlighting more 'well known' personalities or names within the anarchist movement only serves to discredit and undermine the work carried out by 'lesser known' activists. A substantial amount of historical coverage ignores this contribution, as Cores states, "Most of the work which was done was due to the activities of working men and women, most of whom did not appear as orators or as writers in printed papers but sold or gave away innumerable journals, pamphlets, and books, mainly at their own expense, in order to influence the minds of others. They worked at it day and night, everywhere, pleading for the ideal."[54]

This is especially true in the North East.

Kapper didn't move to Sunderland until the end of 1892 – early 1893, and *Freedom* claimed "A new group has been formed in Sunderland and as our energetic comrade Kapper is there now we expect it will soon be a big group."[55] The influence and activities of anarchists were already well established in Sunderland, where on the 28th Jan 1892, as part of a series of weekly lectures at the Monkwearmouth Liberal Club, a David Bell gave a discourse on Anarchism. From "the outset the lecturer protested against the prevalent notion that Anarchism and socialism were identical. The only similarity was that the anarchists and the socialists equally disliked landlordism and capitalism, and that each were eager strivers to seek the abolition of what they termed injustices. The simplest definition of anarchism was "no law", for they wished to abolish all authorities and all government. Opposite to that was the doctrine of the socialists, who wished that the state should have the full control over the productions of wealth. – A discussion ensured, which was participated in by M. Morrison, J. Crown, Gibson, and Watson."[56] Already, as was becoming the trend throughout the country, the differences between the anarchist communists and parliamentary socialists of such organisations as the Social Democratic Federation, and the formation of the Independent Labour Party 1893[57], theoretical differences were naturally coming to the fore.[58]

Meanwhile back in Newcastle, Sunday November 28th 1892, at a meeting of the Independent Labour Party held at the lecture room in the Groat Market, experienced local anarchist speaker Thomas Pearson lectured on the 'Aims of Anarchy' to a large attendance;

> "He said the opposition against anarchism was mainly on accountof the name. He defined anarchism as a society without authority in the political and social relations of the individual, placing its first principle as liberty. It was of necessity opposed to all government by force. Government was an institution to govern or to force individuals to obey a written code of laws. In lecturing in different parts of the country he had often been

asked what would anarchists put in the place of government. This question was asked on the assumption that government was a useful institution and was absolutely necessary. This he denied, as government had shown conclusively that it could not carry out the function it was expected to perform, viz, to prevent crime. The two worst of these were murder and theft. Crime he defined as the infringement of another's liberty, therefore, he contended that the system of government was the greatest crime of the present age. The method adopted by orthodox parliamentarians to stop the crime of murder tended, in his opinion, to perpetuate it. With regard to theft, he contended that the protection of monopoly by the state was the means of preventing the government even trying to put a stop to it. He considered that so long as we had extreme poverty we should always have crime in oneor other of its forms, and government had not been able to prevent it. Was it not a question of cause and effect? Ingersoll said that it was safe to say that government had committed far more crimes that it had prevented. For hundreds of years government had tried to destroy virtue and honesty by force and had failed. Might not the same argument apply to vice? Did we understand the causes that had led to crime? Did not punishment degrade not only the punished but the punisher? Anarchists would put in the place of government free association."[59]

Agnes Henry, an anarchist originally from Tipperary, Ireland, and was associated with *Freedom* paper as a regular correspondent, amongst other activities[60]. On her 'tour of the north' which was predominantly in Scotland, Agnes also stayed in the North East for a number of weeks, agitating as ever.[61] As her 1893 letter to *Freedom* states;

"Although almost a matter of ancient history for these hurrying, scurrying modern times, I feel bound, by the promises I made, to give some account of the tour from which I have recently returned.

On 27th July, I left London for Sunderland, my chief object being to get as near as I could to the mining districts of Durham and Northumberland. In Sunderland I found a very few Anarchist comrades, who had only quite recently known of one another's existence in the same town. There had never yet therefore been any associated action among them. Now, however, they have formed a group, and will certainly do all they can, together with a few more comrades in Newcastle-upon-Tyne, to push the propaganda both in the colliery districts round about and in the towns among the shipbuilders and others.

The great difficulty is the want of an able speaker, Comrade Pearson in Newcastle being the only experienced one among them. But, I may add that Comrade Black of Sunderland bids fair to become a good speaker if he would only persist in the attempts he has made.

Unfortunately, for lack of thorough organisation, I was not able to speak among the miners as often as I would have wished, but nevertheless the thin end of the wedge was introduced in places where Anarchist Socialism had not been heard before. During the three weeks of my stay our meetings were well-attended and elicited intelligent and sometimes enthusiastic interest on the part of the listeners. In short, my experience strengthened me in my opinion that there is no more fertile soil where the seed of Anarchist Communism could be spread than among the miners and the other independent spirited labourers of the North. Meetings were held in various parts of Sunderland and Newcastle, and in the colliery centres of Monkwearmouth, Ryhope, Seaham and Chester-le-Street. Also a fair amount of literature was sold."[62]

1893 also saw the beginnings of worldwide repression of the anarchist movement, following instances of 'propaganda by the deed'[63] including an exploding bomb in the French Chamber of Deputies, and another in a Barcelona theatre. The year before also saw the Walsall anarchists trial where anarchists in the area were framed by police spies for 'incitement to murder' and 'conspiracy to cause explosions', during which protests at these events were held throughout the country, and as Quail notes, papers like *The Commonweal* and other anarchist literature was selling in vast quantities, especially during protest meetings, including Newcastle.[64]

Many anarchists were "resolutely condemning propaganda by the deed as a concept but regularly backing arrestees as victims of state repression".[65] Local anarchists would no doubt agree with *Freedoms* sentiments in that;

> "*Freedom* did not either advocate or applaud outrage; its own policy advocated a continuous and energetic endeavour on the part of the workers, organised in trade unions, co-operative societies and other voluntary associations, to obtain by direct action, such as refusing to work as wage slaves, the control of the means of production; so that the producers and distributors may become their own employers, with the right to dispose of what they make."[66]

Malatesta concluded the sentiments amongst the majority of anarchist-communists;

> "Violence (physical force) used to another's hurt, which is the most brutal form of struggle between men can assume, is eminently corrupting. It tends, by its very nature, to suffocate the best sentiments of man, and to develop all the antisocial qualities, ferocity, hatred, revenge, the spirit of domination and tyranny, contempt of the weak, servility towards the strong. And this harmful tendency arises also when violence is used for a good end. ...Anarchists who rebel against every sort of oppression and struggle for the integral liberty of each and who ought thus to shrink instinctively from all acts of violence which cease to be mere resistance to oppression and become

> oppressive in their turn arealso liable to fall into the abyss of brutal force ........ The excitement caused by some recent explosions and the admiration for the courage with which the bomb-throwers faced death, suffices to cause many anarchists to forget their program, and to enter on a path which is the most absolute negation of all anarchist ideas and sentiments."[67]

Typical of the media frenzy and backlash against anarchists is taken up by a local 'semi right wing biased' rag, stating "The anarchists have succeeded in making themselves the theme of discussion all over the civilised world, and that is just what they most desire. Their theories may not engage the attention they could wish, but their practices undoubtedly do. There is only one way to stamp out Anarchy, and that is by giving as little prominence as possible in the public press to its performances." And that many worldwide are now curiousas to what anarchism actually is "Peter Kropotkin favoured the world with an explanation in a pamphlet entitled *'Anarchist Communism; its Aims and Principles'*, and the pamphlet is generally on sale at mob meetings. Anarchism aims, we are told, at the abolition of all private ownership of land, capital, and machinery. After carefully reading through the pamphlet, which fills some thirty-five pages, I have arrived with a reeling brain at the conclusion that what Anarchy really means is "everything for everybody and nothing for nobody".[68] The diatribe continues with the author equating anarchists as jealous criminals etc.

Despite media misconception and state repression in general, it is with great courage and admiralty that the anarchists continued their activities, discussions, public meetings and written propaganda. "The Newcastle Anarchist Club took part in a vibrant Anarchist agitation on Tyneside and Wearside in 1893-94, holding open air meetings on Sundays with Kapper as a principal speaker.[69] Early in 1894 the Newcastle Anarchists upset the more staid Labour leaders locally by advocating that unemployed workers should raid food shops to feed their hungry children. Beyond Newcastle there were reports that Anarchist journals – *Liberty, Freedom,* and *Commonweal* – were circulating in colliery villages, and meetings were taking place at

Sunderland, Silksworth, and elsewhere.[70]

The local press slander continued early 1894 with a rather frightening, with its hidden implications, heading of "Are Anarchists Lunatics?" which equated anarchists with rabid dogs.

> "That Anarchists, as a matter of fact, are lunatics (says the 'hospital') is as obvious to common sense as that a dog is mad when he rushes at friends and foes indiscriminately, and with frantic teeth endeavours to tear them to pieces. The point of our question is this; Are European jurists prepared to pronounce Anarchists technically insane; and will legislatures enact statutes for their certification and restraint? The medical mind foresees an epidemic of Anarchism in the near future, and its natural instinct is to look about for preventivemeasures. The only preventative measures of any avail to avert severe epidemics of contagious diseases in cattle have been the killing of the infected cattle in the very earliest stages of the malady. In the case of human beings, the very early detection of cases and their prompt isolation have alone been efficient. Our first business is to secure the enactment of a statute or statutes declaring Anarchists and inciters to Anarchy "insane". When that has been done, competent investigators must be set to work to find out every possible British or foreign Anarchist or inciter to Anarchy which our country may harbour."[71]

The article carries on in the same style encouraging the notion that anarchists should be locked up in lunatic asylums until 'cured' or locked up for life if 'un- cured' and concluding "Can we induce any leading MP to take this matter up, and to get this bill through before Anarchism attains to epidemic dimensions inour own country". We may look back at this press report with amusement 125 years later, but for local anarchists at the time it is yet another obstacle in their impetus of organising and their spreading of propaganda. Yet from 1895 untilthe end of the decade it was to become a key period for the anarchists in the North East with the founding of a world-wide renowned venture at

Clousden Hill.

## 1.8 CLOUSDEN HILL: A BRIEF FLOURISHING OFANARCHIST-COMMUNISM[72]

Anarchists throughout the region, under the influence of Kropotkin's writings, were becoming increasingly absorbed with the "interest in the impact of science on agriculture, and the consequent possibilities that might be opened up for production in abundance."[73] "Kropotkin drew attention to the potential of applying artificial heating systems, greenhouses (or 'glass culture') and new fertilisers to land cultivation. *Freedom* serialised an English translation of *The Conquest of Bread* in 1893-94, and anarchists in the North East of England were keen to get hold of copies of the book".[74] *Fields, factories and Workshops Tomorrow* was the actual book refered to, coupled with *The Conquest of Bread,* in which Kropotkin showed "the real material possibility of the Anarchist – Communist ideal of productive units small enough to allow federal organization which would be largely self-sufficient and easily self-managed on direct democratic lines. In place of woolly ideas of the 'simple life' Kropotkin assessed the possibilities of such an existence both economically and technologically."[75]

Kapper, living at the time in Sunderland, began attending conferences by the North East Co-operative Movement, which obviously ignited Kappers determination in showing Kropotkin's theories of mutual aid and basic anarchist – communism could be implemented with immediate effect, as an example of 'anarchy in action'. Buoyed with enthusiasm and the forthcoming financial support from William Key (a wealthy Sunderland 'socialist') Kapper began writing to others within the movement for support. "William Morris's Hammersmith Socialist Society sent money, so did an anonymous "wealthy London Anarchist" (possibly George Davison) "[76]

With sources of finance partially secured, Kapper wrote to Kropotkin with his ideas and request for him to become treasurer. Kropotkin, as well as rejecting the invitation as treasurer as he had his own difficulties in managing his own finances, as well as time itself, also replied;

> "As to your scheme, I must say that I have little confidence in schemes of communist communities started under the present conditions, and always regret to see men and women going to sufferall sorts of privations in order, in most cases, to find only disappointment at the end: retiring for many years from the work of propaganda of ideas among the great masses, and of aid to the masses in their emancipation, for making an experiment which has many chances for being a failure."

Providing a few examples of possible hurdles facing the commune, Kropotkin also stated;

> "In order to succeed, the Communist experiment, being an experiment in mutual accommodation among humans, ought to be made on a grand scale. A whole city of, at least, 20,000 inhabitants, ought to organise itself for self managed consumption of the first necessities of life (houses and essential furniture, food and clothing), with a large development of free groupings for the satisfaction of the higher artistic, scientific, and literary needs and hobbies - before it be possible to say anything about the experimentally tested capacities, or incapacities, of our contemporaries for Communist life. (By the way, the experiment isnot so unfeasible as it might seem at first sight.)"[77]

Kropotkin was by no means completely 'pessimistic' with the proposed project, as he finishes his letter with the comments;

> "Here is, dear comrade, what I had to say in answer to your letter. By no means should I like to discourage you and your comrades. I simply think that "forewarned means forearmed." The better one sees the difficulties in his way, the better he can cope with them. Once you feel inclined to attempt the

experiment, although knowing all its difficulties - there must be no hesitation in making it. Earnest men will always find out in it something to learn themselves and to teach their comrades. Once your inclinations go this way - certainly go on! You have some more chances of success than many of your forerunners, and I am sure you will find sympathies in your way. Mine will certainly follow you, and if you think that the publication of this letter can bring you sympathisers, publish it as an open letter to comrades intending to start a Communist colony"[78].

Undeterred Kapper and comrades forged ahead, eventually finding Clousden Hill Farm and starting the commune, mid 1895. Within its first year, the commune had attracted wide interest throughout the anarchist movement, as well as established public press such as the Chronicle[79] etc. The commune was also host to many visitors, both welcome and unwelcome, from Kropotkin, to Élisée Reclus[80], and Tom Mann "who freely acknowledged that whilst others were wasting their breath in argument, these men were reducing principles to action,"[81] amongst many others, as well as many 'political refugees' fleeing repression throughout Europe. As the fame of the commune grew, so did the amount of visitors 'treating the place as though it was a summer camp'. "There was so much interest that eventually the community asked intending visitors to book ahead and arrive at convenient times, allowing colonist's adequate opportunity to work their smallholding."[82]

Coincidently, Kropotkin again lectured at the Tyne Theatre on the 12th January 1896 on 'The land and what it could produce' stating his view that "the land question was that every country would have eventually to look for its markets athome, and this would mean the wealth of each country being spread more among its labouring population. He said peasant proprietorship in France would have long since disappeared had there not been common lands to keep them together and institutions incidental to communal life which led the peasants to know each other and to co-operate in case of necessity."[83]

Kropotkin also paid a visit to the commune that January and stated "He was much gratified with what he had seen and the manner in which the farm was being worked."[84] Kropotkin also presented the colony with a large volume of a book on horticulture with an inner inscription of "To the comrades of the young colony with heartiest good wishes and best sympathies."[85]

After a few hard worked fruitful years, by 1898, most of the original commune members, including Kapper had moved on to pastures anew, enabling remaining members (predominantly non-anarchist) to work more closely with the co-operative movement, and as such, converted the commune into a business enterprise, eventually becoming Clousden Hill Co-operative NurseriesCompany Ltd, and leading to bankruptcy in 1902.

> "In attempting an assessment of the success of the colony in its promotion of anarchist communism, we must begin by addressing the expectations the colony had for itself. Certainly, Kapper was not naive enough to believe that society wide participation and a return to agrarian living would follow his experiment. Viewed from this perspective, the colony would have been perceived as a form of latter day Owenism, which, moreover, was neither relevant nor practicable to a largely urban, industrial working class. Further, Kropotkin's prediction that the colony would fall victim to its own success proved partly true. A sole venture, operating in isolation, with limited and scarce resources and where seemingly woeful ineptitude of much of the membership in lacking the knowledge and skills of land and livestock management, much less that of seeking to be self sufficient, appears, with the benefit of hindsight, to have been doomed from the outset. Yet we should bear in mind the fluid and mutable nature of socialist politics through the 1890s, where the philosophy was adapting and developing, and where experiments such as the Clousden hill colony were part of the response to capitalism, and a part of this trend in the socialist milieu. As Todd has pointed out, it offered a haven from persecution for political exiles in Europe. It also offered a

> sanctuary for British anarchists, still feeling like outcasts within the wider socialist movement, as a result of the black propaganda of the early 1890s, and as such was a success in itself, if only for a short time."[86]

Whilst a picture is painted of the failings of Clousden Hill, its story has become a 'lesson learned' for many co-operative anarchistic ventures today with its legacy's taken to heart.

> "Where Clousden collapsed under the weight of its debts and lackof internal political cohesion, today's co-ops, though often still struggling, are far more savvy to the risks ..and maintain a significant collectively-maintained set of resources on both ways to run disparate co-op collectives without fermenting immediate splits and ways to sustainably build up projects without running up cash deficits. It's tough on politics, on the rights of housemate's and on the amount of work members are expected to put in, using the experience gained from decades of effort. In that sense the lessons of Clousden Hill and projects like it remain with us, and Todd's bookmeans its activists work was not in vain."[87]

## 1.9 A NEW CENTURY

With the outset of the Second Boer War (11 October 1899 – 31 May 1902) and the sweeping tide of patriotic demonstrations breaking up anti-war meetings throughout the country, coupled with increasing levels of poverty[88] in the North East, local anarchists faced difficulties in their organising and propaganda efforts. This was further hindered with the assassination of American president William McKinley On September 6, 1901 by proclaimed anarchist Leon Frank Czolgosz. The resulting media backlash against the anarchists would have similar repercussions, and the all too familiar echoes of disgust, as it did less than a decade earlier, in attempting to discredit the theory of anarchism.

Joseph Cowen Jnr died 18th February 1900, leaving the *Evening Chronicle* less sympathetic in opening its pages to the philosophy of anarchism. During the same period Newcastle City Libraries, claim that a statue of Garibaldi, which was situated at the front of Cowen,s summerhouse in Blaydon, was destroyed by a group of anarchists in approx 1900. I have previously proved that the statue in question was not destroyed by anarchists but roaming cattle, more likely, and the claims of Newcastle libraries are another usual case of anarchism being continually mis-represented by academic historians for their own personal and , or political gains.[89]

August 5th 1900, saw anarchism locally gain a minor level of support from themost unlikely of places. The reverend Harris, of North Shields, who was curate of Harton Village church in the then outskirts of South Shields, deliver a sermon on 'Anarchism : What is it ? A Christian view' to his regular congregation.

> "The pretty wayside church of Harton Village, nestling amid the gray recumbent tombs of its dead, and yet untouched by city grime and smoke, is scarcely the place, one would think, in which to expect a practical and illuminating discourse on one of

> those greatmovements of social unrest which mark our day and generation." Continuing "His subject was, as I have said, an unusual one, especially so in a church which has never been remarkable for innovations of any kind. It was original; it was interesting. It was refreshing to hear something of a subject too little understood, and from the lips of one who owns allegiance to a religious body so conservative in all its traditions. Mr Harris, I believe, has lived much in Italy and Germany, and this explains to some, though not every degree his liberal outlook, his originality, his choice of subject. With his continental experience behind him, Mr Harris could reasonably claim to know something about Anarchism. Indeed, it was at once easy to see that he was familiar with his subject."

After delving into the story of Samson, Harris continued;

> *"let me die for what I hold to be right"* was the cry of the modern Anarchist also, and the spectacle, said Mr Harris, of probably hundreds of men who were willing to lay down their lives for their cause surely demanded closer attention, closer inspection that it had hitherto got. Mr Harris at the outset rightly condemned hysterical denunciations of the Anarchist movement. These were not enough; they were merely stupid and always thoughtless. The men who blatantly demanded that every Anarchist, Socialist, Communist, and Nihilist should be hanged and quartered were men who did not know what they were talking about. If such a vindictive and unchristian policy were to be followed Europe would run with blood; there would be red war and intestine strife. No words, of course, could excuse murder. The arguments of the stiletto and the pistol were revolting and criminal. But we should never judge movements by their worst features, their abnormal incidents; and Anarchism and all that it entails, had much more to say for itself. What was it, then? It did not mean anarchy. Anarchy was only another word for social and political confusion and disorder; Anarchism, on the other hand, maintained that anarchy at present existed and that the Anarchist's methods

> were directed towards restoring order. Disorder, in the Anarchists eyes, was social inequality. To remedy that inequality was the Anarchists *raison d'être.* Man, originally prone to do good, to live cleanly and purely, to think nobly, and to love mercy, had become grossly materialised by his wealth and surroundings, and Anarchism claimed as its special mission such re-adjustment of the worlds affairs as to let him become once more free from the trammels of riches and position."

The church was partly implicit in concentrating more on an afterlife in heaven as opposed to everyday struggles of humanity, and the church had failed in its duty as more people ( like Samson) struggled to be free and more conscious oftheir own strength, Harris concluded;

> "The life to come and its promises are, in fact, proving useless to- day as anodynes to men who feel present miseries only too keenly; and Mr Harris was more than justified in calling the church's attention to problems of today rather than the shadowy problems of tomorrow. Anarchism and Socialism might, to sum up Mr Harris's reasoning, result largely from ephemeral causes, but so long as the present grossly materialistic order of things prevailed they had to be reckoned with as active political forces."[90]

After the reasonably sympathetic report in the Shields Gazette of 1900 of exploring anarchism through the christian viewpoint, the later assassination of American president William McKinley On September 6, 1901, the paper again vilified anarchists and the philosophy of anarchism on September 12$^{th}$ 1901 in a piece entitled "The causes of Anarchism", the author again equates anarchism with lunacy, that being the lunacy of the assassin driven to despair by his own miseries in daily life.

> "Of late years the success of the assassin has been extraordinary, but he has, throughout, shown more of the cunning of the madman than the self-sacrifice of the patriot or

> the spirit of the avenger of human wrongs. Lunacy, then, is the chief cause of recent notable assassinations. But it has been lunacy connected with a particular sect or creed, and that creed is Anarchism."

In attempting to lay the blame with the decay of theological creeds and the hopefulness of having the present wrongs of the world righted the author concludes;

> "Anarchists, like the old theologians, believe intensely in their doctrines and in their mission. The Ecclesiastics of old burned people at the stake with just as little hesitation as Anarchists "remove" an Emperor or the head of a Republic. Only they acted, or pretended to, within the laws of their time, and they did not direct their energies so virulently against society. But do not let us forget when we argue that atheism has bred a disregard of human life that the ages of Faith cared no more for life than some of us in these doubting times appear to do. They had, it is true, a more heroic temper, a saner outlook, a stronger faith. This Anarchism is the sign and signal of a time when men have ceased to be heroic or large minded, and are absorbed in a morbid contemplation of their miseries."[91]

## 1.10 1906 & THE STRUGGLE CONTINUES

Living amid the disease ridden slums of the then Newcastle, faced with patriotic marches of victory at the end of the Boer War, press slander, and no doubt various elements of police repression, local anarchists were hard pressed to survive everyday life, find employment, as well as each other. It isn't until July 1906 that we find mention of anarchist related activity in Newcastle, where *Freedom's* reported anarchist pamphlet sales received payment from Newcastle Socialist Society to the sum of 3s. 6d.[92] (3s 6d equated in today's monetary terms is a lot of 'penny pamphlets' sold locally). July 1906, *Freedom* was also available to buy from Arthur Cowen, 62 Mary Street, Westgate Road.[93] Who also sold anarchist books and pamphlets from *Freedom*.[94] This no doubt showed the persistence and existence of anarchists, who despite prevailing odds were still agitating locally with propaganda.

Towards the end of 1906[95] the Newcastle-On-Tyne Anarchist Communist Group was beginning to advertise its existence through the paper *Freedom*, its secretary Harry Rubin, sold the paper and various pamphlets from premises at 13 Cottenham St, Westgate Hill. The group met every Sunday 4.30pm at Cottenham St, before moving meetings to 71 Cookson St, Westgate Hill laterin the year. February 1907 also saw the founding of a Freedom Group in Newcastle, which no doubt, had an overlap of membership and possibly co- operation together with the Newcastle Anarchist Communist Group during the same period. R Stuart of the Freedom group wrote;

> "This letter is written with the object of putting the Newcastle Group in the line of march in the propagandist fight for the emancipation of the proletarian. We have now been in existence for the matter of three months, and although few in numbers, yet we are slowly but surely feeling our-way towards the best action which we, think will achieve the greatest results, and that is by bringing, into existence a progressive library of the most advanced books upon Socialism and Anarchism in Hebrew[96] and English, The library will be ' thrown open to the

public at a very nominal charge per week, and from additional promises of patronage we fully trust to recruit members for our group. We have so far not given much attention to open-air propaganda in the shape of lectures, but shall do so after our library scheme has gained a footing: I may remark that P. Kropotkin's "Memoirs of a Revolutionist "Commands the premier position in our future "library arsenal," and the writer of this letter has received unbounded pleasure in the reading of the book."[97]

*Freedom* correspondent and article writer 'Red Rose' from Sunderland was at this time writing from an 'Anarchist-feminist' slant in her defence of lesbian relationships and the scandal surrounding them.[98] Whilst at the same time, the upturn in sales of anarchist books and pamphlets through Harry Rubin and the Newcastle Anarchist Communist Group had increased to 12s, 9d.

Later in the year our 'Red Rose' in an article entitled 'Socialists and Free Love' argues the economic equality of the sexes doesn't equate to the actual freedom from sexual oppression between the sexes, and how Socialists still fear and barely understand the concept of 'free love'.

> "More important even than sending Labour men to Parliament- more important than giving Women the vote, is this question of sex relationship. Sex, I should like to 'tell him, -is the predominant note, of all creation; it affects everything in life; it means joy or misery; it means dwarfed, lop-sided individuals or fully developed and properly poised men and women; it not only - affects life, it is life. And this important matter is the one upon which we are most woefully ignorant; the one question not to be spoken of 'in an open manner, but in whispers, or with a leer, or a contemptuous smile; not to be discussed frankly and fearlessly, but in a mysterious manner that adds morbidity to ignorance. This matter is so, important that mankind can never he happy until it has looked it straight in the face, seeing it to be natural and good, A blessing not a curse; and never can mankind be happy till all barriers, all artificial and legal ties,

> are broken between men and women, for nothing on earth should ever keep a man and woman, together but love and a mutual desire for each other's company, that mutual attraction for each other which will become more powerful in a free society." And concluding "For the present it is necessary to point- outthat the majority of Socialists, partly through lack of study and partly through lack of moral courage, are in a hopelessly mixed state of mind on this question, and are therefore the more unable to resist the attacks of the hypocritical enemy. As an example, take the position of HG Wells, who has been roughly handled by the Yellow Press, and who has been wriggling in a most equivocal manner in his endeavour to save his face over the charge of advocating free love. In his book on Socialism and the family he admits that "one's dream, and perfection is Anarchy," which implies freedom in all social relations. Yet he ranges himself on the side of the exact opposite, that is to say, the imperfection of a Socialism that would ashe expresses it, "concentrate all control in the State."[99]

December 1907 saw the national founding of the International Anarchist Federation of the English Provinces, which was instrumental in the bringing together of isolated groups and individuals throughout the country. The founding conference in Manchester listed delegates from Newcastle and Sunderland. January 1908 saw the joining of the Newcastle Freedom Group, as well as "Our lady comrade who writes under the title of "Red Rose" in *Freedom*, and it at present resident in Sunderland, wrote that she has heard there are some comrades there, whom she intends looking up with the idea of forming a group."[100]

During the second conference of the Federation, in Liverpool, the Newcastle Freedom Group also reported;

> "We are steadily plodding, making the Newcastle Group permanent, with the aim to become a fighting factor in the near future. Although the group last summer was just about wrecked,

yet the remaining ones held together with some tenacity and purpose,for we have now made a few members, young men at that, who are giving promise of doing good propaganda. They have advanced, from the ranks of Social Democracy, viz, State Socialism. One comrade C. R. Crawford, who happens to be, a good speaker, but who has been suffering from a serious illness, hopes to be able to do some open-air work this year. This winter we are quietly meeting together; writing, discussing, and studying the principles of Anarchism. Newcastle-On-Tyne is suffering, like all other congested centres, from an overdose of unemployed. I mean the workless are suffering. We have them marching the city with conspicuous banners, interviewing Councillors, etc; for work; but now leading citizens have started a fund, their names attached to cheques for various amounts. - The poor devils out 'of work may get a "bob" a week for two or three weeks— that may be all; but what more can 'our "city fathers" do? They have done their duty to the "inefficien " ! They have, just appointed a new town clerk at a salary of £1,200, to rise as time passes! An unemployed demonstration took place here on Tuesday night, December 24, in the Bigg Market. Several speakers addressed the crowd, after which the unemployed paradedthe streets. Our group also took part in it, distributing leaflets, such as "Our Great Empire," etc. R Stuart."[101]

Whilst we pick up elements of a minor divide between the more working class street agitations of the Newcastle Anarchist Communist Group and the Newcastle Freedom Group with their aspirations of setting up of 'progressive libraries' and their 'looking down' at the 'poor devils' within the ranks of unemployed during the period, the groups would work together with joint public meetings throughout the coming year.

February 1908 saw "The Freedom Group are working steadily, holding group meetings at which they discuss the principles of Anarchism, and last week they held a public meeting, which was well attended and gave the local comrades much courage" whilst Rubin reported "A few brief lines to show that our International Anarchist Communist Group is still moving. Next March we hope to have John Turner with us, so that Newcastle State Socialists may have a clear exposition of what Anarchism really is. On Wednesday, January 22, at the group's room, a paper entitled 'Anarchism v Social Democracy 'was given by R. Stuart, and discussion followed. Comrade T. L. Heron, a member of the group, will shortly give a paper on "Mutual Aid," to which we look forward with much interest, The Newcastle-On-Tyne International Anarchist CommunistGroup hold their, meetings and lectures every Wednesday at 8 p.m. in 71 Cookson Street."[102]

The following month also saw Rubin stating "The one subject, of discussion here is the strike. That is all one hears in the street; among the crowds at the corners, and those who stroll from street - to street. We have found this a good, opportunity to spread our ideas, and we, are trying to arrange some open-air meetings. Our Comrade Heron has given an address on "Mutual Aid," which was interesting and well received; On the 29th March. we are to have John Turner down to speak at the hall of the Newcastle Socialist Society, 77a Blackett Street, at 8 pm. Subject: 'What Anarchism Really Means.'"[103] *Freedom* also listed R. Goldberg, of 114 Blenheim Street, as being where the paper, along with Rubin, at Cookson St, as available from.

The aforementioned visit of John Turner occurred March 29$^{th}$ 1908. Turner regularly toured the country as National Organiser for the Amalgamated Shop Assistants Union, and "delivered speeches to Anarchist sponsored meetings on the side"[104] Turner, as well as being a regular publisher and member of the London Freedom Group, also published '*The voice of Labour*' during this period, and was 'an able exponent of Anarchist ideas' especially with his feet firmly entrenched within working class labour struggles as a trade union official.

April 1908 and a report from A. Despres in the April issue of *Freedom* states;

"At the invitation of the International Anarchist Group, our comrade John Turner addressed a crowded meeting in the Newcastle Socialist Society's hall, 77a Blackett Street, on Sunday, March 29, his subject being "What Anarchism Really Means". In opening, he showed that an Anarchist can be a Socialist; whilst a "Democrat need not- be a Socialist' in fact, nearly all Tories today were Democrats, but they could not be called Socialists. After dealing with the definition of the term, Turner very cleverly showed, by analogy and comparison, the superiority of Anarchism over political Socialism as a practical social theory. He pointed out that wealth, instead of concentrating into fewer hands, was actually getting into more, and more hands, showing the possibility of the exploiters eventually being able to out vote the workers. In conclusion, he made an able plea for the philosophy and ideals of Anarchism to be more carefully considered by Socialists. The vigorous applause of the audience proved their appreciation of his address. Some few questions followed, which were well dealt with. Then there ensued a general discussion. If our comrade had previously demonstrated his perfect knowledge of the subject he was dealing with, and so ably shown the absurdity of political action, in his replies he positively excelled himself. Repeatedly he was compelled to pause to permit even those he was hitting the hardest to show their pleasure at his replies by their applause. I feel assured that his visit has materially helped the cause in Newcastle. But the pity of it is that we have not more Turners to vindicate by their eloquence and sincerity the truths and ethics of Anarchist Communism."[105]

## 1.11 THE PRINCESS ON RUSSIA

An often unreported, or little known fact amongst the anarchist press, is that Sophia Kropotkin, the 'wife'[106] of Peter Kropotkin, would, for a number of years also tour the country giving lectures on 'Russian Freedom' and 'Life in Siberia' to fascinated audiences. So it was that she would cause quite a bit of an intellectual stir in the North East with her lecture on the present state of Russia at West Hartlepool Town Hall on March 6th 1908.

> "The platform at the Town Hall, West Hartlepool, last night was occupied by Princess Kropotkin, who lectured on "Russia" to a large audience. Princes Kropotkin's husband was imprisoned on accountof his political views. He escaped and since then the Princess has shared his exile in Switzerland, in France, and latterly in England. As the Princess remarked during her lecture, it is a special trait of the Russian woman that she follows her husband in all his distress. The audience, in applauding the remark, were not only expressing their appreciation of the characteristic, but were paying a tribute to the Princess herself, who has nobly borne her part, and has suffered loss of wealth, position, and friends in the cause of Russian freedom."[107]

The Princess often gave accounts of the life and hardships as well as the rigour of the climate amongst the population of Siberia "But these she added were nothing to what the people had to endure from the unscrupulous and corrupt Russian government officials and traders". After describing the beautiful aspects of the country, its flowing wheat fields, fertile and rich in minerals;

> "But Siberia, Princess Kropotkin was careful to add, wants, like Russia to be rid of the present regime which is a calamity for both. Her remarks on the sufferings of the Russian exiles were listened to with sympathetic interest, and it was apparent by the way in which she spoke of many of the prisoners as "my friends" that the Princess keeps in close touch with her unfortunate compatriots. Several pitiable pictures of Russians on the way to Siberia were shown. The number of exiles was given as 78,000 men and women. In conclusion, she said that when she spoke of those who were suffering in Siberia all the hardships one could imagine, she hoped that their sufferings would not be in vain, and that when happier days came to

> Russia and Siberia, they would remember the noble men and women who had suffered for the sake of their country. At the close of proceedings, the audience expressed their sympathy with the Russian prisoners, which the Princess promised to convey to them."[108]

## 1.12 1908

Back to Newcastle and mid 1908 sees local anarchists' now joining forces, dropping the name Newcastle Freedom Group, with R Stuart, R Goldberg et all combining with H Rubin, and H Kaprin, etc, of the Newcastle Anarchist Communist Group under the more permanent name of International Anarchist Communist Group, who were now holding regular lectures and meetings 8pm Wednesdays at 51 Douglas Terrace. R Stuart would also contribute articles to the paper *Freedom* during this period, whilst the paper would regularly list payments from H Rubin from the sale of literature.

The local 'parliamentary socialists' of the Social Democratic Party were soon complaining, more out of jealousy I would imagine, about the growth of Anarchism in and around socialist meetings and events in Newcastle, as amember cry's to the paper *Justice* states;

> "Though we broke away from the Newcastle Socialist Society mainly to form an S.D.P. branch, we had other grievances, chief of which was the prevalence of Anarchists in the society, and this heterogeous membership of the club has given Socialism in the minds of many people such a character in Newcastle and even on Tyneside, as it will take years to wipe out. He expresses the hope that in the possible event of the Newcastle Socialist Society again becoming affiliated to the S.D.P. that Anarchists will be excluded from membership."[109]

Regular sales of literature, public meetings, and no doubt arguments with parliamentary socialists continued throughout the year, and well into 1909.

## 1.13 A TRIP DOON THE TYNE IN 1909

"Who has not heard of that wonderful spot known as "Tyneside" ? Is it not supposed to be one of the pilars of England's greatness? For here are constructed those terrible life-destroying monsters which a senseless, brutal Government needs to maintain its prestige, to defend the interests of capitalism, and to inspire the people with all those false notions of patriotism and glory that blind them to the crime and folly of it all.

Let us glance for a moment at the life centred here and the scenes that meet the eye.

As we descend Pilgrim Street and the Sandhills, we see crowds of people streaming off the Quay, where they had been listening to quack doctors, tipsters talking politics, temperance reformers, Socialists, and Anarchists, their voices mingling with those of the vendors of fruit, ice-cream, sweets, old clothes, newspapers, penny dreadfuls, and novelettes.

A strange sight this Quay on a Sunday morning, the big, stately boats lying alongside looking serene and majestic, whilst below is all bustle, noise, and excitement; an open market-place such as one never sees in any other town.

Here is a short, stodgy figure of a man with an unpleasant face, florid as to complexion, coarse features, and small, cunning eyes; he is made more unprepossessing by having his hair cropped short. On week-days he is a tipster, on Sundays a would-be orator. Someone told me he was a Socialist. I paused to listen, but never a word heard I of Socialism. His speech was the moist dreadful thing I have ever heard, a perfect torrent of vulgar abuse expressed in the coarsest language.

A little further along is a small, lithe figure of a man standing on a portable platform, his face eager, quick eyes deep set, soft brown hair with great natural waves, worn rather long, the whole face and figure betokening fierce eagerness and desperate earnestness. He is telling his crowd of listeners not to put faith in Parliament, but to do things for themselves. He is an Anarchist Communist.

We turn away and mingle with a little stream of folk going aboard the steamer to North Shields. What a mixed crowd it is, we notice as the boat steams away from the Quay side. But now the river claims our attention.

What a marvellous sight is the river! How it appeals to the imagination. What contrasts! The beautiful, stately ships and the mean little quays. Graceful sailing-ships from Norway, schooner, barque, and brigantine, so beautiful with their masts and spars; the pretty landing-stages at all the calling-stations, each with three huts for waiting-rooms, one for ladies only and one for gentlemen; in between these a funny little shop where soiled-looking sweets, penny bloods, and novelettes are sold.

The river was crowded with craft – steamships from Germany, Italy, Spain, Belgium, Portugal; sailing ships from Norway, Sweden, France; one fine old wooden sailing-ship, now so seldom seen, from Norway, spoke of fiords and romantic folk-lore; a steamer from Aberdeen, and one from Leith; tugs innumerable.

Just beyond South Shields the river took on quite a gay aspect, tugs painted green, red, blue, and yellow lying beside great steamers, red and white. This bright patch of colour was a great relief after the terrible grimness we had just passed; first, on the banks the great ugly chemical works and Palmer's shipyard, with the monstrous cranes which have displaced so much labour. In the river, lying side by side, are two torpedo boats and one torpedo-boat destroyer, grey, grim-looking monster's, one mass of treacherous machinery, constructed for fell murder; after these the devilish death-dealing mass, the battleship "Lord Nelson," later the "Invincible," quite as fearful a thing, but not quite so formidable-looking.

These horrible, grim, murderous-looking masses of diabolical machinery are a blasphemous parody on the beautiful, gracious, graceful sailing-ships, the one representing wholesale murder, the other an exchange between and a better understanding of all nations. We are struck by what greed of gain has produced in the way of life-destroying hulks, and what need of the necessaries of life has produced in the swift steamships and the lovely sailing-boats.

We land at North Shields and turn off by the narrow, circuitous lane beside the Quay; dirty and full of smells it is; all doss-houses, cheap eating-houses, and public-houses. Almost every sign bears the name of a foreigner; hung out from the windows are the Italian, Swiss, and Norwegian colours; most of the faces to be seen are swarthy in colour and of any nationality but English; we even meet a group of Chinese sailors.

At last we reach clean, quiet, peaceful-looking Tynemouth; look at its ruined Priory, its little bay; and then back by car to the Quay, where the "great" Hunnable harangues a crowd he seems to amuse vastly.

A day of colour, grace, and contour, of interest in the great heart of humanity, and of grim, haunting horror – all in a few miles on the River Tyne. Bee."[110]

Perhaps the Anarchist Communist heard speaking by Bee on Newcastle Quayside was none other than Harry Rubin himself, we shall never know. Rubin, during the same month also sent a group report to Freedom;

> "Just a few lines regarding the movement here. After a long standstill in the propaganda, the Anarchists have opened a Communist Club so that those Socialists who have lost their faith in parliamentary action, such as Revolutionists, Industrialists, and others, shall be able to work together with us. We hold indoor and outdoor meetings, and sell Anarchist literature. Our outdoor meetings are very successful, our speakers giving very good expositions of Anarchism and Direct

Action, pointing out the futility of political action. We generally get a good crowd; on two occasions our speakers have drawn away the whole audience from the speaker and organiser for the Newcastle Socialist Society. The speaker got very angry and came down from his platform and left the public ground. At the Club during the week we have very hot discussions on Anarchism. Every Thursday night Comrade Tyas conducts a speaker's class, with the object of developing new speakers. Each member of the class reads a certain portion of an Anarchist pamphlet, which is afterwards discussed by other members of the class, which gives very good results. We hope that with arrival of the summer we shall be able to spread our ideal of Anarchism in a much wider circle. Our Communist Club is at 77a Blackett Street. All comrades heartily welcomed."[111]

Pamphlet and book sales were reaching higher numbers, and during June, C.H. Kean was scheduled to visit Newcastle as part of his national speaking tour with subjects ranging from "Direct Action vs. Legislation, Wage Slavery, What is Anarchism, Anarchism vs. Political Socialism, Unemployment and the Remedy, and Government – a Curse."[112]

With a stable base now secured, the International Anarchist Communist Group increased their level of agitation and propaganda spreading, as well as advertising "Comrades who may be in Newcastle on Race Sunday (June 20)are invited to help at a big meeting to be held on the Town Moor that evening. As we desire to make the best show possible from our platform, any speakers who are in the district and willing to help should communicate with G. Grounsell, secretary. Communist Club, 77a Blackett Street, Newcastle-on- Tyne."[113]

C.H. Kean (Charley Kean from Birmingham) on his national speaking tour stayed in Newcastle for the entire week addressing meetings in both the Bigg Market and the Haymarket, and reported in *Freedom* that month;

> "On Sunday June 20th we had a rare time on the (Town) Moor. As the local paper reported "The crowd which gathered around the platform from which the Anarchist Communist speakers intended to set forth their convictions refused to listen. The disturbing element quickly took the upper hand and 'rushed' the platform in ugly fashion. Fortunately the speakers were able to beat a safe retreat, but their banners were seized and torn to shreds, and poles and canvas were smashed before the police restored order". [114]

Kean also described how comrade Despres came on his cycle from Liverpoolto assist with the meetings and that;

> "His description of the Direct Action League in Liverpool was interesting both to comrades and audience. Being requested to speak on Trade Unionism and Industrial Unionism, he dealt with some at a subsequent meeting; and judging by their questions the audience saw some advantage in the new tendency. On Friday, 25th Kean addressed the Communist Club on "decentralisation". Rain interfered with the Sunday meetings a little, but we were able to hold two during the day. The meetings arranged for Monday, Tuesday, and Wednesday evenings concluded our comrade's visit to Newcastle". [115]

The ideas of Syndicalism, and, or Anarcho-Syndicalism, whilst not beginning in 1909, as their influence began a lot earlier, were now starting to take a firmer root in Newcastle amongst the Anarchists.

The build up of syndicalist ideas and practices, and levels of industrial militancy, were always prevalent in the North East with its large working class labour movement, especially in the mines and shipyards. "In Northern England, among Tyneside engineers and shipbuilders, union activists, for instance, found it appropriate or expedient to by sympathetic to syndicalism. In Newcastle, a strong and ultimately city-wide labour movement was syndicalist."[116] These ideas would ultimately come to the fore during the following decade on an unprecedented scale.

After his lecture tour of Scotland, Kean returned to Newcastle and commencing August 5th "Six meetings were held, and all were well attended. The local S.D.P. hall was taken for Saturday night, and our comrade lectured on "Knowledge and Belief." The last night was reserved for a recital of Ibsen's "Enemy of the People." Two meetings were held in Darlington; subjects, "The Failure of Political Socialism" and "Thoughts of a Fool""[117]

Following the attempted uprising in Barcelona in July, known as 'bloody week', the then arrest and state murder of Francisco Ferrer caused international outrage, and the North East was no exception. Ferrer, whose work in the Modern School Movement and its libertarian aspects of education was widely supported by Anarchists and Socialists alike. The Newcastle Communist Club "held two demonstrations on October 31st in connection with the various I.L.P. and S.D.P. branches of Newcastle and Gateshead, to protest against the murder of Ferrer and the imprisonment of his co-workers."[118] Another public meeting was held in the morning at the Sandhill area of Newcastle, and another in the evening with 8s. 5d raised in collections and donations.

**C. H. KEAN'S LECTURES (Newcastle-on-Tyne).**

November 11—I.L.P. Club, 7.30, "Stirner's 'Ego and Its Own.'"
" 13—Socialist Society, "Anarchism."
" 14—Communist Club, 7.30, "The Philosophy of Nietzsche."
" 15—Westfield Hall, Gateshead, "Knowledge and Belief."
" 17—The Café, Newgate Street, "The Chicago Martyrs."
" 18—I.L.P. Club, 7.30, "The Quintessence of Ibsen."

November again saw the return of Kean, with another series of lectures which began on the 9th, and;

> "The first lecture was on 'The Evolution of Man'. After describing the formation of worlds, he traced the evolution of life up to man. The second lecture was on 'Stirner's Egoism'. Beginning with a review of society, and revealing it to us in all its horrible nakedness, he proved that the prevalent feature on

man today was degeneracy, a degeneracy, Kean contended, that was greatly augmented by the atavistic doctrines of Christianity. Further, that if the workers could grasp the fact that the fundamental motive of all our actions was self-interest, they would probably have sense to stand on their feet and demand their rights. In the lecture of 'Anarchism' we haddescribed to us its history. It is a point worthy of note, which Kean specially emphasised, that most of our great thinkers have been Anarchists, more or less. The next lecture was one on 'Knowledge and Belief'. It was pointed out how easy it was to mistake one for the other. All religions were beliefs. The last lecture in the course was 'The Quintessence of Ibsenism'. Kean had a good grip of his subject. He gathered up all the threads of his previous lectures, and then proceeded to show, with the aid of Ibsen, that the individual owed more to himself than to any movement. There was about his remarks a tone of serious cheerfulness, which appears to be much needed in the Anarchist movement. He tried to drive home the fact that the man who went about with a face as long as a Christians – whether he was an Anarchist or an archangel it did not matter – wasjust as much a nuisance to a movement as the person who saw in it just a means of recreation. The ideal man was he who looked life straight in the face, saw clearly what he wanted, and then, with coat off and sleeves up, worked cheerfully for his goal. In the middle of the course Kean delivered a lecture on 'The Philosophy of Nietzsche'. I am unable to sum up his teachings here; there are so many sides to them. There is much contrariety of opinion in the Anarchist movement over this great thinker. Judging from his writings, undoubtedly he himself was an Anarchist. One of his aphorisms reads – 'To live as i like or to live not at all'. But whether he would have allowed others the same freedom is a debatable point. However, those comrades who are not afraid of being hit in a thousand places and awakening up to where one is – metaphorically speaking – should read Nietzsche."[119]

Perhaps reflecting the national growth of Anarchism, or the disassociation fromparliamentary socialists / communists, or more likely losing the lease on the premises at Blackett St, by March 1910, local Anarchist D.C. Thompson, was announcing on behalf of the group that the Newcastle Communist Club will now be known as the Newcastle Anarchist Club and that meetings were to be held every Saturday evening, 7.30pm at Halls Cafe, 37 Pilgrim St, and any correspondence was to be sent to group secretary, c/o D.C. Thompson, 160 Conyers Rd, Byker.

Nationally, the growth of syndicalist ideas and groupings were beginning to take hold throughout industrial areas, one of such, The Industrial League, was the largest of the anarchist influenced Industrial Unionist groupings.[120] One member of the group, W.D. Ponder, would visit the North East, to deliver a series of lectures, with the intention of "putting the anarchist position to the locked out boiler makers", Ponder stayed in Newcastle for the week of October 1st – 6th and "a series of open-air meetings were held in Newcastle, Wallsend, Gateshead, and Byker; with one exception, all were fairly successful. Some thousands of leaflets ('Do Not Vote' and 'What Is Anarchism') were distributed among the audiences, but there was only a very moderate sale of *Freedom*and pamphlets".[121] It was also emphasised that *Freedom* was available to buy every Sunday morning between 11 and 12.30 on the Sandhill, Newcastle Quayside.

January 1911, and the New Year see's Anarchism defended with a 'vigorous protest' letter from a Mr John Pagan in the pages of The Northern Daily Mail.

> "He writes that the "theory of Anarchism is necessarily mild and benevolent, since it talks of a state of society where there shall be no want, no greed, no injustice, no organised inhumanity, no coercion, no violence, no bloodshed. Can anyone imagine a man who promotes and upholds such a theory to be a bomb-thrower, a cut- throat, or a ruffian? As a matter of fact all Anarchists are anti- militarists, because of the force and

> violence for which militarism stands, the bloodshed that follows in its track, the inhumanity of man to man it promotes, and the inhumanity of man to poor women and children that it brings about. To be carried away with the idea that a man is an Anarchist because he commits some insane act in the name of Anarchism is to accept a cannibal as a Christian because he eats a missionary in the name of Christianity." It is true, of course, that many Anarchists are kind and humane men. Their central creed aims at the unfettered self-government of the individual, and they seek the abolition of the instruments of government. It is unfortunate for Anarchists that their theory has become associated with the "propaganda of deed", and many people seem to think that all Anarchists sympathise with the bomb- throwers, who have made the name of Anarchy notorious."[122]

September 1911, and a new group seems to have begun in Newcastle, and G. George, of Sandringham Rd, South Gosforth, reports that the visit of John Turner, Davison, Dick James (Liverpool), and visiting Mexican, Honore J Jaxon,has roused the group into action;

> "Public interest has been centred on the Trades Union Congress, but by the help of our visiting comrades we have been able to focus some attention on the Anarchist ideals and movement. On Thursday evening, September 7, John Turner spoke to a large audience in the Bigg Market, on "Direct Action in the Labour Struggle". At the conclusion there were plenty of questions and a good sale of literature. On the following night Honore Jaxon spoke at the same place on "Direct Action in Mexico" and at the end of the meeting several applied for literature on the subject. At both meetings we gave some hundreds of leaflets away ("What is Anarchism?"), and the sale of literature, including four dozen *Freedoms*, amounted to between 8s and 9s. Through the efforts of comrade Davison, each delegate at the Congress received one of our new leaflets, "Anarchy and the Labour War." Our new group meets on

Thursday evenings (7.30) in No.2 room, Lockhart's Cafe, opposite the Fruit Market, Clayton Street."[123]

George Barrett from Glasgow was due to speak in Newcastle on the 5th – 8th of December as part of his national speaking tour, yet anarchists in Newcastle were unable, at such short notice, to secure venues. At the same time, Sunderland was again, as well as G. George of Newcastle, listed as a point of contact for the obtaining of *Freedom* paper, this being G. Barker of Church St, Monkwearmouth.[124] Both of these contacts were to disappear from the listings section of Freedom by May 1912. This does not suggest lack of activity, as by this time the 'Syndicalist revolt' was in full swing, and I am sure the local anarchists would be deeply entrenched within this struggle.

Late 1912, early 1913, and anarchists, particularly from Glasgow, were calling upon the movement for another national conference with the idea for it to be held in Newcastle. George Barrett was to remark "we have trustworthy friends in Newcastle who can be relied upon to make local arrangements" whilst Dick James of Liverpool stated "The Newcastle boys were keen on the affair the time I met them". Despite national appeals for financial help with the proposed conference, it didn't happen in Newcastle, but was held, instead, in Liverpool.

The Liverpool conference in March included local delegates from Newcastle, Gateshead, South Shields, and Durham, which inevitably showed again the growth of anarchism in the North East, George Barrett, commenting on the conference remarks "The Newcastle district is doing good work and will soon doing much better."[125]

## 1.14 DIRECT ACTION AND THE SYNDICALIST REVOLT[126]

Anarcho-syndicalism has a strong theoretical background as well as effectivemethods of practice used in order to obtain and pave the way for the goal of social revolution. As a backdrop to these ideas I will give a brief history of themovements and the occasional individuals that have sprang from them. Thehistory of anarchism, the roots of which can be traced back to ancient Greek civilisations, is too large a task to be chartered here in such few words.

Anarcho-syndicalist methods of direct action can be traced back to 18th century France, where the roots of the term sabotage can be found. The use of the word 'sabotage' in revolutionary terms came about when "a man was working at his machine in a shop in Paris; his employer had subjected him to an unusual amount of annoyance, and in his rage the workman stooped down, pulled one of his sabots (wooden shoes) from his feet and threw at the machine, rendering it useless. Hence a new word was coined."[127] This view is somewhat disputed by Ford & Fosters theory of the origins of the word. They claim the word derived from Emile Pouget (a prominent French syndicalist) who coined the phrase as meaning 'wooden shoeage' which is to 'work as one wearing wooden shoes' – which in turn may have originated from the Northern English and Scottish expression of 'ca canny', or 'gan canny', (work slow).[128] The use of sabotage also became prominent during the Luddite era of the early 1800's where the destruction of new machinery was common place throughout the country (particularly the Midlands and North). This was done as a protest against what was seen as new technical progress which was viewed to be destroying the livelihoods of the working class involved.[129]

The term 'strike' is said to have originated from the action of "striking," or removing the topsails of ships, rendering them motionless. "In April 1768, sailors in Sunderland prevented ships from leaving port by lowering down the yards (thus "striking" their sails). As a result, the owners and masters of the ships agreed to the sailors' demands for pay rises."[130]

The idea of a general strike was first expounded in 1832 by William Benbow (a follower of local born radical Thomas Spence). In his classic pamphlet entitled *'Grand national Holiday and Congress of the Productive Classes'*, Benbow pushed forward the idea of the general strike and its importance to the working class. It theorised that the workers strength was a powerful weapon, which used with intelligence could gain monumental victories. "Benbow told the workers that if the enforced sale of their labour power wasthe cause of their slavery, then their organised refusal to work must be the means for their liberation."[131] Benbow also "articulated the growing working class hatred towards the capitalist class and politicians. He argued that to expect help from the existing political parties and the middle classes was 'sheer madness', and that the working class could only rely on themselves to bring about change."[132] These methods of direct action against exploitative employers quite often existed around and alongside the growth of trade unionsthat often fought to defend their right to organise throughout the 1800's.

The International Workers of the World (IWW) in America and the French CGT (General Confederation of Labour) played large influencing roles in the rise of syndicalism in Britain. In 1903, anarchist Sam Mainwaring launched a new anarcho-syndicalist journal entitled *'The General Strike'* which won many syndicalists over to anarchism from the S.L.P. (Socialist Labour Party). *'The General Strike'* created a large interest in "fusion of anarchist anti-state precepts with trade union activity"[133]. Unfortunately *'The General Strike'* did not last too long but the ideas it expounded were soon to be re-established.

During 1907, the anarchist John Turner began a weekly paper called *'The Voice of Labour'* which, though only lasting a year, gained popularity with this statement in its first issue, "Direct action..is what we stand for.. We shall insist at every turn that nothing is gained without activity in organisation, in agitation, the Strike in all its forms, and that only by these means will the workers in the end be able to claim their own."[134] Nationally, many anarcho- syndicalists formed groupings around published papers and concentrated activity locally during industrial disputes. "In addition to the hard core of activists working within distinctively syndicalist organisations, there existed a further, more diffuse element of revolutionary industrial feeling, scattered through many other segments of the labour movement."[135]

The natural disposition to fight back against exploitative employers, coupled with the repeated 'let down' from parliamentary socialist wings of the movement, and often trade union betrayal, created a situation where "It is clear that the industrial unrest of this period offered revolutionaries of varying creeds potentially very favourable conditions to advance their political projects in Britain. The emergence of syndicalist ideas in this period seemed perfectly timed to give coherence and revolutionary temper to an evident urge to revolt amongst the organised working-class."[136] These 'favourable conditions' would also advance the propaganda efforts and reception of promoted ideals from local anarchists.

It is often said that the syndicalist movement was given a large boost with the return of Tom Mann, yet the ground was already laid, so to speak, "Economically, working-class conditions were being undermined. The trade union hierarchy remained largely wedded to parliamentarianism and moderation, and as union membership increased it became increasingly bureaucratic"[137]. Mann, after his eight year stay in Australia, was involved in many labour struggles which latter reflected and strengthened his theories of syndicalism. During May 1910, Mann along with London anarchist Guy Bowman travelled to France to speak with members of the C.G.T. of which they were impressed with. On their return they both produced the first issue of '*The Industrial Syndicalist*' which was to last ten months and was quite influential. In December 1910 a founding conference formed the Industrial Syndicalist Education League which was to strengthen syndicalism through many national speaking tours, as well as the distribution of syndicalist literature. The I.S.E.L.'s teachings "exercised a very strong influence, especially among the rank and file of the transport and mining industries, as was revealed in the great strike movements of that period."[138]

With the effectiveness of anarchist propaganda during these 'great strikes of the period', as well as other contributing aforementioned factors "the result was an explosion of industrial revolt of unprecedented extent and sustained power"[139] in which the anarcho-syndicalists played a large contributing role, both through their literature and propaganda, as well as physical involvement.

> "The first shots in the battle were fired in the North East. From November 1909 until July 1910 there was a series of spontaneous strikes culminating in a lock-out by the employers among the boilermakers of the shipyards. In January 1910 there started a three month strike by the traditionally moderate Durham miners against an agreement already signed by their union. The North-Eastern railwaymen struck for three days in mid 1910 which was sufficient to gain them victory."[140]

The strike wave continued nationally and culminated in near revolutionary situations in some areas, particularly Liverpool and Hull, especially during 1912. "In the ten years 1900-1909 the average annual total of days lost due to stoppages (disregarding the exceptional year of 1908 when these amounted to 10,790,000) was somewhere between 2 ½ and 3 million. In each of the year's 1910, 1911, 1913, and 1914 there were around 10 million days lost due to stoppages. In 1912 the figure was nearly 41 million."[141] The miners being on strike is said to have increased the 1912 figures.

As a note of interest, it is also said that George Harvey, local Follonsby (Wardley) lodge miner, played a significant role "in the advocacy of revolutionary syndicalism in the Durham coalfield before 1914"[142] yet the following, written by his own hand may dispel that myth somewhat;

> "It ought to be plainly seen by any thinker that "Direct Action" and Sabotage are reactionary methods of warfare in advanced

capitalist countries, and that their advocacy is a crime against the Labour Movement inasmuch as it spells – the running of the Labour Movement to disaster on the rocks of Anarchism."[143]

The October 1913 conference of the Miners Federation, held in Scarborough saw a resolution proposed by South Wales in favour of approaching the other big unions "with a view to co-operative action in support of each other' demands. In seconding it, Mr. Burton, Northumberland, said he would be in favour of syndicalism, anarchism, or nihilism if, by those means, they could combat Murphyism."[144]

[145]This sustained outburst of industrial militancy, strike activity, and pivotal acceptance of syndicalist ideas and practices amongst the working class, would benefit many anarchist and anarcho-syndicalism groupings with an influx of new members, as well as an increase in the levels of propaganda soldsuch as the new edition of *'Voice of Labour'*, as well as the *'Herald of Revolt'*, and *'Freedom'*, etc. This coupled with agitation outside shipyard gates, the mines, and city centre street meetings, would culminate in the huge spreading of the anarchist ideal. Examples of this anarchist inspired activity would become more evident in the little pit village on the outskirts of the Durham[146] coalfield called Chopwell.

## 1.15 THE CHOPWELL ANARCHISTS

At its peak in 1913, the Northern coalfield (Durham and Northumberland) employed nearly ¼ million people, and produced over 56 million tons of coal every year from around 400 local pits, equating to a quarter of Britain's coal mined nationally. Chopwell colliery began life as early as 1781, and was closed on 25 November 1966, and during its peak output employed upwards of 2000 people.

Much emphasis is given to the life during this period of Will Lawther[147] of whom we won't delve into too much as Lawther was only one of many amongst the Chopwell anarchists of the time, and as much as his early contribution is appreciated, as mentioned earlier in the George Cores quote, many anarchists names didn't appear in any 'limelight' so to speak, therefore why should Lawthers. I give mention to Lawther as during the following chapter, he often put his name forward as spokesman for the grouping of existing anarchists, and perhaps, as was common for the period, because of his Central Labour College education, was possibly one of a few who could actually write (or read for that matter). Basically I see him as being no more 'important' than any other member of the group.

May 1913, and in a report to *Freedom*, Lawther reports "Durham – a few years ago an active Anarchist or 'Workers freedom Group' would have been set down as impossible. But the impossible has been attained, and away among the miners of Durham are what may be looked upon as the forerunner of a real rank and file movement, selling *Freedom* pamphlets and books. At Chopwell, one of the largest collieries is a body of rebels who go out to the outlying collieries propagating the awful doctrine of Anarchism. Two meetings have been held at High Spen, with good sales of literature, and inquiries galore as to our intentions. And, as the Yankee says, it is right here where the workers are, where the real work is to be done."[148] High Spen is the next 'pit village' situated about a mile or so from Chopwell, and was home to the Garesfield Colliery.

Throughout 1913, although activities of the Chopwell anarchists were prevalent within the anarchist press, groupings of anarchists were still existent in Gateshead, Newcastle, and South Shields etc. J. Johnson of Edward Terrace, South Shields was a contact for *Freedom* literature, as well as G.W. Tindale of the Gateshead Group.

June 1913 and in a lengthy article in *Freedom*, the Chopwell anarchists were reporting on grievances within the pit, and how, despite the attempted involvement of the then Durham Miners Association union, the result was, support from "a body of men who pride themselves on being progressive (some of whom call themselves Socialists) not tolerating this action of the men." (24 men had walked out after complaining of a dangerous roof) and concluding "Enough has surely been said now to show how this tragic-comedy pans out, and the final result was that these men had to return to work practically as they had left. But just in so far as 'They never fail who die a great cause', so this struggle will not have been in vain. It points to the need for a policy based not upon the sands of conciliation, but upon the rock of revolution. Conscious effort must supersede the blind instinctive policy of depending upon others to do things that you can do yourself. And until that policy is acted upon, no good can come forth."[149]

July and the group is reporting;

> "Chopwell – A steady and persistent campaign is being carried on here amongst the miners; an active section of the Workers Freedom Group doing the needful. There has not been any stump oratory, but by selling *'Freedoms'* and pamphlets, and by discussion circles, the kind of propaganda that counts is being kept up. Should any comrade that loveth the soap box be coming this way – we would beonly too pleased to find him an outlet for his energies. We want the message of Direct Action carried right throughout the Northern coalfield, and no help is refused. New ground was tackled at Crawcrook on June 7th, a newcomer from the ranks of the political Socialists, R. Graham, taking "the box"[150] with Will Lawther. A good crowd listened to "those hot-headed young miners from Chopwell", and showed their appreciation by buying pamphlets and asking for a return visit. Leaflets were distributed right through the village. On Saturday, the 21st, Stanhope was visited by two comrades, who sold fifty *'Freedoms'* and some pamphlets whilst three of the big guns of the Labour Party were telling the tale about what they had done and what they were going to do."[151]

Fifty copies of an anarchist paper sold, as well as pamphlets is quite impressive in one day and shows the general acceptance throughout local pit villages of our ideals. The Gateshead group pamphlet sales were also on the increase, with that months amounting to 4s.

**Durham & Northumberland Miners' Annual Demonstrations** on the Racecourse, Durham, and at Morpeth, Saturday, July 19. —Workers wanted to sell FREEDOM and pamphlets at these demonstrations. Send your name and address, stating which one you will attend, to W. LAWTHER, 23 Trent Street, Chopwell, Co. Durham; or to J. JOHNSON, 36 Edward Terrace, South Shields.

September 1913, and in another report of the group's activities;

> "Chopwell – The slogan of revolt is still being sounded in this part of the Northern coalfield, outdoor propaganda having been brisk considering the difficulties that beset our path. Spen was visited on Sunday, July 13th when some pertinent questions were asked and answered on our views on leadership and officialism. Saturday, July 19th, was taken to be "the day" on which to move our unearthly ideal right into the heart of the leader's pleasant pastures at Durham, it being the annual Gala of the Durham miners. We made a speciality of the pamphlet *"Direct Action v Legislation"*, advertising it by a poster; and we set the other books and pamphlets out on the grass to catch the eye. Although the sales were not up to the expectations of optimistic comrades, nevertheless we created quite a sensation by daring to sell Anarchist literature to our brother slaves of the lamp and pick. A meeting was held after the big guns had fired off their usual cant and humbug about "the identity of interests between Capital and Labour", and "the wonderful progress we are making". Speeches on the need for direct action and revolution were given by our comrades Jack Griffiths (South Wales), Will Lewcock[152] (Ruskin College), George Harvey (I.W.G.B.), W. Mee (I.W.G.B.), and Will Lawther. Advantage was taken of the visit of our comrade Griffiths to do some propaganda, and meetings were held on July 20th at Chopwell in the morning, and at Crawcrook at night. Westerhope, a colliery village in Northumberland, was visited on the 21st, when a discussion took place in the local

> Working Men's Club. The makings of a fine group are to be found there, where our comrade Will Lewcock is doing good work. Tuesday, the 22nd was comrade Griffiths's last day amongst us, and it was utilised by a fine meeting at Spen. Visits like our comrades will do more to generate a feeling of unity than all the big demonstrations where empty platitudes are rolled off. The workers are eager to lend a listening ear to one who, like themselves, is a worker eager for real freedom, rather than to those whose visits are used as the means whereby they can climb a little farther on to the backs of their fellows. We want them off our backs, instead of lifting more on. This view was well put before a Chopwell audience by Will Lewcock on August 10, when he spoke on "State Capitalism or Freedom?" He showed how the Labour Party's State Mines Bill would not solve the poverty problem for the miner; rather would it tend to create a huge snobocracy, like the mine inspectors whom the State pays today."[153]

The group also mentioned the hope of shortly opening club premises on Derwent St, where all would be welcome to partake in the activities of a 'live propaganda group who are out for freedom'.

George Davison (1855-1930) was the fourth child of shipwright and carpenter William Davison, originally from Sunderland. Davison, who acquired a large amount of wealth through his involvement with Kodak, would siphon much of this wealth through the anarchist movement, funding many a project. These included a study centre / Communist club for the miners at the White House, Ammanford, South Wales (opened October 1913), the Central Labour College in London, which was a breakaway from Ruskin College, the launch of Glasgow paper *'The Anarchist'*, possibly funding for Kappers purchase of the commune at Clousden Hill, and the (Anarchist) Communist Club at Chopwell. "One of the most influential photographers before the First World War, Davison is often remembered for the wrong reasons. The journalist and independent MP Horatio Bottomley attacked him as a Bolshevik corrupter of youth, yet nothing was further from the truth; he was an anarchist who abhorred the use of violence and a communist before the word was associatedinevitably with Marxism."[154]

The Communist Club opened 9th December 1913, "Two weeks into a strike at the Chopwell pit. Indeed, the Clubs influence might well have been immediate as on its opening night 26 coal trucks from a local pit were deliberately set loose to run down a hill then crash, destroying a long section of line and causing £3,000 worth of damage. The local police noted this 'strange coincidence' though there was no direct indication that the men finally arrested (and acquitted) for this act of sabotage had drawn any inspiration from the inaugural meeting at the Chopwell anarchist Club."[155]

Throughout the remainder of 1913 and well into 1914, the Gateshead anarchist group would regularly sell large amounts of anarchist pamphlets, 8s 6d worth in October, 5s 6d in November and 4s 6d in December, and so on. At the previous national anarchist conference in Liverpool, 1913, it was agreedthe 1914 conference was to be held in Newcastle (a room had been secured at the British Socialist Party headquarters on Leazes Park Road) and the February issue of *Freedom*, sees R Cleghorn (of Hyde Park St) from the Gateshead group requesting numbers of attendees, what sleeping accommodation was required, as well as items for the agenda.[156]

Meanwhile, E.C.H.O. from the Chopwell group was reporting;

> "Although no news has appeared in these columns of the doings of this Workers Freedom Group, we have been far from inactive or merely passive Anarchists. On the contrary, we have been verymuch alive, having seen the organised constitutional Durham miners that work at Chopwell Colliery go on strike, without notice or strike allowance, against one of the largest combines in the coal trade. One of the features of the strike was the fact that the paid agents of the men took a very firm stand against the men, just as firm as their "masters". This proved how true has been our indictment of leadership,

showing that the leader exists for no other purpose but to perpetuate Capitalism. It was a fitting climax to the strike that the "house warming" or formal opening of the Communist Club, where the Workers Freedom Group meet, should follow the end of the strike. This took place on January 24th and will stand out as the bright star on the horizon of the workers of Chopwell. After a tea- fight had taken place, the tables were cleared for an open discussion on Anarchist Communism. A good number took part, and the outcome of it augurs well for the movement in this part. Amongst those who took part in it were Comrades Davison, Tindale (Gateshead), Will Lawther, Max Melinger, and many outsiders who supplied the opposition. Sales of literature and *Freedom* have been fairly good, far exceeding the expectations of the most optimistic of our comrades. And to those who think that there is no hope for Anarchist Communism, we point to them the work that has been achieved in this direction. There is no mistaking the tendency of the workers to hear our gospel, read our literature, and accept the ideal and the hope that Anarchy brings into their otherwise dull, drab, and monotonous lives. It is up to those of us who believe in Anarchy to go forward with our unofficial and anti-leadership propaganda, sure and certain of the ultimate triumph of our ideal."[157]

March 1914, and the Chopwell Group again reports "Good meetings have been held this month. Our comrade Warren (Newcastle) on February 15th gave a fine address on Anarchism and Trade Unionism, which gave rise to a fine discussion. On the 21st, Miss Mary McNeill, B.Sc. (South Shields), gave a paper on Edward Carpenter. This opened out a new aspect for the majority of those who were present. Our comrade showed how Carpenter, having seen through the hollow shams of to-day, seeks for a real, sane view of life, and finds it by living and working amidst those who are "salt of the earth". A meeting in the Labour Hall, South Shields, on February 1, was addressed by Will Lawther."[158] The Communist Club would throughout April, hold discussions and study groups every night.

## 1.16 THE NEWCASTLE ANARCHIST CONFERENCE 1914

Never have I seen so much press coverage of an anarchist conference, as to that given to the Newcastle conference of 1914[159], not until that of the Class War international conference held in London 1991. This quite clearly showed the general curiosity, and possibly, the general beginnings and acceptance of anarchist ideas and practices throughout the country, and the world for that matter. "It is not often that Anarchists foregather with such a blare of trumpets, or, more precisely, a press booming. Everyone in Newcastle knew that we were coming, knew not exactly what to expect, and awaited with pent-up curiosity to see what manner of men we really were. Disappointment was theirs, for we were respectable looking, mild-mannered, and did not assume a fearsome aspect."[160]

Proceedings began on Easter Sunday April 12th, 10am at the British Socialist Party's rooms at Leazes Park Road, and from the outset, the press were told that the day's proceedings were private. "Many of the delegates are very youthful in appearance. They number about 40, and represent the Anarchists of Great Britain, the majority being from Edinburgh, Glasgow, and Manchester. The conference meets without a chairman, and beyond the statement of a subject for discussion there are no rules controlling the proceedings. Delegates speak when they like, and on what particular phase of the subject under discussion they please."[161]

> "We started well, for did we not argue with our serving maid over the tea cups ere we had scarce settled ourselves in the town, and very soon afterwards continued the argument with pressmen and local Socialists, whose premises we had taken as our temporary abode. One felt certain misgivings as to the value of long and protracted discussions as a means to an end, but felt, nevertheless, that good work is done by an interchange of opinion upon the many subjects which trouble us; by taking stock of our past years work, and meeting comrades from all parts, many of whom had been hitherto names only. It was

refreshing after many very usual conferences to know that here if one had aught to say, objections to raise, or criticism to make, no mighty chairman threatened if the rules of procedure were transgressed. We knew what we wanted, and discussed it fully, freely, and frankly. A word as to the personnel. They came from all parts, we forget exactly where, but chiefly Glasgow, Edinburgh, Coatbridge, Huddersfield, York, Sheffield, London, Bristol, Gateshead, Liverpool, Stockport, Wales, north and south, and the Chopwell boys came in dozens, each an embryo fighter, from whom more will be heard anon, we hope."[162]

Patronising comments about 'serving maids' from *Freedom*[163] reporter aside, the conference commenced after the delegates battled through the hoards of reporters and curious onlookers. Proceedings began with reports from various districts on activities in their area and;

> "Particularly the inspiring accounts of activities in Coatbridge and Ammonford. Nothing beyond the usual plodding of a handful of comrades, beset by persecution and difficulties, could be reported; but one felt that the Welsh spirit, which can run enthusiastically in so many causes, will find, and in fact is finding a splendid field in Anarchist propaganda. The comrades working in mining districts had certainly the most inspiring reports. Newcastle comrades decided to form a group for more active work. Before leaving we heard that they had met and definitely started the group. We wish them luck."[164]

The rest of the day was taken up with discussions on organisation, the relation of anarchism to trade unionism, syndicalism, the Modern School, a new weekly paper, anti-militarism, literature and pamphlet sales etc, as well as the proposed future International conference, which with the situation in Europe at the time and forthcoming world war, didn't actually occur.

> "The best and most useful discussion of all was the one upon the relation of Anarchism to Syndicalism, Trade Unionism, etc. Whilst there was a diversity of opinion as to the value of Anarchists joining and working through Trade Unions, it was fairly well agreed that some form of industrial action was necessary, and this action and our thoughts could best be expressed by adopting the Syndicalist method of warfare in Trade Unions, thus helping the workmen to put aside their faith in leaders and each become a fighting unit for the emancipation of his class."[165]

These methods were nothing new to the anarchists in the North East, who predominantly belonged and were from a large industrialised urban working class, and had been part of and involved within Syndicalist struggles for years. "If Syndicalism were pure, it was stated, it would be Anarchy, and that movement at present was a step towards Anarchy. Trade-Unionism was good, inasmuch as it went to build up Syndicalism."[166] It can be said that syndicalism in general is the industrial expression of anarchism with the same goals in mind, and that "syndicalism is the means, anarchism is the end" as the old anarchist saying goes.

That evening a public meeting was held at the Co-operative hall, Darn Crook, where one delegate mentioned to the press, on the size and apparent interest of the audience;

> "We do not know that the local people have any names added to the roll. But we take a leaf out of the book of the old Methodist. Many entered their Bethels out of curiosity and stayed to pray. Many might attend our meetings out of curiosity and stop to think."[167]

George Barrett, Doris Wess, G Greensmith, W.D. Ponder, John McAra and Will Lawther etc spoke to an audience of well over 400. Chopwell anarchist Lawther, the first speaker of the evening;

> "Was the advocacy of individual action. He criticised the work of the official Labour movement, and referred to their failure to cope with the present industrial situation. The recent upheaval among the rank and file of the working classes, which had been apparent during the last four years, he said, was looked upon by the Anarchists as a tendency among the masses to throw off their leaders. They as Anarchists welcomed it as a sign of the times. The workers, they thought, had not got themselves into such an economic state of oppression, and had been marking the failure of the methods, policies, and performances of their leaders, that they had at last resolved to fight a way out for themselves Anarchists believed that any movement which aimed at freeing the worker must carry out its propaganda, not in the doss house at Westminster, but at work and where the work was. If workers wished to be free they must depend upon their own initiative, and not upon legislative enactments, but upon direct action. They could not depend upon men who, professing themselves leaders of the working classes, had not the courage to openly oppose the capitalist class. They had seen a tendency among the official Labour Party – and by that he did not mean the band of 'temperance fanatics' adorned by the name of the Labour Party, but the whole responsible trade union movement – not merely to refuse to take a stand on behalf of the oppressed, as in Dublin, but actually to openly further the work of the capitalist class. This had to come to an end, he declared, and it would have tobe stopped by the rank and file realising that the work was their own. He noticed in the Durham and Northumberland Miners Association a tendency among the men to kick over the traces. As Anarchists they welcomed it, and not only that, but they were determined to do everything in their power to further the tendency. Such work was the object of their meeting that evening, to bring the instinct of

revolt into considered action."[168]

Other speakers continued on similar lines of thought including McAra of Edinburgh who affirmed that;

> "They had a logical base for their idea, and their opponents could not refute the fact. There was nothing in Anarchy, he declared, which could not be applied to every form of industry, to every form of mans activity on earth. He stood for the idea of personal defence against brutal oppression. In many countries this brutal oppression continued, and he instanced Scotland, his own country, as a place where some of the worst conditions were to be encountered. These conditions, he declared, were due to the failure of municipal action, principally in Glasgow, Leith, and Dundee."[169]

Of course, anarchist leaflets were freely given away before, during and after the public meeting, one of which set out the objects of the movement as follows. (1) To throw the torchlight of criticism, from an anarchist viewpoint, upon all phases of society. (2) To advocate free association in production, the establishment of Anarchist Communism, and the abolition of all forms of authority.

> "A number of paragraphs on another leaflet give the basis for work among "Workers Freedom Groups". A revolution is advocated to overthrow capitalism, not in order to gain suitable control, but to secure the abolition of control and thereby gain freedom. This work, the statement proceeds, must start in the workers organisations, which should be shaped according to the needs of the future society, and not from the ideas which belong to the capitalist system. The movement does not countenance the establishment of any central governing or administrating body, and in the change to be wrought, politicians and officials will have no part." And concluding "The political change brought about by the coming revolution will be the abolition of the state and its executive, the government, and

> the conduct of affairs by a method of free agreement in other words, Anarchist Communism."[170]

The conference ended with an open air meeting in the Bigg Market, which;

> "Was the more inspiring, and was throughout a battle between a critical audience and the speakers. Comrades Dunn, McAra, and Ponder were the speakers, and the latter's answers to a would-be annihilator in the shape of an S.L.P. critic were keenly taken up and appreciated by the audience. Thus ended a conference which has helped us to understand each other's work and methods, prepared the ground for a weekly paper, and sent us back to work feeling thatsomewhere, at least, good work is being enthusiastically carried on."[171]

The Chopwell group, inspired by the conference events, although we should say – the inspirers of events, advertised the following open air meetings, at local pit villages, on Sundays as follows:- May 3rd, High Spen, 11am ; Rowlands Gill, 7pm. May 10th, Leadgate, 11am ; Consett, 6.30pm. May 17th, Crawcrook, 11am. May 24th, Prudhoe on Tyne, 11am. May 31st, High Spen, 11am. June 7th, Rowlands Gill, 6.30pm. June 14th, Prudhoe on Tyne, 6.30pm. June 28th, High Spen, 11.30am. And July 5th, Crawcrook, 11am.

The convenient outbreak of World War 1[172], 28 July 1914 to 11 November 1918, curtailed these events, just as the anarchists were becoming unified, and forging stronger links with the syndicalist movement. "Many of the left wing elements in the village lost popularity as a result of their opposition to the war. Chopwell showed immense loyalty, with 500 volunteers of whom 200 were later killed in action."[173]

Some anarchists in Chopwell were to continue with activities and anti war stances, October 11th sees a Ferrer Memorial Meeting at the Communist Club with Will Lawther, Will Lewcock, and Adv Staamer as speakers, whilst in December a social evening was held at the Club in order to raise funds for the children of the 'Socialist Sunday School'.

> "Will Lawther took a pacifist stance in *The Spur* (Dec 1914) and involved himself along with his brothers Steve and Eddie in anti-war campaigning, while his brothers Bob and Joe were among the first to enlist in the village. In 1916 Eddie Lawther was sentenced to two years hard labour by a Sunderland court for conscientious objection."[174]

October 1914, and in a sickening example of the local Socialists siding with the state in their support of the war, and of their washing their hands of any involvement to any resistance perpetuated by local anarchists no doubt, Robert Lacon, secretary of the British Socialist Party, Newcastle Branch was to state through the local press;

> "Sir – I am instructed by the Newcastle branch of the B.S.P. to request the favour of space in your columns to make public a disclaimer in regard to recent disturbances caused by the unpatriotic utterances of certain alleged Socialists in this city. These persons are not members of this organisation, and would in all probability have been expelled had they been members, as it is the deliberate and avowed policy of this branch to refrain entirely from even the ordinary outdoor meetings at this crisis in the nation's affairs, thereby doing our bit to assist in presenting a united front to the enemy."[175]

I wonder what happened to the 'united front to the enemy' of capitalism that the 'socialists' purport to adhere to? Of course the war created a massive divide in "The international socialist movement. Most social-democratic parties and their leaders in the belligerent countries supported their own governments and their military efforts. The anarchists had long criticized the social- democrats for collaborating with state power and openly propagated their own anti-militarism."[176] Which brings forth to mind the old saying of, with friends like these, who need's enemies?

## 1.17 WORLD WAR 1

With the declaration of war, dark clouds hovered over the entire syndicalist and anarchist movement. Internal arguments were raging over support for the allies and those who naturally and rightly opposed the wholesale slaughter of the predominantly working classes. Many activities decreased due to enforced conscription and legalised kidnapping into the armed forces (especially in syndicalist strongholds). Meltzer comments;

> "So strong was the syndicalist movement generally in 1914, and so severe the repression against it afterwards, that many believe the Great War was an international connivance to prevent its growth."[177]

History it littered with examples of wars being instigated in order to keep an equilibrium of control for the current state in question, especially when the aforementioned state is challenged to such an extent as in that represented by the international growth of syndicalism and the unifying aspects of the growing anarchist movement. Ernest Bevin was later to recall "It was a period which, if the war had not broken out, would have, I believe, seen one of the greatest industrial revolts the world would ever have seen."[178] With the patriotic fervour of the manufactured war the situation was saved and capitalism could breathe freely again with a sigh of relief. Perlman would sum this up perfectly with his sentence "foreign war, the most ancient method of quelling domestic rebellion."[179]

The senseless slaughter of millions of people during;

> "The fighting between rival imperial systems during World War 1 provides grimly adequate testimony to the way in which the state (not only in Britain) controls and organises the means of destruction, creating mass institutions for the systematic

> regulation of violence and death. Those people who opposed this wholesale killing were branded as cowards, physically attacked and beaten up by mobs which were covertly encouraged and organised by the British government. Conscientious objectors were conscripted and imprisoned, or bullied into becoming stretcher-bearers, which frequently resulted in their deaths."[180]

Those who refused to fight were often sent to the front lines, where upon their refusal, were shot for desertion, and of course these murders were naturally covered up by the state under such fallacies as the Military Service Act, or Official Secrets Act, etc. Meltzer, in his research, highlighted numerous examples of the disappearances of anarchist and syndicalist militants during this period, from Glasgow, Yorkshire, Wales, and "The other stronghold was on Tyneside but there the entire Anarchist grouping vanished from the scene before the war ended. One old militant told me in the 40's that as many others who were not in war industries were drifting south, or enlisting, all were assumed to have done so. Had they all belonged to some tangible organisation, for example, the same church, undoubtedly enquiries would have been made."[181] I can assume the entire anarchist grouping Meltzer mentioned is that of Chopwell, yet some embers of resistance from the area were to persist through the bleak times ahead, and create a small glow of hope.

December 1914, sees the Chopwell group hold an event at the Communist Club for local children, who all received fruit and toys and;

> "Comrade Harry Bolton, in a short speech, pointed out to the fathers and mothers of the children and others who were present how we were going to hold our banner aloft, and keep our principles intact, even if the so-called leaders thought it was a just war. Because, as he pointed out, after all it is not they who believe in war and do the fighting, but the workers; and until the workers have the strength and courage to resist these leaders and war-mongers then the dirty work would still be

theirs to do. Like many other colliery districts in the cold, bleak, North East Coast, we suffer from the war, the pits being laid off whenever recruiting is slack. Of course, that is not compulsion, only it is forcing by starvation those who would nototherwise enlist."[182]

## STAND WE FIRM?

"Some people who claim to have seen through all the schemes that are adopted by the common enemy of mankind – the capitalists – whenever they want to extend their profiteering to-day, believe that the present conflict is not for commercial supremacy, but that, on the contrary, it is a war to end war; in short, a war for humanity to move onward in its progress towards a better system of society. Whilst it is essential to understand the position of our enemy, in order to combat his advances, it is more essential to understand our own position. And to that end must we work, because we now see how easy the workers have been persuaded to forego the fight that they have been waging the last few years.

Many of those who a few months ago were talking of the coming industrial Armageddon are to-day urging the workers to fight, and lay down their lives if need be, in defence of the class whom they are organised to fight against in the industrial arena. And yet these recruiting sergeants of the Labour movement used to say that the industrial worker who voted for other than the official Labour candidate was, politically speaking, a blackleg. So if their line of reasoning be developed, there is now no use for them as Labour leaders, because they have found an enemy more bitter than the capitalist who lives upon them. And stripped of all the veneer that the capitalist press (our enemy) has added to the countries that we are at war against, what remains but the fact that in the interests of a class that is not the working class we are to forsake all the principles and ideals, hopes, and aspirations that we hold dearer than life itself, to fight for our oppressors. Shall we flinch? No, we must not. We repeat the truism that has been uttered for many years: the workers in these isles, but not of these isles, have no enemy except the capitalists who live upon them. Our enemy is here, and how he chuckles to-day to see his "bands" go out, and leave their kith and kin to his tender mercy. A year ago the workers of Dublin were fighting for the right to say what their conditions of work should be. What has taken place since then that we should go through hardships and suffering to defend the property of the Murphy's and the other exploiters, so that they can have a clear field to exploit in other lands?

To us, there can be no other question except our own of how are we workers going to free ourselves from capitalism. It may be that there are other questions; but they do not concern us, and should not transcend the great question that is ever present in the workers war. No one will deny that some are suffering in France and Belgium through the advance of the German troops; but surely what are standing armies kept for? Have not our brothers sold themselves to fight anything and everything that comes in the way, as being what they term "their duty to their king and country"? But then has not there been much unnecessary suffering in England this last few years because they who are asking you to fight and bear arms would not forego their right to rob?

Shall we fight? Yes, we answer, when we have something to fight for; but not to-day. We know of one war only, the battle for freedom, for the conquest of Capitalism. As this war is not for that purpose, it does not concern us.

Must we flinch from the ideals we have always held? No, we stand firm to-day for a land where poverty will be unknown, where women and children shall not want for bread, where men are not treated as if they were things without human feelings. That land is not known yet, but it is our duty to work for it.

Never mind the threats of conscription, never heed the shrieks of the paper patriots; we shall conquer, because we have truth on our side. And that truth is that the workers are exploited by a common enemy who knows neither race nor creed, sex not colour. So we of the working class fight that common enemy, and extend the hand of fellowship to the workers of all lands. Will Lawther."[183]

April 1915, and the annual anarchist conference was this year held in Stockport, to upwards of fifty delegates, including those from Gateshead and Chopwell. An address by the Chopwell delegate on Anarchy and its relation to the War provoked a heated debate, but all eventually agreed that as anarchists, they cannot logically support any government, or any 'governmental war of liberation'.

An anarchist is an internationalist and without that concept of internationalism, anarchism becomes meaningless. War's between nations, is inevitably, a war waged against the cannon fodder of the international working classes. The class war is always being waged between labour and capital, the common foe being that of the international capitalists. The only war worth fighting in that case was that of the international, ongoing, class war, the war to end all wars and an end to the imposed fictitious map lines labelled borders that separate, and to a large extent, control us into neat little sections of the planet. In essence – divide and rule.

During the regional reports of group activities, "Chopwell reported that work had suffered since the war. Some colliery owners had deliberately closed the collieries excepting for a day or two a week, ostensibly to force the miners into enlisting. Among their most promising work had to be reckoned the starting of a Sunday school, which was going well."[184]

The London May Day march of 1915 never occurred, because of the war and restrictions from the state, but the Chopwell group, as ever in defiance, advertised their May Day demonstration.

> **CHOPWELL.**—May Day Demonstration. Open-air meeting, 11 a.m. Open Sunday School, Communist Club, Derwent Street, 2.30 p.m. Roll up! We still believe in Labour's Cause. Labour's Hymns and Labour's Speakers.

The Chopwell group, as well as D.C. Thompson and co of the Newcastle group, and of course the Gateshead group were all regular contributors to various *Freedom* funds and subscriptions throughout the remainder of 1915 and well into 1916 (and into 1918 from G.W. Tindale of the Gateshead group), which still showed some levels of local activity, despite prevailing odds and nationalistic fervour, whilst under the auspices of the 'Defence of the Realm Act' the state was, nationwide, suppressing discontent and sources of anti-war, and anti-conscription literature with repeated raids, jailing many militants in the process.

January 1916, and again the so-called 'socialists' were issuing a manifesto in support of the state, and its virulent attack directed at anarchists opposed to the war. It declared;

> "We as socialists declare that to object to the principle of compulsion when one's native land is attacked, is hypocrisy. Socialism is not a system of "go as you please", socialism is not anarchism; socialism is rather the necessary retort and challenge to the individualist school of radicalism; and we who have fought for many years in the vindication of Labour's rights have now to remind organised labour that direct and indirect compulsion is the keystone of the edifice of Trade Unionism."

After continuing to call any able bodied trade unionist that refuses to fight, andsupports strikes during the period as cowards and humbugs, it concludes;

> "From cradle to grave the whole of our social life is characterised by compulsion. How, then, when millions of ruthless soldiery, led by the most brutal of all tyrannies , threatens our hearths and homes and the destiny of our people, shall a man refuse, in the misused nameof liberty, the duty of discharging, with his fellows, the elementary right of self defence? British workers, we are convinced that this agitation, so far as it is carried on in the name of the masses of British working men, is a slander on the courage and character of the

British masses."[185]

As demonstrated during the period, Labour 'leaders' and the Trade Union hierarchy were actively suppressing any visible revolt and rejection of the war amongst the working classes left to keep the war industry supplied, "Indeed the war could hardly have been waged without these very useful adjuncts of Trade Unionism."[186] Many labour struggles, particularly on Clydeside, were waged without Trade Union recognition and support, but through the shop stewards, despite repression.

"Trade union organisation was the only thing between us and anarchy"

Tory 'leader' – Bonar Law[187]

The unofficial strike, was at times, particularly in time of war, one of the only remaining weapons left to the working classes. Bureaucratic Trade Unions, despite some of their admiral beginnings, had become administrators and managers of any perceived conflict, with an aim of keeping the rank and file workers within industry subdued and contained in the interests of political and economic stability. They serve a purpose of keeping their members in line, whilst they, as the so called 'voice' of the workers collaborate with the state in the interest of capitalist harmony. This collaboration includes negotiating with whatever state induced puppet of a political party is in power at the time to "keep wages down while prices rise, in order to prop up the system and prevent it from collapsing."[188]

Whenever workers use their own initiative and resort to direct action without trade union consent, it undermines the power and privileges of the constitutional trade unionist 'leader', whose job depends on the workers airing their grievances etc through the official channels, and keeping the equilibrium of control. "This explains their dread of unofficial strikes. They frequently spend far more effort in arguing with the workers than with the bosses and whenever the members get out of control and disgrace them by actions unconstitutionally, we see them siding with the capitalists and issuing statements in the capitalist press denouncing the very people they are there to represent."[189] In the larger scheme of events, the unofficial strike can be concluded as "A training session, a salutary exercise that will harden the proletariat for war, in preparation for a final struggle which will be the revolutionary general strike."[190]

March 1916, and in a case[191] typical of the time and under the headline of 'Newcastle tribunal – Anarchist as conscientious objector' the local press reports;

> "An attendant-cook on a dining-car in the employ of the North-Eastern Railway appealed on conscientious grounds, declaring that "he could not take human life, and could not, under any circumstances, help in any war." The applicant said, in reply to a question, that he objected to help the wounded, because by doing so he would release someone else. *The Chairman*: - Do you object on Christian grounds? *Applicant*: - I am not a Christian; I object on moral grounds. In further reply to Mr Woolf, a member of the Tribunal, who pointed out that the applicant was voicing his objections late in the day, the reply was made that "he had been voicing his opinions for the last 17 years." *Mr Woolf*: - it looks as if you are trying to save yourself by coming now. *Applicant*: - I held the same opinions during the Boer War. *Mr Gibbon*: - What organisation do you belong to? *Applicant*: - I have been attached to the anarchist groups in the various towns in which I have lived. *Mr Gibbon*: - But they are opposed to all organisation? *Applicant*: - To all forms of war – yes. He was recommended for non-combatant service."[192]

And more than likely, shot in the back.

Until the end of the war in late 1918, although the effects of the social upheaval and wholesale slaughter were to be felt for numerous years afterwards, poverty and deprivation were rife in the region, food shortages were commonplace. "Throughout late 1916 and 1917 the food problem grew worse and in the bitterly cold winter of 1917-1918 matters reached a crisis." Gas and electricity were restricted and cut off if over used, "Coal was very difficult to obtain so that poorer families froze at home and went without hot food."[193] As unrest, and disturbances, especially centred on the obtaining of food from the few shops with anything left grew, the government "finally hadto introduce compulsory rationing. But the damage had been done. The cumulative effect of deprivation in the war years, observation by ordinary people of the transparent injustice of the system, the complete imbalance of the level of sacrifice, all led to a collapse in confidence in the objectivity of the authorities."[194]

Despite this 'collapse in confidence' of the authorities amongst the working class, times were hard for the local anarchists, especially, like those around them, facing difficulties to survive daily life alone. Not much mention is given to them during this period throughout the national anarchist press, other than that of the persistent Gateshead Group, who would continue, until July 1931, with their contributions to *Freedom*. The remaining pockets of resistance and revolt were predominantly in the industrial sphere, in which local militants wereno doubt involved.

News of the Russian events of 1917 began to filter through and excite the Labour movement, with talk of Soviets, Workers councils etc[195], and the then formation of the Communist Party "was to divert the struggle into parliamentarism and the Kremlin line."[196] Until the horrors and oppressive and murderous brutality of the Bolshevik regime became common knowledge, the Communist Party would entice many militants into its deceitful web. "These little things happen when the people permit new rulers to pose as their saviours."[197]

## 1.18 THOU SHALT OBEY CHURCH AND STATE

The church is another repressive, coercive and state sanctioned measurement of control and enforced obedience, especially in its implementation of the philosophy of control from above. Anarchists hold no qualms with personal religion, but the authoritative indoctrination and coercion in which 'organised' religion imposes its will upon its adherents is obnoxious.

> "Nothing is more natural than that the belief in God, the creator, regulator, judge, master, curser, saviour, and benefactor of the world, should still prevail among the people, especially in the rural districts, where it is more widespread than among the proletariat of the cities. The people, unfortunately, are still very ignorant, and are kept in ignorance by the systematic efforts of all the governments, who consider this ignorance, not without good reason, as one of the essential conditions of their own power. Weighted down by their daily labour, deprived of leisure, of intellectual intercourse, of reading, in short of all the means and a good portion of the stimulants that develop thought in men, the people generally accept religious traditions without criticism and in a lump. These traditions surround them from infancy in all the situations of life, and artificially sustained in their minds by a multitude of official poisoners of all sorts, priests and laymen, are transformed therein into a sort of mental and moral babit, too often more powerful even than their natural good sense."
>
> "There is a class of people who, if they do not believe, must at least make a semblance of believing. This class comprising all the tormentors, all the oppressors, and all the exploiters of humanity; priests, monarchs, statesmen, soldiers, public and private financiers, officials of all sorts, policemen, gendarmes, jailers and executioners, monopolists, capitalists, tax-leeches, contractors and landlords, lawyers, economists, politicians of all shades, down to the smallest vendor of sweetmeats, all will

repeat in unison those words of Voltaire:

> "If God did not exist, it would be necessary to invent him." For, you understand, "the people must have a religion." That is the safety - valve."[198]

The state, as well as using religion as an element of control, at times also fears the preaching's of wayward Christian advocates, who recognise no authority of any government, in essence, a type of Christian anarchism like that of Tolstoy.[199] This was touched upon earlier and demonstrated with the examples of Joseph Barker, and the Reverend Harris of Harton church.

The predominant religion during this period throughout the mining villages in the North East was Primitive Methodism. Whilst being in itself another confusing arm of the different religious sects, the Primitive Methodist church was part and parcel entrenched within the daily hardships of life in working class communities, before, during, and after the war. "Its sphere of operation is, however, much more exclusively among the poor; numbers of whom, no doubt, who probably would never venture to the formal meetings of the other sects, are found attending the out-door preaching or engaging in the cottage services conducted by the Primitive Methodists... The community whose operations penetrate most deeply through the lower sections of the people is the body called the Primitive Methodists."[200] And "Of all the Nonconformist denominations, the Primitives with their emotional intensity had most appeal to the poor."[201]

Within the community, the church, or church hall, is often used in many aspects of communal life and interaction. The misconception that anarchists want to 'burn the churches to the ground' is a fallacy[202]. As anarchists, we would rather the local church was turned into a community social centre for numerous communal activities.

Perhaps alarmed by these elements of support by local churches amongst working class communities, or in a move to tighten the bond between the state and the ruling body of the Catholic Church, or the wayward preaching's of 'radical' Christian anarchists etc, the catholic church would, in 1919 throw the gauntlet of enforced obedience down to its members. Alarmed by the 'ever increasing spread of Socialism', under the threat of excommunication, the following prohibitions were pronounced;

- "It is forbidden and absolutely unlawful for a catholic to be a member of Anarchist or Socialist associations or to give activesupport to such.
- A catholic may not join associations which, although not bearing the name of Anarchist or Socialist, are united with Anarchist or Socialist associations to actively support the same.
- The catholic who has joined such associations or actively supported them is under the serious obligation of renouncing his membership or of ceasing to give such support.
- Wherefore, so long as a catholic is a member of such organisations and has not at least the firm determination to renounce his membership as soon as possible, or so long as he gives active support to such organisations, he cannot obtain absolution from sins and therefore cannot worthily receive any sacrament.
- The catholic who reads professedly Anarchistic or Socialistic publications or attends Anarchistic or Socialistic meetings puts himself thereby in the proximate occasion of losing his faith, and so long as he will not abandon this dangerous occasion he cannot obtain absolution from sins and therefore cannot worthily receive any sacrament.
- The catholic who accepts the teachings of Anarchists or Socialists and is known as such can no longer be considered a member of the church. He must be denied the sacraments so long as he remains an adherent of Anarchism or Socialism.

Catholics! The choice is either for or against Christ, for or against your Holy Faith. The alternative is either catholic or socialist; but to be a catholic and a socialist at the same time is an impossibility".[203]

What more could I possibly add to that? Other than... HOLY SHIT!

## 1.19 1919—1920

In a further denouncement of anarchism to the local press, during the brief national railway strike of 1919, Mr Candler – local railwaymen's official of the National Union of Railwaymen, was to shrink away from any involvement of anarchists during the nine day dispute. The strike was precipitated when the government announced plans to reduce rates of pay which had been negotiated during the First World War. Mr Candler said;

> "They felt there was a lot of misapprehension on the part of the public to the present position, and that an attempt was being made in some quarters to distract attention from the real points at issue. Even the Prime Minister had gone to the length of suggesting that the strike had been engineered by a certain small section of people who were using the trade unions for purposes subversive of the country's weal – that the strike was being run by a body of anarchists. "I want" said Mr Candler with emphasis, "to say, as a law abiding citizen, that I have no connection whatever with any anarchist movement, and that there is no such connection as far as the railwaymen are concerned." And further adding "I want to make it perfectly clear that all this talk about Anarchism and the using of trade unions for the purpose of upsetting the existing order of society, is sheer clap-trap. We know nothing about any such policy, and we are convinced that the men whom we have sent to the Executive Committee to represent us are not the class of men who would commit themselves to any such policy. It is simply a mare's nest."[204]

Nevertheless the government "Went into battle with glee, urging the public on against the "Anarchists" in terms they had previously used against the Germans."[205] After nine days of strike action, the government agreed to maintain wages for another year. Perhaps the threat of further anarchist involvement was to help with the minor success?

In 1919—20 and strikes on the railways, in the docks, some mining areas, and even the police, put forward the notion that revolution was perhaps possible in Britain too. "The average number of workers involved in strikes and lock-outs at this time was 2,108,000, compared with an average of 308,100 between 1927 and 1939. Fighting in Ireland and India only added to the general disquiet"[206]

In summary, the years 1882—1920 showed a gradual increase in the activities of, as well as the rise of the local anarchists in numbers, with their philosophy and practical aspects of anarchism. The natural differences with parliamentary and war supporting 'socialists' became apparent and press misconception's were evidently to be naturally expected.

Poverty, repression, press and public misconception all eventually took their toll on the local anarchist movement, and none more so than the horrifying effects and outcomes both during and after World War 1. It would take thirty years for the anarchists to recover locally to sufficient numbers to again raise their heads above the precipitous parapet in their drive and purpose of perceived rightfulness and pursuit of spreading the message.

In Part 2 (1920—1950) it is shown that there is little evidence of their survival locally, and it is with historical appreciation that local activist Tom brown, with his prolific writings during the following decades, enabled this study to continue both during this period, and the later 1960s.

# PART TWO 1920—1950

## 2.1 EARLY 1920s – NOT A TIME OF PLENTY

From 1920 until the late 1950's, despite some tumultuous times within the country and especially the North East labour movement, there is little remaining evidence of specific anarchist activity. The North East has always had a fluid population, with many leaving the area to seek employment[207]. Perhaps many anarchists did move away, perhaps many were 'killed' during the two world wars, perhaps many didn't want to raise their voices above the parapet of, at times, Communist Party dominance, or ashamed to be in anyway associated with any Bolshevik deemed activities, especially after the horrors they perpetuated were gradually coming to light[208]. Most local protest activities or elements of any literature were labelled by both the press and the state as being communist or Bolshevik in nature, so any anarchist activities were swallowed up within this framework. State and police repression, blacklisting from employers, media distortion, and poverty could have all played out dominant aspects in the lives and activities of the local anarchists.[209] A lot more research is needed in this area, especially around events at both Newcastle and Sunderland's shipyards, to name one example. Despite this, our history will prevail with a few points of interest that have come to light during this research. As for the wider events during these decades, I will only touch briefly upon, as this is not the space to examine the wider labour movement, only general anarchist activity.

1921 and the year seen the miners' go to strike over plans to return ownership of the mines back to the 'coal owners' like the Duke of Northumberland. The strike lasted three months over the summer of 1921 and ended in monetary failure.

"Urged on by the Duke of Northumberland and other property owners who feel the ground shaking beneath their feet, the Government continues to arrest and prosecute Communists and other agitators in all parts of the country. Speeches about the necessity of abolishing the capitalist system, which have been made many thousands of times in the past without any prosecution arising,are now held to be "likely to cause sedition and disaffection," and must be put down by the strong arm of the law. Members of the Communist Party have been specially selected as victims, their offices and houses being raided, and they themselves hauled up before magistrates on most trumpery charges, and fined or sent to prison. *The Communist* of May 28 states that there have been 61 arrests, 32 imprisonment sentences, 7 hard labour, 25 second division, 14 fines from £100 down, 17 are awaiting trial, 6 of these being in gaol. This list does not include the many charges of intimidation or unlawful assembly which have been brought against miners, in spite of the fact that the present struggle has been the most pacific that any one could imagine. Our rulers at one time ridiculed the repressive measures of other Governments, and believed in allowing the people to "let oil a little steam," as they termed it. Their change of tactics shows that they think their position is too critical just now to allow them to take any chances, so the order goes forth: "Gag them!" And as they begin to feel more and more their insecurity they will redouble their persecution of all rebels. The ironical feature of the situation to-day is that whilst the capitalist Governments are throwing Communists into prison, the Communist Government of Russia is doing the same with the Anarchists. All Governments are the enemies of real free speech, and they all use the same argument—the safety of the State, by which they mean their own special privileges and power. This has been pointed out by Anarchists over and over again, but people are very slow to learn the lesson, and still dream of a Government that will bring them freedom".[210]

With the "collapse of the revolutionary wave of 1917-21, the Bolshevisation of the movement, and the repression of 1921, many had been won over to Bolshevik positions, whilst many others dropped out"[211] of activity. During this period, although not strictly anarchist in name, an Anti-Parliamentary Communist Federation was formed, particularly around groupings in Scotland, although it was said to have members in the North of England. This lasted untilaround 1942.

The defence of 'anti-parliamentary communism' and highlighting the real meaning of the term was taken up in a letter to the local press in June 1921, the author, who signed their letter simply as a 'Communist' as they feared victimisation from their employer stated, in defence of a previous letter berating communism "He denounces Communism as Anarchism; a Communist is simply one of the community, and the speakers are out for the good of the community." In the defence of being accused of being just 'grumblers' it was pointed out that all over the country is unemployment, lock outs, and people committing suicide through poverty and starvation, and is this not a case to grumble about.[212]

As mentioned, any perception of any anarchist activity was swallowed up within the wider misconception of Communist Bolshevism; this was demonstrated in a speech delivered by Sir Nicholas Grattan-Doyle, Newcastle 'pre-conservative' Unionist party MP to a local party gathering at Berwick;

> "He warned them against the dangers of a Socialist Government, again such international Associations as Socialism, Bolshevism, Communism or Anarchism, which only differed in degree and which all had as their root and foundation the principle of State ownership as opposed to the personal liberty of the individual. It was not in speeches made in the House of Commons that the danger lay, butat the street corners in Newcastle, Liverpool, Manchester, and Berwick, where they preached their full-blooded policy."[213]

It is an abhorrent notion that anarchism has as its roots the 'principle of state ownership', as demonstrated; this is the exact opposite to the principle and theory of anarchism.

## 2.2 THE CHOPWELL MINERS DISPUTE

During a strike that began mid June 1925 and lasted until December 1926 over 60 miners were to be charged with unlawful assembly, after surrounding the house of a 'scab' called Winship. Over 200 miners were singing the 'Red Flag' and, at the ending of the last verse "We will stop that scab Winship today" was sung. The Chopwell Colliery was in the mean time being run by 'scab' safety men and local officials, who, not being safe in the village, were housed within the pit premises and protected by police. Two of the scabs, who had been 'intimidated' "had been so ill-treated that they had been unable to continue work. It took over 20 policemen to rescue one of the safety men, on one occasion, from a crowd which marched around him singing the "Dead March" and "Lead Kindly Light."

News of the proposed charges against the Chopwell miners spread like wildfire and "the whole of the miners and their wives and families, estimated to number about three thousand, had arranged to march to Gateshead, which is 12 miles distant and back. They were to be met by various contingents of unemployed and bands en route. Information, however, was received at midnight last night that the summons had been unconditionally withdrawn, and messengers were dispatched early this morning to the various centres cancelling the demonstration." Nevertheless, many still attended the Gateshead Magistrates Court "when the magistrates took their seats at Gateshead court today, the strains of the "Red Flag" were floating up from the street below. *What is that song?* Asked the Chairman. *The "Red Flag"* replied the clerk. *Oh, is it,* remarked the Chairman. All the defendants who appeared in court, probably about a quarter of those summoned, were wearing red favours."[214]

After the fining of some of the miners to the sum of £2 each, the magistrate, after receiving assurances from Mr James Robson, President of the Durham Miners Association, agreed to the withdrawal of the remaining charges. The label of "Little Moscow" when speaking of Chopwell has remained ever since, in particular with its streets named after Marx and Lenin. This label is not, as some claim, "a reputation to be proud of"[215], especially today, with decades of authoritarian communism, and it's, at times, barbarity to look back on.

## 2.3 1926 GENERAL STRIKE

This isn't the place to analyse the 'failings' of the 1926 general strike, but to highlight a few local occurrences during the period. "Under massive pressure from ordinary workers, the Trades Union Congress (TUC, umbrella organisation of the reformist unions) was forced to call a general strike. Even with syndicalism at a low ebb, they were fearful that the strike might turn into a revolutionary upheaval, so they refused to use the term 'general strike', with its association with syndicalism. Instead they called the action a 'national strike'.[216]

Labels of what to call the strike aside, and the union hierarchy collaborating with the state out of fear for their position, the workers were rapidly "organising themselves, creating alternative structures under their direct control, such as transport permit committees and hastily-formed councils of action. Had there still been a mass-syndicalist organisation in the working class able to aid and direct this spontaneous action, perhaps British history would have been different."[217]

Warships were stationed on the Tyne and the Tees, police stations were armed in readiness,[218] armoured cars in the pit villages and town centres in anticipation of any civil unrest. During the strike, students and middle class 'scabs and blacklegs' continued to; for instance, drive trucks, buses and trains. These were met with successful picketing, particularly the railway lines running throughout the North East. Nationwide "buses and lorries were overturned andoften petrol bowsers were fired. In some towns huge car parks were formed of blackleg's vehicles and their drivers were often taken prisoner."[219] At Burnhope, near Gateshead, a farmer's tractor trying to manoeuvre past picketswas overturned, whilst other moving vehicles throughout the region had their tyres slashed.[220]

The general strike was to last nine days, yet for the Chopwell miners, it was part of an ongoing dispute which was, until the national strike, operating for nine or so months. A Chopwell Council of Action was formed within the village for the purpose of setting up food kitchens, food distribution, credit for strikers at local shops and permits to allow produce vehicles from local farms safe passage. "They ran sports days, community dances and events for children. 'Collectors' visited farms around the area to seek produce for the soup kitchens. Even the village poachers were collectivised to offer their due portion to the common pot."[221] Fuel was sought from small surface coal mines and raids upon coal company wagons. Police were drafted into the village from as far as Wales and Nottingham, yet were unable to put a stop to the 'thievery' of coal, and in one instance, in the case of a loudly vocal anti-strike police sergeant, his own personal coal bunker was also rightly raided.

The earlier Chopwell (anarchist) communist club was sold by 1921, but its ideas were to still largely prevalent within the village for years to come.

> "The Chopwell example would seem to suggest the conscious development of a distinctive anarchist strand whilst showing tolerance and free intermingling with numerous left movements. The element of community is all important. To quote one former resident: 'Now all say that somebody else should deal with it, the police should deal with it, the social services should deal with it, but not ourselves, that wasn't the case in Chopwell. It was a community which was dedicated to getting rid of the capitalist system and substituting for it the kind of society that William Morris had dreamed of'."[222]

Trains travelling through the region, particularly in Northumberland were regularly stoned by locals who viewed them to be driven by scab labour. After instances of this, the Flying Scotsman, on its regular journey through Northumberland had steel plates fitted in place of windows.[223]

Cramlington, Northumberland, and 15-20 miners from the Dudley pit (it is said that some miners from Chopwell were amongst this group, yet I can find no evidence of this, other than hearsay)[224] were on usual picket duty and monitoring the local railway line. It was agreed that no scab coal train shall pass.

In an incident of direct action, against what was perceived as an oncoming coal train, a section of line was removed, to "stop everything on wheels" – "Weplanned the job and did just that. We took the rail up in record time but, we thought it was a coal train that was coming. We were amazed when it turned out to be 'The Flying Scotsman'."[225] The driver of the train, because of instances of previous stone throwing, was driving at a slow cautious speed; hence as the train became derailed and turned over on its side, out of 5-600 passengers, only one person had minor injuries. Nine miners were sentenced to up to eight years 'penal servitude' for this. The level of anti-scab militancydid not stop, with further instances of stone throwing at trains occurring in other areas on the outskirts of Newcastle and in Northumberland.

The end of the strike also brought a lot of state repression, police baton charges on assembled strikers, and prosecutions brought against those, including Chopwell, producing strike related literature.

The strike ended 12 May 1926, not through 'drifting' back to work, but the reluctance by trade union leaders to carry on the fight to the end , thus losing their positions, with a well prepared government, yet the miners, undeterred, would carry on the fight for longer.

Perkin would sum up the end of the strike;

"The crisis of class society in Britain was averted not by the triumph of the government and the employers over a potentially revolutionary labour movement, which could have only been temporary, but by the common interest of professional managers, professional union leaders, and increasingly professional politicians and civil servants in keeping the system going and avoiding crises. This did not mean that they did not have their own separate, competing interests which they severally tried to foster at the expense of one another and of their constituents and the general public. On the contrary, they also had an interest in conflict, in the sense of the competitive collective bargaining which displayed their skills and made them indispensable. But their fundamental interest was in keeping the game going, for without the game they had no *raison d'être.*"[226]

## 2.4 TOM BROWN & A SNAPSHOT OF STRUGGLE

The aforementioned Tom Brown's (1900 – 1974) early immersion into local labour activities came in the midst of the Syndicalist revolt of the period of 1911 and his participation in the School Children's Strike. After his state education, like many in the area, Tom was soon serving his engineering apprenticeship within the shipyards where "he was quickly drawn into militant industrial activity"[227] It is at the shipyards that "he gained his considerable talents as a speaker, organiser and shop steward. Brown initially entered the Socialist Labour Party in his youth, and became for a short period, the Communist Party's regional industrial organiser, once it had consumed the SLP. Later however, Brown's disillusionment with Bolshevik Russia and his own experiences of the British Communist party led him into conflict, and his departure followed soon after.[228]

Moving to Coventry, Tom had secured stable employment in the Motor industry, and it is said it is here that he "was attracted to Anarchist and Syndicalist ideas"[229] After the General Strike of 1926, Tom returned to the region for a number of years before ending up in London during the mid 1930's, where he had secured work on aircraft.

The following, written by Tom Brown is worth including in full as it gives a fascinating glimpse of the period, particularly that of the area concerned. After losing his job in Coventry, Tom returned to the North East and resided in Birtley, Co Durham for a couple of years after the general strike of 1926, and the following is from *Direct Action* vol.4 no.7 (25) July 1963, and is entitled "Into battle with the bazooka bands".

> "One way of writing history is to take a social group, in one place and at one time, leaving the broad drama of great events, and treating the subject as a microcosm, letting the minutiae of humble lives interpret the greater story. In thus taking one corner of the Durham Coalfield as my subject I might as well be writing of the coalminers of Scotland, South Wales, Yorkshire or almost anywhere."
>
> "When the General Strike of 1926 ended, I lost my job in Coventry. Four weeks after the Strike I decided to go North, but at Coventry station I was told: "We can issue a ticket to Derby only. The railways are so disorganised we cannot guarantee any travel beyond that distance." So, with three tickets and four trains, I reached Newcastle (about 185 miles) in 18 hours. The Government had boasted of their skeleton blackleg service and this was the result, even four weeks later."
>
> "From Newcastle I went to live in the small mining town of Birtley, part of the urban district of Chester-le-Street in Durham, and found and made a home in Elizabethville (though not in the Congo). Here in 1914 about 600 temporary houses, a school, church and hospitalhad been built for Belgian refugees, hence the title. In 1919 the refugees went home and the government locked the empty buildings and – the village was surrounded by high spiked iron railings – the heavy iron gates

and refused to allow homeless people to occupy the huts.[230] Then, in the course of three days the place was taken over, mostly by ex-soldiers and the gates removed and dropped in a brook. The police were ordered to expel the squatters who promptly formed a defence force and posted round the clock sentries. After a few months, authority decided it was better to accept the fait accompli and charge their unwelcome tenants rent – 7s. 9d. a week."

"When, on May 21 1926, the national lock-out of coal miners took place, Durham had already been out for two weeks on a county issue. That and a long series of single pit strikes had left the strike fund broken (at that time each mining county in England had a separate union, linked in the Miners Federation of Great Britain). But Durham went, with the rest, solidly into the battle."

"How, then, did the miners' families live? There was a national miner's relief fund which was big, though not nearly as big as the distress it was to relieve. Durham received its share but there were 120,000 men plus wives and children to feed, clothe and shelter and most of that had to be found at home. The Guardians gave relief to the strikers but soon that was drastically curtailed. The Boards were under the control of the Minister of Health who ordered all relief to single or married able-bodied men to cease. Relief, and not very much at that, was to be given only to the wives and children."

"The County Council, with a majority of miners, gave free breakfast to schoolchildren over five years of age. The same body had formed clinics for children under three. Here a fortnightly medical check of the babies was made and a weekly allowance of one pound of full- cream dried milk and a bottle of cod-liver oil given for each baby. Children's clothes were sold at cost price. The garments were almost half the price the mothers would have paid in the shops and the goods were certainly superior. Most of the work of these clinics was organised locally and done by volunteers."

"Then someone discovered that an Education Act allowed the Council to institute primary schools for children between three and five but without supplying the money for such a venture. So it was put to the Council that they could pass a resolution to establish primary schools for the under fives without fixing a date, then give school meals to the primary scholars. This legal hocus-pocus was carried out and the kids got their free meal quite legally."

"The local co-operative, with some backing from the CWS, [Co-operative Wholesale Society] was able to give some credit to the miners' lodges – as always. And, always, such credit was repaid weekly, from the second week of the return to work, until the whole of the debt was paid. There is a strong traditional streak of Puritanism in Durham and the repayment of such debts of honour was considered not only just, but sound business – there is always a next time."

"The local co-op was small; nothing like the city giants, but like many small co-ops was efficient. It owned the only large store in town and the only cinema. It had meeting rooms and a hall, a barber's shop, a billiards saloon, allotments, a farm producing fresh meat, milk and eggs, with cottages for its labourers."

"Rent did not trouble the majority as long as the strike lasted. Many lived in coal companies' houses and a rent strike was automatic. Any attempt at eviction would have been met by a thousand-strong picket. Coal was got by searching the waste heaps which, like youngmountains, adorn the coalfield scene."

"There was recreation, too. There were village fiestas, without the feasting. A procession led by at least one excellent brass band, a meeting, a sports day with athletic events for children and adults (first prize, a bar of chocolate) and, in the evening, an open-air dance or a concert. There were ladies' football matches and comic football matches between teams of boisterous clowns and comic boxing shows – at times everything comic. But frequent meetings were important too, for they served the part of a Press."

"Rival to the silver bands, some well known, were the bazooka bands, the "bazooka" [kazoo] being a sixpenny instrument one hummed into. About 40 of these, with drums made quite a noise. Allthe bands – there must have been a few hundred of them in the country, including children's bands – were in costume, a condition being that the costume should not cost a great deal. Sometimes 20 bands would take part in a local carnival, tramping miles to the site. I recall one fat man who, dressed as a sultan in the remains of a bedspread, marched at the head of his "harem" of 40 women, a very proud sultan he looked, and the "Tramps", each wearing a battered bowler and spats, who played their tune, then sang, "We're on the road to anywhere" like a choir. There were bands of Zulu warriors, Red Indians, knights in tin can armour, battalions of Fred Karno's Army, bands of mermaids (the most difficult of the lot) and of pirates (the easiest)."

"But as that long, warm summer began to fade into autumn, the struggle became grimmer. The first serious blow was made, against the Chester-le-Street Board of Guardians, who had refused to obey the Government's order to cease relief to single men. The Tory Government deposed the elected Guardians, whose work was unpaid, and put in their place three highly-paid commissioners. The new regime stopped all relief to men, single or married, who might be able to work. The only relief was to wives, 8s. [Shillings] a week, and children, 1s. a week. Thus a family of six received 12s. a week in the form of a food voucher, no money, compared to the dole of 29s. a week. This measure of economic terrorism was applied not only to strikers but to all unemployed "on relief", miners and other workers, and was continued after the strike for a few years. Following the strike, these people without money were dunned for rent. The only ways to get money were to sell part of their meagre rations, or pick coal from the waste heaps and try to sell it. 4-5s. for a week's hard work, less to the unlucky."

"The police acted against the strikers picking coal from the heaps; the men went in larger groups, the police were reinforced. The miners began prospecting for coal in the fields like gold diggers but this meant spreading out. Pressure increased with the coming of cold weather. A nearby wood of commercial fir, belonging to Lord Lambton, was completely felled and sawn up. A coal owner magistrate, whose large house on the North Road had three tall gateposts of 18in. square oak, found, one morning, that they had been sawn off six inches from the ground."

"Then the Notts. Miners' Association, led by Labour MP G. A. Spencer, broke away from the Federation and returned to work. Heavy police reinforcements appeared in Durham, the biggest, heaviest constables from distant counties; and attempts were made to re-open strikebound pits. Scarcely a miner, with the exception of a few in South Shields, could be found. The blackleg gangs were token forces of bankrupt shopkeepers and of professional layabouts from the town."

"The pits were usually closed after three days. Sometimes after the first day, and the owners resorted to surprise but there was always a strong picket awaiting the scabs at the end of their morning shift. Scouts took to following on bicycles the truckloads of police: this in turn led to the police making dummy concentrations to lure the men to the wrong pits but there were always enough pickets to go round."

"News travels fast in a mining area and even the sound of

running feet and a shout would bring out men, boys and women in a mass picket – yes, women pickets, and punching ones, too! It was hard, bitter fighting: usually, before the scabs could be reached, the charge of six-foot-plus, 15-stone policemen swinging batons in arm- breaking, skull-cracking blows had to be met and broken."

"The pattern was for the picket to gather early, to prevent a surprise getaway. The police would try to disperse them, but would soon gather about the pit yard. The scabs would wait at the pithead for 2, 3 or 4 hours, then the police would make their big charge and the main battle was on. A prisoner always went to jail for 6-12 months. The wounded were, if possible, carried off by their comrades."

"I recall one such episode on the old North Road near Gateshead; where a colliery had "reopened". The Birtley men gathered there. Two tramcars came to pick up the scabs, the police were pushed back, the trolleys pulled off, all windows broken, starting and steering handles removed; one tram derailed and the tramway men sent home, all in a few minutes. We hung about for three hours, and then half a dozen scabs dashed from the back of the yard, down the hilly fields, towards the new North Road."

"From the hedges sprang small, slim, youthful figures, who ran like hares after them and did nothing but trip them up, then pounding behind came heavier figures and in two minutes the scabs were unfitfor work for a week or two. On the main road the fighting broke out again. At night some of the scabs who lived in Gateshead were visited in their homes; they did not return to the pit, which, in any case, closed after three days."

"At another pit, which lasted only one day, a sergeant lifted his baton high to give the signal for a charge and was at once felled by a stone. At another a sergeant (the supers, like the

Duke of Plaza Toro, led their armies from the rear) appeared to give an order to charge and rushed into the crowd, while his men stood still. I never found out where he went to."

"One surprise nearly succeeded, but a few young fellows, very early in the morning, went to the "reopened" pit, to be charged by treble the number of police and sought refuge on the waste heap. These heaps of loose stone are tricky and one runs up them zigzag fashion. The police tried to run straight up and every man started hisown avalanche. The men on top helped these, too, and pelted the constables, but they were marooned in a sea of blue serge. Then, after several hungry hours, they saw columns marching from every village for miles around. Luck now was relieved."

"All this time hunger was growing. Over a nearby hill a miner's wife was picking late blackberries. She was hungry, ate some without washing them and died of poisoning a few days later. Said the coroner: "There is no doubt that the poor woman was very hungry."

"In December, a national ballot of the miners favoured a return to work, except in Durham, which voted by a big majority to stay out. In the face of a national return, however, the E.C. [Executive Committee] had to disregard the vote. Out from mid-April to December, the miners went back; the strike was over, but not the fight. Their union was intact, their spirit unbroken."

"Yet, apart from the social war, it was a peaceful community, more peaceful and ethical than London W.1, though the police were regarded as an occupying army. A woman or a child could walk alone in the dark, doors were left unlocked. A sociologist, speaking of this and the following period in Durham, said that the absence of crime was the most remarkable feature of the depression and attributed this to "steady living and the steadying influence of the

Union." (Charles Muir, *Justice in a Depressed Area*, p. 32-33 1936). Later, the Pilgrim Report said that there was here little self-pity, but a determination to fight the effects of poverty and unemployment. Yet, it said, 71 per cent had been out of work for 5 years or more, compared to Liverpool's 23 per cent and Deptford's 3 per cent. (*Men Without Work*, 1938)."

"It was a consciously working-class community, self-reliant and ready for spontaneous action, best when its leaders were in London. There was, of course, a deal of petty gossip and such in a "Coronation Street" way, but in struggle they were loyal to one another and in some local pit disasters – even unto death."[231]

## 2.5 LEAN TIMES OF THE LATE 20s

As mentioned, times were hard for local anarchists with state repression, being perceived as Bolsheviks, press misconceptions, poverty, and so on. Until the late 1950s there is little evidence of existence, but then again, not every anarchist grouping or anarchist individuals advertise their existence through the national anarchist press. A fine example of this is during the 1980's there was an explosion of activity and anarchist groups on Tyneside, yet barely a mention is given to much of this to the paper *Freedom* at the time as we shall discover. With this considered, we have a few items of anarchist related events to document.

Late 1927, and in yet another attack directed at anarchists by the church see's Dr Hensley Henson, the bishop of Durham deliver the annual Masonic sermon at Bishopwearmouth Parish Church, Sunderland. In the sermon he emphasized the danger to modern civilisation was threatened "by atheism, unrest, and the forces of anarchy";

"There is a beating against civilisation, a destructive hood of anarchic forces. The old restraining banks are beginning to show sinister indications of weakness. What are the banks behind which modern civilisation exists and develops? Government, with its machinery, legislative and executive, is but the symbol of that instinct of order and justice which in dwells the minds of citizens. Civilisation includes far more than its institutions – traditions of law abidingness and patriotism, the salutary disciplines of home and locality, religion and morality which springs from it, the faith, culture, and power which enables the civic service of individuals. These are the tactics which hold back anarchy and make it possible for civilisation to come into existence, grow rich and strong, and develop in evermore wonderful variety. If these grow weak and fail, the time must come when the pressure of anarchic forces will have grown too strong to be resisted, and the vast fabric of society sinks into revolution and ruin. Despite the great material improvements in the conditions of popular life during the past century, there was less contentment, less happiness, and less security in society. Large sections of the people were so hostile to the conditions under which they had to live that they were in the mood to change them at almost any cost and even to shipwreck society itself in the attempt."[232]

Of course the suggested solution was obedience to the authority and teachings of Christ almighty, but we may wonder, with the numerous examples given in this history, at the lengths in which the state instructed the church during periods of national discontent to utilise their infrastructure for more of a dominant control of the populace.

## 2.6 BASH THE FASH

The early 1930's symbolise a time of extreme hardship for the North East. Industrial decline, closing steelworks in Jarrow etc, high unemployment, decline in shipbuilding and a slump in coal output. Nationally, in the two years between 1929 and 1931, steel production fell from 9.6 million tons to 5.2 million tons. In 1930 coal output in for the country stood at 257,906,802 tons, by 1931 this had fallen by nearly fifteen per cent to 219,458,951 tons. "In the early months of 1929 unemployment had been around 1,250,000. A year later it was round about 1,750,000, and in the early months of 1931 about 2,6000,000." These years "developed into a severe and prolonged depression which sapped the strength of Trade Unionism, without ever becoming quite deep enough to provoke extremes of revolutionary feeling."[233]

The decade also saw the state protect more of its privileges with more repressive acts of parliament, such as, the Public Order Act, the Incitement to Disaffection Act, etc. "Suppression of criticism, raiding of halls and even dances, and so forth, were both more easy and more frequent. Attacks were rarely made on official Labour organisations, but left-wing Socialists and Communists were regarded as fair game."[234] No doubt local anarchists were encompassed within this too.

The 1930s also saw the prevalence of The National Unemployed Workers Movement in the region. Although a front for the Communist Party, locally it was a grassroots organisation and had some monumental and impressive struggles against authority and capitalism in general. From instances of the whole community turning out to resist bailiffs, to helping each other out with food and clothing, education, and other support. Numerous protest marches, which quite often resulted in clashes with police, were also quite prevalent.[235]

The group would also be instrumental in their fight against local fascism and encouragement for the volunteering for the International Brigades in revolutionary Spain in 1936. It can be said the movement was well respected in the region amongst the working class suffering from extreme poverty and thrown on the scrapheap by capitalism, but I may wonder to what extent this respect and support was given to the 'leaders' of the 'movement' from the majority of local working class people, a lot of whom possibly didn't know it was a front for the Communist Party. In highlighting the reasons for unemployment, and poverty, and how this is then inter-connected with capitalisms exploitation of the masses is admiral work, but then to 'by the way, read Daily Worker' or 'Join the Communist Party', 'obey our rules / leader' bares echo's of that aspect of the left that we love to hate, and where it becomes obvious that the 'Party', and more importantly the 'Party line', becomes more important than the struggle it purports to support or endeavours to be a part of.

On a personal note, my great granddad during this period was 'lucky' to secure work as a Coal Trimmer, shovelling by hand coal onto ships, to level it, on the Tyne, backbreaking work for little pay. On payday, he would have to fight his way home across the bridge to Gateshead through gangs of muggers eager to relieve him of his wages on a twice weekly basis. It can be said hard times breed hard people, which was a useful trait in the forthcoming years in the physical fight against the rising tide of fascism.

Fascists in the North East, until the 1930s, were predominantly oddballs on the fringes of the ruling class like the Duke of Northumberland. With the rise of fascism in Mussolini's Italy, Hitler's rise to power, and the beginnings of a new party by a "wealthy, disaffected ex Tory, then Labour politician named Sir Oswald Mosley"[236] coupled with the economic climate of the times saw more of a working class following slowly begin to crawl out of the woodwork in support of the nauseating fascist doctrines of the British Union of Fascists. Of course, local resistance to any sign or attempted public show of the fascists was swiftly dealt with by the local populace and no doubt any remaining anarchists in the region. A few examples of this will follow;

> "In 1934, 1935, and 1936 the British Union of Fascists, with Sir Oswald Mosley as leader, sprang out of insignificance. Lavishly supplied with money, complete with black shirt army, anti-semitic propaganda, and other dangerous and brutal devices of Continental Fascism, it had some appeal for the idle, reckless, venal, savage or despairing of all classes – including some of the working class."[237]

The British Union of Fascists was formed in 1932, yet "as early as 1931, for example, before the BUF was formed, the Sunderland branch (of the National Unemployed Workers Movement) reported that it had been 'instrumental in breaking up the local branch of Mosley's bright young things'."[238] It was Hitler himself, who during his speech at the Nuremberg Congress on 3 September 1933, was to emphasise "Only one thing could have broken our movement — if the adversary had understood its principle and from the first day had smashed, with the most extreme brutality, the nucleus of our new movement."

Indeed, this was taken up with relish by the majority of the working class in the North East.

The attempt by the Blackshirts to hold a street meeting outside Sunderland Boilermakers Hall, March 1933, saw locals chasing them out of the area. "Newcastle staged an enormous public meeting at the City Hall in May 1933, called by 130 political, industrial and religious leaders, to condemn Nazi anti- semitism in Germany. Sunderland also held a large meeting." June, 1933, and after the partial victory of holding an open air meeting at Newcastle's Marlborough bus station, the fascists then attempted to hold another at the Race Weeks speakers corner, "accordingly, five Blackshirts arrived with a lorry for a platform and opened their meeting. The crowd noticed that the fascist speaker 'bore a striking resemblance to Herr Hitler' and reacted by overturning the lorry and hounding the Blackshirts 'continually'."[239]

It was a natural disposition to oppose fascism in the North East with its traditionally diverse mix of a labour force composed of numerous nationalities;

> "Added to the relatively cosmopolitan outlook, there was another local tradition crucial in understanding working class opinions. Towns and villages clustered along the two rivers had bred strong organisations in the form of trade unions and co-operative societies, not to mention the myriad of religious chapels and recreational clubs. The occupations of these communities, such as coal mining, ship building, seafaring, and engineering, generated a keen sense of solidarity since mutual support was vital to survival."[240]

Sunday September 10th 1933 and just down the road, what has since become known as 'The Battle of Stockton' was to ensure. The BUF had made previous attempts to hold meetings in Stockton, but they were frequently heckled or attacked by anti-fascists. It was therefore decided by the BUF to make a showof strength.

> "The town, along with the rest of the North East, had been hit by the great slump and unemployment that followed the Wall Street Crash of 1929. The new jobs being created at ICI's Billingham works were effectively cancelled out by the loss of thousands of jobs in the shipyards and marine engineering works that lined both banks of the Tees downriver from the Victoria Bridge. Joblessness stalked the town, and the impact of this was plainly visible in empty streets.
>
> It was that town that on that day provided the stage for one of the first British outings for a new and menacing political force - Oswald Mosley's British Union of Fascists - the 'Blackshirts'. Mosley was a decidedly odd character. A Public Schoolboy, his career was one moulded, in his eyes at least, by the concept of 'action'. Like his political friend, Hermann Goering, he had been a world war one airace, but unlike Goering, he found a political home, for a short time, on the Left as a Labour MP.

However his messianic tendencies and his sense of being marked out for a mission soon led him on a journey to the far right and the formation of a British Fascist Party in his own image.

Believing that liberal democracy was finished and that the west was headed for destruction, his party, he decreed, was not to be overly exercised with the mundane work of organisation, canvassing and electioneering that marked out more conventional, democratic, parties. Not for them the slow, patient job of trying to elect councillors or MP's. The job of the BUF, said Mosley, was to seize power - and, like their counterparts in Italy and Germany, to seize that power from the streets.

By early 1933 the BUF had established a small nucleus of an organisation on Teesside, centred on Stockton. This followed a seemingly set pattern. Small towns and semi-rural areas hit hard by unemployment were seen as prime areas for recruitment for Mosley's fascism. Minus the strong opposing political culture of the big industrial cities which partnered a local well-organised trade union and labour movement, they were seen as easy pickings for theBUF's populism.

On the morning of that day, fully loaded motor coaches carrying, according to Warburton, over 100 BUF members from Tyneside and the Manchester area, set off for Teesside, and in mid-afternoon, their coaches met up at Victoria Bridge, allowing the disembarked black shirted and jack-booted phalanx of Mosley's army to begin their march along Stockton High Street.

They were not alone however. An opposing crowd, according to contemporary press accounts some 2,000 strong, was ready and waiting in ambush.

The BUF managed to get as far as the Town Hall building in the middle of the High Street market place but any further progress was halted by the sheer weight of numbers of their opponents.

The whole of the High Street then began to resemble nothing more than a medieval battleground. The Northern Echo and other local press reported the use of weapons on both sides. Wooden staves and pickaxe handles were wielded, and stones —and more lethally— potatoes into which razor blades had been studded were thrown intothe Black shirted ranks.

The BUF, minus their injured foot soldiers, made it back to their hired charabancs, and, to a chorus of ribald insults, jeering and cheering drove off into the gathering twilight. 'Non Pasaran'— they did not pass."[241]

The unique use of potatoes with inserted razor blades bares testimony to the hatred felt by local people directed towards the fascists, and quite rightly so.

The remainder of 1933, and throughout 1934, saw tit for tat skirmishes with fascists. Their public meetings were regularly attacked in both the Bigg Market of Newcastle, and the streets of Sunderland, whilst the fascists tried to increase the intimidation of their opponents, including the 'brave' act of smashing left wing bookshops windows etc. The proposed assembly by the fascists at 1934,s Newcastle Race Week was postponed by Mosley himself because of the fear of violence.[242]

Before his move to London, Tom Brown was also involved with local anti- fascist struggles and confrontations, and it is said[243], was instrumental in the setting up of the local Anti Fascist League to provide protection to 'left wing' meetings in the area, and to co-ordinate the local and natural anti-fascism of the regions populace. Later commenting on events he recalls;

"One May morning I was near the Labour Exchange on

Windmill Hills[244], Gateshead. A few small groups of men were chatting or waiting for their time to sign on and a few, less than a dozen, were listening to an Independent Labour Party speaker. Suddenly thesounds of men's voices singing the Italian fascist song were heard. Then a party of Mosley's fascists wearing black shirts rounded the corner; giving the Mussolini salute and chanting M-O-S-L-E-Y, M-O-S-L-E-Y. In quick march with threatening voices they strode to the I.L.P. platform. Then came a rush of men as the groups and the dolequeue broke up to run and defend the platform. In a few minutes the fascists were scattered. The fallen ones were begging for mercy until they were rescued by some members of the Gateshead Labour Party.

After a few weeks a small party of Blackshirts came in peace and were not molested. But some workers realised that a much stronger fascist party would not be so peaceful and a band of them formed the Anti Fascist League in Newcastle and Tyneside. Good open air and indoor meetings were held and new members recruited. Marches showed that the older men remembered their military life inWorld War one.

The ancient hall of the Smiths Guild in Newcastle was hired and the people who lived nearby kept an eye on the premises at night. Manyof these good people were street sellers and offered their barrows and carts to form quick barricades to keep the fascists in if they attacked. Some of them, such as the newspaper sellers who worked in and around the Central Train Station, were able to keep us informed of fascist visitors to the area.

Our meetings, especially in the Newcastle Bigg Market and on the Town Moor, were well attended and applauded. The Newcastle police were courteous to us, even though our support was almost exclusively working class with fifty % of that out of work. The Labour Party said "Don't do anything about it, just leave then to the policeto deal with". The Communist Party said "Just ridicule them – shout Mickey Mouse at them."This deadly weapon had been suggested by the national leadership of the C.P; it referred to the fascist rank and file uniform of black shirts and light grey flannel trousers.

Only two prominent members of the Labour Party supported us – they were both full time officials of the Transport and General Workers Union. Our members singly, or in pairs, interviewed fascist recruits and in most cases persuaded them to pack it in. At first members of the Jewish community appeared interested, but they changed when Mosley was interviewed by a Jewish delegation. They reported that Mosley had given an assurance that neither he nor his party were anti-semitic. With this they were very happy. The trade union movement, the Labour Party and the middle –class Liberals also returned to their slumbers. Only when Mosley put up new party candidates against the Labour Party were trade unionists, for a short time, roused to anger. To oppose fascism was never popular in such circles."[245]

Further encounters with the local fascists came thick and fast and quite often violently so. A lot of emphasis is given to the 'Battle of Cable St' in London, Sunday 4 October 1936, and the day's confrontations and events, yet this was happening in the North East on a regular basis.

"The BUF on Tyneside dwindled rapidly. In a matter of six months, most of the members had left - few, if any, public appearances were made and the small number remaining were little other than a club, and so it remained for years. The Anti-Fascist League, poor and "un-influential" had, by its devotion and courage, proved that Fascism can be fought and defeated."[246]

Whilst there is no direct evidence of the involvement of local anarchists during this period, and their lack of 'advertising their existence', the participation in grass roots organisations and activities, such as the Anti-

Fascist League is a natural disposition, and so it can be assumed their direct involvement was encompassed within this struggle, like many before and after, including the Spanish Revolution of 1936.

## 2.7 FROM THE STREETS OF GATESHEAD TO THE FRONTLINES OF REVOLUTIONARY SPAIN

Whilst this is not the space to delve into the pre-ceding history and build up to events which shaped the Spanish revolution of 1936, nevertheless the role and participation of people from the North East is worth a brief overview, as the revolution is such an important event and example of a social revolution, and aspects of anarchism in action.

July 1936, and military generals Mola and Franco hatched an uprising against the then 'left wing Republican' government of Spain. The working class of Spain rose in response in another continuation of their struggle against previous brutal regimes of monarchists, Catholics, and now fascists backed by Mussolini and Hitler's troops and equipment of war. The world-wide implications of the 'war' bare testimony to a narrative of dirty deals, non-intervention, the priority of retaining valuable resources of iron and copper etc over human life (Britain and France), the murderous backstabbing brutality of states more concerned with 'dealing with their enemies' and extracting as much gold as possible out of the country (Russia) and those of a fascist disposition intent on a reign of supremacy and global domination (Germany, Italy).

For the Spanish anarchists, at the forefront of the resistance to the fascist onslaught, and later defence against communist backstabbing, deceit and murder, the battle was not only in any defence of the republican government against fascism, but also for the ongoing social revolution taking place throughout large sections of the country.

> "Indeed in this sense anarchists view Spain not only as a period of civil war, but primarily as a time of social revolution and transformation. For the anarchists in Spain the idea of fighting

to restore the republican government was absurd as the two had been enemies in constant conflict before the fascist uprising. The struggle against fascism was an extension of the Spanish class struggle anarchism and not a replacement. Both the fascists and the republican government stood between the organised working class and their revolutionary aims. The anarchists fought Franco with the intention to pave the way for revolution, the state and government were also their targets. For the anarchist militias the civil war was meaningless if it did not challenge and overthrow capitalism whether in a democratic or fascist guise."[247]

Sixty years after these events, a commemoration pamphlet was produced by Tyneside Anarchist Group. Included was an article entitled "The North East people and the Spanish civil war" which is reprinted here in full, firstly as it is a local endeavour shedding a minor light on the happenings during the period, and secondly as it is not from an academic left wing based study of the revolution, but a local grassroots anarchist interpretation of events.

> "In this present 'Age of Cynicism', it is very difficult to comprehend the enormous response that the war in Spain produced. There were basically two ways to help defeat fascism in Spain. Either volunteer to fight for the republic, or organise in Britain to campaign against the non-intervention policy of the Chamberlain government and to send arms and aid to the Spanish people. People in the North East did both.
>
> In total around 120 people went from the North East to fight in the Communist Party organised 'International Brigades' (IB) which in total formed an important part of the Republican army. There were many misconceptions propagated about the motivations and origin of these volunteers both at the time and subsequently. Firstly, you did not have to be a Communist to join the International Brigades and this was especially true of the North East. Nationally, around 50% of IB volunteers were

CP members, but in the North East this figure was around 37%. Many were involved in the National Unemployed Workers Movement which became a massive organisation in depression ridden Britain, especially in the unemployed black spots in the North East. Others were members of the Labour Party or of trade unions, but the factor which combined them was their determination to defeat fascism in Spain; many had been involved in action against Mosley's Blackshirts at home, as well as hunger marches and the campaign against the Means Test.

Also, the picture of the Spanish Civil War as an 'intellectual's war' is very misleading. As with the country as a whole, the overwhelming majority of those who volunteered in the North East (around 80%) were of working class origin. Direct involvement in the struggle could take other forms. For example, Francis Gill, a young working class boxer from Sunderland, volunteered on the 'Alice Marie', a ship breaking Franco's blockades by taking essential supplies to the Republic.

So the majority of those who volunteered were both working class and politically active. Yet the right wing press at the time and certain right wing historians since have chosen to denigrate their commitment by suggesting that they either had a financial bribe, or were suffering from some form of mental deficiency, The *'Daily Mail'* specialised in stories of tramps being recruited with promises of food and money. These slanders understandably angered volunteers. Even today, the volunteers from the area that are still alive are quite clear about the reasons they volunteered; they saw fascism clearly, and were determined that it should be defeated in Spain. In total, around 24 people from the North East died whilst fighting in Spain and their loss was to have a serious detrimental impact on the working class politics in the North East.

Many, of course, had to look after children, jobs or other responsibilities which meant that they could not take such a direct role in the struggle. However, this did not stop them from campaigning on the issue at home. The left political parties, the communists and the ILP (Independent Labour Party) were both energetic in their collections of food and money for the Spanish people as well as organising debates and rallies on the subject, but both parties were very small in the region and so were unable totake a lead in the activities.

On the other hand, many of the Labour Party and trade union leaderships distanced themselves from the issue as they were more worried about short term electoral prospects and fearful of being seen to collaborate with 'communists'. The North East had quite a strong working class Catholic voting population; so many local leaders chose not to mention Spain in order not to offend these potential voters. Consequently, there was little Labour support forthe 'Aid Spain' activities and this was crucial in an area like the North East where the Labour Party dominated. Key North East leaders that did little or opposed intervention included Shinwell and Dalton. However, this did not stop Labour Party members in the North East from campaigning actively on the issue, and perhaps as many as 90% were supportive of the Republic. Other important figures in the Party from the area, Ellen Wilkinson and CP Trevelyan were vocal in their advocacy of support for the Republic and bitter in their criticisms of those who refused to oppose non-intervention for short term party political reasons.

The same was true of many of the unions. The Transport & General Workers Union in the North East did little to help; the example of Bevin was hardly inspiring. Other trade unionists came round to supporting the republic after initially supporting non-intervention. Will Lawther, vice president of the Miners Federation was one such person. He had a personal interest in the conflict as his youngest brother Clifford was an IB volunteer who was killed at Jarama in February 1937. In addition to the miners, the national initiative of Voluntary Industrial Aid was supported locally by the Amalgamated Engineering Union which requested members to donate one hour of overtime a week. Workers at Vickers Armstrong factory in Elswick reconditioned old motorcycle combinations and ambulances for Spain. Gateshead Trades Council, like others in the area, paid for the housing of 30 Basque refugees and actively raised funds throughout the period.

Because the other left parties were too small to take the lead and theLabour Party had no wish too, the way was left open for ordinary people to come together and organise around the issue themselves. In the North East there can be observed the growth and development of a mass movement in support of Spain, despite the fact that there was no central co-ordination or lead from a particularpolitical party or grouping. Perhaps the most striking feature of the 'Aid Spain' movement was that it encompassed people from all classes and of almost all political complexions and religious persuasions. In fact, the 'Aid Spain' activities in the North East were positively benefited by the fact that there was no one party or interest group dominating the issue; instead, there was maximum room for across-the-board co-operation which necessarily sprang up in *ad hoc* manner as the circumstances demanded. It was left to individuals from all kinds of progressive organisations; NUWM members, most political parties, churches, and so forth to co- ordinate and act to help the Spanish people and this they did from a shop near the Workers Bookshop on Westgate Road. The local papers of the time are packed with reports of fund raising activities all over the North East.

Many contemporaries highlighted people's generosity and support and lack of party division as two key features of the 'Aid Spain' movement in the North East. Many who had never been previously involved in campaigning and collecting in this way were to become so. Within 'Aid Spain', what was especially noticeable was the extensive involvement of women at all levels.

The response received by collectors was not only a testament to the genuine heart-felt sympathy people had for those suffering at the hands of Franco, but also a very clear indication of the fear and hatred most people had for fascism. The Tyneside food ship stands as the single most tangible example of the sympathy people in the North East had for the suffering of the Spanish people. In February 1938 Tyne and Wear became one of twenty nine areas to send a food ship to Spain after £3,450 worth of goods had been collected in only two months.

An article in the North Mail commented that the ship was; 'One of the North's greatest efforts' and 'an act of the highest humanity'. It elaborated; 'A little girl at South Shields brought in a bag of biscuits and miners wives, with no money, rather than not give anything at all have handed over food from their scanty larders'.

The tremendous contribution that all sorts of people made to the cause of anti-fascism in Spain is both a testament to their generosity and far-sightedness. In contrast, many Labour leaders and the incompetent and disgraced Chamberlain government were blinded by short-term political expedients and failed or refused to recognise the terrible danger that fascism in Spain meant to all; "Bombs in Madrid today and London tomorrow" as the saying went. Yet, as with the rest of the country, ordinary people in the North East recognised this danger and acted on it giving, in some cases, their lives to the struggle against fascism."[248]

## 2.8 SOLIDARITY NOT CHARITY

Another local act of solidarity was the 'taken in' of refugee Basque children, 20-30 of which were housed in Tynemouth, and a smaller amount in Hexham,Northumberland.

The local liberal left historian's who glorify and bleat on about how great we were for taken in these children in their labour journals, essays and books on the subject; fail to mention the horrific and barbaric fact that only children approved by the Catholic church were accepted. "Furthermore those children who have nothing in common with the Church or who are CNT-FAI[249] children are naturally not as well treated as the others. But there are other methods of "respecting" the children's political ideas. CNT-FAI children are sent to rich people's houses, are waited upon by servants: in other words treated like little bourgeois!" This was done in an attempt to stifle their natural sense of recognising injustice and a sense of solidarity.

The children of anarchists received special attention in order to 'recondition' them. A letter from a child states, after asking for anarchist newspapers to be hidden carefully, because only fascist orientated papers were allowed, that "I do not know very much about politics because I am still a small boy, but it is necessary that we should begin to understand fully the Spanish situation for we are the men of tomorrow who must continue the struggle in Spain." And in another, a child concludes;

> "Besides, you must know that the son of a worker must not live in that manner because firstly: in Spain the war has been brought about through the capitalists wanting to keep us as their slaves, or rather, to serve them, and here the same thing is happening that we wish to keep as slaves the servants. And this cannot be, especially as we are sons of fighters who are defending the cause in the name ofa new Society and a new way of living amongst the workers—Juan, come for my sake as

well as my sister's —Every time I think of all of you I cry in despair, and ask that I might go with you and my friends ... Do not think that we are badly cared for, on the contrary it is because they treat us in the same way as capitalists, and a good comrade of the C.N.T. as I am, and furthermore, the son of a worker, it must not be so. Salud! Viva la C.N.T.! Your friend Emilio."[250]

Horrific and barbaric I mentioned, because the stark fact is that some of these children, whose only 'fault' was having a progressive and natural sense of right from wrong, which is today encouraged in children, because their parentswere anarchists, because their culture was a one of mutual aid and an aversion to any injustice, a disrespect of enforced authority in an alienating culture whilst suffering from loss of family, friends, and home. The disgusting fact remains that those deemed as 'wayward' or of the 'reformatory kind' were repatriated back to Spain, and no doubt, back to a certain death. Put that in your fucking history books.

Whilst many volunteers left for Spain, and campaigns were underway to supply food and medicine, what the predominantly anarchist inspired unions, such as the CNT (Confederacion Nacional de Trabajo) really wanted was not volunteer unemployed labourers from a Gateshead housing estate, looking for adventure from an otherwise dull existence of poverty, but arms, weapons, andexperienced military personnel, such as those who could fly and operate fighter planes, those who could care for and adequately use weapons without precious time of training. They would rather the anti-fascist and ultimately the libertarian struggle was continued by militants in their own country, to put pressure on their own governments. They didn't particularly want food sent, they wanted people to stay and continually supply weapons when possible, whilst spreading the message of social revolution through propaganda.[251] This is somewhat of a kick in the teeth to those who romantically exemplify the heroic sacrifices of the International Brigades, yet it was a hard, cold fact.

After his recent arrival in London, Tom Brown was soon deeply immersed within the anarchist movement, where he occasionally wrote for *Spain and The World* during the Spanish Revolution and regularly for *Revolt* and *War Commentary* during the War years, as well as his close involvement with the Anarchist Federation of Britain. His comrade Albert Meltzer was to later comment;

> "Further mention deserves to be made of Tom Brown and his role in re-establishing an anarcho-syndicalist presence. He was a working engineer and shop steward who could express syndicalist ideas in plain and simple language. Inheriting, as it were, the Newcastle traditions of factory syndicalism and recognising their significance in the modern anarcho-syndicalist trends, particularly as expressed in the Spanish revolution, he could speak and write on the subject free from jargon and be a voice from the workshop."[252]

Tom Brown was also actively involved with CNT-FAI Spanish Aid Committeesin London with Emma Goldman, Albert Meltzer, Ralph Barr, and Marie Louise Berneri etc. This was the group instrumental in the publishing of the anarchist paper *Spain and the World,* which was published a couple of times a month for just over two years. There also existed, at the time, an Anarcho-Syndicalist Union in which Meltzer, commenting on Tom Browns involvement states he;

> "Had been a shipyard worker in Durham[253] and had drifted south to work in aircraft, was a perceptive comrade generally, and he gave a bit of life to the Anarcho-Syndicalist Union into which he brought a breath of the workshops. He was one of several excellent speakers the ASU had at the time."[254]

> "At one meeting in the Conway Hall in 1937 we had an entirely new speaker, quite different from the "name" speakers at an Emma Goldman meeting, who spoke directly from the factory floor. Tom Brown. It was the first time he spoke in London (being a newcomer to London, if not to the movement, having

> been a syndicalist for many years previously in Durham). He had a fine commonsense delivery and spoke wittily and logically. Many of Emma's meetings had failed in the sense that while calling passionately for action to help Spain, they made no clear lead other than to make a purely political appeal for arms or medical supplies. The National Government had no intention of lifting the arms embargo and no resolutions would make it do so. Tom Brown's case was a logically argued one for industrial action, which dismayed the I.L.P. politician's at the meeting."[255]

*Spain and the World* in its notes of financial contributors would occasionally listthose received from a G. Fryar of Durham, as well as a letter from Blyth, Northumberland. The paper would also regularly publicise aims and events of the Anarcho-Syndicalist Union, including a report of its meeting in London on 7th April 1937, where after an opening by Emma Goldman, another member, quite possibly Marie Louise Berneri, who answered on the objectives of the ASU in this country "the gathering together of all individuals and groups of Anarchists and Syndicalists in England. An appeal to those who, realising the injustice of the present social system and being dissatisfied with the political labour movement, feel the imperative necessity of a unifying principle on a social and economic basis which transcends politics."[256]

Marie Louise Berneri was the daughter of Camillo Berneri, an Italian professor of philosophy, anarchist militant, propagandist and theorist, who was murdered in Barcelona by Stalinists. "It was her influence that helped (bringing together) the Anarcho-Syndicalist Union group, the youth groups, and even some of the older members of the *Freedom* group."[257]

To what extent and influence, the membership of the Anarcho-Syndicalist Union had outside of London, particularly in the North East, I have been unable to ascertain. It can be said that it was a forerunner for the later formation of the Syndicalist Workers Federation (later the

Direct Action Movement, then Solidarity Federation), which had a definite support locally.

## 2.9 CNT MILITANT INTERVIEW

Fifty years after these events, July 1986, was the 50th anniversary of the Spanish Revolution, and to commemorate the occasion members of anarcho- syndicalist grouping Tyneside Revolutionary Syndicalists (more on whom later) met with Miguel Rico (an active CNT militant during the Spanish revolution, and at the time residing in nearby Middlesbrough) to carry out a small interview, which was then published in the July 1986 special supplement of *The Syndicalist* number 7.

> "It was during the Spanish revolution that the ideas of Anarcho-Syndicalism were not just political theory but a practical reality. In many areas of Spain the CNT was faced with the problems of fighting the civil war but also with restructuring the whole of society based on the ideas of libertarian communism.
>
> During the post civil war years under the dictatorship of Franco the CNT and libertarian communist influence was almost smashed. Since the death of Franco the Anarcho-Syndicalist movement has come out of hiding and is again beginning to grow, though at this point in time it is obviously a shadow of its former self.
>
> For the first time documents, reports and eye witness accounts of problems the CNT faced and the solutions arrived at are becoming available. Unfortunately no real attempt has been made to translate these documents and make them accessible to the English reader – that is until now.
>
> We interviewed Miguel Rico who witnessed these events firsthand about some of his experiences.

*Syndicalist*– When and where were you born and how did you become involved with the anarchist movement?

*Miguel*– I was born in the Hospitalet area of Barcelona on the 1st October 1919 but when I was very young my father found work at a cement quarry in a place called Villanueva y Getru. It was there that I was raised and educated. When I was 16 I joined the FIJL (Federation of Libertarian Youth).

*Syndicalist*– Was that the average age of the members of the federation?

*Miguel*– Some were younger but most were 17, 18 and 19 years of age.

*Syndicalist*– How did you become involved?

*Miguel*– You did not just join, things were not done like that. At that time the police were trying to infiltrate the movement at all levels and there were many informers everywhere. In our town you became a member of the Libertarian Youth on the recommendation of an already respected member. This is what happened to me. I was recommended by an older person who knew my views and beliefs and knew I was to be trusted. I then joined. My brother who was two years younger than me joined by the same method.

*Syndicalist*– How many were in the Libertarian Youth, and what activities did you engage in?

*Miguel*– At one time there was as many as 200 in the Libertarian Youth in our small town. Our activities were mainly propaganda, getting our ideas across to the workers but also raising funds for the movement. We would also hold a meeting, as I said we had to be very careful so although the secretary and committee could meet in safe cafes and bars our full meetings were always held outside of town. You see at that time it was very common for people to go on picnics in large groups at weekends, this was what we would do.

*Syndicalist–* In 1936 the revolution broke out. How did this affect the Libertarian Youth in Villanueva y Getru?

*Miguel–* The first affect that it had was that the older members joined the militia and went to the battle front. We who were leftknew that the work of the Federation had to go on, the fight against the fascists was not just at the front but also at home, a rearguard was needed. A new committee was elected and the work went on. Atone time I held the position of local secretary. Once I was delegated to attend a conference in Barcelona it was at the time that the anarchists controlled the city. It was then that I saw what was really possible, how things could be organised with true equality andfreedom. We as delegates were booked into one of the biggest hotels in Barcelona. The dining room provided free meals to the delegates. It was here that I met a fellow anarchist nicknamed 'Zupa'. He was once one of the best pickpockets in Barcelona. I'll always remember the time that a group of us went to a restaurant that before the revolution was considered very posh, a place that only the rich could afford to eat in, but now it was run by the workers it provided cheap meals to the people of Barcelona as well as the militias who were passing through. The restaurant still used the silver cutlery that it had used before the revolution. While we were eating our meal we noticed that the knives, forks and spoons began to go missing one by one. We all knew it was 'Zupa' but we could not catch him in the act. When we got outside 'Zupa' put his hand in his pocket and took out all the missing cutlery "'Zupa,' we all said "'you don't need to steal anymore." "I know" 'Zupa' said after he had taken them back "I was just practising." *Syndicalist–* How long were you secretary of the local Libertarian Youth?

*Miguel–* About four months and then I joined the militia. I did not tellmy mother that I was going to join because I knew that this would upset her.

*Syndicalist–* What was the name of the militia you joined?

*Miguel–* I joined the Hortiz Column which was sent to Caspe in Aragon. After that we were sent to help in the battle for Belchite butin order to do this we had first to take a small town called Fuen de Todos. As we entered the town a machine gun started to cut down our comrades. The firing came from a priest who had mounted a machine gun on top of the bell tower of his church. We had to send for a Republican plane to bomb the church, it was the only way that we could take the town. It was during the battle for Belchite that Iwas wounded, we lost many comrades there.

*Syndicalist–* You were wounded more than once. Is that right?

*Miguel–* Yes, after I recovered from the wound I received in the Battle for Belchite I rejoined my Column but was wounded again. I was taken to the hospital and the doctor told me that I was being sent to a recuperation centre and then on to the army barracks at Olot. This was at the time that the Communists were trying to militarize the militias. I told the doctor that I would go home until I was fully recovered and then report to the barracks at Olot. After about three weeks I went to report and was arrested for collaboration with the fascists. I was taken before a court martial and found guilty. I just could not understand it, but later I found out that the communists were doing this to anarchists everywhere. I was put in a cell to await sentence. Eventually I heard the keys in the door and was convinced that I would be taken out and shot. This was the first time that I was really scared. Everyone is scared when going into battle but you tell yourself that somehow you'll survive but this time I was convinced that I was about to die. The door of the cellopened and there stood a Colonel who said 'release this man'. I then recognised him as a Colonel who we had fought beside in Aragon. He was only there to inspect the new recruits but had heard that a prisoner was being held and had insisted on seeing me. On his word I was released. There was no doubt about it this man saved my life. Under the communist advisers from Russia the militarization went on and I ended up in a communist led brigade.

*Syndicalist*– Do you remember the name of the brigade?

*Miguel*– If I remember rightly I was sent to the 134 Brigade 10th Division First Company.

*Syndicalist*– What were your experiences there as an anarchist in a communist dominated brigade?

*Miguel*– Well I kept myself to myself after my experiences at the barracks in Olot. I thought the best thing to do was keep very quiet. By my actions it was clear to everyone that I was not a communist member. One day I was approached by a captain (who I found out later had been a centurion delegate in an anarchist column), he explained that it was not safe for anarchists and that I should be careful what I said and did. I stayed with this captain as his assistant. The collapse of the Republic was soon to follow and I managed to cross the border into France.

*Syndicalist*– How were the refugees treated by the French Government?

*Miguel*– The refugee camp that I was in was just like a concentration camp. People there starved. There was food in the camp but the guards made people barter for it with any possessions they might have left. There was no medical treatment so disease spread through the camp. Many of the very old and very young died.

> Miguel went on to fight against the Nazis in the French army and eventually with the British troops in North Africa. We finally asked Miguel if he would one day write a book about his life, he replied, "maybe one day I will but at the moment there are more important things to do like translating as much material as possible."[258]

Franco entered the capital of Madrid and declared victory on 1 April 1939, and the mass graves of his murderous regime are still being uncovered to this day. For the anarchists, the underground resistance and struggle against Franco was to continue for decades.

Rudolf Rocker, concluding his writing on events, August 1937, was to profoundly emphasis;

> "For twelve months a brave people has been sacrificed to the selfish interests of imperialist robbers and their Russian henchmen. It is high time for the Libertarian world to understand that and to wakeup to the fact that the fate of Spain will be the fate of Europe. Never has a people fought for its freedom more heroically. Never has a people been worse betrayed by open and secret enemies. It is Spain's great tragedy that she has hitherto been so little understood: the story of the sufferings of a people that is bleeding from a thousand wounds and still will not give up the fight, because it knows that it carries in its breast the precious growth of freedom and human dignity on which the future of all of us depends."[259]

## 2.10 REVOLT! AND THE WAR YEARS 1938-1950

*Spain and the World* ceased publication towards the end of 1938, and a new paper *Revolt!* was to become the new national publication. The first issue contained details of a monetary contribution from a J. Bastock of Middlesbrough, as well as what would be the first of a series of article contributions from Tom Brown, who was also on the editorial committee.[260]

Tom Browns first article was a vociferous attack on conscription and national service being implemented with the onset of approaching World War 2 entitled "Easy steps to national serfdom" where it was stated "Let no patriotic worker think conscription as to defend his home against a bloodthirsty foreign foe. The armed forces are used not to protect workers homes but to combat foreign capitalist competition, to subdue the colonial peoples and threaten the workers at home. Military conscription laws are used to crush strikes and force down wages." Before concluding;

> "Now in Britain the T.U.C. agrees to operate National Service and discipline the union bodies who resist. Let us vigorously support the unions and trades councils which refuse to prepare their members for the blood bath. Let us as in the last Great War build in each factory, pit and mill, workshop committees with rank-and-file initiative to resist each step to National Service the sweet sounding alias of National Serfdom."[261]

Issue 2 see's an article 'The State', giving a brief historical narrative of its formation.[262] Further articles were on 'Cripps and the people's front'[263], and a lengthy piece 'Unemployment is hell' states "Localities such as Jarrow and the coalfields were, a few years ago, buzzing hives of industry. Most of the wealth was taken to the South of England or the more pleasant scenery of the Mediterranean coast. Now, unwanted by the absentee owning class the silent factories and mines seem like the blackened, poisoned stumps of a senile giant, — but the population remains." And "The unemployed will not find a solution of their problems in sympathy of monarchs, the charity of an overfed bourgeoisie or the cribbed "schemes" of intellectually bankrupt politicians. Their own arms, though weakened by hunger, yet have the means to shape their own destinies."

The article goes on to encourage the workers to take back their own mines, factory's, and mills etc for their own use and production for themselves, as "Miners shiver from cold or spend a day's labour picking a bucket of coal froma waste heap while living on some of the richest coal seams in the world, textile operatives in Yorkshire may be seen without overcoats in winter though surrounded by mills able to produce cloth to cover the whole population. Land once fruitful is given to weeds or half cultivated and agricultural workers go to the towns to swell the ranks of the enforcedly idle. The unemployed miners must be put to work producing coals for themselves and their fellow unemployed, the idle land must be taken to produce the vegetables, bread, eggs, and milk, the shortage of which is sapping the lives of the workless." Concluding;

> "It may be said it is better to press for a slight increase of dole. Doles are increased for political expediency; they are cut for the same purpose. But faced by the revolutionary direct action of the class conscious unemployed, the rulers would shower doles on them. The ruling class is moved by fear — not pity— let them fearthe unemployed."[264]

Issue 5 see's Tom lament his wrath against outdated Trade Unions and their continued support of the state by incompetent bureaucrats in 'The problems of unofficial strikes'. Before given examples of how trade unions can be partly implicit in more of a division of the workers into separate industries, the article concludes;

> "Trade unionism suffers too from its association with the state. At first the state opposed unions then sought to win them over.

> Now every state committee from unemployment assistance to Royal Commissions have trade union "representatives." In the hour of crisis they are faced by two loyalties, the state or the workers, the state usually wins. Syndicalism would be free of political parties, unhampered by state loyalty. Unofficial strikes threaten too the vast accumulation of funds, usually invested in capitalist concerns or war loan. On top of their other tasks the unions undertake to pay, old age pensions, dole, sick and death benefits. The possession of the funds to pay these makes them lame and conservative. In Germany this led to the unions not resisting Fascism for fear of losing their treasure. Without paying such benefits unions could be run on a subscription of three pence per week. All this is but a brief survey ofa few of the differences between the out-moded organisation, trades unionism and the newer, syndicalism or revolutionary industrial unionism. The outbreaks of unofficial strikes make it possible for us to build in every factory, pit or mill, workers' committees linked by industry to one national solid whole, but such a movement can only develop in so far as it has a well thought out strategy. Syndicalism supplies that. Such a movement must not be controlled from above but from below, by the workers assembled at their place of work. They must decide what is official and what is unofficial."[265]

The prolific series of articles would continue in issue 6 with a scathing attack on Winston Churchill and his horrendous record of human rights abuses, both at home and the wider world.[266] These years also saw Tom Browns involvement with the Anarchist Federation of Britain, which is said to be also the precursor to the later Syndicalist Workers Federation. During World War 2 the articles would continue through the paper *War Commentary*[267] as well as numerous public meetings in his harangue against the war and the state in his unique Geordie style.

February 1941, and *War Commentary*, as well as advertising a new Freedom Press pamphlet *'Trade Unionism or Syndicalism?* By Tom Brown, would also carry an article, where under the same title would state;

> "The opponents of Anarchism often tell us we cannot have Anarchism overnight. We know that well. Everything must be built up, but the time to start building is now. As previous societies decayed there developed within them the embryo of new forms of societies, so within capitalism we build the framework of socialism: the syndicates. From every struggle and from our daily work we must learn how to run industries and services. We must develop the class-consciousness, the knowledge and self-confidence of the workers, until the embryonic society bursts the shell of capitalism. As the I. W. W. preamble put it: "By organising industrially we are forming the new society within the shell of the old." Capitalism threatens to destroy society with itself, and the only force that can save humanity is the revolutionary workers. The Anarchists call the workers to the syndicalist revolution: Revolution of Construction."[268]

May 1941 and Tom Brown was on the speakers bill at the London May Day events and in March 1942 was speaking at the Freedom Press rooms on 'Counter-revolution in Russia', whilst the March issue of *War Commentary* see's an article on the roots of *'The Internationale'* song and how it was changed and corrupted by the Bolsheviks.[269]

Locally, and The Morpeth Herald is reporting in March 1943, on the annual conference of the Morpeth Divisional Labour Party that;

> "They were warned against appearing at public functions with representatives of 'proscribed organisations', examples named being Anarchists, Syndicalists, and Communists. According to my dictionary, a proscribed organisation is one which has been put out of protection of the law (in this case Labour Party law), banished, exiled, rejected, denounced as dangerous. Our civic chiefs must now lead uncomfortable lives, for every invitation they receive to grace a platform with their presence will have to

be subjected to microscopic scrutiny as a safeguard against danger of infection from political heresy."[270]

August 1943 and Tom Brown is lecturing again at the Freedom Press rooms on 'A.E.U. and the Engineering Workers'. Followed by a lengthy article on the 'Rail Strike of 1919' in the papers 'pages of labour history' series.[271]

The November 1944 issue of *War Commentary* is of particular local interest as firstly it has a front page article on the return to work of the;

> "Newcastle Dockers on October 31st after they had been on strike for six weeks regarding payment for the removal of hatch covers. T he Dockers decided to return a fortnight ago, but their return was deliberately delayed and caused much hardship, by discussions regarding the administration of the new union branch formed by the National Union of General and Municipal Workers. The Dockers original union branch was closed down when they refused to recognise it. During the last six weeks it is regrettable that troops have unloaded and loaded vessels so efficiently that officials and employers deprived the men of work until they gave assurances as to the constitution of the new branch. When the men turned up for work on Monday morning they received a notice from the local Dock Labour Corporation. This stated that the Corporation had been informed by the Union that the Dockers had given a written undertaking to observe union rules and honour all agreements. Among these agreements they had undertaken to /accept in full the Dock labour scheme for the Tyne. Their attendance at control points,however, was not to be taken as indicating their acceptance. Even now there is not enough work for all. But those attending will get attendance money. Each man has lost about £30 during the strike. Itwas a great effort— -they did well."

Another report was given on the then dispute at the Walker Naval

Shipyard over different rates of pay for various skilled and semi-skilled workers. Whilst another report from the Tyneside shipyards states;

> "Here also the overtime situation has come well to the fore. At many yards on the river big demonstrations have been staged demanding a 2% per week increase. Small strikes are taking place everywhere. A number of sheet-metal workers stopped work to emphasise their unwillingness to see more dilutee labour come into the industry; about 100 riveters also struck work because they maintained that they were not even receiving the minimum wage for the class of work which they were doing. These incidents are symptomatic of the general trend everywhere the men are restless, they see the inadequacy of the unions, and are taking matters into their own hands."

And down the road on the Tees river in Middlesbrough;

> "Here again the men are restless, although there is rather more work on hand owing to the demand created by the war in the Pacific. For this reason the men seem to think that they can afford to lie back using the constitutional methods of demanding wage increases."

The letters page also contained a return of our old friend G.W. Tindale from the Gateshead anarchist grouping, who reminisces of his participation in response to Tom Browns earlier article on the 'Rail Strike of 1919'.[272]

The later 25th November edition of the paper includes a continuation of the 'pages of labour history' series with a piece on the strikes of 'Black Friday 1921' by Tom Brown, and more interestingly contains details of monetary contributions to *War Commentary* funds from four separate people in the Gateshead area, as well as one from a R.M.H. in Stockton on Tees.[273] These contributions would continue until April 1945. Whilst this does not necessarily confirm anarchist activity in the region at this time, it certainly shows the support for anarchist papers in the area.

Obviously, any anarchist related activity would be under threat of state suppression given the period, so I can assume these wouldn't have been 'advertised'.

There was during this time a Newcastle War Resisters Group in which;

> "John Morley and Jack Sadler, conscientious objectors from the First World War, were the main inspirers of the Newcastle War Resisters Group of conscientious objectors, with its motto, 'The highest morality is the greatest expediency.' The majority of its leading members were members of the Independent Labour Party (I.L.P.), opposed to what they viewed as being an imperialist, capitalist war. It was one of the largest of such groups in the country. Taking an absolutist stance on objection to the war, many of its members appeared before the courts in the Moot Hall. The organisation met weekly in the Theosophical Hall and attracted an average attendance of around 60. *The Word*,[274] an anarchist newspaper, described its meetings as instructive, enthusiastic and convivial and its approach to pacifism as mainly political and humanitarian."

The group was active from 3 September 1939 to 2 September 1945, and included a wide range of people within its ranks, including "business men, clerks, tradesmen labourers, typists, and housewives", and local anarchists no doubt. "Up to November 1943 the group members had received 28 prison sentences, a number which was to increase considerably by the end of the war."[275]

Before departing company with *War Commentary* December 1944 and Tom Brown is writing on the current debate of giving support to trade unions, while on a report from the Sunderland shipyards states;

> "The bosses are quick to take advantage of any opportunity of tightening their control over the workers. Since the beginning of the war the sounding of works-buzzers has been banned under the War-time Control of Noise Order. Last week the Shipbuilders Association were granted a certificate of exemption

from this Order by the local police authority. The bosses argue that the sounding of works buzzers should do something to stop the tendency of men to arrive late and knock off early in the place of no watch and no knowledge of the correct time."[276]

The Newcastle Boilermakers of the Walker Naval Shipyard were clashing with the forces of 'law and order' and in an endeavour to prosecute them for being on an 'illegal strike'. "On the day of the hearing several hundred boilermakers from Tyne and Blyth areas did not attend work in order to be able to express their solidarity with their fellow workers by demonstrating outside the City Police Court." On January 5th the men again appeared in Court and were found guilty of "unlawfully taking part in a strike" and sentence was deferred until the following day at the suggestion of Mr. Rutledge, defending, so as to enable all the 505 men involved in the dispute to hold a meeting. "What the defendants have done they maintain was right and in their interests as Trade Unionists. Whatever fine or costs are imposed will not be paid. Beyond that, I have nothing to say." 125 men were found guilty and 'ordered to pay a fine of £10 each or alternatively 31 days' imprisonment. "The Newcastle boilermakers have certainly made a stand for a principle and deserve the support of all sections of the working class."[277] The strike wave was not just confined to the shipyards as;

"The "Evening Chronicle (10/1/45) reports a stoppage of 700 men working on the goods handling and goods and passenger parcels delivery staffs at Newcastle Forth Goods Station, Newcastle New Bridge Street Goods Station, and the passenger parcels department at Newcastle Central Station." And on the 27th May;

> "On instruction from the Fuel Ministry, the management of Sleekburn Colliery, Northumberland sacked all its 1,200 miners for deliberately cutting down output. On April 21st, the men struck work over a wages dispute. During the negotiations, the owners say, the miners adopted a go slow policy with a resulting fall in output. Another shut-down order has been

issued by the Durham Coal Controller and is being challenged by 1,600 miners at Whitburn Colliery. Ninety-two veteran miners, some of them who ore over 70, have been declared redundant and have received their notices. It will be seen that mine-owners are not losing time in celebrating Victory Day, in their own fashion. Miners who dare to resist them or who are too old to exploit are summarily sacked."[278]

Alongside unemployment, tuberculosis was also to play another key role in the bleak deprivation at this time in the region. A report by the North East Branchof the Socialist Medical Association stated that the borough of Tynemouth stood the highest in incidents and outbreak. "We are reaping the fruits of the wasteland of depression during which large parts of the North were distressed areas. Even as late as September 1935, when the government of the day was proclaiming a recovery there were 91,974 unemployed persons in the seven principal towns of the North East. In the mining industry 8,000 Northumberland miners and 37,000 Durham miners were unemployed. In the Tyneside shipbuilding industry 58.7 % of the men were out of work. The purchase of good food in these circumstances was not always possible. We had scarcely turned the corner before the Second World War was on us. Long hours in the workshops badly ventilated because of the black-out aggravated the situation and no doubt contributed to the numbers of tubercular patients." The suggested answer was "since prevention is better than cure, better housing is a prime necessity, rents in the future should not be so high as to restrict expenditure on the purchase of good food."[279]

Meanwhile on July 19th 1945, and a commemoration meeting, held in London, of the Spanish Revolution, Tom Brown "dealt with the futility of parliamentarism. The only effective method of struggle for the workers was working-class direct action, with the aim of workers control of industry, as carried out in the Spanish Revolution."[280]

For the remainder of the late 1940's there is little evidence of anarchist related activity in the North East, yet a presence was still evident as

*Freedom's* press fund and monetary appeals listed N.G (Ashington) Jan 1947, R.M.H. (Stocktonon Tees) regularly until 1952, G.D (Gateshead) May 1947, CWD (Ashington) Dec 1947, JBW (Stockton on Tees) Jan 1948, J.B. (Houghton Le Spring) May 1948 and A.B. (Houghton Le Spring) August 1950.

February 1949 and "Top marks for tenacity go to the Education Department of the Ashington Co-operative Society, where regular Sunday lectures on all subjects under the sun started in the dark days of depression after the first world war, are still going strong. Anything from 50-100 people assemble for each session." "Last week a talented young lecturer from Kings College (Newcastle) gave a typical purely informative description of the British Constitution and how it works, but before he got through the job his audience had involved him in discussions on Communism and Anarchism."[281] Ashington is a mining town on the Northumberland coast and was once known as the "world's largest coal-mining village", and as evidence suggests, had a knowledgeable anarchist presence, or a presence sympathetic to the cause.

October 1949 and *Direct Action* (Organ of the Anarchist Federation, soon to be Syndicalist Workers Federation) was beginning to list a series of pamphlets written by Tom Brown, including *"Trade Unionism or Syndicalism"*, *"British General Strike"*, and *"Social General Strike"*[282] Whilst in an article in the December issue;

> "Revolutionary workers in Britain are appalled by the present seeming apathy of the workers. Wages are frozen, then reduced by devaluation, the workers are pressed for more production and goaded to revolt by managerial insults, yet, apart from a few "unofficial" strikes they patiently endure it all. The truth of this is, andwe are sorry to admit it, that the great majority of the workers are patient because they believe that the Labour government in some way represents them. They would never have put up with so much from a Tory government. Patiently and stoically they claim that, having elected this

> government, they must give it a "fair trial", so they endure rising prices, shortage of tobacco, enforced teetotalism and work drives, because they feel a high sense of public responsibility. We regret this and hate the thought that such a fine spirit is misplaced by trust in a political outfit that is no better, or worse, than the rest." Tom Brown would also deliver a lecture 'Workers Control – A Syndicalist Approach' Dec 29th at Trade Union Club, 12 Great Newport St. WC2.[283]

"There was growing disillusionment with the Labour Government[284]. Many workers had genuinely believed that the new administration heralded the dawnof a socialised society. They were soon to be brought back down to earth, not least by the Labour government's readiness to use troops to break strikes, which were still illegal under Order 1305."[285]

So ends the bleakest period in our study of anarchism in the North East, a movement virtually wiped out, predominantly by war. Capitalism won again.

Despite the 1950s beginning relatively quiet on the local 'anarchist front', a worldwide resurgence was in the air which would build steadily throughout the late 1950s to an explosive climax of activity and groups of the 1960s and later produced literature of the 1970s. The time was ripe and ready for the taking, or so it was felt.

# PART THREE 1950—1980

## 3.1 THE 1950s

> "At a special conference of the Anarchist Federation of Britain, held in Manchester on August 6th, the urgent need in this country for an organisation which would concern itself with syndicalist propaganda and action was fully discussed. As a result, it was decided to dissolve the A.F.B and to form the Syndicalist Workers Federation."[286]

By November 1950 *Direct Action*, the newly produced paper of the Syndicalist Workers Federation, is publishing the beginnings of what would become Tom Browns future pamphlet *The Principles of Syndicalism*, with a piece entitled

'Not Centralism but Federalism' followed by 'Economic Federalism' in December[287], then 'Abolition of the Wages System', 'The end of the Money Trick', 'To Each According to his Needs', 'Workers Control of Distribution', 'The Commune', 'Defending the Revolution', and 'First Fruits of the Revolution'in future issues.

From March to May 1952 a D.C. Wilson is advertising in *Freedom*, if anyone in the area is interested in forming a group to contact himself at 3 Norman Terrace, South Bank, Middlesbrough, whilst RMH of Stockton on Tees would remain a regular contributor to *Freedom* funds throughout the decade. Both of these contacts were pretty close together, so I may wonder if they eventually found each other and formed the group.[288]

By October 1953, and anarchist activity in the region is given a further boost with the formation of Tyneside Anarchist Group, who held meetings every other Sunday, 7.30pm at the home of D. Boon, Louvaine Place, near Sandyford, Newcastle.

The month would also see a letter from the aforementioned D.C. Wilson of Middlesbrough to the pages of *Freedom*, where in a response to an earlier letter states;

> "From his letter (*Freedom* 10/10/53) I conclude that E.G. of Worksop is inclined to my own view that, the most suitable ground for sowing the seeds of anarchist propaganda lies where the dissatisfied and disillusioned leftists gather on the fringe of the Labour Party. Perhaps this is because I came to anarchism from this kind of socialism myself and feel that there are many left behind without the psychological "scars" of a break with Catholicism or Marxism to impede a smooth and painless transition from an authoritarian to a libertarian viewpoint. I think that E.G's suggestion of an advertisement should be acted upon. I do not, however, share his optimism concerning public libraries. Mine is a "strong, industrial" area and an anarchist paper in the local library reading room was not possible even when there was an anarchist librarianin the place! It isn't the librarians who choose the journals to be shown but library committees, i.e. local politicians, imitation Churchill's and Attlee's. Curtains for anarchist papers E.G.? Quite. But try if you like, other places may be different. I couldn't even get them to buy Richards' *Lessons of the Spanish Revolution*, the North Riding Head Librarian offered me a pro-fascist book instead and if it wasn't for the fact that he lives so far away, he'd have got a brick through his front window. Being a Yorkshire man, I am not so keen on free copies. As long as you are willing to give away, they won't buy. Freedom may not be perfect, but it's too good to give away.[289]

Midway through the decade, and a now retired 'Sir Will Lawther' is publically denouncing his anarchist past. In sounding like an apologetic turncoat he informs us;

"As a result of my time at the Labour College I came back to Chopwell having adopted the then fashionable philosophy of Anarchism. Nowadays this political creed is so stale and outmoded that I doubt if one person in 100,000 would care to subscribe to it. But to us it was new and exciting. It was the ultimate in extremism, the demand for direct action, and the professed disgust, not only with the class-ridden social structure, but also with all gradual means of getting rid of that form of society. I think now that the adoption of this philosophy was the logical development in the outlook of the fighter for social progress, particularly among the young men. Things couldn't go fast enough for us, and thus we reacted violently against the slow process of political democracy. Of course, now I believe we were wrong headed but I see no reason to be ashamed of the fact that as a young man I did not have an old head on my shoulders."[290]

Renouncing any involvement in varying aspects of anarchist deemed activity forthe sake of following a career, or denying any involvement for the sake of a monetary career is an episode that occurs both locally and nationally in the decades to follow, and to this day, in the case of those following 'academic careers'. Using anarchism as a stepladder to success, especially when too many have gave their lives (Spanish revolution as one example) is despicable and I believe aspects of this activity, and the natural habits of the leech species bare resemblance.

There is not much remaining evidence of anarchist activity during the 1950s in the North East. It can be said that sometimes the anarchists are so entrenched within their own community, to a certain extent, that they can, at times, barely venture out of it. Whilst being so busy working away through example or encouragement of instigating inherent and inbuilt aspects of mutual aid, natural solidarity, and an aversion to authority, why raise their head above the parapet and announce their political belief in publically stating "I am an anarchist"? Whilst this is in no way anything to be ashamed of, it can lead to minor ostracism within a close working class community, estate or environment (either through lack of understanding[291], continual state conditioning, and media distortion). After all, anarchism promotes the concept of true equality, so therefore, if an individual is an anarchist, this then makes them no 'better' than any other within the community.

It could also be said, why give a label or compartmentalise a natural and social way of being? Of course it is also natural to seek out like minded individuals and groups to further develop collective endeavours and thus fulfilling communal instincts. It can also be stated that this is particularly true in the North East, where anarchists occasionally come together for shared activity and / or purpose, at times under a shared name, and at times not, whilst not making this a permanent endemic. For example, the name Tyneside Anarchist Group or Tyneside Anarchist Federation has been used in different decades, with different aims, aspirations and precedence of activity type, without the same lineage of people involved in such groups, or even knowledge of previous existence of name.

Remaining activity in the form of monetary contributions to the paper *Freedom* for the latter half of the 1950s include contributions from the following; G.D. and J.D. (Gateshead), D.C. Wilson , P.E. and ARH (Middlesbrough), D.G. and J.G. (Billingham), H.B. (Newcastle), and RMH ( Stockton on Tees), and last but not least 'A GEORDIE'.[292] It was also emphasised, during 1959 (and the early sixties), that *Freedom* was available to buy from G.M. Bremmer Newsagents, at Bigg Market, Newcastle.

Developments in the wider world, the Cold War, Hungarian events of 1956, the situation in South Africa, the advent of more nuclear power programmes, and seeing events unfurl within the civil rights movement in America, all served to gradually build up sections of the populace, predominantly from the 'left' who wanted to change the situation of events.

> "They came together in a casual protest march to the nuclear base at Aldermaston. These marches grew into the first protest

> march movement since the thirties, and on a higher level when one considers the subjectivity of the latter; though inevitably a bureaucracy, with Labour sympathies, grew up with the Campaign for Nuclear Disarmament, the protests against that bureaucracy signified the increasingly libertarian nature of the Committee of One Hundred, many of the latter had moved to anarchism from the ideas of international non-alignment; distaste for the Labour Party; and a moving forward from pacifism by virtue of their own experience confronting the police."

The older anarchist generation, whilst trying to point out the futility of 'asking a Government to ban the bomb', would also welcome a;

> "Large number of the C.N.D (Campaign for Nuclear Disarmament) rank and file. Indeed so impatient with the leadership were many of the latter that they lined up behind the Anarchist banner so that they would *not* co-operate with what was – so far as the nuclear dividing line was concerned – the loyal opposition. More than one development took place at the same time; suddenly there was an entirely new generation, that grew up in its own struggles and through its own experiences and came over to a position we had clearly defined but which they had not accepted on a platter. It did happen occasionally that some found it hard to give up on some shibboleths of the peace or labour movements – hence some inconsistencies, such as the occasional group thinking it could be anarchist and still support the Vietcong government for instance, but by and large the British Anarchist movement leaped forward with this generation to become, somewhat to its own surprise, something to be taken seriously in an assessment of the political scene."[293]

And so the 1960's were to unfold.

## 3.2 THE NOT SO SWINGING SIXTIES 1960—1963

The North East was accustomed to marches, particularly those of the unemployed during the 1930s and protests through the streets of Newcastle against apartheid, against the bomb and nuclear power, as well as the annual May Day march, which all were commonplace during the late 1950s and early 1960s.[294] Whilst these were predominantly organised and participated in by the local 'liberal left' many anarchists were also naturally drawn to such events, or some were eventually drawn to anarchism through such events.

The local folk music scene, particularly at places like Birtley was thriving, and as a backdrop to events one participant of the time recalls "I learned a whole repertoire of traditional and contemporary songs. There were a lot of IWW songs like, *Union Maid, Solidarity for Ever, Joe Hill,* and *Which Side are you on?*"[295] This showed the local recognition of, admittedly American, syndicalist struggles and the philosophy of direct action. "If there was a motif for left wing youth politics round 1960 it would be direct action. It stretched from sit downs through large marches and small marches, long marches and short marches, to poster parades, wall daubing and fly posting. Conventional meetings and resolutions were almost a sub text. This took place inside a deep cultural shift embracing music, poetry, fashion and a loosening up of attitude to sexuality and authority. This shift continued through the 60s and 70s but the direct action upsurge tailed off through 1963 as the General Election drew close."[296] Putting faith in parliamentary solutions as a matter of protest, or the aim of your protest, or worse still to put it in the hands of 'leaders' to protest on your behalf, tends to do that I am afraid.

Far from 'tailing off' in 1963, anarchist related activity was certainly too largely increase towards the latter half of the decade. Perhaps losing faith in self- styled 'leaders' was the predominant instigator of this. It could also be said, that after World War 2, and the perceived stability that this then created, could possibly be the reason for the upsurge of 'war time' babies coming of age during the latter 1960s.[297]

To many anarchists in the region, the influence of 'music, poetry and fashion' played little, or not so much of a prevalent part in the decade to come. Whilst these may have brought in extra numbers of people during certain periods, and the new 'counter culture' was to play a significant contribution to the general recognition of anarchist idea's locally at times, the main arena of the decade's battle, as I shall show, was in the militant industrial sphere, just as it was in previous decades, and future decades to come. Certainly, there was a gradual increase of 'university' groups during this time, but whilst some may have stayed in the region after their particular course of education ended, the majority didn't. Again, this is a scenario repeated in decades to come.

Coincidently, one of the first signs of activity I can find at the beginning of the decade is;

> "Dear Comrades, I am endeavouring to 'comb out' Anarchists (Libertarians) in the Durham area – primarily with respect to the proposed University Libertarian Movement, for which internal propaganda is best suited, but any sympathisers outside of the University would be greeted with open arms. If it is at all possible maybe you would insert an advert to this effect in *Freedom*. With many thanks for your assistance. Sincerely yours, Eric Adam's. Musgrave Gardens, Durham City.[298]

Prior and succeeding to this evidence of support remains, as shown by contributions to *Freedom's* monetary appeals throughout the decade with example contributions from D.G. & J.G (Billingham), HN, CM, HRR, HB, BP, BC, RR, BB, & RN, (Newcastle), G.D, Mrs D, JH, & D.D, (Gateshead), H.N. (Jesmond), K.T. & P.E. (Middlesbrough), DM, LF, IG, & R.P, (Stockton), V.B,(Darlington), G.E, (Sunderland), B.C, (Hartlepool), S.C, & E.A (Durham), B.M, (South Shields), and J.H, (Birtley).[299] Whilst some of these were occasional, most were regular contributors.

Tom Brown was at this time still in London and active within the Syndicalist Workers Federation and was to chair a public meeting in 1961 "to commemorate the (1936) Spanish workers social revolutionary struggle against fascism" on July 16th.

October 1961 and much respected local Labour historian Ray Challinor, (1929-2011) who whilst not being an anarchist himself, was quite sympathetic to its philosophy at times, was to post the first of a few letters to *Freedom* in the oncoming decades. Ray at this period was involved with Campaign for Nuclear Disarmament (CND) and the Committee of 100, attending the first anti-nuclear Aldermaston March in 1958.[300] The letter, in response to an earlier *Freedom* editorial state's;

> "Dear Comrade. Your editorial, which discounts the danger of war occurring through accident, overlooks the incontestable fact that Man has a natural propensity to make mistakes. To err is human. A drunken colonel in 1940, by ringing a hand bell, caused military authorities throughout East Anglia to think the Nazi invasion had begun: a misread signal resulted in the Luftwaffe's attack on Rotterdam, killing 30.000 people; and, as is notoriously well-known, birds have been mistaken - for missiles on radar screens. Today, with the fate of millions of people literally at your finger-tips, the nervous strain must be immense. Not only is this true of military personnel, but it must be even more true of the politicians. No wonder so many have buckled in under the heavy responsibility. Khrushchev reliably informed us, in his 20th Party Congress report, that Stalin was mad. With German troops at the gates of Moscow, be sat morosely twirling a globe about in the Kremlin. Professor Trevor-Roper tells us that Hitler, as the Allied armies came closer to Berlin, went out of his mind. While in 1946 the American Foreign Secretary, Senator Forrestal went completely insane and jumped out of a skyscraper window shouting. "The Russians are here". In other words, during the past 20 years three politicians who, if they were alive today would have the destiny of Mankind in their hands, have gone stark, raving

> bonkers. Would you suggest that our present-day politicians are any less mentally unstable? I think they are making extremely rapid progress towards the lunatic asylum. Yet, only one person in a position of nuclear responsibility has got to go insane for the big bang to occur—and *Freedom's* financial worries to be over for good. Having said all this, I would argue that there is a chance of a Third World War being started by accident. Viewed historically through the passage of time, it grows to a possibility, a probability, and then almost a certainty—if the present situation is allowed to continue long enough. Yours fraternally. Raymond Challinor. Newcastle, Sept. 21."

In response the editors of *Freedom* replied;

> "We do not agree with our correspondent just because we do not believe that the fate of millions is at the finger-tips of a few button- pressing individuals. The decision to launch a war is a much more complicated affair, taking time as well as involving a large number of individuals and groups. The examples he cites of the fallibility of human beings refer to accidents once war has actually started, which is quite a different matter, as we pointed out in our article "War by Accident" when we wrote that "The dangers of 'accidental' war are only conceivable when war is in any case imminent, when the professional soldiers are given more power to take spot decisions, and this delegation of power will obviously be greater in a press-button war than in past conflagration which involved much slower land forces". Any individual who imagines that he is capable of taking decisions for millions of his fellow beings is obviously "bonkers". Anyone who is so obsessed by the fruits of power and who in the process loses the capacity to enjoy the simple things of life is also "bonkers". (But so too is the man who works himself to his grave in order to be able to keep up with the Jones!). Our argument is that the decisions are not in fact taken by these people. Stalin may well have sat in the Kremlin twirling a globe while German troops were at the gates of Moscow. If Stalin was all that powerful it is extraordinary that

the Germans didn't in fact take Moscow; and in spite of the fact that Hitler was out of his mind it is curious that the Germans did not resort to bacteriological warfare when all was lost. After all they had the means to."[301]

Discussions aside on how "bonkers" politicians are, in the industrial sphere things were beginning to heat up where in March 1962 Tom Brown, again at the forefront of industrial militant agitation emphasises;

> "Millions of workers are in pay dispute with their employer at this moment. The Governments pay pause directly affects only those workers employed by the State, civil servants, postmen, telephone engineers, teachers, State dockyard men and also, the workers in nationalised industries, rail, power, and some road transport and the miners. In this field alone does the Government have power to deny a wage increase, this should give thought to those unions who are always passing resolutions to "nationalise the industry", or calling for State subsidies. But the Cabinets stand against the annual wage rise also encourages those employers who may have felt strong enough in any case to resist the regular wage hike. Chief among these are the engineering and shipyard bosses with about- 3,000,000 workers. It is natural, then, that there should be speculation about a General Strike, for if all workers now in dispute acted together, by design or accident, the number on strike wouldbe greater than that of 1926. The Communist Party, trying to cash inon this situation is calling for a General Strike, but, like the man whowants to get to the moon, they wouldn't know what to do with it if they got it."

Tom then goes on to show how there is little chance of a general strike at the moment as workers are so divided by too many unions, quite often within the same industry, and how, whilst some engineers called a one day strike over a particular dispute, the clerks within the same workplace refused, thus blacklegging their 'paying' members. Again, divide and rule springs to mind. The article continues;

> "Of course, Communists and various groups of Trotskyists are calling for a Labour Government as a means of getting around the "Tory wage pause", they want us to forget that the Labour Government of 1945-51 operated with the aid of the unions, a much harsher wage freeze, and these same people had called onthe workers to return that Labour Government."

And it is stressed;

> "With or without an impending election, with a Tory or Labour Government, the leaders of the trade unions and the Labour Party are opposed to the General Strike in any circumstances." As these methods of worker controlled direct action were not conducive with any government or trade union body, and should not be tolerated, before concluding "Only when a Rank & File Movement has been built in every industry will the Great Strike be fought to victory. If you believe in the General Strike you've got to start now, in however small a way."[302]

Late 1962, early 1963 would also see the formation of Tyneside Anarchist Federation, which comprised of those hailing from a 'more working class constituency' to those who rejected the pacifist position of Tyneside Committee of 100 and thus naturally drawn to anarchism. Other Anarcho-Syndicalists, from previous groups were soon to join its ranks. The group, with their red and black banner, inscribed with their name were quite vocal and visual on the 1963 May Day march through Newcastle city centre.

During the same month, Durham students were again advertising "Will anarchists in and around Durham interested in forming a discussion group, please contact Owen Wells, St Cuthbert's Society, University of Durham."[303] There were anarchists in the Durham area at this time, as I shall show, but to what extent they involved themselves with University discussion groups seems very limited, if at all. Perhaps differences of class or differences of culture played a part.

Tyneside Anarchist Federations (TAF) advertised meetings, alternate Thursdays 8pm; upstairs at the Adelaide Pub, Newgate St, Newcastle were soon attracting numbers, including a newly formed student group from Kings College. June 1963 and the group were soon hitting the local newspaper headlines where;

> "There was widespread speculation among students at King's College, Newcastle today about the existence of a strange new sect calling themselves the Anarchists. Some students described them as left-wingers, Communists and nuclear disarmers. Others said they were "right wing anarchronists". But whichever wing the anarchists support, they were today lying low after making their stormy debut on the Town Moor. No one in the college appears to have heard of the anarchists until last night's traditional Race Week husting's they whipped up a tirade of abuse against two Conservative MP's. They tried to prevent Mr Fergus Montgomery, MP. for Newcastle East, and Dame Irene Ward, M.P. for Tynemouth leaving the ground. Police had to throw a cordon round their car. Martin T***, a 22-year old student who was there but 'emphatically not as an anarchist' – said *"I think there was no trouble until the police* told the anarchists to take their banner down. They needn't have done that. After all it is a free country".[304]

This was actually the Tyneside Anarchist Federation, supporting the then few students behind their banner. Despite the prevalence of TAF during this period,other anarchists or anarchist groupings existed in the region, for example, the Federation of London Anarchists annual summer school of 1963 listed, together with a hundred or so others, delegates from Durham,[305] whilst the later Syndicalist Workers Federation conference of December 1963, also held in London, included delegates from both Sunderland and Stockton on Tees.[306]

This year would also see the continuation of CND / Committee of 100 type activities; these were centred mainly in and around the folk and protest scene's at places like the Bridge Hotel in Newcastle, whilst "In the same year anarchistsfrom South Shields ventured south to take part in the mass occupation of the fallout bunker at Reading to highlight the governments contingency plans in the event of nuclear war."[307] Charlton, in his 'cynical brush off' of anarchists in and around the Tyneside Anarchist Federation at the time would state, on discussing Dave Douglas's role that "Dave belonged to a young group of people who became active in 1963-64 when the mass movement, the Committee of 100 and indeed CND itself, was in decline. By mid 1964 Dave and his group, self – labelled flag- toting anarchists were centred on the ILP (Independent Labour Party) rooms in Byker..But soon the wild and often drunken behaviour of the 'revolutionary youth' drew the unwelcome attention of the police and hostile neighbours".[308] As mentioned earlier, the perception by this author of an apparent decline in local activity is debatable, or matter of opinion.

In Dave Douglas's view, "The first attempt to expand the existing University Anarchist Group into a Newcastle Anarchist Federation ended in us the workers walking out, and the psycho Wallace hoying a broon ale bottle at the 'snotty bastards'. The aborted meeting at the Adelphi divided into snotty bastards and the Tyneside Anarchist Federation. The city abounded with ANARCHY and REVOLUTION, SMASH THE STATE, and WORKERS CONTROL.

In midnight raids, darting from shadow to shadow, we hit city centres with the whitewash night after night.We sought to advertise our existence and create an agenda of debate among the Toon folk."[309] It was the Adelaide Pub, not the Adelphi that Dave mentioned. Wallace, was Dave Wallace from South Shields, and along with Dave, was to be the contact for TAF in the *Freedom* and *Direct Action* listings / contacts section during the latter half of 1964.[310]

Reflecting the period and influx of students into the city;

> "The developing counter culture centred around Free Verse poetry and Jazz brought together the anarchists from both groups in a social setting. Social gatherings were moreover, a salient factor of both groups composition. Notwithstanding, TAF

> remained a predominantly activist syndicalist group which, while also a product of the 1960s retained links with an older tradition. In contrast, the university anarchists reflected the counter-cultural face of 60s anarchism, bohemian in character and predominantly middle class in makeup. While coexisting, these differences came to a head by the mid 1960s when, on TAFS suggestion to form a unitary federation on Tyneside, a meeting was held at the Adelaide Pub in Newcastle ended, with the students being ejected for their apparent lack of political will or interest. Despite these apparent contradictions, the anarchists flourished on Tyneside."[311]

Peter Ridley of Tynemouth, a regular financial contributor to *Direct Action* would in October 1963 add to the anarchist debate on voting in parliamentaryelections with a letter[312] to *Freedom* where he argued;

> "With reference to the forthcoming general election and proposed anti-parliamentary campaign by libertarians, may I remind comrades of the necessity of registering and voting- I do not mean by this that one should put one's mark by any of the candidates' names, but that one should 'spoil' one's paper by writing for example an anti-parliamentary slogan across the ballot paper. The traditional anarchist tactic of abstention is too negative: already a sizeable proportion of the population abstains through apathy ratherthan conviction. Why should we allow ourselves to be associated with this indifferent mass? 'Spoiled' papers are counted at elections, and a sizeable number would affect not only the opportunist politicians but people everywhere."[313]

Whilst this tactic is debatable, it has been used by anarchists, amongst other tactics, many a time. The line I certainly disagree with, as I am sure many would, is "Why should we allow ourselves to be associated with this indifferent mass?" well for starters, we are and always will be part of this 'indifferent mass' without putting ourselves on pedestals of importance as anarchists. I also find it inspiring that 'a sizeable proportion of the population abstains' from this circus of supposed democracy by the act of a cross on a piece of paper every four or so years, whilst behind this political facade, the perpetuation of capitalism remains. Ultimately no matter which political party sways the populace with their false promises, no matter who wins, the state and all it purports in its control of the status quo always triumphs.

## 3.3 1964

1964 and the list of pamphlets by Tom Brown has increased, with additions of *'What's Wrong with the Unions?'* And *'Nationalisation and the New Boss Class'* and on the 29th January Tom would also give a talk on 'Civil Rights in the USA' at the White Swan in London, whilst writing an article on similar themes, incorporating the assassination of President Kennedy and delving into the history of slavery.[314]

In his summary of the pamphlet *'Nationalisation and the New Boss Class'* Tom would vividly emphasise "Socialisation, the ideal born of the early Labour movement, can come only from the workers and not from those who have a class interest in the preservation of capitalism. It is not State ownership, but the common, social ownership of the means of production and social ownership implies control by the producers, not by new bosses. It implies Workers' Control of Industry—and that is Syndicalism."[315]

The contact for Tyneside Anarchist Federation at this period was H.D. Nash of Queens Rd, Newcastle, and later Simonside Terrace, Heaton.[316] Perhaps, because of instances of Brown Ale bottles being thrown at middle class students, TAF meetings were, from February, now being held Wednesdays, 8pm, at the Trent House pub.[317]

The February edition of *Direct Action* see's Tom write in an article entitled 'Who are the Workers?' where he shows that there is no distinction between 'blue collar workers' or 'white collar workers' under capitalism. Both sell their labour power, and both can and are subject to exploitation. "To talk of "blue collars" being one social class and "white collars" another is like an anthropologist classifying the races of mankind by the colour of their socks. A white collar, even an old school tie, does not protect a worker from low wages,redundancy or injustice." Before concluding;

> "In the Revolutionary Industrial Union—or Syndicate--there must be room for every person, who is not a delegate of the boss, who plays a part in the production of that industry or service. Tradesman, labourer, clerk, scientist, draughtsman, tea-maker. White collar, blue collar. No collar. Black socks, red socks, no socks. One in, all in."[318]

March 18th, and Tom is giving a talk on 'Aspects of Workers' Control', again at the White Swan in London. March, April, May & June would also see four articles in *Direct Action* on 'Lenin and Workers' Control', the bulk of which was from his pamphlet of the same name.[319]

April, 1964 and Scottish anarchists are commenting how their numbers were boosted during a march and mass action at Rosyth dockyard by the Tyneside contingent of the Committee of 100, where up to 700 police were present to try to contain events.[320] In linking the disarmament of nuclear weapons, to essentially stating how this must encompass the disarmament of the state, this month's issue of *Direct Action* would devote the majority of its front page on the issue of unilateral disarmament and showing that "an anti-War movement must be international. That is obvious. It must oppose war as such, and war preparations in every country. If it selects certain targets rather than others itwill be seen not as an anti-war movement, but as an agent of -the powers whose weapons it does not oppose."

> "Unilateralism as a principle is revolutionary. This is why it is opposed by some, and why we must insist on it. Nuclear weapons are both the product of an authoritarian society and a symbol of its brutality. The H-Bomb was not built by accident;

> and we cannot talk about removing it without considering the system which produced it... The society we live in is a class society: the vast majority of the people are exploited and oppressed by a minority, the ruling class, which uses its control over the means of production to impose social priorities which are in its own interests. The state is the iron glove of the ruling class: its laws, its police force, its prison system to enforce its will – as the Committee of 100 has learned. H-Bombs are a part of the defence system of the ruling class; to end them we need a social revolution."

And concluding the feeling of the majority of class struggle anarchists during the period;

> "For us the struggle against the Bomb is the struggle for a classless society, If war is the health of the state, then we shall achieve peace only when we replace it by libertarian organisation. If class society has produced nuclear weapons, we must destroy class society. Peace, freedom and social justice are one and indivisible."[321]

By August, with his Lenin series of articles finished Tom brown next gives us an eyewitness account of the shop stewards' movement on Tyneside during the First World War in a piece entitled 'School for Syndicalism', which is reprinted here in full for local interest and the glimpse it gives us of the period and the early life of Tom Brown.

> "One's first day at work is an important day. In my case it was also a very long day. Hurrying along the damp, dark streets at 5.30 on a winter's morning, with a tin tea can and a parcel of bread (there were few canteens at that time); I felt like a workman, though a very small one. The first world war was still raging and my first inside view of the factory was of rows of 60-pounder and 18-pounder field guns, anti-aircraft and mountain guns, tanks and anti-sub artillery, then lines of machines turning gun barrels or milling breech blocks.

It was noisy, bewildering and rather threatening, but youth is buoyant and I soon adapted myself to my new environment. I soon learned that some persons were jolly, some indifferent and some aggressive. Many of the latter wore bowler hats and thick watch chains, one was known as Simon Legree[322]. The jolly men taught me that when you are pushed, you push back. I was an apt pupil. I was too small to do any actual heaving, but, like most of the lads, developed a form of public relations which appeared to be basedon ju-jitsu.

But it wasn't always like that. There was one foreman who claimedhe remembered the days when his like were allowed to strike apprentices. One day he found six of his boys warming themselvesin the smithy. Taking a hazel rod from a pickle tank, the proverbial "rod in pickle", he crept up behind the boys and lashed out at them. Though taken by surprise, they quickly recovered and four of them held him down while two lashed him with the hazels, to the sound ofhis yells and the laughter of the smiths.

I soon realised that the new life I had entered was a kind of social war, the scene suitably furnished by the ever-present artillery. On theone side were the overseers, the lowest agents of the invisible but powerful enemy, the informers, the anti-unionists, the few who hankered after being scabs and who whispered, "Don't trust unions and such like, keep your nose clean and you'll get on", and the management. Facing them, bold and contemptuous, were our people. I was learning sociology without books.

I soon went on to learn that there were issues in this conflict that a man or a small group could not win by themselves and men turned to "the Union." This I thought I understood. I had seen the pictorial banners of Northumberland and Durham miners, the favourite picture showing a boy trying in vain to break a bundle of about a score of sticks and an old man breaking his sticks one at a time. Theslogan beneath proclaimed "United we stand, divided we fall", or "Unity is Strength".

But while we had one enemy, the employer, backed by "the authorities", and we were one in circumstance and purpose, "the Union" was really many unions. The craftsmen had their own unions, each craft at least one separate union, the engineers several unions for one craft, and the "semi-skilled" machinists their union. The "unskilled", after generations of being shut out, were now in several general unions. But women, now nearly 50 per cent of the labour force, were not allowed to join any union and had to form one for themselves. Only some of the draughtsmen were members of a union and the clerks disdained to be organised, accepting a lower wage in return for an intangible "dignity".

Even worse, the machinery of the trade unions, like the Labour Party, had become part of the war machine, giving away all hard-won rights. My school-bred and newspaper-fed patriotism was cracking at the edges, for the class enemy had not suspended his predation. What had happened to the banner and slogans of unity?

But "Union" was more than officers and organisation, it was an idea. Almost within living memory, men and women had died on the scaffold for that idea and still men knew that Union meant bread, human dignity and the hope of liberty. War or no war, the social struggle went on. I learnt two new terms, Syndicalism and Revolutionary Industrial Unionism. Soon they seemed to mean the same thing, though I was some time in understanding them. The firsthad a 1789 sound, I thought, like the Committee of Public Safety, but the latter seemed apt to engineering.

Later, when I became involved, I found that the new ideas stemmed from European Syndicalism and the IWW, the latter having small groups in Britain and support from Wobbly seamen from the US and Australia. The Socialist Labour Party also advocated industrial Industrial Unionism, having been affiliated to the IWW, which theyleft after having disagreed with the "without affiliation to a political party" clause. The Syndicalist, like the IWW groups, were small but the influence of all these groupings was enormously greater than their numbers would seem to justify. Little wonder that the Government and the employers imagined a vast and wealthy organisation, plotting against the powers that be. But a little leaven leaveneth the whole lump.

I recently read in *Anarchy* the pontifical statement, "it seems to me that Malatesta's main contentions still hold good that those anarchists who are prepared to act in the industrial sphere should work within the existing unions rather than propagate the idea of a new union movement." (*Anarchy* 40, p. 173)[323]. Unfortunately, while many of us know of Tom Mann, James Connolly and Larkin, no one knew about Malatesta and his alleged advice. A man without a pope is apt to be a pragmatist, so these grimy workers just did the best they knew – and very effective it was.

Firstly, the trade unions, through their officials, had gone over completely to the side of the State at war, and were as much a partof the war machine as were the Brigade of Guards or the Royal Navy. With a stroke of the pen, all the rights won by a century of hard fighting were signed away. While rents and prices soared, there was to be no wage increase. Safety measures were swept away, a working week of more than 66½ hours was compulsory, industrial conscription was agreed to by the unions, with penal measures against the rebellious or weary. Military conscription reinforced this dictatorship. Even the Webb's had to admit, "The individual workman realised that the penalty for any failure of implicit obedience to the foreman might be instant relegation to the trenches". (*History of*

*Trade Unionism*, p. 639)."

In return, the employers' war profits were to be limited (to a certain, highly inflated, standard), but this "Munitions Levy" was never enforced and within a year was formally abolished.

On the Clyde, factory committees of syndicalist and IWW form were created and, because their ideas suited the needs of the hour, spread with rapidity to Tyneside, the Mersey, the Midlands and throughout the land. Life would not wait until the paralytic unions resumed business, "after the war".

The "new union movement" overcame at one bound the hundredfold division's of the workers. All crafts, the semi-skilled and unskilled, the boys and the women, were drawn together in frequent mass meetings. They elected and withdrew their delegates, now known as shop stewards, whenever necessary. They acted as one force. In the factory in which I worked were number of Belgian workers; they, too, joined in, as did a body of soldiers who, because of their skill, had been drafted to the works.

We were now powerful. We struck work, we demonstrated, we hoisted our wages and curbed the overseers. State and employers consulted our delegates, after threats of prison had failed. The impetus of this movement has lasted until this day. Now every worker knows the value of a workshop organisation to his daily bread. It remains for us to broaden the ideas of this valuable experience. Our factory movement may not have been pure enough for coffee-bar revolutionaries, but we answered the plain man's question: "Does it work?""[324]

The arrest of Scottish anarchist Stuart Christie and Spaniard Fernando Carballo Blanco in Madrid on August 11th, 1964 on charges of 'terrorism' and the 'attempted assignation of General Franco' sparked worldwide protests and campaigns for their release, including

Newcastle.[325] The local press would report;

> "Spain's national flag is to be burned in Dean Street, Newcastle this Saturday outside the Spanish Consul's office. Representatives of five Tyneside organisations will be protesting against the trial of 18-year old Stuart Christie. Christie of Glasgow was gaoled for 20 years in Spain on charges of terrorism. A joint committee of the five local organisations met in Newcastle last night to discuss the trial. The Tyneside Federation of Anarchists, the Tyneside Committee of 100, the Youth Campaign for Nuclear Disarmament, the International Socialists, and the Young Socialists were represented. A spokesman said after the meeting; "We deplore the fact that the rights of a British subject have been overlooked by the British Government. We are demanding a fresh trial in a civil court. We will march from Eldon Square to Dean Street on Saturday and burn a Spanish flag outside the Spanish Consul's office as a protest."[326]

Dave Douglass and his version of events, reminisces;

> "When the news came through that wor comrade Stuart Christie had been kidnapped and whisked away to a Spanish Jail, an impromptu gathering in Eldon Square on a rainy Saturday afternoon and a determined push onto the road to march to the Spanish Embassy culminated in a march of above 1,000 as friends. Comrades, shoppers and 'Saturday afternoon beats' fell in behind the march. 'Free Stuart Christie' became a slogan the city kids understood within 48 hours. And within 48 hours the Spanish Embassy on the Quayside sat toothless as all the windows went through, and we hadn't done it."[327]

Stuart Christie would eventually be released September 1967; Fernando Carballo Blanco would suffer 12 years before release.

## 3.4 1965

1965 and the year starts with another lecture by Tom Brown on 'A Page of Labour History' on February 12th, at the Lucas Arms, Grays Inn Road, London.The articles would also continue, with this month's on 'Abolition of the Wages System'[328]. The month of March is the same with another lecture under the same title on the 5th, and a further article on 'The paper-chase after wages' which looks at wages and pay freeze's before concluding;

> "The only wage defence possible now is the direct action of the workers at their place of work--by themselves, for now they see their trade union leaders are in the government contriving wage control. But, let us repeat, wage struggles, can have only limited objectives. The only way for the workers to enjoy the enormous increase in productivity, present and possible, is by becoming the owners of the means of production, That is possible, of course, only by common ownership--the day of the village blacksmith and peasant has gone. Syndicalism is not all negative; it is revolutionary reconstruction, it shows how modern developments have made possible, indeed imperative, Workers Control of Industry and the abolition of the wages system."[329]

April 2nd, and the talk is on 'Strikes I Have Known' followed by an article on 'State Steel, Mussolini Style', May 14th's talk is on 'Wage Freeze' and June 4th's is on 'Philosophy & Syndicalism'. Mays issue also mentions the participation of local anarchists, where it was reported "As USUAL, the first two days of the Easter March went off mainly "very well"~quiet and orderly. Well done CND. We'll let you march again next year if you behave yourselves. On Monday the strong contingent of red and black banners spread across Kensington Gore to enter Hyde Park for the lunch break, making a fine sight. Besides the banners of the Syndicalist Workers' Federation and the Anarchist Federation of Britain there were local groups" including Tyneside.[330]

Activity in Sunderland was also on the increase where Geoff Edwards was holding regular Anarchist Discussion Group (Syndicalists welcome) meetings at St Georges Terrace, Roker. Geoff would advertise these meetings through the national anarchist press to encourage new members.[331]

*Direct Action* June & July 1965 and Tom Brown has a lengthy piece 'Trades Councils: Rise and decline' and 'Trades Councils: Rise and decline – strangled by bureaucrats'. August, and in a commentary article about current Labour councils, the following, quoted in full as a matter of local interest.

"The lowest plunge, something of the shape of things to come, has been taken by the Labour-controlled Newcastle City Council. Newcastle-on-Tyne is the first city in Britain to adopt the American principle of appointing a City Manager. Its manager will bear the title "Principal City Officer with Town Clerk." The proposal came from Councillor T. Dan Smith, one of those very Left persons who believe you should get into the Labour Party to make it more radical, etc. Dan, a clever man, has already secured -the job of Chairman of the North Regional Economic Council, Now, who is the democratic revolutionary force who has secured the job of City manager?" This month would also see the beginnings of contributions to the paper from Peter Ridley of Tynemouth, the first being 'Law and the Worker'. Future issues would also contain regular writings on local North East industrial happenings from 'Direct Action reporter'.[332]

*Direct Action* October and Tom Brown is writing on the 'CIA' as well as a historical look at 'The Luddites' and a couple of local disputes *Direct Action* reporter mentions include "Two hundred alert engineers shocked the management of Churchill, Gear Machines, Blaydon, on August 27. They walked straight out without approaching the management and giving no indication of when they would return. This happened when one man was offered more to operate his machine "to fuller advantage" to boost productivity for their export drive. This kind of action has more than local significance. Approaches of this nature made either individually or collectively can be expected more often in the future. These workers will not tolerate differentialsof this kind and realise that once a standard wage is reached other things count for more than the extra odd shillings a week for a few."[333] Also mentioned was an unofficial strike by 30 Newcastle Dockers over a pay dispute.

These minor snapshots of writing show us the general feeling and tone of the local working class, and their struggles and disputes of the period, more than some lengthy intellectual tome of a book ever could, and I include these for that exact reason and as examples of our 'history from below'. Whilst evidence suggests no direct anarchist involvement, who's to say there wasn't? Certainly the ideas and philosophy of Syndicalism was still prevalent within the region, and as I've already stated, because of blacklisting, misunderstanding, and even personal choice, at times one's own personal politics were kept to oneself.

November 14th, and in a report of the Syndicalist Workers Federation's national London conference, included amongst the 50 or so delegates were those from Tyneside, with apologies read out from those unable to attend including among the number those from Gateshead. After a lengthy and livelydebate on Trade Union membership,"it was resolved that "Members shall, where consistent with Syndicalist activity, work within their appropriate trade union and, where possible, become shop stewards." [334]

*Direct Action* in November would also report "Workers from most major sectors of industry took part in a lively and informative discussion on "The Shop Stewards and Unofficial Movement in Industry" on October 4. The meeting was held at the Conway Hall, London, and organised by the industrial action sub-committee of the Syndicalist Workers' Federation. Discussion ranged from instances of both successful and unsuccessful strike action to the current efforts by the bosses, union leaders and Labour politicians to bring the unions under further state control. It seemed generally agreed that workers' control of industry was not something to be won without a struggle, and " thatit was necessary to counteract in every way the false schemes of those who wanted to reduce this revolutionary' idea to a mere seal set by the workers on their own exploitation. The meeting was ably opened by Joe Thomas (Print) and Tom Brown. (Engineering)." 'Direct Action reporter' mentions Newcastle Dockers winning their dispute, how academic 'scabs' did the jobs of striking technician colleagues during their dispute at Durham University and striking musicians in Newcastle's Northern Sinfonia Orchestra. The paper would also highlight a quote from local newspaper *The Journal* which stated 2.1.0.65. "The Labour Party Conference ended as usual with the notes of *"The Red Flag"*. Labour leaders take the song's sentiments about as seriously as they do Father Christmas, but it's a nice token of respect to a Socialist past." It seems the anarchists are not the only ones to see through the Labour Party's apparent'socialist illusions of grandeur'.

Of course Tom Brown was also adding to the agitation with an article 'One Product, One Union', where it was pointed out;

> "If UNITY IS STRENGTH, 'twere folly to have half-a-thousand unions. There was some public discussion and wonderment when it was revealed that Ford's workers were divided among 22 unions at the Dagenham factory, but there only one commodity is produced. I have worked in more general engineering factories where twice that number of unions were "organised". Syndicalism, as one of its many principles, says, "Let us first have one union for each industry." That makes sense to most industrial workers and in any case is more dignified than twenty-odd sets of union officials, jostling to be head of the queue into the firm's office. Revolutionary industrial unionism, or Syndicalism, is easy to understand. First a factory produces a certain commodity, such as a motor car, or a number of related commodities, say clothing. The goods are not made by one person but by many, each adding his work at the appropriate stage - machinists, assemblers, packers, store men, clerks,' cleaners and others, all needed to produce; a commodity which is the fruit of a social process. "Why should they not all be in one union? This is clearly seen by workers.

'Who opposes it? " it is pointed out that if the unions were to accept algamation into one, then hungry power seeking union officials would have no place, and concluding "Is industrial unionism possible? Suppose that all trade union officials suddenly died of a mysterious disease, that all the union offices fell to the ground and all union treasure melted away. There would still be a labour movement. At their places of work, the workers would still be aware of their common bonds, there would still be shop stewards and factory committees and the ability to negotiate wages and conditions. There would still be the power to strike. Life wouldgo on, but that movement would be free and independent and it would develop. Born of industry, it would be the industrial union."

As a further note of interest, the paper would also include the following announcement "TYNESIDE YOUTH AGAINST THE BOMB—-Folk song social. 5th November, 7.50 pm, Bridge Hotel, Newcastle. Admission 2s.6d."[335] Later commenting of events of 1965, Dave Douglass would state "the anarchists were the most dominant force among the young activists"[336]

## 3.5 1966

1966 and another eventful year which begins January 6th and Tom Brown giving a talk on 'Methods of Struggle', whilst in the North East these were being put into practice. *Direct Action* Reporter is commenting on union bureaucrats falling out on Tyneside and remarks "their corner of the labour market is threatened, or needs to, expand... These persons are not unionists, but middlemen, selling you and; me and using their disposal of our labour- power as a bargaining - counter. They cannot work to give us greater strength on the factory floor- because to do so would be to release us from our dependence on them." Another report on a dispute with Boilermakers at Hebburn going in circles as "One of the stewards: "The official negotiating machinery is choked with red tape. 'Nothing ever comes out of it. The management can manipulate it to delay the settlement of legitimate pay claims; after months of stalling you are told: go back and settle it at yard level. Then you are back where you just started... The only action left was to walk out."" [337]

> **A FORMER Tory candidate for Consett (Durham) has just joined the Gateshead Labour Party. When interviewed about his reasons for this apparent change of colour he said, "I have fought Socialism all my life."**
>
> ***DIRECT ACTION* REPORTER**

In a February article on shipbuilding at Clydeside, Tom Brown now in his late 60's reflects on his youth "I was born of a shipbuilding family, in the midst of one of the world's biggest concentrations of shipbuilding capacity and apprenticed to marine engineering; at work as a boy in the bowels of a great ship, I vowed to get out of the proud craft of my ancestors as soon as I was 21.. The vow did not quite come off. I had to wait until I was 23 before I managed to shake the rust of the shipyard from my boots after trying marine engineering at the other end of the country. My advice to young men and as many old ones, as can manage it is, get out while you can. You'll never regret 1t."[338] Perhaps they wouldn't, and perhaps Tom was wisely foreseeing future events as between 1960 – 1966 six shipyards were to close for good in the region, with many more to follow in the coming decades.

The North East coal mines were also suffering during this decade. The Durham coalfield would lose half of its pits and workforce, and Northumberland would also suffer from closures during the period. In March our *Direct Action* Reporter is stating;

> "A certain amount of activity is under way in the North East at the moment, largely confined to the coastal pits and mainly, but exclusively, among craftsmen. Morale in the inland pits is low; such pits, being on the edge of the coalfield, are shallow and the seams are short, making working and modernisation difficult and costly. Pitmen struck at Annfield Plain, Consett recently over equal pay and the terrible working conditions. It is pits like this which are closing fast--it is estimated that there will not be one left to the west of the Great North Road by 1970, a staggering change in the economic and social life of Durham." And in another quote "The Lodge Secretary at Easington: "We have men in this pit taking home only £8 15s a week, out of which they have £2 to £3 a week rent to pay, and if they live in Peterlee, there are bus fares too. There are men today who get more money for lying in bed than some who are working in the pit. We have men working on jobs described as *"borstal"* on stone flight work and on the belts. These men are only receiving £1, 18s. 11d a shift."[339]

This month would also see Tom Brown deliver, what I personally believe, to be one of his most evocative sermons, which, in order to rescue from oblivion I quote in full...

BEYOND THE STRIKE

"SUCCESS is more difficult to bear than failure," said the pessimist, perhaps because he expected too much too quickly. Some working class militants are showing signs of falling to the spell of this aphorism, even after a series of successful strikes and threats of strikes. "'We are just fighting on bread and butter issues. We are winning, but is it worth it? Surely we should have higher aims than that." Certainly, "man does not live by bread *alone*" but he cannot live without bread. This is something we have to consider in perspective, remembering that history is greater than man's longevity."

"Turning back in thought to the beginning of this century, or even 40 odd years ago, a time that is in the memory of millions of persons now living in this country, we see tremendous progress made, largely by workers' direct action, in even half a lifetime. In 1900, even 1920, millions were short of bread, *without butter*. In 1910 there was no dole, no sick pay or national medical care, no old age pension; these were brought in later, as Lloyd George said, "as an insurance against revolution". Children from overcrowded homes were often cast out or deserted to live in the streets. Families were evicted from their poor homes, separated, and imprisoned in the dreaded workhouse."

"Jack London in *People of the Abyss* wrote with horror of his visit to London, where he saw "men pick up orange peel from the spittle-drenched pavement and eat it." Hunger not as an appetite to satiate, but an agonizing pain, was the experience of millions. I recall seeing a deadly-pale young man carried away from a dole queue and hearing the gloomy remark of his mate, "it's the Hunger." I believe the capital H letter is justified."

## GREATEST WAS APATHY

"Against these vile conditions only some workers were rebellious. Others were without hope: "it's always been like this, it always will." Many lived a traumatic life of toil, drinking, quarrelling and unstudied copulation. Others, in their proud poverty, were ever willing to die for their King, their mythical country or that wonderful Empire-—which they would never see except along the sights of a rifle—even in 1920 after the greatest and certainly the least justified blood- bath yet known."

"These were the powers the agitators fought against, and the greatest of these was apathy. Without the work of thousands of unknown agitators, nothing would have been accomplished. Not always clever, not always right, yet, by and large, all the work of these agitators, spoken in eloquence or crude phrases, in anger, hope, hatred or compassion, by word and deed, was to one end, to arouse hope, combat and confidence in their fellows."

"They might be forgiven if they had spoken only of bread-without the butter- but they pointed their propaganda even beyond this necessary to the hope of a new society, in an almost evangelistic spirit of "These things shall be."

"Perhaps we tend to forget that the first century of working class organisation affected only certain occupations and regions, the very poor and the very respectable remained, largely, unmoved. Now everyone is learning the value of organisation and direct action. Some jobs which were once the lowest paid are becoming the highest. "Salaried" men once too proud to rebel are using Syndicalist principles to pay off their mortgages; jockeys, teachers, bank clerks and technicians use the strike weapon, rabbis and cantors have just joined the surging throng."

## OUTSTRIPPED IDEOLOGY

"We have won not only a larger slice of the national cake for less toil, but greater protection, more job control, more respect. There are even places where the old order is reversed, and the foremen walk in fear of the men. But all this is not enough. The next big step is overdue. Already, it seems that the limit of real wages has been reached, that higher prices and steeper taxation will rob us of every wage advance-the latter is the avowed aim of the Labour Party. Even from a narrow, materialist point of view, a new aim and strategy is needed. Most shop stewards must feel this malaise. Now we have won this round, what next?"

"The present shop stewards' movement (I here use the term movement in the sense of a social tendency, a series of incidents moving to one end) differs from that of the second and third decades of our century. The earlier was a conscious, planned, and purposeful movement; the latter sprang from the earlier, but at such a speed and so widespread, as to evoke the term "prairie system". Because it was originally, so well laid and so suited to our present needs, its growth outstripped any existing means of ideology and social propaganda. This is more painfully evident when the need of a radical social change and a rational social philosophy are considered."

"If the workshop movement is to be anything more than a blind giant, a conscious, reasoning, studying, acting organisation is necessary. We need the scientific method in our class relations at work as much as we need it in our technical problems. This cannot come from men acting in personal isolation. Ideas, philosophies are social products. The workers of Britain lack that organisation: those who refuse to help bring it to stature should not sneer at the fruit of their own indolence and self-seeking."

## FORMIDABLE THREAT

"We of the Syndicalist Workers Federation are seeking to build such an organisation. It can start only in a small way. "Great oaks from little acorns grow", we wrote in our school copybooks, and it is true. We know of the comrade who is tired of being, apparently, the only rebel in his small town, butthe steadfast witness of one most often, in the long run, attracts others, sometimes those who themselves are self-styled lone wolves."

"This country is divided into about 630 parts, almost equal in population, about 84,000. Surely there is one militant in each of these areas. 630 revolutionaries in a hundred groups, working together while at the same time generalising and preserving every valuable experience of our class, would be aformidable threat to the ruling class, because its work and the ideas given to it by the experience of the masses, would be adopted by the people."

"But if you neglect this struggle, then others will, too, and that will be the fruit of your arid cynicism? Reaction, War, Nazism. Is that better than "mere breada butter struggle"? Remember, social revolt has often started over a fight for bread. But don't blame the other fellow, he's blaming you."[340]

For this reason, local anarchists, as a matter of course, would publicise and, at times, participate in workplace strike actions and agitations, throughout their history. As Tom states...from small acorns etc. Naturally where we can sow seeds of discontent, and watch our libertarian ideal grow, we will lovingly water and feed it to hopeful fruition.

April 1966, and *Direct Action* Reporter emphasis that the role of militant women within industry is much alive;

> "Protagonists of the sex war claim that women have no talent for industrial organisation or militancy. This myth may have originated because women predominate in sections of industry where organisation has, in the past at any rate, been poor. This generalisation has always been strained, as anyone seeing "The Match girls" musical will know. In the North East it is manifestly false. Only the other day hundreds of women workers offered support to one department at Ericsson's telephone factory, Sunderland, in an unofficial wages dispute.

At the end of last year shop workers at Binns Stores, Newcastle, won a 6% rise through strike action earlier in the year; and union and non-union teenage girls at the new Rank radio factory at South Shields, struck to get their (male) steward reinstated. This month women at the Blaydon wire works came out on strike to get their steward, Mrs. Doreen McNally, reinstated."[341]

In May Tom is writing on 'Trotskyists and the General Strike' whilst Peter Ridleyis sending in an interesting report from North Tyneside;

"THE. SCENE: waste ground by Woolworths, North Shields on a Saturday morning. The sound: "Prices and Incomes, God Save the Pound, East of Suez, Productivity, Prices and . . ." The Labour candidate, Dr. Gordon Adams of the Coal Board, is addressing himself to "the bored and bewildered population . . . *"And now, are there any questions?"* A young man who has been quietly leafleting the crowd steps forward. He is refused the microphone. *"Would you agree that the way you sold the Incomes Policy at the last election, as a means of enabling lower-paid workers to close the gap with the higher-paid, has worked as a fraud on such people who voted Labour, since the policy has amounted to an attempt at a general wage freeze?"* Not a very good question. It gives the candidate too much elbow room ". . . teeth. Wait till we've got it going." What is more, before letting him answer, the agent, who has now read oneof the leaflets, gives the questioner a few unasked-for words of abusive introduction to the crowd . . . *"Syndicalism went out of date eighty years ago . . . has no place under a socialist government . . ."* The young man shouts back, *"Do I look as if I went out of date 80 years ago?"* And the crowd start reading the leaflets. Try again. *"Wl1y can no Labour Government let people get greater job control?"* Bull's eye! The candidate has obviously never heard of job control. There are a few fumbling moments of consultation. The agent steps forward. *"And now our next question is from a Youth Leader, who wants details of our Programme for Youth."* He reads the question from a typed list-and the candidate rolls out a few more unctuous platitudes. The original question remains unanswered. The point is not missed by the crowd. The questioner distributes the last of his leaflets and a general discussion breaks out between him and bystanders. People turn their backs on the intruding amplifier. The meeting comes to an end without further questions. People disperse, reading their leaflets and arguing. Leaflets were also distributed house to house in North Shields and also throughout a monstrous grey-brick council barracks. Syndicalism is kicking hard for an octogenarian ghost."[342]

**NEWCASTLE SYNDICALIST GROUP** meets every Thursday, 8 pm, at The Adelaide, Newgate St., Newcastle-on-Tyne.

By the summer, and things were certainly heating up in the region. Mick Renwick was advertising in both *Direct Action* and *Freedom* that those interested in the area should contact himself at Mowbray St, Heaton, and Tyneside Syndicalists / Newcastle Syndicalist Group meet every Thursday, 8pm at the Adelaide.[343] Mick Renwick was of the same generation as Dave Douglass, who, after Mick's death would reminisce;

> "First up at Heaton CND then in the faction that became the Tyneside Direct Action Committee and later the Committee of 100, demonstrating up at Holy Lock on the Clyde and down on numerousAldermaston marches against the H Bomb and Atom Bomb which had come to the very wire of nuclear war and we were convinced our premature departure from life before we had the chance to live it... Mick had been born into a unique and dying community, for his Dad wasn't simply a Northumbrian pitman, he was a Geordie pitman, he worked at the Rising Sun Wallsend. Mick lived in back to back Heaton,

miners, railway men, and shipyard workers. He was raised in the strongly militant trade union tradition of the miners union and communities... We both became enthusiastic founder members of the Industrial Workers of the World when it re-founded in Britain and it was this organization that Mick heart and soul has worked for in the last fifteen years."[344]

Tom Brown writing on how the General Strike of 1926 did not finish on the publicised official date, but continued;

> "Rail men, bus, tram men and Dockers refused to start work. In Manchester, 30,000 rail men demonstrated with great spirit. In Hull, 150 tram men were sacked and rail men, other tram men and Dockers stayed out on strike on their behalf. Two days after the strike, more workers were on strike than on any other day, by at least 100,000. Thursday was to be the first day back to work, but rail terms were not agreed until Friday — and on Saturday the rail strike was still on. Some had fallen, but the counter-offensive of the employers was defeated by the solidarity of the workers. State and employers were taken by surprise by the sudden turn of events. A new spirit seemed to be developing. That spirit was manifested by the miners who refused to return and fought on against State and mine owners for several months. A new General Strike seemed about to break out. This could have happened, but for one factor. There was no national revolutionary organisation to co-ordinate, to draw together, to inspirit the nascent movement. What was needed was a Syndicalist movement on a national scale, even a small organisation, to be the necessary linkage. Such did not then exist, nothing else would have done, nothing less will do. Because of my experience in the General Strike and in the long, bitter, bloody struggle of the miners in 1926, I am a Syndicalist."[345]

Tom would also give a talk on 'The Economic Fallacies of the Left' to the SWF crowd in London, July 16th.[346]

Capitalism, in general and the high ranking industrial leaders within it, alarmed at the rise of militant disputes and workplace agitation throughout the country, would set up their own bureaucratic firms specialising in recognising industrial militants, communists, anarchists, and syndicalists etc with the purpose of black listing. Firms could now consult with these outfits and check on their own staff, or potential employee's. The anarchist press at this time were highlighting this, *Freedoms* response;

> "The Economic League' is an informers organisation which assists employers in a number of ways. It gets a lot of its information by subscribing to the different 'left wing' papers and the rest from informers within certain organisations such as unofficial rank and file committees. The Trade Union leadership, in general, has failed to do anything to combat the League's activities. The only way to do this is to show the League 'up' for what it is and warn other workers of its activities."[347]

*Direct Action* states "One of the most vicious of witch hunting journals is IRIS. It intervenes in every important trade union election, by naming the candidates who are either communist or reputed to have communist support. The Economic League is a member of the same league."[348] *Direct Action* would also, in later issues, give more lengthy and detailed writings on this under the title of Organised Witch-Hunting.[349]

Throughout the anarchist press and movement in general, because of this upsurge in recognition of black listing and later fascist and special branch police monitoring of activists, and their names and addresses if possible, many would only now use initials, aliases, or more predominantly just group names when writing for the libertarian press. Of course this makes it at times difficult for the 'historian' of such times and events / groups, but as later times were to show, when far right fascists started publicising people's names and addresses in their '*Red Watch*' magazines of the 1980s - it is quite understandable. For this reason, as a matter of security[350] to the many in our history who are still alive and / or active only initials, if needed, will be used. The only names to be used will be those where, for instance, they wrote a book in their own name, i.e. Stuart Christie, and their name is a matter of public knowledge anyway. For those of us who were around at different periods to follow, I am sure those will know whose initials belong to whom, and for those that don't, well, as a well known anarcho-punk band once said – 'Tough Shit Mickey'.

In the later months of 1966 *Direct Action* would see articles from Tom Brown, 'Geordie', and '*Direct Action* Reporter' on such items as Franco and Gibraltar, the TUC congress, Councils of Action, Inflation, Aberfan Pit Disaster, and Wage Freeze's, as well as snippets of news on some local industrial disputes. Despite no North East listing in the contact section of the paper (from December 1966) the 8th National Conference of the Syndicalist Workers Federation, held at Manchester on Sunday, November 13th was attended by well over 50 delegates, including those from Tyneside.[351]

## 3.6 1967

1967 starts in s similar vein, with regular articles from Tom Brown on such topics as 'Wage Freeze', 'Peasants Revolt', and in an article entitled 'China's Workers against Mao' it is stated;

> "One can only understand the nature of the Russian Communist State when one realises that it is the result of a demoniac lust for power. If one looks, as Marxists usually do, for some anthropomorphic "historic purpose" in the development of society then one will find it in the more "efficient" development of the previous, Tsarist State and the development, at any cost, of Russia into a big, heavily industrialised country, even at the cost of that country's greatest treasure, its agriculture. But these are but conditions of the primary aim, to take and keep the power. The same is true of Chinese Communism, except that Mao has leaned more heavily on the peasantry—the same method. the same age-old tactics of oppression, the same end. Now the ideologues are putting themselves up for auction; who pays the most, Moscow or Peking? And like the medieval Schoolmen they search for differencesof doctrine. Lenin, Trotsky, Stalin, Mao—what's the difference, is onebutcher better than another?"[352]

March 29th of this year also see's Tom give a lecture on 'The Russian Revolution' at the Lucas Arms, London. *Direct Action* also contains the 'North East Notes' regular column and an article by P.R. (Tynemouth) on safety at work, which also emphasises;

> "One of the striking features of capitalism is that it is burdened with internal contradictions. In particular, the spending of time and care on any job conflicts with the need to produce more at less cost, and to do this the worker must control his environment, which in turn conflicts with management's parasitic need to control the worker. Similarly, the need of

> management to keep a docile but alert and minimally healthy work force cannot be fulfilled, since a man cannot be involved and apathetic at the same time."[353]

Mid 1967, and whilst the perception of the period is of 'free love' 'Technicolor,flowers and happiness', the North East tells a different story, as highlighted by *Direct Action* Reporter who in a brief window of the time tells of student strikes and how "A march was held through the city; only one banner supported the government, it was carried by a University "Socialist"—-he was set upon." And on the industrial front mass disputes were happening at Vickers Walker Yard, Blyth shipyard, and Doxford Yard, Sunderland, whilst "at Durham Gaol 300 prisoners staged a sit-down strike in the workshops on February 27 over the sadistic treatment and conditions" ,"Meanwhile a South Shields mother blamedthe damp in her prefab for the death of her baby. In January another baby died in the same estate. The prefabs were condemned ten years ago."

> "Tyneside railwaymen were staging one day strikes in support or Yorkshire colleagues, and where "Regional representative Frank M**** reporting to a mass meeting said "Wakefield are trying to do by unconstitutional means what we have been trying to do constitutionally for three years. Evidently this is the only way to do things with British Rail because we have got absolutely nowhere. . . " Since then all 200 wagon repairers at South Shields have walked out in sympathy with their charge hand because he was sacked after ten years. They will not return till he gets his job back." "Workers at North Eastern School Furniture, Darlington, have just won the right not to clock into work. But for doing this as part of a work-to-rule campaign over differentials, draughtsmen at Caterpillar Tractors, Birtley, have been locked out. The degrading practice should be dropped everywhere; in the meantime, its abandonment is a useful aid in any campaign of non-cooperation, though it could be taken further for example, by refusing to start work until top management clock in, in the

> morning and after the lunch break" Bus drivers disputes were also mentioned and "At C. A. Parsons, Newcastle, 650 draughtsmen recently got four weeks' holiday after a 15-week strike." "Six thousand "manual" workers at Reyrolle's Hebburn have now changed their tactics in pursuit of longer holidays, from token total stoppages to guerrilla lightning strikes at key points in the plant without warning to the management. The new campaign started on May l6 when all met in Hebburn Park to unanimously approve the decision, to agree to a general levy to make up the wages of those involved, to call a district conference on "the Third Week" for all Tyneside convenors, and to take the afternoon off!" Whilst "On May 1st 13,000 shipyard workers held stop-work meetings outside the Tyne yards in support of the shipyard draughtsmen, locked out nationally because of an official strike at Swan Hunters. Ten days before, 200 shop stewards, meeting under the aegis of the Tyne and Blyth Confederation of Shipbuilding and Engineering Unions, had unanimously decided on a full day's strike involving 6,000 workers.""Perhaps the scabbiest act of all was the launching of the *Amasone*, during the lockout, by Boilermakers' President, Dan McGarvey. This took: place at Charlie Clore's Furness Yard on Teesside despite the fact that the only clash between police and draughtsmen throughout the lockout took place there when draughtsmen persuaded drivers not to deliver and despite a direct appeal to him by the DATA Branch at the yard. What an omen for the future: this was the first- ever launching by a union official in Britain!"[354]

Tom Brown was also adding to the agitation with pieces on 'Ballots' and 'Equality' and a lengthy piece on 'Workers Control and Syndicalism', where in an effort to dispel myths on the principles of syndicalism and the true nature of 'workers control' states;

> "Once again, "Workers' Control" is having a tempting sound to the political cuckoos—to the general confusion of the political novice. With Socialists, Communists, Trotskyites, Liberals, Welsh

and Scots Nationalists and journalists it has become a sociological In-term. Let us clear away a little of the confusion. Syndicalists desire a society in which the means of production and distribution are held in common-—social ownership-- where all are socially equal, with the guiding principle: from each according to his ability, to each according to his need. This projection of a future society is not, of course, the invention of Syndicalists. It was understood in England 600 years ago, it was practised in Biblical times more than 1,300 years before that. But while it was first desired as an ethical principle, it has now become an urgent economic and social necessity. The scientific and technical developments of the means of production are in conflict with the property relations of capitalist society and it's State. From this conflict follows, not only the war of the classes, but the daily struggle of groups and persons to gain a fortune or a loaf of bread. A conflict which brings, in a condition of "permanent crisis", the confrontation of nations and groups of nations, the development of weapons of total destruction at the cost of the starvation of millions and even a tortured self-struggle within the individual, who is at once urged to be a moral citizen and yet grab all he can in the name of Success. Not only the stones, but the machines cry out for social ownership. Many who are not of us will agree with this social principle. We ask them to face the issue, not only who owns but who shall control. At present the vastly greater part of the means of production is owned by a quite small class of persons. They, by virtue of that ownership and not because of ability, knowledge or moral character control industry. In a society based upon common ownership, as in any other society, industry, the means of production would be controlled by people, by persons. Who must control? Obviously not the capitalist class; they would no longer exist as a class. The State? That is an organisation brought into being by the very social conflict and torture we are seeking to end, an armed force- to keep the slaves in subjection and to keep within certain bounds the destructive struggles of the rulers themselves. The new society will not be one in which some men govern other men according to the territory in which they live. It will be concerned with the administration of things. Without deep, widespread social conflict the State is unnecessary; it will be broken. Who, then is left? Only the people. An economic process requires an economic organisation. Persons who work in industry (We include not only factories, but transport, offices, schools and all the complexes needed for production) find themselves in a certain occupational relationship to one another; they are, willy-nilly, organised. Why create another, an artificial organisation to control industry?... Men and women economically organised in their work are, in their struggle with the employing class, turning to the true industrial union through their shop stewards, shop committees and shop mass meetings. From this widespread primary organisation should come the organisation of the working class which is already passing from the ineffective, orthodox strike to the manifold strike actions of Syndicalism, leading to the stay-in strike and the general lock-out of the capitalist class." And concluding "But, we must ask, if no capitalism and no State, what social organisation for industry other than Workers' Control? There can be no Workers' Control of industry short of a change in the basis of society. It cannot come about, piecemeal or otherwise, within the framework of present property relations, State and capitalist ownership. Any "united front" to further the cause of Workers' Control could only come about if it was a front of those who believed thus. One may have a united frontof diverse elements on a single issue general to many, a temporary arrangement to further a single point. But it would be folly for Syndicalists to be lured into a united front on basic, fundamental principles with those who were opposed to those principles. Any person of understanding who favoured Workers' Control would already be a Syndicalist. Politicos cannot honestly support such a cause. Imagine a united front between Socialists and Tory capitalists to spread Socialism. Some or all would have to be lying. Or an alliance between Atheists and Christians to- spread the Gospel. Or a united front of vegetarians and the Butchers' Federation to spread their common aims. One is as daft as the other."[355]

June 1967 and Bobby Lynn and the Glasgow anarchists are reporting of a lecture held by Tom Brown at the Trades Council Club, Glasgow, where despite lack of advertisement etc "about forty people attended the meeting which was the best meeting of any other meeting of its nature." And "The goodthing about the meeting was, it brought some old comrades who hadn't been around for years. It's now hopeful that we shall see more of them."[356]

July, and 'Control of Industry' article concludes;

> "Whether or not we like it the social conflict is with us every day. Syndicalism offers not only a means of taking and holding the means of production, but its principles are daily proven as not only the best but often the only means of winning the struggle to solve our day to day problems. But this phase of the social war becomes only part of the daily round, without ultimate meaning, unless we fight in the knowledge that it is but a step to a greater end, the solution of the social problem." [357]

1967 ends with the news of the Labour Party's plans for more pit closures in the Durham and Northumberland coalfield, in favour of oil and nuclear power. 74 or so pits in the region were closed for good during the 1960s, with a further 19 or so in the 1970s. Commenting on the Labour Party betrayal in *Direct Action*, local writer 'Geordie' emphasises;

> "Will Calvert, chairman of Silksworth Miners' Lodge, Durham, expressed the view of most miners when he said in a BBC-TV interview, *"For years Durham miners have been the backbone of the Labour Party. Now that same party is actually going to destroy the miners . . . I would not go out of my house to vote Labour next time."* Silksworth has given a lead to all miners by at once leaving the Labour Party, and withholding the political fund. The decision was unanimous by 1,000 members; the

> money now withheld is £400. "Treachery", and "Stab in the back" are general comments, anger the constant mood. At South Shields 400 miners met in Armstrong Hall to hear the Wilson apologies recited by local Labour MP Arthur Blenkinsop. For an hour they listened to speeches, then the platform announced, "No questions will be allowed?' 350 miners jumped up shouting; picking up the tables and chairs they threw them to thefloor as they stormed from the meeting. . ,"

Before summing up "Labour Party rank and file are like the married woman often found in Victorian novels, who says of her husband, "*He starves me, bashes me, insults me, steals my money and spends it on drink and harlots, but he's my husband and I'll stand by him.*" No party needs to placate the ever- faithful; it's the floating voter the politicians watch." The author also recommended the following actions as the "only possible plan of resistance for the miners...

1. Withdraw from the Labour Party and, individually and collectively,withhold the political levy from that party.
2. Refuse to vote for the Labour Party.
3. Organise at pit and lodge level, federating into regional and national councils, for industrial action.
4. Form Councils of Action of miners and all others in the country who will suffer by the Anti-Coal Mining programme."[358]

It is roughly about this time (late 1967 – early 1968) that Tom Brown was involved in a pressure group of local Paddington residents opposed to a 'Mafia style porn club' opening in their area. As a result of this he was targeted by 'mobsters' and beaten severely, with iron bars, on his way home from a nightshift. This would affect Tom's health for the remainder of his life, and unable to work as a result of the beating, was soon to return to the North East with a move to Low fell, Gateshead.

## 3.7 1968 / 1969

1968 see's a gradual decrease in the output of articles from Tom Brown, who, now living back on Tyneside, would still contribute the odd occasional piece of writing and would keep the North East Notes column of *Direct Action* going, and in January is commenting on eviction of miners from National Coal Board owned houses, due to closures and highlights a quote from local Craghead (Co. Durham),miner ""They are putting the clock back 40 years when coal owners put you on the street when you lost your job—-this time it's our own people doing it.""[359]

The next couple of months of *Direct Action* include articles on 'The Story of the Syndicalist Workers Federation – Born in Struggle' a short piece on the groups history by Tom which concludes;

> "Some complain that the SWF has not changed its principles. That, in a world where Socialist politicians change their principles far more often than their raincoats, ought to be welcome. But the principles of capitalism have not changed: we live in a society which is still founded on rich and poor, war and class war still go on, men's lives are still governed by property relations. What has happened to all those fabulous developments which made Syndicalism and Revolution "irrelevant"-—the H-Bomb, Affluent Society, Automation? The old problems are still with us. Capitalism has no answer. The case for Syndicalism remains unanswered. It is no answer to go looking for a new butterfly to chase."

Geordie is writing on 'Wilsons Economic Crisis' and how in "Consett, Co. Durham, 300 lorry drivers, including shop stewards, members of the TGWU, have resolved to cease supporting the Labour Party and have cancelled their political levy. Other districts are expected to follow." March, April, and May, sees a small pieces by Tom on 'Foreman's', 'Labour Party Wage Freezes, economy etc' 'American Civil War', whilst DA Reporter covers the strike of South Shields bin men and drivers.

Geordie again covers the 'Wage Freeze' and the region wide bus strike.[360]

Meanwhile, November 1968 and *The Journal* reports;

> "The day Harry Hope lowered the flag he signalled the end of his job. Instead of celebrating Prince Charles's birthday on Thursday, Mr Hope a maintenance engineer, was sacked on the spot. Because he *"strongly objects to Prince Charles being forced on to the peopleof Wales."* Mr Hope, aged 38, hauled down a Union Jack fluttering from a Shotley Bridge hospital building in honour of the young prince's birthday. When a hospital porter tried to hoist the flag again, Mr Hope slashed the rope. He was summoned before Mr Alex Lawther, North-West Durham Hospital Group secretary and sacked. Mr Hope, a self –styled anarchist and atheist said: *"This was not a foolish prank, but an action which was politically motivated. I am completely opposed to imperialism, and as the flag was my enemy, I could not accept walking past it during the course of the day."* Mr Hope added that he could easily have cut down the flag when it was dark but he had nothing to hide. *"I do not regret what I have done and in similar circumstances I would undoubtedly take the same action,"* he said. On the point of his alleged remarks insulting the Queen, Mr Hope said: *"There was nothing personal in this. The Queen as a person is a nonentity to me but I have strong objections against the whole question of royalty."* Although he was not surprised when he was dismissed, Mr Hope thought he had been harshly treated especially as he had worked at the hospital for three years."[361]

Early December 1968 and the student anarchists are hitting the local headlineswhere Conservative students, angry that anyone dare protest at their events,are writing to the local press "We have witnessed for the first time a Left-wing attempt to prevent a man from speaking his own thoughts in public. We refer to the heckling of a group of anarchist dissidents who stamped, jeered, howled, and sang while Mr Patrick Wall, M.P. for Haltemprice, was addressing the Durham University Conservative Association on the subject of foreign policy. Our feelings at this are best described as being a mixture of anger and sadness – anger, since a man was deprived of his right to speak his firmly held beliefs in front of a university audience, an audience, which one would think, would be used to open discussion free from pressure; and sadness, since the very people who were so vociferous at that meeting in their demands for observance of the principals of humanitarianism in Vietnam, Rhodesia, and elsewhere seemed quite determined to be as malicious as possible in their attacks on Mr Wall." Whilst another disgruntled student complained "It is the activities of this revolutionary and intolerant clique which catch the headlines, and not the activities of the great majority of students, whatever their political views, who continue to uphold the accepted standards of behaviour."[362]

January 1969 begins with local outrage at the proposed 'lecture on economics' by right wing conservative Enoch Powell at Rutherford College, Newcastle. Local anarchists, students[363] and other protestors blocked all entrances to the building in defiance, leading to scuffles with police trying to gain admittance for Powell. Unable to do so, they resorted to smuggling him in by at first pretending to drive away, then sneaking him into the rear of the building. *The Evening Chronicle* 'reporting' on events called it a 'blatant threat to democracy' and;

> "Something outrageous and sinister was prevented in Newcastle today. A man was almost denied freedom of speech by the blatant threat of possible disorder. To circumvent trouble, the authorities had to resort to a degree of subterfuge. Better that, however, than senseless violence. Mr Powell's lecture was on economics – quite unconnected with his views on race. But, in trying to prevent him from speaking, the student faction has made itself notorious in three ways. It has violated the principle of free speech. Voltaire once said: *"I disapprove of what you say, but will defend to the death your right to say it"*. The student reply is virtually the one dictator's and anarchists

> have given through the ages; down with all opposition. The student faction also sought to flout authority."

The right wing diatribe continued with the assumption that despite the fact that Powell was a racist, he, as a 'leading economist' was invited to speak and therefore should be allowed to do so, before concluding that thirdly, the students involved in the protest have succeeded in bringing the entire student body into disrepute, and that steps should be taken "to guard against being misrepresented by a noisy and dangerous minority."[364]

This front page editorial instigated numerous letters of objection with its terminology and assumptions, including a (heavily edited) response from D.A. of Beaconsfield Rd, Gateshead, who writes "I would like to protest at your recent editorial which linked dictatorship and anarchists as opponents of free speech. Many thousands of anarchists have died fighting dictatorships of both "right" and "left", Spain and Russia being but two examples. Freedom is the basis of anarchist philosophy. We wish to see a society based on the co- operation of free individuals, a world without war, racialism or poverty." [365]

For the rest of the year, local anarchists are meeting etc under the current name of North East Anarchist Group, with both Peter Ridley of Whitley Bay, and Mick Renwick of Heaton as contacts, whilst the remainder of the decade see's monetary contributions of support to *Freedom* from S.C. (Durham), P.G. & B.P. (Newcastle), JMJ (Stockton on Tees) and G.D. (Gateshead).[366]

## 3.8 1970—1975

The decade starts with Durham anarchists hitting the regions newspaper headlines with their participation in a grassroots demonstration against city centre traffic congestion and pollution by local residents.

> "Traffic blocked Durham City this weekend while demonstrators marched against traffic congestion. A swelling column of students and residents was split by police motor-cycle riders as traffic stopped in the city streets. Now new demonstrations are being planned by Durham Anarchists, who want all traffic banned from the city centre. Police pushed demonstrators gently on as they blocked streets."[367]

Perhaps buoyed with a sense of success, less than two weeks later the Durham Anarchists are again in the news, with "a warning was given last night to anarchists and students hoping to cash in on a demonstration planned by 500 Durham civil servants. Mr F** S**, secretary of the Civil and Public Services Association, has threatened to call off the march if any outsiders interfere. Staff at the National Savings headquarters in Milburngate house to march tonight from their offices to Durham bus station in North Rd in protest at the city councils failure to provide a crossing over a busy main road. Mr S*** said last night that he had been approached by the anarchists and students. "*We are not interested in any help from them.*"[368]

Up the road in Gateshead, during a protest about the Industrial Relations Bill at the Town Hall, local paper *The Journal* is again berating anarchists and 'left wing students' present at the protest, with such patronising comments as "There was the anarchist from Hatfield College, Durham, in his mauve blouse, beads, bell, crucifix and fur coat." And "It was a day on which believers in individual freedom, the anarchists, told the Tyneside worker what he had to do. Turn a deaf ear to Harold Wilson and the TUC General Secretary." The paper was also unsympathetic to any of the workers out on strike during the period, with comments about how much time they spent in the pub as opposed to any protest or picket line. Anarchist paper *Freedom* did get a brief mention, along with *Morning Star* and *Militant* which were all on sale at the protest.[369]

*The Evening Chronicle* and its morning offshoot *The Journal*, once bastions of free speech and free space for 'progressive' idea's, would now have founder Joseph Cowan turning in his grave with disgust at the repeated semi right wingeditorials and slander against any protest in the region.

Again, 1970 see's both Peter Ridley of Whitley Bay, and Mick Renwick of Heaton as contacts in the area in *Freedoms* listings, whilst its list of monetary contributions of support include B.P, B.B, and R.B (Newcastle), D.A. (Gateshead), S.C. (Durham), and F.W. (Hartlepool).[370] Later in 1971 the paper lists G.K. (Saltburn) and B.S. (Durham)[371]. Durham Anarchists are also advertising their presence with adverts and encouragement to contact Mike Mogie[372] of Mavin St, and later, Neville's Terrace, Durham.

The aforementioned Durham Anarchist Group are vividly and amusinglystating at this time, with their descriptions of kangaroo courts for police chiefs;

> "Just to let you know that there is an anarchist group in the N.E. The group, which is only three weeks old, is holding its own embryonic revolution in Durham. We have several projects under way which wethink might be of interest to anarchists in other parts of the country. To begin with, Durham is a reactionary little bundle of houses and shops which is almost totally owned by the church, the council and the university. In the past the 'honourable gentlemen' of these establishments have hindered the building of youth clubs, dance halls, adventure playgrounds and many of the other types of amenity which make people happy. We are determined to radically change this state of affairs. The arrival of the group has come as a bit of a shock to the local bourgeoisie, up to now they had never had anything more radical than the Labour

Party. We are very happy to say, however, that the town's people have reacted favourably towards us. We are now working on several projects and have had some success. We are organising adventure playgrounds and youth clubs in the worst parts of the city. We are also trying to form rent committees, and we hope that these will take a militant stand against the forecasted Government legislation on rents. Local young people are very interested in what we are doing, and a lot of them have said that they will help us fight the local oppressors. We are now engaged in a struggle to get the local War Museum closed down. So far we have forced the Museum curators to take down their most gory pictures and a symbolically peaceful demonstration against the Museum will take place within the next few weeks. Bill Dwyer wrote in *Freedom* last week about the Durham drug squad taking photographs of people in the public gallery of the local courthouse during a drug case. This photograph-taking follows months of police harassment against drug takers (to escape from the oppressive environment is a worse crime in Durham than in most other parts of the country). At present we are carrying out a campaign against the drug squad. We managed to get some stories in the local newspapers—including Thomson press! — Which really has slammed down on the drug squad. On Thursday night we burnt an effigy of Sgt. Brown, head of the drug squad. We suspended this effigy on the end of a long rope from a local bridge, held a mock trial, condemned him to death and then burnt him to the cheers and heartily vocalised abuse of all the local heads. This was at midnight and afterwards a group of about sixty people staged an impromptu march on the prison, registering disapproval in the usual way and with a black flag raised on the prison flagpole. Following this we marched through the town, an almost unprecedented event in the peaceful Wear-side village of Durham, and one which caused concern and loss of sleep among the local pigs. The Durham Anarchist Group is off to a good start, getting more followers each week and we will definitely have more to inform you of within the very near future. D.A.G."[373]

*The Evening Chronicle* is later picking up the story;

> "Search Michael Mogie but you are unlikely to find any home-made bombs ticking in his coat pockets. Nor will he be found hatching some sinister plot against law and order – although he will be quite happy to see a little less law and rather more order in society. For Michael, aged 19, sacked student, ex-journalist and now Durham anarchist leader, says he doesn't believe in violence. *"People who think anarchists go round plotting to blow things up are out of touch. The bombers were a long time ago in our history and were in fact extremists we would be happy to forget. The anarchist movement realises a violent revolution is unlikely to succeed. It's got to be a revolution of the mind"* he said. This distaste for violence extends to all things military, ranging from the Vietnam War to the Durham Light Infantry Museum. This should be abolished and the building turned over to art, says Michael. He thinks guns and tanks have an unhealthy effect on the minds of schoolboys visiting the museum. Violence is out so Michael and his Anarchistic Association use modern methods to convert followers to their beliefs in a society free from politics, bosses, police and money. He has twice been on television and has taken part in demonstrations – one of them to protest at the way traffic has hold of Durham's ancient City Centre. Now on the dole – his grant to study A level's at Durham Technical College was stopped – Michael has refused jobs because bosses have told him to get his shoulder-length hair cut. He edited a student magazine at the college and helped to "reorganise" the students' union. *"I haven't been a member of any political party but I started by being interested in the Labour Party, the International Socialists and then the Communists,"* he said. *"Now I 'am an anarchist for socialistic reasons and I believe society can be ruled without politics."*[374]

Mike Mogie would remain the contact for Durham Anarchist Group, for the rest of the early 1970s, whilst in Gateshead 1971 see,s B.S of Ely St seeking further people to form a larger group in the area. Not much more information is obtainable for the next couple of years of activity in the region. 1973 and *Libertarian Struggle,* the paper of ORA (Organisation of Revolutionary Anarchists) mentions having a contact in the Newcastle area, contactable through the paper.[375] Newcastle meetings at this time were being held at rooms above Cradlewell Books, left-wing bookshop, at 235 Jesmond Road, also the meeting place of the local Socialist Society.

The exact date remains a slight mystery, I do know that he visited London soon after 15th May 1972, more than likely on Syndicalist Workers Federation business / and or for a SWF social, but by the early summer of 1974 the motivational speaker and 'down to earth' writer that was the large influence of Tom Brown, would quietly pass away at his home in Low Fell, Gateshead.[376] The national anarchist and syndicalist movement was unable to mark his passing with tribute, as his death wasnt discovered until later publications and letters addressed to Tom were starting to be returned to sender marked "deceased".

In his final years in the North East Tom would continue his SWF activities with contributions to the Federation, as well as "several lively contributions, on libertarian subjects on local radio"[377] Ray Challinor would also interview Tom for the North East Labour History Society[378] on the various struggles he participated in during his life.

> "It was partly as a result of Brown and the SWF's contribution to activism that anarchism maintained a working class perspective, which provided the foundation for later variants. As such, Tom Brown's importance was in passing down the heritage of previous a generation into modern British anarchism, and he has remained, a doyen of the movement."[379]

## 3.9 1976 – Squats, Punks, & Publications

1976, and Cradlewell Books was fast becoming the centre of local protest activity, meetings, distribution of literature, including community paper *Tyneside Street Press* and later *Tyneside Street Sheet*. Although these publications were not strictly anarchist they were often libertarian in nature.The shop did sell anarchist papers like *Freedom*, *Black Flag*, and Canadian *Open Road*. The bookshop "had been set up by the Tyneside Socialist Centre. And the socialist centre really, was a very active political initiative that was trying to cross sectarian and party divides and trying to involve not just political party activists but trade unionists, active trade unionists, reaching out to the women's movement, reaching out to the environmental movement, it's ambition to become a sort of organising, focus for radical activity on Tyneside, and the first practical thing it did was to set up this small bookshop"[380] Naturally this attracted the attention of the local National Front who were instrumental in the odd brick thrown through the shops window.[381]

When the council decided to increase rents in North Tyneside by 60p, local anarchists, who were active in many of the grassroots campaigns happening throughout the region at the time, were also soon involved within the protest activities of North Tyneside's Housing Campaign Committee. The press was as usual quoting anarchist activity as communist activity and vice versa, when if fact it could be both or either, or even neither.

> "Card carrying members of the Communist Party were among demonstrators who disprupted a Tyneside council meeting, the council leader claimed today. Coun. Jim B*** leader of North Tyneside said *"I think that wasnt just a show against rents increase. It was anarchism."* Police were called to the council chamber in Wallsend to eject more than 50 singing and banner waving protestors from the public gallery. Coun. B*** said; *"I know there were members of the Communist Party there, who have stood as canditates in local elections. It was a disgusting*

> *and disgraceful performance. If it hapens againwe will clear the gallery again."* He said. He added the demonstrators were a tiny minority of the 30,000 council tenants in the area, and were being stirred up by a hard core of demonstrators who have been active in the area for about a year. Mr Joe D***, secretary of the Council Tenants Protection Association, based on the Battle Hill estate at Wallsend, read out the statement on a loud hailer, protesting at a 60p a week rent rise. Today ambulanceman Mr D*** explained why he acted out of character, *"I am normally one of the quietest men you could meet. What I did last night took a lot of doing, but it is time a halt was called to these sort of actions. This was most undemoncratic and a thing which is endemic in the Labour Party at the moment"* said Mr D***."[382]

MS was at this time the contact within the pages of *Freedom*[383] and also as 'Durham Freedom Group' in *Black Jake*[384] for any anarchists in the area, at Front St, Sherburn Village, Durham where he was a student, before later taking a job at Cradlewell Books and then later at Days of Hope bookshop in Newcastle. Although I won't mention any names[385], MS was like predecessor Will Lawther in his eagerness to put his name to everything, including group pamphlets. The comparison was also prevalent between the two in how, after becoming the 'limelight' so to speak, they both were to publically denounce anarchists and their anarchism, as we shall see. But for the moment MS was to play a key role in forthcoming events.

Newcastle Anarchist Group, who despite the name would also have members in other areas of Tyneside, were becoming the prevalent group within the region at this time. The group would also be known as the Black Jake Group due to the production of the two magazines they produced under said name.

The First issue of *Black Jakes Occasional Organ*, produced early 1977, is I believe, the first anarchist magazine produced in the region by a local group, as opposed to relying on national endeavours like *Freedom* etc to sell. This was becoming the trend throughout the country and an activity that would explode into precedence in the following decade. Printed by Newcastle printer workers co-operative Tyneside Free Press at Charlotte Square. Issue one would list Newcastle Anarchists contactable through Cradlewell Books. The main feature is a write up of the recently opened anarchist squat "The Mosley Street Free Hostel" which would hit the local headlines with fervour and highlight the City's homeless problem.

The local press reports "Anarchists yesterday invaded an empty city centre office block and threw open the doors to the homeless. The squatters marched into the building in Mosley Street, Newcastle, by opening a side door with a key. *"We couldn't have more room if we had taken over Buckingham Palace",* said one of the self-confessed anarchists who came to the *Journal* offices to announce the occupation. *"The place has been empty for seven months while homeless people walk the freezing streets at night. We think this is a disgrace and will stay as long as we can."*[386] Whilst a later press report states *"An anarchist group was today* spending its second day as squatters in a Newcastle office they have thrown open to City homeless. The 15 strong group which claims to be part of Newcastle Anarchists said it wanted to use the building to house people who had nowhere to sleep. Last night it scoured City streets looking for down-and-outs and was able to provide shelter for three people in the four story block. *"I think we were unable to find more people because we left it too late and didn't really know where to look,"* one of the group said today. *"We'll do better tonight and by then we should have some heating for the building."*[387]

The groups own version of events was published in their magazine as follows;

> "On Friday January 28th, the Newcastle Anarchist Group occupied a four story office block in Mosley Street. This building had been empty since July 1976, and while this and other similar places remain unoccupied, many people are homeless.

Some are able to get a bed and shelter at hostels run by groups such as the Salvation Army or Cyrenians, but these organisations cannot hope to provide beds for all the homeless. As a result, many are forced to sleep in derelict houses and other similar places, which can provide at least some sort of shelter. The Mosley Street offices were occupied in an attempt to provide shelter for some of these people, and also in an attempt to show how a Free Hostel system can work. The Free Hostel was run with a minimum of rules, people being free to come and go as they pleased, and genarally being encouraged to help in the running of the place. In this way we were starting to build a friendly community, and the skippers (the name 'tramps' use for themselves) were beginning to run it on their own behalf. This contrasts with the situation in other 'official' hostels, where skippers are seen only as passive recipients of charity, who ought to be properly grateful and do as they are told. In the Cyrenians they have to be in by 8pm, and if they go out after that they are not allowed back. They are sent out again in the morning and have to spend the day outside. At least in the Salvation Army hostel thay can stay in during the day, but they just have to sit around, while other people run the hostel and their lives.

The common attitude to skippers seems to be that they are just idle layabouts who deserve all the shit they get. This is illustrated by Labour councillor Abraham's comment that there is no homelessness problem in the city, but "only irresponsibility". One policemen we spoke to couldnt understand why we bothered to help people who 'chose' to spend their money on meths or surgical spirits. In fact, few skippers 'choose' their way of life consciously. They are genarally forced into it by various circumstances, such as domestic problems. One thing they do have in common, of course, is that they come from the most oppressed levels of society, the lowest paid sectors of the working class. Just to say a skipper 'chooses' to go on the road is a vast simplification of the real situation.

> The Free Hostel gave shelter to skippers in a way which, we hope, offered a basic degree of dignity through self-management. It wasn't a charitable institution, with 'us' generously handing out succour to 'them'. It offered some self-respect to society outcasts. The Hostel is now closed. On Thursday 17th Febuary, the police came into the building to arrest four outsiders who were allegedly trying to rip lead off the roof."[388]

The police, eager to end the situation as, embarassingly for them, the squat was not far from their Market St police station in the city centre , and no doubt orders from the top to end the much publicised squat were eargely put into action. The opportunity soon came "Four men who started jail sentences today are unaware that their crime helped police to solve a squatting problem in Newcastle. The 20 squatters took over empty offiices in Mosley Street more than a fortnight ago, backed by an anarchist group. Under the present law police are unable to turn them out. When the four accused – who were not squatters – were spotted on the roof of the building, however, officers had to be allowed in." "Today squatters complained that the police had been working in collaboration with the estate agents." "Mr B** W**, aged 23 said; "*We were locked out and this is a civil offence. Only the court has the right to order squatters out.*" The press report goes on to mention the sentences of three months the people stealing the lead recieved, whilst "In a seperate case R**S**(36) of no fixed address, was jailed for six months for trying to force the door of the building after it had been boarded up."[389]

> "Theft of roofing lead from the city centre office block occupied by anarchists three weeks ago has forced the end of the squat and put four men in jail. The ex-Sun Alliance office block on the comer of Pilgrim Street and Mosley Street was taken over by 20 members of the Anarchist Federation of Newcastle, to which the University Anarchist Society is linked. During the last three weeks, the building has provided accommodation for about 30

homeless men, who would otherwise be forced to sleep rough. The police were unable to evict them under the law until four men were spotted on the roof of the building stripping lead last Thursday. Police moved in and arrested the four men without any hindrance by the Anarchists who were out at the time. When they returned to the building, the police had changed the locks and boarded up the entrance. On Friday some of the Anarchists complained that the police or the Estate Agents had confiscated some of their belongings. Both organisations apparently deny this. Three of the men arrested last Thursday were jailed for six months and the fourth for three months at Newcastle Magistrates Court last Friday."[390]

Prior to above press report, in an interesting insight into to some of the debates surrounding the Mosley Street squat during the period, the following letter, under the heading of "This week Mosley Street next week the world" by someone directly involved in events, is worthy of a reprint.

"I write in response to your remarks in "Comment"- in last week's Courier where you described an argument between a Young Liberal and an Anarchist at the Mosley Street occupation.

It is regrettable that such an incident should have taken place, for there is little doubt that the Liberal concerned received somewhat shabby treatment at the hands of the Anarchists: regrettable that such a trivial matter should have been enough to make the Young Liberals disassociate themselves from the squat which they had previously supported.

We Anarchists are saddened that a wedge should have been driven so easily between us and the Liberals, when after all we make common cause on many issues although differing in our choice of methods: doubly saddened as many of us feel that the publicity, which the row was about, is of secondary importance, being simply a means for letting people know what is going on.

Of primary importance are the practicalities of supporting' the squat, not just serving the soup, but all the other seemingly endless jobs such as trying to raise money for blankets and heating; buying in food; answering the door; and generally making sure the facilities are always manned, night as well as day.

It is a basic Anarchist tenet that actions speak louder than words. Rhetoric and propaganda can and should be taken with a pinch of salt, but not committed action. In this respect the Anarchist involvedin the argument has shown his true colours. He has become the backbone of the squat, spending nearly every night there (when others of us were beginning to find reasons for being somewhere else), and being the first to tackle the less savoury tasks such as shovelling up vomit or restraining the drunken violence of a "skipper" with too much surgical spirit inside him.

He has shown himself by his actions to be less interested in the "ego tripping on the publicity and aura surrounding the squat", and in letting off catch phrases about "smashing the system", in the endless debate of noble ideals and in cosy student political-clubbing and more concerned with facing up to the realities of life by responding to need with action.

Can not the Liberals do the same, bury the hatchet and join us whennow their help is needed most? Yours etc., Ann R. Chist."[391]

Whilst the 'corporate core' of the newly emerging punk 'movement' were beginning to sing about 'Anarchy in the UK', or painting circled A's on their brand new leather biker jackets whilst espousing rebellion and forgetting the original principal and general idea of punk itself[392], it seems the Newcastle Anarchist Group were practising what they preached, namely the ethos of direct action, mutual aid, and solidarity. The squat may have only lasted just over two weeks, but the ideas it perpetuated and the philosophy it practiced were to have lasting influence. Well attended public meetings at Cradlewell Books being one example.

The emergence of 'Punk' and in particular the later elements of 'Anarcho- Punk' in the region were to run alongside and in participation with the local anarchist groups / movement and continue to do so until the present day. Dual participation in both camps was a natural progression, especially for the young punks and other 'disaffected youth' of the time.

The local anarchist groups would gain an influx of new participants in activities, membership, and, in some cases, lifelong friends. Whilst some elements of the punk scene were to go on to become 'famous' and forget all principles that they once had, the North East punk scene was predominantly a grassroots and 'down to earth' affair. Some examples will follow, and certainly, the history and activities of the local punk scene from this period onwards runs parallel with the history and activities of the anarchists, and will continue to do so in this history.

## 3.10 1977—1978

*Black Jakes Occasional Organ* Number 2 was released in time to criticise the regional build up to the visit of the queen as part of her jubilee celebrations and tour of the North East in July 1977.

> "Considering the vast resources currently involved in selling the Silver Jubilee to the public and the recurrent references to it on TV, radio, in advertisements and in the shops; considering all this, there has been surprisingly little discussion of the matter in the pages of the radical press. This is a pity, because the Jubilee is a very interesting and significant phenomenon on all sorts of levels. It is a major propaganda exercise, it is a godsend to the ad-men (how many Special Jubilee Offers have you seen this week in the local supermarket?) and it is a good gauge of the distribution of ideas and loyalties which only serve to bind people to the structures which oppress them." The article continues "The Queen may be 'only' a symbol of the nationstate, of national identity and national unity, but as such she is a tremendously important political factor. This is not the place to argue in detail an anarchist case against the State, but I would contend that the State is inevitably oppressive; that it is inevitably a tool of minority domination over the majority; that any ideology which preaches loyalty to the State, or identification with the nation, is inevitably reactionary. Anything which serves to buttress the continuing ascendancy of the State, and popular acceptance of it, should be taken very seriously. And royalty does just that. There are several ways in which this function is performed. Firstly, the Queen and royal family are a convenient focal point for nationalist appeals. Nationalism today is not strident and jingoistic as it once was, but is a far more subtle sentiment, which is kept alive, simmering softly, by the politicians and industrialists and trade union leaders and media. We all know how the 'national interest' is repeatedly invoked in support of a policy or' party; how we are told that we must "all pull together", "work like

> beavers" and "tighten our belts" or "the country" will go bust. There is, in other words, an ongoing process whereby problems and solutions are always discussed in a national framework, whereby it is tacitly assumed that "really" we are all British and thus all have the same interests. The presentation of royalty is a part of this process, gently reminding us all the time of the existence of this 'special' family, and thus of the values it symbolises. We see them at horse-shows and functions, we follow the childrens progress and love-lives, we read fulsome biographies in glossy magazines. If we are really lucky, we see them in the flesh at some State ceremony. And gradually, subtly, the idea seeps in that we belong to something ancient and hallowed called "the Nation", and that we have something colourful and ceremonial called "the State", and that they are closely related to eachother and are both very good things." Before concluding "Mrs. Windsor is coming to Newcastle on July 15th. Are we going to give her an appropriate welcome?"[393]

There was a small protest during the visit in July by anarchists, although I have been unable to find a 'write up' of this.

*Black Jakes Occasional Organ* Number 2 also contained an article entitled 'Egoism and Anarchism' by TJ. This would be the first of many writings, in both the local and national anarchist press from TJ. Originally from Luton, now living in Newcastle after being a student TJ would be an instrumental participant in many future anarchist groups and activities in the decades to come.[394] The issue also contained acknowledgement of the support it was gaining from other areas of the North East; i.e. South Shields, Sunderland, and Durham.

Another article on government cuts to services concludes;

> "It's not good enough just to say "Fight the Cuts". We have got to stop going to the Government and asking it to do things for us - we've got to start doing things for ourselves, replacing State-run social services with self-managed community services.

> Instead of a health service of 'expert' doctors and nurses, who dose people up and send them back to work, we need a health service that emphasises the distribution of knowledge, and seeks to prevent rather than 'cure' illness. Instead of schools (State or private) which teach irrelevant subjects and subordinate the pupil to the teacher, we need Free schools which allow kids to decide their own priorities, and to develop their individuality as they do so. Direct action is the way forward, occupation and grassroots democracy, not only restoring services but bringing them under community control. Let's step out of line. Let's forget the slogans of the unions and the lefties and all the other trendy defenders of the Establishment. Let's start doing things for ourselves."[395]

Needless to say, the North East's chronic housing 'problem' and homelessness, poverty, and the regular 'cuts' to public 'services' during this period, was all occurring during the 'reign' of a Labour government. A further five shipyards were to close for good during the period 1974 – 1979, leaving only eight remaining at the end of the decade. This was coupled with pit closures. The blind perception that such a Party as Labour would eradicate these 'issues' still prevailed locally, in an area renowned for being the bedrock of the Labour movement. "Against this background, the unions and militant workers alike floundered. The reality was that reformist politics no longer offered any solution, and following reformism was now all they knew."[396]

A few doors down from the Tyne Theatre, where Kropotkin had famously, previously lectured; 115 Westgate Road was to become the new home of Cradlewell Books under the new name of Days of Hope Bookshop. Later, speaking on the bookshops name change;

> "The name was taken, some people will remember this, Ken Loach had a TV series that I think went out in 1975 or '76 about left politics, radical politics, around the time of the First World War, actually very apt for something, now that we're going through the centenary and that was called Days of Hope

and it was about conscientious objectors and radical opponents of the war, and it wasjust a great title, so people in the socialist centre seized on it, I guess they got Ken's approval, because he's always sort of been a friend and supporter of the bookshop and radical causes."[397]

This was now the publicised contact address for the Newcastle Anarchist Group / Black Jake Group[398], and would became the centre of activities, meetings, and of course the distribution of libertarian literature for the group. It would also become the 'home' for many new groups to come.

This period also saw the release of *National Liberation and State Power – An Anarchist Critique of the MPLA in Angola* by MS. The pamphlet stated it was printed and published by the Black Jake Collective. The "intention in this paper is to examine the development of the MPLA (Popular Movement for the Liberation of Angola), the most 'left-wing' of the three major national- liberation movements which arose in Angola during colonial period, and the movement which was finally successful in establishing itself as the government of an 'independent' Angola." Interesting stuff for some at the time I am sure, the pamphlet would go on to conclude;

> "Anti-Imperialist struggle merits our support. What does not merit our support is "national-liberation" struggle which is based in Western concepts, a Western vision of history, and Western priorities. A true anti-imperialist struggle involves opposition not onlyto socio-economic and political oppression, but also to the the subtly-related techniques of cultural and ideological oppression. National-liberation movements generally are blind to this, seeking only to replace personnel and programmes, while retaining theimperialists' institutions and values. It is up to revolutionaries to criticise such movements, rather than endorse their confusions and hypocrisies. Meanwhile, the best thing we can be doing to help the oppressed populations of the underdeveloped countries is to work right here, in our own

> particular niches within the imperialist metropolis, against the exploitative and authoritarian structures which oppress us all."[399]

May 1978 saw the release of *Region 1*, again published by the Black Jake Collective, but again credited to MS. Described as 'An examination of the State's plans for repression in the North East', the introduction explained;

> "The British State has been laying contingency plans, to deal with emergencies, for centuries. The classic "emergency" of course, has always been the threat of foreign invasion, and the modern system of Home Defence (or Civil Defence, for the terms are interchangeable) has its origins in pre-First World War anti-invasion precautions. But for our present purposes it is interesting to note that really <u>detailed</u> plans were not laid until <u>after</u> the war, when the State was threatened not by invasion from without but from resistance from within." "What we want to do here is to give a general outlineof the various emergency systems which the State has constructed in the name of "Home Defence", with special reference to Tyneside and the North East. We know that these systems <u>will</u> be used not only in the event of nuclear attack or natural disaster, but also in the event of a serious internal threat to the power of the State. The systems exist not to defend "the people", but to defend the State, against the people if necessary."

Over 30 pages of exposed council / police / military / and government contingency plans etc later, the pamphlet would conclude;

> "What we have tried to do here is to give some idea of the range of measures taken by the State in this Region, for its own defence. We have pursued the discussion on a number of levels, examining at one moment the everyday activities of the police and at another the existence of secret Government shelters..Obviously, the State always wants things to appear

"normal", and will resort to such drastic measures as calling in the troops, or activating the Regional HD system, only when absolutely necessary. But it is important for us to realise that these drastic measures are still only points on a continuum, and that the routine work of police surveillance, or the mundane activity of Emergency Planning Departments, or the regular process of Army counter-insurgency training, are also points on the same continuum. The State is preparing now for a situation where it may have to take on vastly-extended powers. If a situation developed where ordinary people started taking matters into their own hands, the authorities would react. They would throw the whole weight of a biased vocabulary at us, and they would add to it the physical burden of State repression. The State is ready to meet and repress our autonomous actions. We must be ready to meet and resist the State."[400]

Mid 1978 and more than forty anarchists attended a founding conference held in Leeds on 22nd June to establish the North-Eastern Anarchist Federation. Delegates attended from Newcastle, Sunderland, Wakefield, Huddersfield, Sheffield, and Leeds. It was agreed at the conference to rotate the secretary role throughout the various regional groups, and publish a monthly bulletin to keep everyone up to date with future activities / protests etc, as well as to encourage the communication between the various groups. Reports were "also given on the recent raids[401] in Huddersfield by armed Special Branch officers looking, without success, for evidence of bomb making conspiracies. There was a heated discussion on methods of combating fascism. We judged the conference a success and are optimistic about the future of the federation."[402]

December 1978, and replying to a request from *Freedom* on the publication and content of the paper, see's a letter from John M** of Newcastle, a long time subscriber and member of the Newcastle Anarchist / Black Jake Group, encouraging groups around the country to send in regular reports of activities. "You publish national and international listings of anarchist groups, which is useful and necessary. However, surely it would be nice were some of these groups actually to send you reports of their activities and plans. I think *Freedom* should become, more than it already is, a general, non-partisan, anarchist disseminator of information. Certainly, vital issues, e.g. ABC (Anarchist Black Cross – Persons Unknown) trial and Torness[403], are covered, but, as the Nat West says, our roots are our branches."

To this end, as promised by John in his letter, the same issue includes an interesting and illuminative group report from Newcastle.

> "The Newcastle Anarchists main concern at the moment is Region 1, the regional seat of government. We have discussed what we could or should do about its whereabouts and uses. Last weekend we helped to distribute some leaflets concerning the regional seat of government. Also, full details are being published in this week's edition of Durham Street Press (28/11). On Monday, 20 November, Albert Meltzer addressed us [404] at length on the history, role and prospects of the Spanish CNT. The meeting (open) was well attended and the talk most illuminating. An informal discussion ensured. One of us travelled down to London for the Direct Action Movement conference on 11/12 November. The main impression we got was that the DAM was disunited and unorganised, arguing at length about the definition of a worker, whether students were parasites and hearing various highly individual personal testimonies. Some things emerged, however. For the moment, DAM intends to work within the trade unions and will charge a registration fee for its next conference. Black Jake has been made the official contact for DAM in the North East of England. On Saturday, 16 December we are holding an all-day event in the Bridge Hotel, High Level Bridge, Newcastle. Attractions include Clapperclaw, a feminist theatre group."[405]

The following issue of *Freedom* contains a Black Jake group report, which mentions (prior to above report) a few earlier activities from the end of 1978. The report, originally from the North Eastern Anarchist Federation Bulletin No 3 states;

> "Black Jake (current secretaries of North Eastern Anarchist Federation) held quite a successful meeting on 23 October with two speakers from the Persons Unknown support group in London. The discussion centred on the case of the comrades in Brixton, but also broadened out to wider issues about the developing police state. About 30-35 people came along; we managed to collect £14 for the support group and sent a message of solidarity to the people in Brixton. On 11 November we organised a picket of an exhibition put on by British Nuclear Fuels Ltd in the Eldon Square shopping centre (of Newcastle). It all went off surprisingly quietly, but we attracted quite a lot of attention. We are planning to launch a publicity campaign on the whole area of 'Home Defence' starting off by revealing the location of the Sub-Regional Control. Mass leafleting and press publicity are planned. We are currently working on a supplementary to Region 1 and a pamphlet on computers and how to fight them."[406]

The outcome of the proposed pamphlet on 'computers' is unknown, however, *Region 1 Supplementary* was published April 1979 and described as 'further information on the State's plans for repression in the North East: the Sub- Regional Control; County preparations in Cleveland, Durham, and Northumberland; the Special Branch, etc.'

1978 also saw the release of the inspirational protest record from local South Shields punk band the Angelic Upstarts, entitled 'The Murder of Liddle Towers / Police Oppression'. An angry and much sought after[407] attack on local police murderers, the record would be instrumental in voicing the local hate felt by many. Liddle Towers died as a result of a beating he received at the hands (and boots) of Northumbria police, late January (the beating) and early February (died the 9th, Dryburn hospital as a result of injuries) 1976. An ineffectual inquest, as well as local protest ensured. The Liddle Towers Action Committee issued a pamphlet highlighting the case in June 1977[408] which continued and encouraged further protest in the region, including the Angelic Upstarts... "Mensi (singer on record): "Liddle Towers was our protest single. It was the story of a boxing coach who was arrested for being drunk and disorderly. He was examined by a doctor and was perfectly healthy. Then in the morning was discovered dead and had injuries which the police surgeon described as being similar to that of a person who had been in a serious 70 miles-an-hour head-on collision. His injuries were absolutely horrific. He was basically kicked to death. We done a couple of shows and got the money together and we pressed 500 singles, and then Small Wonder/Rough Trade re-released it, and it got to number one in the indie charts. With no radio play. Apart from John Peel, nobody else played it, and it was actually banned off any sort of play list in the northeast." Further 'stage shows' from the band included episodes of pigs heads, attired with a police helmet, being kicked about on stage, led to the band being banned from Newcastle venues for seven years.[409]

The venomous hatred felt towards the local police, especially after further incidents of police beatings and physical fights in cells, and the backs of police vans, would continue for decades to come, and would forever inspire and channel hatred felt into future activism. Many more instances of police brutality and 'deaths in custody' would also reverberate around and incite the simmering anger felt by many.

**NEWCASTLE UPON TYNE, Monday 23 October. Black Jake meeting on the theme "Are we moving towards a police state " with special reference to Persons Unknown case. Bridge Hotel (near High Level Bridge), 8 pm.**

[410]

## 3.11 1979

February 1979, and John M** is the author of an examination in *Freedom* on anarchism, homosexuality and gay liberation, and how they are inter-relatedin their struggle, "One gender must not exploit the other in the name of sex, nor may any organisation exploit sexual relationships or define them." "We must eliminate this exploitation from ourselves and from the system under which we exist. Only then will the worst atrocities of the state be clearly seen to be committed in the name of irrelevance." And concluding "This article should not be interpreted as meaning that sexual liberation is all that matters. Rather, it should appear that no freedom is real or valid without concomitant sexual liberation. The essence of homosexuality is a challenge to the state."[411]

MS is also writing at this time on the elections of the European Economic Community and encouraging the boycott of the forthcoming election of June 1979.

> "The elections are purely and simply an exercise in legitimation. We are being asked to confer the mantle of democratic respectability upon a power which is already established, and whose aims and objectives are already very clear. We are being asked to express retrospective approval for the emergence of the new western European techno-bureaucracy, and for the planning of production on a continental scale in the interests of growth, profit and capitalist stability." Whilst calling for a boycott, it was also encouraged to make contact with European comrades at the same time, "In this way, we can use the spurious 'internationalism' of the EEC to help us create a <u>real</u> internationalism of the European movement."[412]

The articles coming out of Newcastle are continuing with another by TJ on 'Thoughts on Sexuality' where he looks at relationships and the "normal Christian-type monogamy-ownership crap" sexism within them, and 'propertarianism' within relationships.[413]

March 12th and 13th 1979 the Litman Studios, at Newcastle Polytechnic would host 'A Farce – The Accidental Death of an Anarchist' by Dario Fo, presented by the touring theatre group 'Belts & Braces'. The show, described as "a farce based on Italian police corruption and the subsequent cover-up, after our comrade Giuseppe Pinelli 'jumped' four floors to his death on 15th December 1969 while in police custody in Milan."[414] A later London showing was reviewed as "a great show by Belts & Braces, who ad libbed it up to date. You will laugh from beginning to end, if at times somewhat grimly. It is called a farce, and indeed we are living in farcical times. It is a robust and enthusiastic performance, and it was good to see the establishment being kicked in every part of its anatomy before a packed audience."[415]

The Newcastle Anarchist / Black Jake Group, in the face of oncoming general election hysteria, would host a public meeting 'Don't Vote; Fight Back' at the Bridge Hotel, Newcastle, on Wednesday April the 25th, 8pm. In conjunction with the North Eastern Anarchist Federation, posters ('Whoever you vote for..The government gets in') and leaflets ('Vote for me quick') were produced and distributed on local streets and through doors. The group would also report "specifically anarchist activities are restricted at present, due to energy being put into the North East Anti-Nukes Group, etc."[416]

The result of the general election of May 1979 would herald in the beginnings of the Thatcher years and the Conservative Party's relentless psychotic endeavours against, and near destruction, of the working class. As stated, local anarchists, with the election over, now turned some of their attention to anti-nuclear activities, and the (then) perceived urgent threat to both human life and the planet from its nuclear destruction. The concentration on anti-nuclear activities is due in part, to the (then) proposed construction of a nuclear power plant, less than eighty miles up the road from Newcastle and thirty miles east of Edinburgh at Torness Point near Dunbar in East Lothian, Scotland.

> "In May 1978, after it became clear that a lethal new reactor was planned at Torness, 4000 people marched the six miles

from Dunbar to the proposed site for an anti-nuclear festival. The Torness Alliance, a network of anti-nuclear groups and individuals, was formed to stop the power station being built. In May 1979 10,000 people took Part in another festival and following this 1500 entered the fenced-in site a mile away. They proceeded to disrupt surveying, re -landscape earthworks, design huge anti-nuclear slogans and damage equipment. 400 got inside the central machinery compound. Various actions on a small scale have occurred since, and a recent poll showed that 90 per cent of the local population are against Torness."[417]

The events of May 1979 caused a bit of a split within the Anti-Nuclear Movement with those who favoured methods of direct action, such as those who participated in the actions within the inner compound, damaging machinery etc. These were being labelled 'wreckers' by the more conservative elements of the 'movement'. Lengthy discussions were also to ensure amongst the anarchists.[418]

MS, commenting on events would stir a bit controversy with;

> "I went up to the Torness gathering over the weekend of May 5th-7th and overall thought it was really good. A very constructive, worthwhile event. But the bit I want to discuss here is the episode on Sunday, when a small group of people broke into the machinery compound and started damaging equipment. The reason why this episode is relevant to us is because these people identified themselves, and were identified by others as 'the anarchists'. The issue at stake is not whether it's 'right' or 'wrong' to damage property: I have got no objection to sabotage of equipment which is going to be used to build a nuclear reactor. The issue at stake concerns our attitude towards working within a broad movement such as the Torness Alliance. The fact is that the Alliance is the nearest thing to a working libertarian organisation that we've seen in this country for quite a while. Decisions made at national meetings have been criticised, and it's true that properly

representative structure needs to be worked out for these meetings. But on the actual site over that weekend, we had a working system of grassroots democracy, at which mandated, recallable delegates (spokes) represented their affinity groups, and reached consensus decisions on that basis. There were obviously individual problems and inadequacies, but the Alliance is a concrete example that libertarian forms of organisation can work. However, it seems that some avowed anarchists regard even this sort of structure as a bourgeois con-trick. On the Saturday night, at a long spokes meeting, a consensus was painfully hammered out concerning the nature of the occupation which would take place on Sunday. Despite this, some avowed anarchists went off and did their own thing. This raises the whole question of what we mean when we call ourselves 'anarchists'. Do we mean that we are libertarian socialists, prepared to abide by collective decisions which are reached in an open, democratic and unbureaucratic fashion? Or do we mean that we are unaccountable individuals, who will abide by no collective decisions, and insist on following our whims and moods? I know where I stand, I am a libertarian socialist, and I'm prepared to listen to and work alongside other socialists or liberals or environmentalists or anyone, so long as they're committed to the struggle against nuclear power. I believe we have to build a broad movement, and this will inevitably embrace many currents and tendencies. I am interested in helping to create that movement. I am not interested in the petty poses and gestures of individuals who use an event like the Torness gathering in order to play at being 'militant', whether they call themselves 'anarchists' or anything else. The point is this: if these individuals were genuinely committed to a campaign of sabotage against nuclear installations, then they shouldn't be arguing about it at Torness. They should be organising a secure cell-structure and obtaining explosives. But to wait for someone else to call a peaceful gathering, and to use that gathering for a trivial exercise in fence-cutting and tyre-deflating, is to indulge in parasitical politics of the worst kind. There's two sorts of anarchist,it seems.

> There are anarchists who want to understand the world, and to organise to change it. And there are anarchists who want to make individual gestures of protest. And between the two, there is a large gulf."[419]

Of course many disagreed, including the 'Reading Anarchists' who emphasise "Many of us in the anti-nuclear movement, faced with this situation and with the clear danger to life and liberty presented by nuclear technology, feel that sabotage, and the destruction of machinery and property, are justified. We feel that this course of action is entirely consistent with the principles of non- violence. It does not hurt people; nuclear technology does."[420]

The 'argument' would go back and forth for the next couple of months with reply's and responses to and from MS, with one conclusion from DM of;

> "It is our contention that an unrepresentative Alliance bureaucracy is developing (witness instant statements to the press, deals with the police etc) which much be opposed. The 400 or so 'elitists' were acting in the spirit of the movement while others were either taking other forms of action (building a croft, planting flowers, digging holes, constructing signs etc,) or were being shepherded together by would-be leaders and given a lecture. This lecture warned of "*extremists, wreckers, not in the Alliance, going against the spokes decisions, we must tell the nice journalists and police immediately to CONDEMN them*". I enjoyed Torness, as did my colleagues, and respect all the activities and personalities I encountered there. But I will NOT be CONDEMNED by anyone. That is the State's function, which is why I am an anarchist."[421]

Another would state, on the debate over 'violence' and 'non-violence' that "Most of the Alliance saw the occupiers of the compound as 'wreckers' determined to destroy the nuclear site. They saw this as 'violence' – so they sided with the police" and "Violence is what the

Torness reactor will do when it's built". "The Alliance as a whole look at nuclear power as a single issue, rather than in the wider spectrum of State oppression."[422]

In a further response to MS, DC would also state "I have every sympathy with MS when he declares himself on the side of the democratic anarchists as opposed to those who argue for total individual freedom and fuck everyone else's rights. However, even to an outsider, it is obvious that the Torness Alliance is by no means a beautiful example of anarchist democracy at work. And the decisions reached were obviously not based on 'consensus', as he claims, and obviously the delegates were not truly representative. Quite the contrary, it seems from the letter by WSS that we have here a typical example of domination by an informal elite of activists who are neither proper delegates nor even conscientious about their accountability."[423] Further events surrounding Torness follow in 1980.

Monetary contributions to the running of anarchist papers, predominantly based in London, were starting to decrease towards the end of the decade. Why contribute to national papers when local ones, demanding financial and physical input were on the increase? A few noted in 1979 are JM and FWK (Newcastle), DH and JAJ (Sunderland) to *Freedom*, whilst *Black Flag* would have DAS (Washington, Tyneside).[424]

The regions blossoming and strongly DIY and un-commercial orientated punk scene was given a further boost when local Gateshead punk band Total Chaos along with others, like the Model Workers etc were given use of a disused garage space on the ground floor of community groups 'Them Wifies' premises at Bells Court, Newcastle. This became the area's first 'truly independent venue and space'.

> "Remarkably 'Them Wifies' gave us carte blanche to do it up as a venue. Thus we spent lots of our time clearing it out, painting the odd circled 'A' around the place, building a stage and a disco area. The building remained suitably grotty with one toilet (which gave the Newcastle constabulary reason to close it down

a year and a half later), and we had the responsibility of opening / locking up, cleaning it, running the gigs, advertising, fly posting etc."[425]

The first gig at the Garage, as it was to be called, was in June 1979 to a small audience of 15 or so, but was soon attracting hundreds. A friend of mine later commented "that it was the best 25p you could spend on a Sunday night in Newcastle".

Total Chaos, who despite the name, were anything but, would state "We have always been called Total Chaos which we believe is an alternative phrase for 'absolute freedom', taking 'chaos' in its original Greek 'xaos' meaning 'before regulation'. Basically we are anarchistically minded pacifists believing societies problems are caused by inequalities within human society. These inequalities are brainwashed into our heads as being the accepted norm. These laws are upheld by the agents of social control – the police, the courts and state education to keep the mindless majority happy. The royal family are kept to teach us that there is a class system. In our ideal society everyone would respect each other with equal love and no-one would give out orders; Utopian maybe, but beautiful. Even today, by working together in music collectives, political projects, peace movements, housing associations and buying allotments collectively we can snatch back some of our basic human rights – to LIVE OUR OWN LIVES."[426] And further stating "This political vein is not followed through in the lyrics because we believe it is wrong to brainwash people with personal beliefs. However, some songs reflect our concern over media manipulation, corruption and mindless violence. Total Chaos or "absolute freedom" are a band who engage in music for enjoyment and nothing else. Therefore music alone is our aim and not stardom with music."[427]

The ethos of being —at one with and not apart from—the 'audience' was aptly demonstrated when playing at another venue, after being asked to leave, "we suggested to the crowd that we continue the gig back at the Garage... every punk in the place picked up various bits of equipment and walked about half a mile to the Garage, which was opened, the gear set up and a great night had by all. And not one bit of the gear was nicked en route."[428] Total Chaos play further roles within our history and will appear again.

By October MS is beginning to show his disillusionment with the anarchist 'movement', where in a book review on another subject, tells us;

> "The overall message of the book is that there are many experiences and traditions from which we can learn. The anarchist or libertarian tradition is one of them, but only one. We have to face up to the fact that there has never been a mass, consciously anarchist movement in Britain, and the prospects for one don't look good: those comrades who insist on calling for a 'new national anarchist organisation', or who claim that they have already built one, are condemning themselves to sectarian irrelevance. What we do have is a growing number of people who define themselves broadly as 'non-aligned socialists', and who don't identify exclusively with any single tradition. There are people who have come from Leninism, from feminism, from the labour movement, from libertarian politics, and from elsewhere, and they all feel dissatisfied. By opening a dialogue between these people, we can start to create not a party, nor even a 'movement' perhaps, but a loose community of socialist thought and action. Of course we should be aware of the continuing differences – we <u>should</u> remember Kronstadt, and we shouldn't have any starry-eyed expectations of some grand libertarian alliance emerging. But at least let's get the dialogue going, and see where it leads."[429]

Some local anarchists were present in London for a march, and possibly later when "Violence erupted at a 'stop the cuts' protest meeting yesterday. Fighting started when anarchist D**H** tried to address the platform, which included Labour leader Jim Callaghan at the Central Hall, Westminster." The meeting was held after the previous day's march of 26,000 against cuts on transport, housing and education.

> "As H** made a plea for free speech – surrounded by 30 other anarchists, many of them punk rockers with multi-coloured hair, Labour party stewards moved in. A brawl broke out and the scuffling went on for about five minutes with people being pushed to the floor and punched. Police arrived and the anarchists gave the signal to leave. They screamed *"We'll be back but next time there'll be more of us."* Mr H**, a 26 year old postman from Hackney said, *"I admit I'm an anarchist but all I was doing was trying to have my say. This was not organised. Nothing would have happened if the stewards had not sat on me. I am not associated with the other anarchists who joined in to help me"* Mr Callaghan had arrived 30 minutes earlier to an explosive mixture of boos and cheers."[430]

And on that note, so would end another thirty years of build up and struggle for the local anarchists and the precedent was set for the beginning of the 1980s and the confrontational onslaught of the coming 'Thatcher Years'.

Part four (1980-1992) takes up the majority of this fascinating history. As we shall show the decade would herald in an unparalleled amount of produced literature, groups, and actions throughout the region, which has since never been surpassed.

# PART FOUR 1980—1992

## 4.1 1980 — A DECADE OF DISORDER?

Despite the fact that a bunch of psychopaths have taken over the reins of 'running the country', the decade starts off relatively quietly on the local anarchist front. This is not to say that it is because of lack of activity, just the lack of advertised activity in the national anarchist press, an all too often recurrent theme.

Hull have now taken over the secretariat role of the North Eastern Anarchist Federation from the Black Jake Group, whilst in London, the Persons Unknowntrial had ended with the defendants acquitted. One of such, Ronan Bennett would stress;

> "It was anarchism that was on trial. It was anarchism that had to be on trial since the lack of solid evidence—and hence the use of the conspiracy laws—inevitably brought to account the defendants' attitudes and ideas. But if anarchists have won the day, we have still to win the decade. The authorities will do everything they can to prevent such humiliation in the future. How long, for instance, can we expect to maintain the (admittedly fragile) protection of a jury system?"[431]

Locally, and January sees a letter from Jesmond, Newcastle requesting "I am researching Anarchism in relation to the Visual Arts (especially 19$^{th}$ century) and am seeking a pamphlet by Charles MALATO[432] on the subject of urban and rural workers (published in Paris, 1888). I would be grateful if you could help me locate this or suggest other relevant material. AC."[433] The outcome of this is unknown, I hope they had luck.

MS is also again in the letters pages discussing the Anti Nuclear Campaign and stating;

"At the moment it lacks a clear organisational structure and a clear way of reaching decisions, and this means that far too much poweris in the hands of strategically -placed individuals. The need now is to establish whether the ANC is going to be another London-run campaign, occasionally mobilising demo-fodder for a ritual rally or whether it will provide a service to, and links between, autonomous local and regional anti – nuclear groups. The issue has not yet been decided. Of course, I'm not a disinterested observer. I'm on the Interim Steering Committee, and I'm doing what I can to develop the ANC in North East England. My experience so far is that the launching of the national campaign has provided a real boost to theanti nuclear movement in this area, encouraging a degree of cooperation which never existed before. There is the chance to build a strong regional movement here, so that even if the ANC does become highly centralised -will be able to resist being co-opted (or 'recuperated'). There's a more general lesson in this, I think, which has to do with the contradictions of all forms of organisation. I've written before in *FREEDOM*, with reference to the Torness occupation last May, about the ways in which the slogan of 'libertarian autonomy' can become an excuse for a new sort of elitism. Similarly with a body like the ANC: even if it is a national, centralised organisation, it can nevertheless provide the means for a greater degree of local unity and autonomy. Things aren't as black and white as some comrades like to think. The contract between 'centralisation' and 'decentralisation' isn't an absolute, but must be analysed anew in each specific context."[434]

Despite the monetary contributions to *Freedom* this year, including those from DM (Darlington), RGB (Newcastle), GD (Gateshead), and AD (Sunderland)[435]. Despite the existence of anarchist groupings and individuals in the region, the contact page in *Freedom* would cease to mention or publicise any local group from March 1980. Perhaps blame could lie with MS, who is writing this month how he would like to be no longer associated with the label 'anarchist' in a letter which states;

> "There seems to be an emerging political style, which aggressively identifies itself as 'anarchist', and which bases itself on disrupting events organised by the Labour Party or trade unions. Some time ago there were scuffles at a big march against the cuts, and in the latest issue of *Freedom* (29/3/80) we had a report from 'K. Ronstadt' on the disruption of the so-called 'Debate of the Decade'. I don't want to question the sincerity or commitment of the people who are adopting this approach. I do want to question their assumed political objectives. What do they hope to gain by it? There is no hint in K. Ronstadt's article of any strategy underlying these tactics; just a crude resentment of anyone who is perceived as a 'leader', and a delight in disruption for its own sake. Nor is there any hint of realisation that, by adopting this approach, K. Ronstadt and friends are simply becoming part of a new spectacle. The scuffles on the cuts march made the national press, and the disruption of the Debate was discussed in the left-wing press. This whole approach isa real gift to the bourgeois media it can be used to demonstrate, in general, that lefties are always squabbling among themselves; and in particular that anarchists are (as God-fearing citizens always suspected) a bunch of trouble-making loonies. As to the Debate itself, I wasn't there, but I had encouraged Hilary Wainwright to attend when she was invited (Hilary is a friend of mine). I think that any exchange of ideas on the left is potentially useful, and I would defend the right of socialists to attend debates of this kind without being interrupted and harassed. From the reports I have heard, there was just about unanimous opposition to the disruption, and I find it depressing to reflect that, for many socialists, this experience must have been their formative impression of 'anarchists'. I would also like to distinguish between K Ronstadt and friends on the one hand, and the H block protestors on the other. They at least were drawing attention to a real struggle, a war in which people are dying and in which basic human rights are being flouted and denied.

What lies behind all this is a whole political vision. The final part of K. Ronstadt's article makes it clear that s/he views 'the left' as part of the enemy, and s/he calls for an 'Independent anarchist movement in industry, in each locality, etc., etc. ' S/he goes on to admit that the anarchist movement is characterised by 'confusionand inability to develop a revolutionary strategy'. Exactly. And this, the latest in a long line of calls for a new 'independent anarchist movement' is a classic symptom of that confusion. The year is 1980, the country is Britain. There is not, nor has ever been, a strong anarchist movement in this country. There is a strong labour movement, with all sorts of creative and libertarian currents in it despite its bureaucratic leadership; there is a strong autonomous workers' movement; there is growing militancy among blacks; in many areas there are campaigns developing to oppose the cuts and defend basic services; and there is a growing anti-nuclear movement. Many more areas of struggle could be identified. We don't want, and in any case won't get, a new 'independent anarchist movement in industry, in each locality, etc., etc. ' we do want a consistent libertarian in-put into all these struggles, a creative libertarian contribution which demonstrates its validity through practice" But of course this means (horror of horrors) working alongside people who aren't anarchists or even libertarians, people who may belong to left-wing parties or reformist pressure groups. For K. Ronstadt and friends, this of course is out of the question: far better to retreat into sectarian purism, attacking other socialists as if they were the main enemy and dreaming of a new 'independent anarchist movement' Maybe some people will see these arguments as an over-reaction, and will say that I simply ought to let K. Ronstadt and friends follow their inclinations as I follow mine. But it isn't as easy as that, because their aggressive insistence upon their own anarchist identity immediately implicates anyone else who adopts the label 'anarchist'. I have been approached by non-anarchist friends and comrades, who have witnessed these 'anarchist disruptions' and who come to me for explanations and justification which I cannot provide, so I am pushed into a

> situation where, in order to distance myself from political practices which I think absurd and destructive, I am ceasing to identify myself as an anarchist. I imagine a lot of other people, also with strong libertarian commitments must be finding themselves in the same situation."[436]

In a response to MS, which, in all honesty I am more inclined to agree with,Belfast Anarchists would argue;

> "We were enraged to read yet another downer on Anarchism, by MS, namely his letter to K. Ronstadt (*Freedom*, April 26th). As far as we are concerned the 'emerging political style' is that of MS and non-anarchist friends - an attempt to bring together the passive fragments of the disillusioned left, a 'libertarian current', characterized by a need to be seen as respectable and overreacting against any disruption by others which is plainly 'not cricket'. For instance, MS says that the disruption of the debate and the scuffles on the Cuts march was 'a real gift to the bourgeois media'. Since when have Anarchists been tailoring their political action so as to getrespectable coverage in the national papers. Seeing as many dastardly deeds are put down as the work of anarchists we would suggest that this is a lost battle anyway. Our energies should be spent in devising and maintaining our own forms of communication. Angry people, for whatever reason, unlike his cultured socialist friends he's so worried we'll offend, are disruptive .... they chant they block roads, they walk miles in demonstrations, they picket, they occupy what they don't do is sit around most of the time talking cosy politics and calling themselves the vanguard of the revolution. We also object to the definition that H. Block is a 'real struggle' and the 'disruption of the Debate' (an attack on Labour and support for the H. Block hecklers) as not. For the record, Anarchists have been involved for ten years here now in broad fronts on the left from strikes and women's issues to internment and political status. We certainly don't think 'horror of horrors, I spy a Trot', but we do bearin mind that the groups

we are working with are ultimately out to seize power. A view which probably sounds distant in Newcastle or London but is part of the reality of life here particularly with regard to Sinn Fein, many of whose members, especially in rural areas, are not even socialists. As Anarchists we have to counter this as best we can through propaganda, pushing ideas at meetings and by showing in the way we operate that a society can work on the basis of cooperation, mutual aid and horizontal organisation. Anarchists here are involved in all the movements he mentioned, as Anarchists, in rank and file groups in the trade unions, the women's movement, and they are heavily involved in the anti-nuclear movement, particularly the anti uranium campaign going on in Donegal. Anarchists haven't 'frightened off' the local people. .it is the latter who are physically preventing the drilling: and sabotaging the machinery and offices of Irish Base Metals. . (And it was these same Anarchists who were amongst the group criticised by MS at Torness in 1979) Like MS, we were not at the 'Debacle of the Decade' and can't say whether it would have been more profitable to give out the ritual leaflets and remain seated, although the latter would not have given rise to such discussion. The concept of such a debate sounds a bit contrived to us and if fellow Anarchists thought that the co- ordinating committee was mystifying and manipulating, they had every right to heckle. Of course, we want an Anarchist movement. As MS says himself 'what lies behind all this is a whole political vision. We want everybody to become an Anarchist and share in that vision. Sure there are differences, in all political groupings, it's not a peculiarity of Anarchism, but that does not dilute the essential message or make us reluctant to call ourselves Anarchists. The sooner those who threaten 'I am ceasing to identify myself as an anarchist', do so, the better."[437]

The debate would carry on for future issues in the letters pages of *Freedom* and July would see the last of any (known) correspondence from MS where he concludes "Anarchism is libertarian socialism and it only takes on any meaning when it starts relating to the broad thrust of the class struggle..."[438]

National calls for another occupation of the Torness site were being issued for the 3rd of May. It was hoped it "will be an exciting event a necessary continuation of the opposition to Torness at a time when millions all over the world are joining in the struggle. Everyone horrified by the construction of yet another nuclear power station is urged to take part."[439] This time the state was well prepared,

> "Over 150 people turned up for the occupation over the weekend of May 2nd. On the first night (Friday) attempts were made to pull down some of the fencing. The police were out in force - up to 800 of them with helicopters, dogs, motorbikes, etc. On Saturday 3rd, after someone had thrown a black object with BOMB written on it in white over the fence, the picket of the front gate was attacked fairly brutally by the police and 27 people were arrested."[440]

In a prelude to forthcoming cruise missile bases throughout the country, particularly Greenham Common, "Torness has become a demonstration of the security forces, who are making it clear to everybody that protest will be limitedto a point where it does not affect the progress of the building work"[441] or the smooth running of the operation. A show of strength from the authorities executed with military precision, and in cases, usual police heavy handiness.

Meanwhile, our friends Total Chaos would see their first vinyl output with the track 'Psycho Analysis' on the compilation album 'Bullshit Detector 1', released on Crass records in 1980, which was a compilation of 'unsigned' 'punk bands' from received demo tapes. "Centred around the work of the band Crass, anarcho-punk asserted a belief in the politics and practice of punk 'as itwas always supposed to have been' – autonomous, subversive and free from commercial corruption. Embracing the politics of anarchism, anti-militarism and pacifism, Crass worked to popularise the notion of a consciously revolutionary punk rock culture. It was an approach that inspired many thousands to immerse themselves in the highly distinctive 'do-it-yourself' milieu of anarcho-punk and to commit their energies to what were recognised as the critical political struggles of the house."[442]

> "Anarcho-punk reclaimed the notion of punk autonomy – rejecting all approaches from the pop industry, establishing in their place the movement's own record labels and distribution networks; working directly and collaboratively, without agents or intermediaries, to set up tours, produce publications and record music."[443]

This would herald in the beginning of an upsurge in the amount of DIY fanzines[444] and booklets being produced locally, and of course, self produced music, and as already demonstrated, self run venues like the Garage. A couple of notable local zines during this period were '*Protesting Children*' from Stockton on Tees, and the forthcoming '*No Comment*', produced by Total Chaos and friends from Gateshead.

Against the already existing backdrop of high unemployment[445] in the region on September 12, 1980, Consett Steelworks closed for the last time. Despite demonstrations and protests, the British Steel Corporation deemed that the plant was no longer 'commercially viable', and it was shut with the loss of 4,500 jobs. Thatcher was beginning her onslaught.

## 4.2 1981

Leeds have now taken over the secretariat role of the North Eastern Anarchist Federation, and locally the year begins with the formation of Sunderland Anarchists / DAM (the recently, 1979 revived Syndicalist Workers Federation offshoot the Direct Action Movement) group, who are contactable at Durham Rd, Sunderland. This group would also join together with others in the region to form Tyne & Wear Anarchist Group (TWAG). The grouping covered an "area stretching from North Yorkshire to the Scottish Borders, incorporating several anarchist and syndicalist groupings."[446] This included the remnants of the Newcastle Anarchist Group, who despite the departure of a few 'leading lights!!' were still going strong.

The summer saw an explosion of rioting throughout most major cities. Unemployment, deprivation, poverty, and particularly police repression within the inner city communities were all put forward[447] by many 'social analysis's /sociologists', and other middle class commentators in their semi derived apologies for what was really an upsurge in working class anger, a fight back against years of enforced domination, and a lashing out at all authority. The disaffected, the discontented, the disenfranchised, the downtrodden, the dominated, disbanded and downright delightfully devious arose and awoke in a show of proletarian participation in shared struggle. No longer passive consumers and observers.

The state induced illusion and enforced concept of 'Great' Britain, and it's racist, sexist, and homophobic conditioning of divide and rule was blown to smithereens.

> "The fact that in the summer of 1981, women here were seen in the riots fighting, in however relatively proportionally numbers, alongside men was a memory the spectacle of Greenham Common came to repress.. The temporary defeat of a common enemy – in '81, the cops – develops men and women's consciousness of their *real unity*, their strength & sensitivity, & always wipes out the most superficial hierarchies between men & women, which has been manipulated by ruling morality in order to divide and rule, fragment, isolate and repress. The defeat of the cops on the streets helps to defeat the cops in our heads: In Brixton April 1981, gays fought alongside 'straights', black alongside whites, men alongside women...It is *this* unity that neither misogynist macho-stereotypes norfeminist stereo-type-casters ever talk about because it would mean the end of their 'perfectionist' models of human behaviour."[448]

Tyneside would remain relatively unscathed despite higher levels of unemployment than other 'riot torn' areas. One explanation would state;

> "Some of the most comprehensive YOP (Youth Opportunity Programmes) innovations started life on Tyneside. It was one of the first areas to introduce "21 hour benefits" enabling unemployed youths to attend up to 21 hours of FE (Further Education) without forfeiting their social security. The quantity of experiment particularly to self-interested empire builders connected with the unemployment industry savours amid the theatrical plenitude, of human fulfilment. The area has for Jack G**, trade union NATFHE Liaison Secretary at South M and T College "learned to use unemployment creatively" (!!) But the MSC's Regional Representative for Special Programmes expressed a more disillusioned and accurate view. When asked what was the point of an extensive programme when so many kids will only wind up back on the dole, he answered that, at the least, it prevents violence on the streets.
>
> The YOP strikes in the Tyneside and Consett region experienced during the summer of 1981 helped defuse an anger that could have been as intense as Liverpool. The extensive YOP programmes must have had some impact on minimizing the rioting in the region. In fact the blanket YOP schemes pioneered by these seemingly impregnable Godfather-like Labour party citadels where every unemployed school leaver even in 1980 was within six weeks "offered" a place on a YOP course, must now appear as a prototype that the Thatcher government, in response to the riots, applied to the rest of the country. Even the newspapers were frank enough to admit that unemployed school leavers would now be "under considerable pressure" to take up YOP places by Unemployment Review Officers. The same could have been said of Tyneside, which anticipated under the auspices of the Labour party dominated local state, the national trend by at least one to one and a half

years."[449]

**Toxteth riots,England,1981.** During a lull in the action a leftist militant climbs on to a box and addresses the crowd on the subject of the coming socialist utopia. Her promise that there will be jobs for all is met with derisory laughter from a group of young rioters. As the speaker details other reforms, the group begins a mocking chant,"Bigger cages,longer chains! Bigger cages, longer chains!"

[450]

The riots may have largely by-passed the region, but the Sunderland Anarchists are soon commenting on events;

> "During the summer a wave of riots swept the country (missing Sunderland). As usual the media has provided us with a simplified version of the events, just in case we think too deeply about the issues involved. On one side our brave and overworked bobbies, fighting against violent, petrol-bomb throwing thugs and looters. All of course, blacks and white criminals (not forgetting the anarchists). If we do form impressions its preferably in favour with the forces of 'law and order'. Any reasonably intelligent person can see its not as simple as that. These riots dont just happen every now and then simply to allow people to let off steam, mid summer madness and the like. There are certain contributory factors, many people realise this. After Toxteth, MP's and others spoke of unemployment, bad housing and bad community / police relations. Obviously these factors are significant, but they are not the root cause. When crowds of people, most of whom are normally 'decent respectable citizens', go out on the streets, and take part in a massive demonstration of force, it is not only because they have no jobs etc, neither is it a racial issue

(Southall the exception) It just happens that black people live in these area's. St Pauls, Brixton, Toxteth and Mosside saw rioting and looting by people of all ages and races. Remember the old white man in a wheelchair, looting a supermarket in St Pauls, Bristol?

The riots occur because people have a justified resentment against the way THEIR lives are run. Also against the "system". The government does nothing to alivate the pressures, strain and problems of living in inner city ghetto's. This coupled with police harrassment and general victimisation of individuals doesnt help matters. It only takes a minor incident to spark off a riot. This releases all the frustrations and anger built up inside people. The police obviously bear the brunt for they represent authority & the establishment in general. After all they are the TOOL of the state anyway.

When the smoke has cleared and the debris swept away, the state severely punish a few people to make an example. AN ENQUIRY may be set up to discover the causes of the riots. What a laugh, as if the people did'nt know why they did it, and as if the state is going to do anything about it anyway. Riots should be seen as showing that there is anger and resentment, and anti-establishment feeling in everyone, many of whom are normally unable to express or understand it." And concluding "Riots also demonstrate what ordinary people can do when their rage is united. Its not enough justto beat up a few cops. Its important to make sure the people's righteous anger, your anger, is directed at the real enemy. The STATE and its repressive system. We cant tell you to riot and we dont want to lead you. Your future is in your own hands. FIGHT BACK AND TAKE CONTROL OF YOUR OWN LIVES."[451]

June also sees a report from Sunderland on the groups activities;

"There has been a remarkable resurgence of anarchist activity

> on Tyne and Wear with the formation of the 'Tyne and Wear Anarchist D.A.M.' group comprising anarchists from Gateshead, Newcastle and Sunderland. Comrades attended and leafleted Newcastle and Sunderland T.U.C. May Day marches and demonstrations. The four black and red anarchist banners were a prominent feature of the marches attracting much interest and attention. An anarchist bookstall at the Sunderland demonstration sold a fair amount of literature. Newcastle and Sunderland town centres have been fly posted. The regular production of 'Dutch Wallpaper' posters is being planned whilst anti-royal wedding posters are being 'distributed'. An anti-monarchist leaflet is just off the press and a leaflet specifically for distribution at C.N.D. events is being drafted. A public meeting is being held in Newcastle on 14th July 1981, when DT, D.A.M. National Secretary, will speak on Anarcho Syndicalism. A heartening feature of the Group is the youth involvement. Members of the Gateshead punk band, 'Total Chaos', have associated themselves with the Group and are enthusiastically in the forefront of activity. These comrades produce their own paper, *'No Comment'* and in cooperation with older members of the Group are publishing a leaflet explaining anarchism written to appeal to teenagers. DH."[452]

These leaflets were distributed at Total Chaos gigs throughout the region, and in particular at The Garage. The venue was attracting larger amounts of people interested and open to new ideas expounded by the local individuals and bands involved within the Garage scene. One of such 'Big Toot'[453], possibly alarmed at the amount of young punks turning up at gigs with swastika's adorning their clothing (after the Sex Pistols Sid Vicious was seen to) would also issue a leaflet and article, In the Total Chaos zine *'No Comment'* which was addressed "To the Garage people" and began;

> "Have you ever wondered why you wear anarchy signs? It shows you do not accept the system as it is. Anarchy isn't violence. The minority think anarchy is telling old people to

fuck off and smashing telephone boxes. It is not. Anarchy in the UK would mean living in a free non-violent society. We do not need authority or violence. The two main purposes of anarchy are to free violence from human relationships and to free your mind of the systems control. Don't be misled by police, teachers, politicians etc, who say that in a state of anarchy there would be utter CHAOS and it would be like civil war...This is not true. It is a big fucking lie. The people in power tell you this because they are shit scared of losing their authority and power. They want to keep you down trodden and anarchy threatens their status. Don't be misled by the shit media. Don't notice it. By noticing it you are accepting it is there, thereby giving up. Youth is divided up by the media because they are scared. Punks, mods, teds, etc are all names invented by them so we fight amongst ourselves and not the people in power. Fight the system but don't impose anything on anyone or else you are being a total hypocrite. YOU haven't the right. As soon as you impose anything on anyone you are being authoritive. Anarchy is against all authority. Another mistake people make is to wear swastikas. It might be to shock but the swastika stands for oppression and not punk. The NF are a bunch of heartless morons. They are worse than the police or the Thatcher regime. If the NF were in power we'd all be in the army to serve our use to them... Anarchists would be shot probably. Destroy all forms of power and have respect for the individual but not the system. ANARCHY IN THE UK. BIG TOOT."[454]

The aforementioned DH in the previous Sunderland report is Daryl Hepple, "A conscientious objector in WW2 and a lifelong pacifist, who cut his political teeth in the Independent Labour Party and the United Socialist Movement. Becoming an anarchist via association with CND and the Committee of 100 in the 1960s; subsequently enjoying an almost 30-year relationship with numerous anarchist groups around the country, until his untimely death in 1987."[455]

July, and in another report to *Freedom*, DH is telling us;

> "Clown Prince Charles visited Newcastle-on-Tyne on July 1st. We staged two anti-royalist demonstrations. Six of us were arrested for conduct likely to cause a breach of the peace. Prior to the first demo we had distributed anti-royalist leaflets. Several characters nearby were acting in a bizarre manner indicative of lunacy - heads down, furtively talking to the lapels of their trendy sports jackets. One of these muttering paranoiacs approached and cautioned us. Surprise, surprise, he was a special branch officer. As Charlie passed in his car we shouted sundry uncomplimentary slogans and displayed placards bearing the greetings: Balls to Saint Pauls, Rot All Royals, Stuff the Wedding, Workers Power Not Shirkers Power. We were not arrested. No aggro from the police. Only from a choleric union jack waving middle aged lady. The second demo was staged just as Chuck left the local polytechnic. Again we raised our placards. A tornado of plain clothed cops descended upon us with the charm and finesse of a ferret let loose upon rabbits. Uttering the war cry 'fucking bastards' they seized us, tore the placards from our hands and destroyed them. One zealot in his enthusiasm for legalised vandalism got his hand embedded with splinters much to the delight of a comrade who had been receiving a rough time from this neo- fascist. Manhandled into a quiet side street we were spread-eagled face up against a wall and frisked. Our anti-royalist leaflets, copies of *Direct Action* and other anarchist leaflets and pamphlets were confiscated and not returned. In the wagon en route to the Station permission to smoke was politely requested. This was refused with the added injunction, 'Smoking is bad for your health', 'so are you buggers', replied a comrade. At the Station we were not charged with any offence. Nevertheless we were separated and locked up for two hours. We then appeared individually before two detective- sergeants who said that they had not made up their minds whether or not to charge us. We were then released. As we were being escorted from the Station we were slyly and "without our permission"photographed."[456]

DH would also report the following throughout the national anarchist press;

> "Following an Anti-Royalist demo culminating in the arrest of six comrades Northumbria Police are harassing members of the Tyne and Wear Anarchist/D.A.M. Group. Recently the anarchist punkband 'Total Chaos' distributed an anarchist leaflet at a gig. The police warned one of the band members against further distribution on the grounds that it was conducive to incitement to steal. After the gig the comrade was shadowed by a plain clothed policeman for a considerable period of time. Comrades street selling *Xtra* have also been subjected to police interference. Alleging that the paper was probably seditious they confiscated a copy saying that it would be scrutinised to see if there was anything they could 'get you for' when a comrade raised the issue of freedom of expression the reply was: 'You are as free as we permit you to be. 'During this episode an individual kept furtively appearing and disappearing among the pedestrians snap-shotting the sellers from different angles. A well attended successful public meeting on anarcho- syndicalism was addressed by DT, National Secretary D.A.M. in a Newcastle pub. Prior to the meeting the police pressurised the landlord in an attemptto cancel the hire of the room. A copper's nark infested the meeting. It is hoped his limited intellectual horizon was broadened."[457]

"*Treason: A Local Anarchist Paper* was launched in October 1981 by anarchists living in Sunderland, Tyne & Wear, who were previously involved in the production of an earlier paper called *Communard* which ran to a single issue." Based around the local polytechnic, the editors were soon joining up with other 'locals' in the formation of Sunderland Workers Group, "and subsequently *Treason* was born."

> "*Treason* and Sunderland Workers Group became affiliated to a sub-regional anarchist federation, Tyne & Wear Anarchist Group, which was part of the larger North East Anarchist

> Federation. TWAG was comprised of many different people who chose to work under the broad anarchist umbrella. There were syndicalists and anarcho- syndicalists, communists and libertarian socialists, pacifists and individualists, punk rockers and those who defied description. However, despite the differences, the group was very active; holding public meetings, attending demonstrations, leafleting, paper selling, book stalls and occasionally getting arrested. One notable incident involved an abolish-the-monarchy demonstration against Prince Charles who was performing an official opening ceremony in Newcastle. I think 5 or so of us got nicked. We were held all day and released without charge. A bizarre urban myth developed that HRH personally intervened. Who said the days of royal pardons were a thing of the past!"[458]

*Treason* would only run for one issue, before later changing its name to *Black Star* in 1982. The first issue stated "*Treason* is not a blue-print for revolution, or in fact is any anarchist paper. We are simply offering an alternative lifestyle to the present authoritarian system which runs our lives. We believe that an anarchist society is the salvation of the human race. A free, equal, classless, and self-managed society. The means to achieve this is in our own hands."

The issue included articles on the recent 'riots', 'prisoners & anarchism', as well as a piece on 'crime & punishment' which concluded with the reprinted leaflet ("that deals with theft and was distributed at a gig") from Total Chaos, described as the Gateshead section of TWAG, which states;

> "Easy to say but really hard to do. If you're at school, don't and I must say it again DONT obey teachers and prefects mindlessly. Mindlessly is the key word. Evaluate situations for yourself; think whothe law or rule or orders are advantageous to. For example, think why they ask you to wear uniforms? Could it be that they want to depersonalise you-keep on thinking, I've got a mind, brain, and personality of my own. Just

because someone is older than you or wears a shitty badge it does not mean that should tell you what to so. Don't join in the school games. This is a big con – to make you think in a competitive way. If you win and beat people you are glorified and rewarded in the forms of medals and certificates. This is artificial. You don't really want to run around a field to 'win' a piece of metal. It's all part of the system which makes some of us winners and most of us losers and all of us mindlessly satisfied. If you are on the dole – make sure the bastards behind the counter be-little-you if the queen can get millions off the state why the fuck shouldn't you be entitled to a measly £20 a week? – In fact, if we did away with the queen and her hypocritical parasites – people on the dole would get twice that amount. Remember when you sign on that's your money. You are entitled to it. This world is a shit place fora young working class kid on the dole and that's because of the people in power, therefore the world owes you a living so keep fucking asking for it. Don't obey crummy little laws – if you're genuinely hungry and you need something to eat go to a big supermarket and take it because that is also yours. Will it make any difference to the fat London capitalist who owns 33 Tesco stores whether you steal a mince pie? If you are hungry and the fat capitalist isn't then that pie doesn't belong to him it belongs to you. Keep on spray-painting – if you work you pay tax and your parents and some of you pay taxes. Therefore most of the buildings around you belong to you, so fucking cover them with as much graffiti as you want. Say fuck to church. Say fuck all authority. Say fuck to all exploiters. Believe in yourself – adopt an anarchist stance. It's your life NO-ONE ELSES so let's all be self-righteous. Don't be taken in."[459]

Beautiful in its naive simplicity, but remember that this was written in 1981 by young punks from Gateshead housing estates, embracing and endeavouring to articulate their flowering rebellion - not learned anarchist philosophers.

Virtually running parallel to each other was the founding of both the Gateshead Music Collective (GMC) in October 1980 and the Sunderland Musicians' Collective (SMC) in September 1980. Although the collectives were not anarchist by name, they certainly were by their nature and un-hierarchal structures.

> "In 1981, the council gave the SMC the lease on a room situated above the council's community garage at 60 Borough Road, Hendon. It was an empty room, which suited us. The SMC formed a committee and put on benefit gigs at the local Art College and various pubs and clubs to raise funds for materials. The local media became interested in a bunch of scruffy punks and other misfits who could organise themselves into a DIY collective. The Sunderland Echo and Tyne Tees Television did articles on the SMC, so when the council's Environmental Health department said they were closing us down for "excess noise", we had already had positive media exposure. When we went to meet with local councillors, we were organised, and we put our case to the Education department. Our plan was to try and encourage other community groups to share the building, and the council offered us the upstairs of a Victorian school.
>
> We painted the walls of the main hall in camouflage style, and got some fishing nets from the docks. Then someone said: "it looks like a bunker." The name stuck.
>
> It comprised four large classrooms centred around a main hall, with two smaller classrooms on the upper floors. We rented classrooms to various groups, including Ford and Pennywell weightlifters, Sunderland Youth CND and Springboard Drama Group. The main office would be the base for the Sunderland Musicians' Collective and what would become the Bunker Collective."[460]

The first gig at The Bunker was later, in September 1982. Over in

Gateshead, the GMC were now meeting at the town's main library and approaching the council for premises and other various 'trusts' for monetary help. "The council came up with the Police Club beside the council buildings. The main aim of the collective is to provide rehearsal space and recording facilities at a very cheap price. It is also hoped that by the start of next year that gigs can be held at the Police Club with bands playing for nothing and admission being cheap."[461] Hence The Station was born. ""Ironically enough, after their first venue was shut by the police, the Gateshead Gig Collective ("After hassling some local council suits") relocated to The Station, which was actually the old Gateshead Constabulary clubhouse!"[462]

Both venues were prominent in the emerging 'anarcho-punk' scene developing locally and nationally at this time with many fine bands playing both The Bunker and The Station. Not only would they be a place of music, they would become a place of meeting with mutual ideas and emerging communication with like minded individuals, especially for the increasing amount of 'youth' feeling alienated from an everyday life of 'non-existent work', pressure to conform to society's expected standards, pressure to obey, to create a happy nuclear family, to get a mortgage..TO BE NORMAL!!!

> "The atmosphere at these gigs was amazing. It changed a lot of punks in Sunderland. We had already seen Crass and a few other anarcho-punk bands, but for young punks who couldn't get into gigs, this was their first chance of seeing these bands live. So it was life-changing for young people to feel safe at a gig, to hear the music that mattered to them and be able to be part of an event. People would stay behind at the end of gigs to help out with the tidying, humping the groups' gear back into vans, and most importantly meeting the bands. None of the anarcho-punk bands were like pop stars. They were different; they always had time for the fans. With no interference from adults, it must have seemed "too good to be true" to some – and our ranks swelled. After four months of gigs and events, the Bunker committee had grown. More people were taking

> part in the general running of the building, not just the hardcore group of us who had been there from the beginning. At the second Bunker AGM on 15 November 1982, 34 people turned up, 15 of the attendees were girls (only one girl had been involved at the first AGM in January). We always wanted a large and diverse group of people to run the project; the committee wasn't just punks either, it was made up of all kinds of musical tastes."[463]

Lifelong friendships, solidarity, communication and co-operation between the Tyne and the Wear, against the expected norm of division and regional difference between the two were now taking place. "Anarcho-punk led to more friendly relations between our neighbours from Newcastle and Tyneside. Before it was still that stupid football tribalism that stood in the way of our getting to know people. They had the Garage in Newcastle, and then the Station in Gateshead, and we all would support each other's venue. Punters started turning up from all over the country and, by the time we had established the Stockton Road Bunker, punks were moving up to Sunderland to live."[464] And of course, this further increased the numbers within the regions anarchist groups for years to come.

Days of Hope bookshop was attracting media attention with its selling of *'Towards a Citizens Militia – Anarchist Alternatives to NATO & the Warsaw Pact'* "Coun. Derek Conway, Tory leader on Tyne Wear Council, said he would be taking up the sale of the book with the government and Chief Constable of Northumbria, Mr Stanley Bailey. The book *Towards a Citizens Militia* was bought by Coun. Conway in the Days of Hope bookshop, in Westgate Hill for £1.50. It contains sections on principles of armed resistance, organisation and conduct of guerrilla warfare and organisation and operation of the civilian resistance movement. The book is published by Cienfuegos press, with addresses in Orkney and Michigan, USA. Coun. Conway said the book included information on organising unrest, physical violence, sabotage and ambushing vehicles. He said *"It is unbelievable that they can peddle this rubbish and it is hardly surprising that the police are facing well organised attacks with literature such as this available." "Towards a Citizens Militia* subtitled *Anarchist Alternatives to* NATO & the Warsaw Pact', is thought to have been written by Stuart Christie[465], a leading anarchist. The Home Secretary Mr William Whitelaw has already said police are investigating an allegation that the book is subversive. One bookshop worker said he felt Coun. Conway just wanted to make political capital by attacking them. "but it would be at our expense we have had threats before" he said."[466]

The next day's media response, under the title of 'Author defends riot book' would state;

> "An anarchist's handbook on sale in Tyneside may have been usedto direct recent riots, its author said yesterday. The Police Federation said they were certain the book, or others like it, had been used by riot organisers in Liverpool, Manchester or London. Tyne Wear Tory leader Coun. Derek Conway bought *Towards a Citizens Militia* in Newcastle's Days of Hope bookshop. He wants the book banned. But a spokesman for the Director of Public Prosecutions Office said the book had been examined last year and they were not taking the matter to court. The £1.50 publication shows how to ambush airfields, fuel depots, power stations and security force vehicles. It details ways of sabotaging cars, disabling guards, caring for firearms and fighting security forces clearing mass demonstrations. Author Stuart Christie came to prominence during the Angry Brigadeanarchist's trial and was the subject of last night's Radio 4 Profile Programme. He told The Journal *"It's entirely possible it may well have been used. People should be in a position to defend themselves."* Mr Christie added he was disturbed by the looting and criminal damage which had accompanied the recent disturbances. *"We certainly wouldn't withdraw the book if it has been used by rioters; it is the only way out as far as they are concerned."* He said. A Police Federation spokesman said they were against banning such books but there was no doubt that extremists of both Left and Right had used such

> publications to work out riot tactics and strategy."[467]

Albert Meltzer would comment "There is nothing remarkable in the book except that it takes seriously the possibility of people defending themselves against aggression and outlines methods of resistance. Indeed one might ingenuously think that it would accord with current Tory monetarist thinking, in dispensing with the need for an expensive Government-controlled Army and showing how one can, without cost to the generality "do it yourself". That thinking's all right for Education or Health, not for the sacred cow of Defence!"[468]

Stuart Christie defending the "reason for publishing *Towards a Citizens Militia* at this time" would tell us "we believe there is an alternative to the threat of nuclear holocaust or worldwide genocide as a result of chemical and biological warfare, from both East and West, and the alternative is one of a citizens defence force along the lines of the Yugoslav, Swiss and Israeli models. An organised and defended population would be a lot more difficult for an aggressor to subdue than a professional elite subject to all sorts of class, political, and personal interests – After all, it's now the 40th anniversary of De Gaulle's call to the people of Occupied France to disregard the Petain governments surrender to the Nazism and continue the struggle against the invaders. Perhaps if the peoples of Europe had been organised in Democratic Citizens militias the rise of Fascism, militarism and all the attendant horrors of war, genocide, torture, then the history of the 20th century and the future for civilisation would have been a lot healthier." Before concluding "I, as a publisher feel very strongly that it is my civic duty to defend those few democratic freedoms we have left and I feel that there are many more people who would feel the same if and when faced with tyranny and injustice."[469]

This wouldn't be the end of the saga as;

> "A Newcastle bookshop has received bomb threats after publicity over an anarchist leaflet sold there, according to a councillor. The threats to the Days of Hope bookshop in

Westgate Road were revealed during the council meeting by Coun. Steve Cohen (Lab). The leaflet *Towards a Citizens Militia* was denounced recently by Coun. Derek Conway, Tory leader on Tyne Wear. Coun. Cohen said he hoped Coun. Conway would also condemn members of the National Front who had threatened members of the bookshop staff and people wearing Federation of Conservative Students badges who said they were going to bomb it."[470]

In a letter so far removed from actual 'events on the ground' so to speak, froma BJD of Newcastle, published in *Freedom*, tells us;

"As someone who has only recently come to take a personal interest in anarchism I've been surprised at the lack of articles by anarchists to be found on the subject of feminism/women. Having come to anarchism academically (like many today from what I can gather), I soon concluded anarchism to be the oft quoted doctrine of the absurd as regards large scale social change. Having said that I have not found myself in agreement with those critics who, though not without some anarchist sympathy, consider it to have nothing significant to contribute to socialist theory except for its critiques of authoritarian socialism and the dangers of bureaucratization — in other words nothing positive. It appears to me that it is just where anarchism can make most sense that it has had very little to offer, i.e. as regards the relations of women and men, women and women and men and men. For an 'ism ' that concerns itself so, rightly with the individual it is incredible" that so little writing is to be found on personal relations —surely the basis of any useful social theory. Yet there is a bulk of literature to be found on themes like the State."[471]

Perhaps if BJD was to actually contact and talk to existing anarchists in the region at the time, instead of 'observing from an academic high horse' then he could have been educated on the vast amount of literature dealing with the "relations of women and men, women and women and men and men".

The contacts section of *Freedom* at this time listed both Sunderland Anarchists /DAM at Durham Rd, Sunderland, as well as a new entry of Tyne and Wear Anarchist Group / DAM Thomas St, Ryhope, Sunderland. I do believe this was the same group of anarchists in Sunderland. Monetary contributions to *Freedom* include the regulars DH & AD (Sunderland), GD (Gateshead), NB & PML (Newcastle), and a new contributor of JW (Thornaby).

After a mass march by CND in London, some sections of the anarchist press were full of letters debating the pros and cons of 'heckling' and the whole concept of marching as opposed to more of a direct action stance at the time. This doesn't concern our history here, other than as a conclusion to 1981 and the publishing of a letter from Jarrow, Tyne & Wear. The letter states;

> "As someone who has recently become interested in anarchism and one of the thousands on the CND march in October, I wish to give my observations to the 'Rally Debate'. Many letters have attacked the so called rowdies and chanters. Well just for the record, I'll throw my lot in with them any day. Their contribution to the rally was the most constructive thing all day. This was also the belief of the large group of punks and skins I was standing with, as well as nearby 'straights '. As far as anarchist literature was concerned, there was no shortage. I managed to buy *Freedom, Xtra, Black Flag, Direct Action,* and *News from Nowhere* and picked up a leaflet from as far away as Glasgow. (Reckon the person from the Glasgow book collective must have fallen asleep along with a hundred thousand others.) Next time round I'd like to see the anarchists go a step further and take over the platform and call for the marchers to march on the MOD and have a sit-in, 250,000 people would be quite effective. Although it won't abolish the bomb it's a start, and a damn sight more positive than listening to bloody Michael Foot and Co. Best Wishes, John, Anarchist punk and school student"[472]

The year would end with an interesting letter from Durham, regarding previous pre World War 1 'Syndicalist' struggles in the pages of Direct Action.[473]

## 4.3 1982

The year begins with local anarchists busily preparing for the forthcoming North Eastern Anarchist Federation conference to be held in Sunderland. The current sectariat for the NEAF, namely Doncaster, South Yorkshire, would advertise;

> "The North Eastern Anarchist Federation has just entered its second year since being restarted. Its third conference was held in Sunderland, on the 13th March. The NEAF have groups in Newcastle, Middlesbrough, Sunderland, Leeds, Hull, Huddersfield, Askern (Doncaster) and Keighley. We are also in contact with comrades in Bradford and Sheffield where it is proposed to hold our next conference in September. We are involved in many activities in the north east and several of our groups publish local papers; *Angry* (Hull), *Seditious Whispers* (Doncaster), *Kaos* (Middlesbrough), and *Treason* (Tyne and Wear). We would be pleased to hear from any isolated comrades or groups in the area who would like to maintain contact with the NEAF and attend future meetings. We would also like to hear from any other regional federation in Britain with a mindto exchanging information and contacts."[474]

AD is also recalling events (and wrong date) "Organisationally, 1982 was a big year. In May Sunderland hosted its first major anarchist conference in the East End Community Centre, close to the Town Moor, venue for the town's annual May Day rally. Earlier in the month TWAG (Tyne Wear Anarchist Group) had a large contingent in evidence at the said rally. A fine display of a least a dozen red and black flags was a stirring sight to behold. I also ran a successful bookstall, selling a wide range of anarchist titles, mainly from Cienfuegos and Freedom Press."

"The conference was attended by around 60 delegates, observers and guests. Attendees hailed from Newcastle, Gateshead, Sunderland, Middlesbrough, Darlington, Keighley, Hull, Leeds, Doncaster, Huddersfield and London. Messages of support from comrades in Spain, Sweden and the United States were also read out. The conference endorsed commitment to the revolutionary overthrow of capitalism and the ensuing class struggle. From a publishing point of view a wonderful array of journals was on offer: *Treason* (Sunderland), *Angry* (Hull), *Seditious Whispers* (Doncaster), *Kaos* (Middlesbrough), *Common Cause* (Darlington), *South London Stress* (Brixton), *Black Flag* (Anarchist Black Cross), *Anarchy* (Anarchy Collective) and *Freedom* (Freedom Press). Following a conference decision *Treason* was expanded, and would now be produced by TWAG as opposed to exclusively Sunderland Workers Group. Along with editorial changes came a name change. A historic day indeed, *Black Star: Paper for Independent Working Class Organisation* was born. Ironically, comrades from SWG were delegated the task of editorship, with input from the wider group. The editorial group numbered about 6, and became known as the Black Star Collective.

*Treason / Black Star* had always been a very broad based publication with a mish mash of ideas and themes which reflected its diverse membership. At times it appeared to have no real identity or direction. Issues 1-6 contained articles which covered mainstream issues such as CND, militarism/war, racism, nuclear power, police brutality, crime and punishment and rioting. Classic texts from Kropotkin, Berkman, Bakunin et al were also reproduced, along with a lot of anarchic 'smash-the-state' type rhetoric. Workers struggle and class warfare were merely paid lip service. Reports on industrial action and left-opposition in Eastern bloc countries occasionally appeared, but these were few and far between. Syndicalist orientated

> input never really got beyond another anarchist obsession of extolling the virtues of the CNT, the Spanish anarcho-syndicalist union. The papers content was in general terms, organisationally and theoretically weak, with little analysis and a naive grasp of the essence and concept of class struggle. Again, a reflection of the diversity of TWAG at the time."

Of course, it is easy for AD to look back with hindsight, later writing in 2003 to 'pick faults' with what was, during the period of the early eighties, an influential paper for many during the period. The author himself continues on the 'mindset' of the time;

> "The papers seemingly apparent obsession with CND, anti-war issues and racism, can, I believe be explained by the political climate of the day; the Thatcher years, war in the South Atlantic, rejuvenation of interest in CND, peace camps and a general rise in xenophobia."[475]

The 'state', alarmed at the level of discontent, riots, rebellion and other forms of autonomous resistance to capital and wage slavery occurring throughout its empire, despite its attempts at divide, rule, and seperation would, as hinted at previously before World War 1, enter a new phase of creating nationalistic fervour and patriotic fallacy with the onset of the Falkland-Malvinas War (2 April – 14 June 1982). Just what capitalism needed – instill a bit of national pride back into our daily exploitation. We can sell more arms back to Argentina after they have utilised the supply we supplied them after firing on 'our boys', and did somebody mention the prospective undersea oil fields in the area?

The conflict began on 2nd April, when Argentina invaded and occupied the Falkland Islands, followed by the invasion of South Georgia, in an attempt to establish the 'sovereignty' it had claimed over them. "If we were unprepared, how is it from next Monday, at only a few days notice, the Royal Navy will putto sea in wartime order and with wartime stocks and weapons?... preparations have been in progress for several weeks."[476]

> "After 1981, the show of State power in the South Atlantic not only made death seem attractive, not only made sacrifice seem brave, not only demoralised the massive rage which clearly hoped for a qualitative extension of the '81 riots into '82, not only demoralised millions into an overwhelming sense of retreat and helplessness, but based this intimidation on the horrific sense that if they can get away with that they can get away with anything."[477]

The conflict lasted 74 days and ended with the Argentine surrender on 14 June, returning the islands to 'British Corporation Control'. In total, 649 Argentine military personnel, 255 British military personnel, and three Falkland Islanders died during the 'war', and it is said, would be instrumental in the winning of the next general election by Thatcher. There is nothing like the scent of victory on the battlefield to boost parliamentary proceedings and procure support. A stench of death permeates the ballot system of supposed democracy. A senseless slaughter for victorious votes. Absolutely Vile.

April would also see a letter from Tyne & Wear Anarchist Group / DAM commenting on, previously suggested, ideas in the production of *Freedom*. Amongst many points raised, a few worthy of note are "that what is needed is an agitational paper which could act as a news network concentrating on meetings, action, strikes, international information and calls for support. This should, in the main, be written in a short to the point style. If this was the case then the occasional longer, detailed background article would be welcome. We believe that this is an important point if we are to create a movement inthis country (yes, we do want a movement). For too long in this country the political philosophy of anarchism had been treated as a joke and many of those who tend to call themselves anarchists but who are just playing at it, should stop getting in the way of those who want to get on with the real work." And concluding;

> "We feel that if *Freedom* cannot fulfil the need for a paper on which others can assess the state of the anarchist movement in

> this country then another will, and *Freedom* will then become just a name in the history of anarchism in this country. If your answer to all this is that you can't be 'all things to all people' then why not start producing a paper for anarchists?"[478]

Of course criticisms of this letter would follow, including comments such as "I would like to dissociate myself from the current wave of criticism of *Freedom* coming from these barren northern wastes, especially as a few 'democratic centralists ' in the NEAF seem motivated by a desire for their opinions to be voiced as the collective judgement of us all" And "Besides the cloud-cuckoo land aspect there is also the prolier than thou attitude in these letters—an obsession with strikes, demos, action. Talk about Rent a crowd! And no smilingplease, because according to Tyne & Wear, the revolution is too serious a business."[479]

Despite perceived minor frictions between the North East and *Freedom*, the monetary contributions to the papers funds would continue throughout the year with those from JW (Thornaby), PC (Bishop Auckland), MB (Darlington), GD & BH (Gateshead), JW (Middlesbrough), and PC (Durham). The contacts section would list Cleveland - Liverton Crescent, Thornaby, Also produces *Common Cause*, local anarchist paper.' And later at Box A, c/o Victoria Road, Middlesbrough. Sunderland would remain contactable through *Black Star*, Thomas Street, Ryhope, Sunderland.[480]

The Newcastle Anarchist Group was now contactable through the growing Newcastle Anarchist Youth Group (NAYG) at Priory Court, Gateshead. The group was developing alongside regular gigs at The Station, and meetings at Gateshead Central Library with the Gateshead Musicians Collective. The anarchist meetings would soon move to the back room at the Nags Head pub on Gateshead High Street. They are soon advertising "Newcastle Anarchist Youth Group requests info, news views etc, to be used in the production of a SERIOUS Anarchist paper for youths, from all groups and individuals etc, especially from the north east."[481]

Newcastle Anarchist Youth Federation, with a contact of MP, Grosvenor Place, Jesmond, Newcastle, which I believe are related to NAYG in Gateshead would release an A4 double sided typed leaflet during this period entitled 'Self Determination For The People of The World' and began;

> "Firstly, contrary to popular belief, anarchy is not chaos, violence or destruction. We are led to believe that we need authority to maintain society. If authority disappeared we are told there would be a breakdown in society and there would be violence. It must be stressed that this is not true. Anarchy is a viable constructive alternative to our present system/society, which is not based on competition and violence. Anarchy is order, natural order, not the enforced order, which is really State-imposed disorder. Anarchy is unity, pure liberty and strength in oneself. It is the means whereby people will realise their own potential and individuality, thus begin torule their own lives, without any political leaders. On a practical level it is the means by which the workers take over the factories, where, at present they have little or no control. The alternative is anarcho-syndicalism which is a practical theory based on workers control over their work, i.e. by means of workers councils escalating to committees headed by workers representatives, who are compelled to recall if they unsatisfactorily represent the electorate. This theory has become a reality e.g. Spain 1936 with the agricultural collectives and industrial syndicates."

The leaflet carries on in the same vein, looking at different aspects of society from an anarchist viewpoint. "The media is nothing more than a conditioning, propaganda machine which is controlled by the state. It creates barriers and instigates violence." Pop stars, politicians, parents, and property are also analysed in a short to the point style. Sexist roles, education, militarism, patriotism and religion get the same treatment, before concluding;

> "The worker is the slave to the capitalist system. The worker

does not reap the benefits of his own labour. The capitalist management use the proletariat and reaps the benefits. The capitalist system is founded on profit and not need, whereas the work should be based on the needs of the community. In a truly humanitarian society the production and manufacture of goods would be run on a totally co- operative basis as a collective. There would be no need for bosses but there would be a need for more organisation, through workers councils and a much more co-operative approach to each other.

We are a group of young people who disagree with the present system and feel an urgent desire to change it, to create a better society, based on mutual co-operation and trust. Above all, EQUALITY AND FREEDOM. Our aims are to educate people, through talking and leaflets, and to provide a viable alternative to modern life under authority. We would like to create a better understanding of Anarchism, a practical socio-political idea, especially to the young.

Pay no attention to the representatives of state control. Put more emphasis on personal control. It's your life, no-one else's, live it now. The individual must take control of his or her own life, then he/she can reject the state. This must come from confidence in oneself. ANARCHY IS THE REJECTION OF THE STATE. As man seeks justice in equality so society seeks order in anarchy. Government is tyranny, so anarchy is liberty."[482]

The advent of cheaper travel, hitchhiking, etc also increased levels of participation by anarchists from the North East in other cities throughout the country, from conferences to marches, peace camps to gigs, and especially anti-fascist call outs and counter demonstrations. One example being;

"Over the weekend of June 5th-7th members of the Direct Action Movement, the North East Anarchist Federation and the South London Anarchists took to the streets of London in several demonstrations. On Saturday 5th a picket was placed by NEAF on the Soviet Embassy at Palace Gate, North Kensington. The picket which was in support of the Russian anarchist Arkadiy Tsurkov[483] lasted for over an hour and was supported by both NEAF and DAM members." And on Saturday 6th "a group of over 200 anarchists many of them members of the DAM led the Waterloo section of the CND march to Hyde Park. This march which was led by the NEAF banner received great attention from the various police and press photographers along the way." Much to the annoyance of CND officials who asked police to remove the anarchists from the rally. "The anarchists who had now swelled to over 500 decided to march down Oxford St in protest against the murder in the Falklands. This march which was quite peaceful was attacked by large numbers of police from the SPG (Special Patrol Group – or 'riot police') near Bond St tube station where a street battle took place between these persons trying to protect the anarchist banners & flags from being damaged (the NEAF banner was damaged and the South London banner was lost) and the cops. Many comrades were injured by police batons & 48 comrades were arrested and charged with criminal damage, assault & obstruction. A defence committee has been formed to defend the "Oxford St 48"."

The weekend of action would conclude with "On Monday 7th members of DAM, NEAF & South London Anarchists took part in demos outside the American Embassy protesting against the visit of Reagan to Britain. Only one black flag was present as police stopped all persons carrying black flags & took their names & addresses before telling them to get rid of their flags or be arrested. This was in marked contrast to the great number of banners from the pathetic left."[484]

In what looks to be a letter regarding the recent protests in London, MB from Darlington is commenting;

"Dear Comrades, 'Brique Leflic' and 'Benvenuto

Baldelli' (*Freedom* 12.6.82), among others, illustrate beautifully what happens when anarchists tail end protest movements. When they inevitably find it is leading nowhere they suddenly find they are lost, particularly if the captive audiences provided by the priests and professors are not obeying the empty calls to 'direct action '. It has been a constant complaint of anarchists that the politics of protest are bankrupt — but still they go on the marches and the demos until in frustration they end up by accident or design, in sterile confrontations. Onlookers ask pointedly—'is this what you mean by direct action?' Ifsitting on the grass in the sunshine can be criticised as just 'doing something', then exactly how much more effective is getting your head kicked in by the SPG—10%, 30%? The only serious practical threat to the state's war preparations comes from the prosecution of the class war. That means taking the bosses and their minions on in struggles over homes money and day to day survival; the only thingsthat matter to the great majority of us. NO MINORITY can do that on behalf of the rest. It will only happen when things get intolerable, materially or otherwise, and that can't be predicted. All we can doas a minority is to argue our case, show the connections, spread the word, use our imagination, struggle for ourselves and raise our consciousness together. The rest is bullshit, anarchists playing at 'leaders' under a false banner of 'direct action', telling the 'apathetic masses' what they 'ought' to be doing—in other words doing exactly the same as all the other politicians." no wonder no one listens. This sort of 'anarchism' is just protest with knobs on, entertainment for Scotland Yard, mild amusement for the passing throng who bother to stop and look."[485]

Over the weekend of 26 & 27th June, "The Direct Action Movement held its second conference of the year in Leeds. Comrades from Newcastle, Hull, Leeds, Huddersfield, Manchester, Burnley, East Anglia and Doncaster were present. A general discussion was held into industrial organisation and syndicalism, it was agreed that there was a need for pamphlets to explain the DAM position on a number of particular issues, the conference agreed to the publication of a pamphlet before the next meeting in the autumn."[486] The North East delegation was the Newcastle Anarchist Group, who also took part in a later meeting to set up the co-ordination of national anti-militarist groups, under the banner of 'Resistance'.[487]

*Black Star* are also advertising their latest issue (5+6) with articles on: CND — the debate continues, Tyneside Soviet -1980, Multi-Nationals, and Are you man enough? plus lots of other local news and views. "*Black star* 5 & 6, a double issue, upped the stakes by announcing in its editorial, in the most categorical of terms – 'In view of the escalation of state attacks against working people the editorial policy of the paper will be moving towards a more class-struggle stance'."[488]

AD from the *Black Star* Collective is also writing within *Freedom* at this time with an update on the case of Arkadiy Tsurkov and the nationwide growing support. A mention of a leaflet produced by the Black Star Collective highlighting the case is also mentioned.[489]

Another conference was held by "the Direct Action Movement-International Workers Association who held their final conference of 1982 in Leeds over the weekend of the 30th October. The conference, which was the best attended fora number of years, had delegates from Burnley, Manchester, Huddersfield, Hull, Middlesbrough, South London and Leeds DAM—IWA groups. There were also a number of comrades from the North East Anarchist Federation, Newcastle Anarchist Youth and the Doncaster Anarchist Group present."[490] This increase of activity would further flower into the next year...

## 4.4 1983 THE STRIVE TO BE FREE

In what was to become its penultimate issue, *Black Star 7*, with its lurid pink cover "further declared its intention with a large banner headline on the front cover, 'Direct rank-and-file control of the struggle is the road to workers self- management of society'. Part of a Syndicalist Workers Federation pamphlet on workers control was reproduced, an article on the workers revolt in Szczecin, Poland in 1970 and a series of short items on various workers struggles around the world appeared."[491] The issue would also look at the aftermath of the Falklands conflict, 'to strike or not to strike', 'Electro Convulsive Therapy' and 'the State as murderer', which interestingly concluded;

> "Where the State is concerned, murder is a crime in theory only – verbally condemned but widely practised for economic and political purposes and impossible to eliminate until the State itself is destroyed." "No longer does the State have to rely on relatively crude methods of repression which characterised earlier tyrannies. Advances in science and technology have provided a whole range of sophisticated instruments of repression for those in power – and they threaten us ALL. 'Domestic' genocide is a reality for too many people TODAY and the threat of nuclear genocide between nations remains a distinct possibility on a scale that will make Hiroshima and Nagasaki seem mere child's play. As long as the States retain control independent of the people our very existence is threatened."[492]

This 'distinct possibility' of nuclear holocaust was a predominant factor for many during this period, especially when America began the implementation of stockpiling cruise missiles at their bases throughout the UK. Delicate relations between American and Russian capitalists in their eager strive for world domination, control of its resources, and their sickening lust for power would fast forward the possibility of the planets destruction.

The state in its efforts to dominate and influence every aspect of our daily lives would also make moves for more of a control of the airwaves. How dare we listen to what we wish? Spring 1983, and "New legislation on pirate radios is about to be introduced. Soon illegal transmission could mean a £1000 fine as well as prison sentences. During the last couple of weeks the cops have made raids on several radio stations, including 'Our Radio' (London) which has an anarchist hour."[493]

Some from the Bunker collective in Sunderland would host Persons Unknown radio, and a participant gives a fascinating insight;

> "The idea started in spring 1983, M from Community Arts in Hendon spoke to the Bunker committee about us having a station to promote the local music scene and the Bunker, M had helped us from the beginning with the Sunderland Musicians Collective and the Bunker, he had connections with some pirates, so arranged a trip to a pirate radio conference in Sheffield, you had to be invited to these things, as you just couldn't turn up, what they were doing was highly illegal. We were given our introduction and attended workshops over the weekend, only then could we purchase the equipment we needed. We decided not to do live broadcast as this was too risky, so we pre-recorded the programme in the studio at Community Arts. We agreed on our broadcast frequency should be as close to Radio One as we could 89mg-htz, Radio One was 90mg-htz, this would block out their top 30 chart show anywhere where we would broadcast from. Our first test run was from Tunstall Hills in Sunderland just outside the town. The equipment was a car battery, transmitter, tape deck and aerials, the tape recorder was started and we left the scene, keeping a watch with binoculars from the next hill, the rest of us got in a car and drove with a radio on to see how far we were transmitting, fuck, it was miles. No one came to stop us. So

from then on we started broadcasting from summer 1983, we never broadcast from the same place twice, the GPO, the Radio Licensing authorities and Police would be hunting us down, we broadcast the show from the top of tower blocks to friend's attic flats. We had a P O box so people could contact us, send us tapes and requests, the show built up a following in Sunderland, we let other people who came to the Bunker to pre record their own shows and the Radio station went to 2 broadcasts a week, Thursday and our slot on a Sunday, this would be a 90 minute show, with one of us having to go back to the transmitter to turn the tape over. This went on for over a year until late summer 1984 when a group of younger punks decided to broadcast from the same position for maybe 3 or 4 weeks. Of course they were caught, with the confiscation of all our equipment and the lad's record collection from where they broadcast from, we held a benefit gig at the Bunkerto pay the fines, but we had succeeded in blocking out the charts for over a year, with our brand of music and political sedition."[494]

The forthcoming May Day marches, general election, propaganda, conferences, anti nuclear and other activities, etc were keeping local anarchistsbusy. Early March, and anarchists in the Darlington area are advertising "Darlington election farce. Some of us hope to become involved in the farce at Darlington and we would be grateful for any idea and/or material. Also if there are any comrades in the far North who want to help...c/o Ia Box A, Red & Black Bookshop, Victoria Rd. Middlesbrough."[495]

Late March, and an amusing group report by IA in the pages of *Freedom* informs us;

"The farce at Darlington continues apace. We have been doing the usual – fly posting, leafleting etc, but what has really got up the bastards noses is the 'Darlington Free Radio'! At the present time this only consists of a beaten up old megaphone, but it has been very effective. Our inaugural broadcast was at a

Foot[496] rally which was attended by over 1000 people. We set up our outside broadcasting unit (a broken down Fiat) outside the hall. Apparently nice Mr Foot was in the middle of his rousing electoral address when we went on the air. The audience immediately burst out laughing (or so we're told) and took no notice of nice Mr Foot's speech. (He was lost and couldn't regain his audience's attention, until he remembered the magic word – unilateralism, whereupon the passive hacks rose from their seats and cheered the great leader). We remained on the air for two minutes urging people not to vote etc. All this time our outside broadcasting unit was under attack from the party thugs, and as it was only borrowed from a friend we decided to retreat. However we did return twice more to disturb the proceedings.

At our next broadcast we made a great tactical error. The occasion was the Labour Party march to highlight the closure of the Shildon Wagon Works. We started off alright and the crowd was very attentive. However within 30 secs we had 20 to 30 party hacks threatening to lynch us. The words that upset them were, 'Don't vote Labour as they are a pack of hypocritical parasites'. Some of the thugs comments were rather illuminating:- 'This is not a political issue', 'We have marched all over the place without any trouble until you lot turned up', 'We want to keep politics out of this', These and other comments were relayed to the crowd, as we continued broadcasting. This upset the hacks even more.

Although they were the ones who were screaming abuse, trying to relieve us of our radio, flags etc, it was we who were threatened with arrest if we opened our mouths anymore that day. Talk about Russia! Even though the press were present in abundance, we can guarantee that not one word will be printed about our demands for freedom of speech; that this is how dissidents the world over are treated. Keeping our mouths shut we attempted to leaflet the march as it disappeared up its own arse, but again were threatened with a thumping. The Labour Party does believe in freedom and democracy!

The campaign continues, but we would urge, in the run up to the general farce that all comrades obtain a 'Free Radio Station', because as that rat Rodgers said, 'We have free speech in this country', but would he let us have a go of his megaphone. Would he fuck!"[497]

March also see's DM of Middlesbrough defend a few publicised criticisms of the DAM after it was expressed previously that they were 'unable to progress beyond the 1936 Spanish experience'. DM, a long time contributor and participant in the regions DAM activities would respond;

"The Dam hasn't progressed beyond the '36 Spanish experience? What a red herring. Dam members live and work in Britain 1983, their ideas reflect that. It's not a matter of spending your time reminiscing about the Spanish Revolution. It's just one important part of our propaganda. One of the concrete examples of anarchism in action. Workers controlling industry and the land is important. The people armed are important. Aren't they? Then the Spanish experience and its lessons have to be publicised among British workers and learnt from. Its symptomatic of the British 'anarchist' movement that some of it thinks that anyone who was literate and lived before 1968 is a 'nineteenth-century wanker', while others spend their time in a time-warp around 1921 or 1936, and yet others are pedantic pseudo-theorists. What a circus." And further stating on the dislike of the DAM in some quarters "a disorganised, too much precisely because that organisation is about what anarchism really is and not the parody some would like it to be."[498]

One of a few responses to DM would state;

> "He may suggest that a woolly-minded and irrelevant anarchist movement is not going to like an anarcho-syndicalist organisation because that is what an anarchist organisation is all about. I would say, that not only is it an elitist statement but the NEAF & NWAF (North East & North West Anarchist Federations) are also other forms of anarchist organisation, and the only ones that do not seem to be stagnant. I would also suggest the reason that some people hate the DAM is because of certain people's insistence, and fanatical rantings, on building a mass movement before any real action could be taken, instead of going out there and trying to put their argument to the workers, All the time and not just during a strike. The DAM could be an excellent organisation if the talkers did more action and they 'got rid' of the small group of trot minded people."[499]

May and Newcastle Anarchist Group were reporting their activities;

> "Just a short report of our actions during Anti-Militarist Week (14-21 May). On 14th May we went around shops that sell war toys handing out anti-militarist leaflets. On 16th May we distributed leaflets outside army & navy careers offices and job centres, and on 18th May sprayed the doors of the Territorial Army, as well as a tank and army tractor, with anarchist and peace slogans. We haven't come to a stop with the end of Anti-Militarist Week and are planning future actions."[500]

May also see's the final *Black Star* produced in the region with the release of number 8 as an A3 free two sided broadsheet. "The last issue! After a short life of a year, launched as *Treason* in Nov '81 the collective have now gone on to Black Star Book Service whose literature can be obtained from Red & Black Bookshop, Middlesbrough."[501]

> "We had hoped to build a strong anti-authoritarian / statist, libertarian, class struggle orientated grouping based around the paper. The paper being an organisational focal point and a

platform for action. Unfortunately time has shown that this was not meant to be; a painful, disillusioning, and frustrating experience. The time had now come to take a positive, critical and analytic look at ourselves, the paper and our own regional political environment. Many questions were raised; did we really justify our own existence or were we merely advertising our existence as revolutionaries to ourselves? Had we achieved our original objectives or even gone part of the way to doing so? Had we done justice to the libertarian communist cause and the anarchist ideal?

Other less complicated and practical problems had also to be brought into perspective: the ever declining number of people involved and willing to get involved in the collective. The ever-present shortage of funds, these being necessary to hold our ground in the turbulent arena of social democracy, authoritarian socialism and reformist trade union politics. All told we had to face reality, so according to the general consensus of opinion the decision to cease publication was taken. Production of a final issue was deemed in order as it was felt we owed it to our readership if not to ourselves."[502]

This would not be the end of the story for *Black Star* as it resumed publication after two of the collective, DH and AD relocated to the Milton Keynes area.[503]

The region was also given a mention in *Black Flag*, when "The plaque commemorating the Royal opening of the Tyneside £14 million Redheugh Bridge was damaged within hours of the ceremony."[504] Looking at the plaque today, it has continually suffered ever since.

A further mention of the Cleveland Anarchist Group talks of more disruption to local election meetings, minor confrontations with local police and special branch and "Our star moment was when a 'solitary anarchist' heckled and ruined the Roy Jenkins meeting, thereby achieving nationwide fame on 'Newsat Ten' and TV am (not forgetting the local rags) suspiciously aliased as 'Peter Black'. Following this the pigs had a message in the local paper saying that they would be taking measures to counteract the secretive Middlesbrough based anti-election campaign idiots."[505] The group also gave mention, and 'adverts' were starting to appear for *Strike Back* (later to be called *Strike*) which was the agitational free bulletin of the local Middlesbrough DAM.[506]

The local contact for the DAM[507] paper *Direct Action* in Newcastle at this time was GJH, who was also the secretary for the Syndicalist Alliance. This groupingof 'revolutionary syndicalists' were keen to emphasise;

> "One thing we would like to clear up now is our situation now in England vis a vis other libertarian workers groupings. We are a propaganda and an education league, and we have no intention of threatening the existence of other organisations, like the anarcho- syndicalist DAM or the industrial unionist IWW (Industrial Workers of the World). Quite the contrary, we hope to work with these brother organisations where possible. We are not geared to recruitment in the same way as they are."[508]

Although not specifically anarchist, or even anarcho-syndicalist the group produced an interesting *Bulletin* and various leaflets. Issue 2 of the *Bulletin* contained a short history of the IWW, an article on the nature of the IWW, a couple of pages titled 'Roots of militancy; A piece of class heritage and local history', which was basically a reprint of a longer pamphlet by Dave Douglass entitled *'Pit Life in Co Durham, Rank & File Movements and Workers Control'*. An article 'On Anarcho-Syndicalism' which was a talk given by Sam Dolgoff in Canada 1980. A letter on 'councilism', and an interview with Swedish Syndicalists of the SAC.

In their leaflet 'Giz a job not a bomb – a syndicalist perspective' given out at Newcastle march's under the same heading of 'Giz a job...etc' the group showthe link of unemployment, capitalism, nuclear threat and the causes.

> "We must change the whole basis of society to guarantee a

> future of peace and a world without wars. Therefore, the existing system of world capitalism must be abolished. The struggle against nuclear weapons is the struggle against the warfare state. Whilst having great sympathy with the Greenham Common peace women and similar we feel the fight against nuclear weapons can only be effectively conducted by an organised working class. As syndicalists we advocate direct industrial action – strikes, go slows, blacking, non-cooperation and sabotage by those workers involved in the manufacture, development and transportation of nuclear weapons and sympathy action by others."

Concluding on unemployment;

> "We view the fight against unemployment in the same light as the struggle against nuclear weapons. Ultimately we must eradicate the root causes, i.e. the system of wage-slavery and capitalism. Replacing it with a society based on direct democracy and self management; collectivisation and federalism – a society where labour, production and distribution is socially motivated and geared towards need and not profit. We don't want 'a fair days pay for a fair days work' we want to reap the full benefit of our labour. We want to see an end to exploitation, wage-slavery and capital. In such a society the spectre of unemployment will never manifest itself."[509]

## SYNDICALISM, REVOLUTIONARY SYNDICALISM, ANARCHO- SYNDICALISM...A BRIEF EXPLANATION

Having already mentioned the terms syndicalism, revolutionary syndicalism and anarcho-syndicalism numerous times, I believe a brief explanation[510] of their differences is in order. These three strands of syndicalism, sounding the same, have existed in semi-alliance with each other since the term was coined from the French 'syndicalisme', which basically translates as 'trade unionism', yet the terms do differ in certain aspects which further adds to minor confusion in local study of the various groups under the syndicalist banner. For example, the Syndicalist Alliance, previously just mentioned, classed themselves as revolutionary syndicalists, and the soon to come in our history Tyneside Revolutionary Syndicalists were, despite the name, an anarcho-syndicalist grouping.

Syndicalism can be used as a simple term of rank and file, organised trade union activity. "The syndicalist union is a parallel organised structure, not a vertical structure, the power will always remain in the hands of the members, they are the ones who shall decide when to strike, when to negotiate. Naturally such a union is bound to be much more militant than the collaborationist unions."[511] Where this syndicalism differs from that of revolutionary and anarcho-syndicalism, is that the members of the syndicalist union in question are more concerned with the well being of its own members whilst striving to achieve political and economic gains as opposed to creating a long term view of the reconstruction of society as a whole. Many syndicalists of this nature were predominantly members of parliamentary political parties.

The revolutionary syndicalists are those 'seen' to have taken the next logical step from basic syndicalism. Revolutionary syndicalism is based on the conviction that all problems in society are caused, and are the result of the formation of political parties and the governments they form. The revolutionary syndicalist rejects all political parties, no matter how socialist / communist / liberal they appear to be, and the government or state dictatorship that is created from this parliamentary fallacy. The revolutionary syndicalist believes in the class war, and see's the economic field as the main arena to wage this war upon. "To the revolutionary syndicalist the union was all important and the working class must be organised inside these economic combative organisations. Their struggle was directed against capital and the state."[512]

Despite the perceived struggle 'against capital', local revolutionary syndicalists, such as the Syndicalist Alliance seem happy to work within the framework of capitalism with their proclamation of;

> "Our immediate demands to alleviate some of the problems and pressures on unemployment must be:- A shorter working week / complete overtime ban / a national minimum wage / a reassessment of 'new technology' / job sharing not wage sharing / campaign for higher benefits and greater social facilities / the creation of a national federation of unwaged workers groups. These demands must be implemented and organised by ourselves, through the collective decision making of workers committees of recallable delegates, independent of political parties, trade union officialdom, state and management."[513]

Unlike basic syndicalism which "rejected preparing for workers control or using direct action, but sought parliamentary backing",[514] or revolutionary syndicalists who concentrate solely on the factory as a means to the revolution, anarcho-syndicalists believe in involving the whole community as well as the workplace in the creating of a new society which will benefit all included. Anarcho-syndicalism "combines the more relevant aspects of syndicalism and the revolutionary aspirations of anarchism."[515] Anarcho-syndicalism has a central "focus on the need for workers and the community to collectively control and transform the work process."[516] This would be the predominant aspect in any attempt at the reconstruction and change of society. The anarcho-syndicalists do not want to seize control of capitalist industry to 'manage' it better, but rather, as Rocker shows throughout his writings, anarcho-syndicalism is a programme based on the abolition of capitalism and the re-organisation of the whole community based on the concept of social-self management, which on a larger scale encompasses benefits for all in society.[517]

August 1983 and anarchists in Teesside were also producing Northern Star, a 2 page broadsheet which included articles on the 'elections', 'fascists', 'religious nutters' and 'police brutalities'.[518] The Newcastle Anarchist Group were producing a range of leaflets on the 38th anniversary's of the atomic bomb being dropped on the city of Nagasaki (9th August 1945) and the earlier Hiroshima devastation (6th August 1945).

A further leaflet was produced for the Sunderland, Stratford Ave, section of NAG. This was on 'CND and the state'. Others produced during this period were 'You and the Law', 'the real meaning of May Day' and 'Why Vote?' which emphasised;

> "This is to counter the current campaign by the various political parties for the forthcoming council elections. The various leaflets you have probably been receiving over the last few days will differ in context between each party but are basically the same; in all cases another person is "representing" you, when in fact the only person who can represent you, the individual, logically is yourself. The promises made by these people are merely a ploy to give politicians the power to control the lives others. Think about how much your vote actually says in the running of your life within this society. Once the party you have voted for is elected you have no further say in what they do. It's all very well criticising the political system but what alternatives are available you may ask?? It is possible to peacefully coexist with each other, without restrictions imposed upon us by government, as an example; the workers, instead of being exploited by the management, could run places of work themselves; i.e. workers councils / co-operatives, without the hierarchy of the trade unions. Why should this idea stop at

work? Why can't we run our own lives without the authority of the government? WHY VOTE? TRUE DEMOCRACY FOR THE INDIVIDUAL CANNOT COME ABOUT THROUGH GOVERNMENT."[519]

The local press were also taking an interest;

> "Anarchists yesterday gave peace campaigners a rocket after being thrown off an anti-nuclear demonstration. Nine youngsters from the Newcastle Anarchist Group were told by march organisers they would not be allowed to carry their banner, on a city centre protest to commemorate the dropping of a nuclear bomb on Nagasaki in 1945. When the group tried to join the tail end of the march – without their banner – a policemen told them they would not be allowed to take part. A spokesman for the group said: *"The police said the march organisers had asked them not to let us join the march. It's absolutely disgusting. These people ask for solidarity and support and then turn us away."* The march, organised by the Tyneside for Nuclear Disarmament and the Greenham Common Support Group, attracted about 50 people. It was led by 12 women dressed in black pushing empty pushchairs with placards bearing the names of children who died in Nagasaki. BS, one of the organisers, said the march was intended to remind people of the horrors of nuclear weapons and the need to stop the arms race. *"We weren't aware any group – such as the anarchists – wanted to join the procession. We wanted this to be a march totally dedicated to Nagasaki Day and not a mass rally."* She said. *"I did not realise* the police had told the anarchists they could not join the march.""[520]

The financing of worldwide wars in the Middle East, Southern Africa etc, and the threat of further conflicts forever present on the horizon, "Meanwhile, the major banks of the USA and Western Europe are imposing vicious cuts on the working and peasant people's living standards in the Third World." "Much of this rapidly deteriorating situation can be traced back to the financial institutions based in the industrially advanced countries, which provide a billion pounds or more a day to finance military expenditure, and in whose interests most wars are fought. 'The City' area of London is one of the major centres of these institutions. In the light of this situation, there are plans to STOP THE CITY on September 29 1983. This is the day when profits for the summer are reckoned up. It is a chance to show that the will of the people is stronger than the institutions of war and destruction."[521] Local anarchists would attend these, and subsequent further 'Stop the City', events in both London and later Leeds.

The Newcastle Anarchist Group are also beginning to advertise their compiling of a group library, "donations, leaflets, papers wanted. They have also put out various leaflets on Hiroshima, police bill, etc."[522] Self education as opposed to oppressive and indoctrinating state education has always been an important factor for anarchists groups in the region. Towards the end of October the library is now listed as being contactable through Wingrove Rd, Newcastle as opposed to Priory Court, Gateshead.[523] Not only would the library list an impressive array of libertarian literature (eleven a4 pages long), internal detailsof the role and duties of the librarian, as well as pages on the role of the library itself and guides for how to borrow a book. The group also produced 'Secretarial duties and format of meeting's of the Newcastle Anarchist Group'.

A lengthy guide to 'a few well known anarchists or libertarians' with biographical sketches some 9 pages long was also freely available and included Arshinov, Bakunin, Berkman, Bookchin, Borkenau, Bourne, Comfort, Courbet, Durutti, Eichenbaum, Godwin, Goldman, Goodman, Guillaume, Henry, Herzen, Kropotkin, Leval, Makhno, Malatesta, Walter, Morris, Orwell, Pelloutier, Proudhon, Read, Spooner, Stirner, Thoreau, Tolstoy, Ward, Tucker, Wilde, Woodcock, Christie, Graham, Magon, Meltzer, and Berneri. A guide to anarchist literature held at Newcastle Central Library, and which section it was located in was also internally publicised. Another internal document entitled 'What anarchists believe', which covered what anarchism was, a look at 'state and class' and 'liberalism and socialism' was also produced.[524]

Another group was beginning to meet during this period. Unnamed at first the group eventually decided on Anarcho-Syndicalists (Tyne & Wear). After a cancelled British National Party march through Newcastle, 10th September 1983, the group was instrumental in proposing a 'broad based non-sectarian group' to monitor and co-ordinate anti-fascist activity in and around Newcastle as "there is still appreciable fascist activity in Tyne & Wear, from stickers and slogans to paper sales and racist attacks and harassment." The letter to interested parties also stated "I would hope that groups and individuals who participated would do so simply as anti-fascists, rather than seeing such a group as an opportunity to sell their respective political literature or recruit people into their own organisations."[525]

Further fortnightly meetings to the remainder of the year would discuss involvement in unemployed workers groups, local strikes – including the decision to take two bottles of whiskey down to Westoe Colliery, South Shields to share on the picket line of a local NUM (National Union of Mineworkers) dispute, and anti fascist activity.

The group also received an invitation to re-join the DAM and it was decided "a), no interest in rejoining DAM at present, but solidarity with any activity in accordance with our aims & principles, b) we are not the Syndicalist Alliance, c) an invitation to a future meeting (DAM Leeds)." Further discussions centred on pressure for better books at Days of Hope bookshop, and proposed films atTyneside Cinema.[526]

December meetings decided upon the need to produce some literature. It was agreed to discuss this further in the forthcoming year and decide what format, frequency of production, content, costs and price etc. Members of this grouping would eventually become the nucleus of Tyneside Revolutionary Syndicalists and produce *The Syndicalist* (later *The Tyneside Syndicalist*) newspaper which ran from late 1985 to winter 1987, and will be covered in due course.[527]

1983 would also see an explosion of local zines produced. Some were political, some were not, some educational and some barely readable. Some just concentrated only on punk bands and their music, whilst some were poetry and article based, but all were important for the communication networks they were part of and adhered to, with a strong emphasis on 'Do It Yourself' underground culture.

A few notable zines during this period include; B41984 (Sunderland), would you like an enema? (Darlington), 1st, 2nd, 3rd *edition* (Newcastle), *Total Protest* (Newcastle), *Our life our world* (Newcastle), *Testament of reality* (Darlington), *Stepping out* (Newcastle), *Hate & War* (South Shields), *No Comment* (Gateshead), *Under the net* (Newcastle), *Pyrrhonic* (Newcastle), *Have a good laugh* (Newcastle), *Still Dying* (South Shields), and *Acts of Defiance* (Sunderland).[528] "There were more fanzines in The Toon (or even Sunderland!) in the early eighties than there are in the whole of the UK today"[529]

*Acts of Defiance* informs us, whilst doing a regional round up of gigs and other events that during a benefit gig at The Station "Newcastle Anarchist Group made about £70, which will probably be used to print the next batch of leaflets, or go towards buying some badly needed literature."[530] Again this shows the inter-connecting links and mutual co-operation between the local punk 'movement' and the local anarchists, especially during this period.

1983 ends with Teesside Anarchist Group informing us;

> "Nuclear energy: It'll cost the earth. Nuclear power, like nuclear weapons can only bring death and destruction to the world, at first the working people of the world. Nuclear power is not a cheap source of electricity. Power stations are built at high profits – at our expense. Employing few workers, once built, nuclear reactors are easily controlled by Governments looking forward to the day they can do without troublesome coal miners and other workers in the power industry. A primary

reason for nuclear reactors is to provide the raw material for nuclear bombs. The Government plans to dump its nuclear garbage under Billingham, a direct threat to the people of Billingham and the generations to come. Oppose the plans; organise to build a better safer world."[531]

## 4.5 "What are we going to be doing now its 1984?"[532]

Nationally, and anti-nuclear protests were on the increase, with for example; in Berkshire, RAF Greenham Common has now become a permanent home for thousands of people, and in particular women protesting at the stock piling of (American) cruise missiles at the base, and similarly at Faslane Peace Camp a permanent peace camp sited alongside Faslane naval base in Argyll and Bute, Scotland, where camp residents regularly breach the security of the naval base by getting inside the fence, canoeing or swimming into the base, successfully disrupting the road transportation of the Trident missile warheads by blockading the two gates etc.

Locally, and Newcastle Anarchist Group are still active and contactable at Priory Ct, Gateshead, and Middlesbrough DAM and the Teesside Anarchists are contactable through Red & Black Books, Victoria Rd.

In a letter to the national anarchist press, PR[533] of Tyne & Wear is writing;

> "After an absence from politics of almost four years I read your last edition of *Anarchy* with pleasure and excitement. You have helped to renew my commitment. I did, however, see various letters with which I became enraged and disgusted. As a male anarcha-feminist and committed anarcho-syndicalist I must protest in the strongest terms at the letter of 'Alf' who writes, quote "There is an almost total lack of debate in the Anarchist movement. Pacifism, syndicalism, feminism, are in ascendancy,

all in my view totally irrelevant to the advanced capitalism which we in Britain live under." First of all the oppression of half the human race by the other half is not "irrelevant". The struggle of women is a subject which all anarchists should be involved in, regardless of sex. To anarchist women freeing themselves from male oppression is seen as the primary front upon which they struggle. It's no good keeping the fight against sexism till after the revolution. It's got to be fought here and now, on a personal, as well as political level. I have noticed since my return to the British anarchist movement from Canada and the US, a lack of commitment on the part of male anarchists to the struggle against sexism which verges on sexism itself.

As an anarcho-syndicalist I also take exception to being called part of an "irrelevant" movement. 'Alf's' views of "advanced capitalism" seem to me to be a cop-out in order not to be involved in day to daystruggles. Anarcho-syndicalism is still the industrial wing of anarchism and the fact remains that so long as the majority of the population of the world are wage slaves, so long does anarcho- syndicalism have relevance. Of course, world capitalism has changed since the beginning of the century but this still does not negate to the syndicalist organisation and methods of struggle. They may not be perfect but they're the best we've got."[534]

The letter continues with encouragement for the creation of a British Anarchist Federation to 'co-ordinate all anarchist activity in the fight against Thatcherism and the state'.

The year also begins with local anarchists busily preparing for the forthcoming North Eastern Anarchist Federation conference to be held in Newcastle. The current sectariat for the NEAF, namely Sheffield, would advertise "A conferenceof the North Eastern Anarchist Federation will be held on the weekend of 4th and 5th February in Newcastle. Anarchists from Northumbria, Tyne & Wear, Co Durham, Cleveland,

Yorkshire and Humberside are welcome at the Bridge Hotel on the Newcastle side (North) of the High Level Bridge, and starts at noon on Saturday. A discussion paper has been circulated."[535] I can find no other report of the outcome of this conference.

Early 1984 also saw the final issue of Sunderland zine *Acts of Defiance* with number 8 being a double sided free a4 sheet explaining its ending. Subtitled 'the magazine for the converted' it went on to explain how current zines, anarcho bands etc were all repeatedly 'preaching to the converted' over and over again with their messages of anti war etc. Now was the time to 'get out of the anarcho ghetto' so to speak and begin to spread our ideas further afield. "Although we may have had some impact on a few people, the audience of fanzines is generally far too limited to allow any real impact to be made."[536] Other projects beckoned, The Bunker, and Housing Co-op etc. "Unless we start to think again about what we're doing and why then we will remain isolated, lone voices shouting hopelessly in the dark." And ending on a more optimistic note with "but despite all the problems we must overcome there is still hope. As long as you believe in change then change can come."

Another leaflet distributed during this period, produced by 'The Anarcho- Hopefuls, North of England', would echo similar sentiments of defeating isolation and constructively enabling anarchist groupings to function more effectively. Entitled 'Are Anarchist Groups Self Defeatist?' the leaflet would firstly give a brief description of what anarchism is before analysing the role of the anarchist grouping within the struggle. "The anarchist group may play a big part in your fight against the state (an anarchist group could never, by itself, change the state) and this just may or may not start the ball rolling onto bigger and better things, if people are prepared to work for it."[537] Further advice is offered to anarchist groups on how to not fall into apathy, failure, disinterest, and lack of communication, whilst offering minor solutions. A leaflet slightly ahead of its time in certain aspects.

March, 1984 and a letter from Middlesbrough DAM, whilst debating previous raised points in a letters page about support for industrial struggles and anarchist involvement would conclude "As anarcho-syndicalists we know that we must wrench workers' allegiance away from the reformist unions and the only place that that can be done is where the workers are in struggle, in the workplace, in conflict with the employers. That is why we involve ourselves in workers' struggles and do not stand on the side-lines like cartum comrades."[538] Without 'wrenching' workers away from their union, this natural solidarity and anarchist support and involvement would become precedent during the recently begun miners' strike.

> **EARTHWORKS**
> **The Newcastle Anarchist Group has produced its first issue of a paper entitled *Earthworks.* Contents include an article on the Tyneside Unemployed Workers Union, Retrieving North East Anarchist History, Mental Hospitals, May Day & more. 10p from *Earthworks, PO Box 10, Forest Hall, Newcastle upon Tyne.* Stamped Addressed Envelope / Donations no doubt appreciated.**
> ***Source: NEAF Bulletin July 1984.***

Some of the Newcastle Anarchist Group are producing a magazine at this time called *Earthworks*. Issue 2 would contain lengthy articles on '1910-1912: The workers fight back', 'Social control in schools', 'the use of troops as strike breakers' , 'Joseph Cowan – a Tyneside radical', 'Mutiny at Kinmel Park', and 'Labour scabs' which interestingly highlights how; "The Labour Party was supposedly set up, or so we are told, to fight on behalf of the working class in parliament (a thing that could never work out), a sort of working class political arm. This however is a lie, the Labour Party are part of the Elite that manipulates and exploits the working class and defends Capitalism with every chance. The Labour Party could never defend the working class against the harsh conditions of society as it is the capitalist manifestations that create the worsening conditions and it is the Labour Party that defends Capitalism. It is the working class and only them that can defend themselves against the state machinery." Numerous examples of Labour Party hypocrisy are then given including war time support, nuclear bomb making programmes, as well as support on the side of oppression during the 'troubles' in Northern Ireland, etc etc.[539]

"We had to fight the enemy without in the Falklands. We always haveto be aware of the enemy within, which is much more difficult to fightand more dangerous to liberty."[540]

*Earthworks* No 2 would also contain a current analysis of the, then beginning, miners' strike, some of which is produced here at length in order to give an insight of local anarchist thought during the period, not to mention local historical posterity.

> "The miners' strike has been going on now since June. Since that time the State has done all it can to undermine the strike, what with the publicity, the total abuse of laws and use of the D.H.S.S. etc. Thisis a political strike they scream, of course it's a political strike, it's theworking class versus the state.
>
> The strike began way back in June with Macgregor being sure of an easy victory, thinking that the miners had no fight left in them to strike. Stocks of coal had been built up since 1977 when a productivity agreement was pushed through between the Labour Party and the N.C.B (National Coal Board), this was an agreement that the miners were totally opposed to and they voted against it. Even though the agreement went ahead, coal stocks which had beenbuilt up made Macgregor feel even more sure of a victory, he could very easily sit out a long strike. These coal stocks are getting very very low now and Macgregor has lost control, he is putting his foot in it left, right and centre.
>
> When miners at Cortonwood Colliery heard of the decision to shut the Colliery down within four weeks (they had been earlier told that the pit had many years of mining left) the miners took immediate action. As soon as the strike began there was a massive media campaign which was to call for a democratic National Ballot, thiscall had nothing to do with democracy but

to try and separate miners from their own solidarity and so try to stop the increasing power of the strike.

Miners have been offered redundancy payments of £1,000 per year in the mining industry. Nice if you are nie on 60 and at pension age. That job is not for selling, it does not belong to one person and they have no right to sell it. When a job is lost that is it, there is nothing left, no future work for the unemployed and the young. Macgregor does not have time on his hands anymore, it is now rapidly approaching the dark and cold nights when lights are lit most of the time and fires are burned through the day. His coal stocks will very soon be non-existent. Macgregor is getting so worried that he has been sending personal letters to miners appealing for them to return to work. This has been a total failure and made Macgregor look even more of a total fool than he had already been seen to be. The miners cannot win the strike alone, there can only be a successful victory when the working class stand shoulder to shoulder against the state.

Pits in the North East coal field have been closed down for years. Since 1947 181 pits have been closed. These have closed by not one government but two, it is not all down to the big bad Tory Party, and there have been almost an equal amount of pits closed with the loss of around the same amount of jobs by that so called working class party (sic) the Labour Party.

In 1947 until 1959 there were 38 pits closed with a loss of 17,977 jobs. This was not all Labours doing, but it was they that started the ball rolling, they were ousted from power in 1951. 1964 once again saw the Labour Party in power; by 1965 they had begun to close pits. By 1969 they had closed down 66 pits and put 46,831 miners out of work. This was to be the largest amount of pits closed in one period in the history of the North East coalfield. In this period the rundown of the coal industry is very similar to todays.

Today the Tories feel that Nuclear Power is the fuel of the future (despite the dangers), there will be a smaller workforce who will have been vetted on numerous occasions so a less likely chance of disruption from the workers. In 1965 the fuel of the future was to be oil which the Labour Party felt was cheaper. Coal powered power stations were converted to oil. After oil producing countries raised their prices and the oil crises led to a three day week power stations were converted back to coal. The working class having been manipulated once again by a capitalist government.

In 1975 the coalfields of the North East were once again attacked from a Labour Government. On this occasion 10 pits were closed with a loss of 3,918 jobs. During this period the Labour Party launched the 'Plan for Coal' and Tony Benn the then Energy Secretary not only supervised it but also launched the plan for nuclear power, giving the go ahead to the building of many more nuclear power stations. As has been already mentioned in the nuclear power industry there is a less likely chance of disruption of the workers and if there is a threat to production it can be quite easily handled as Tony Benn showed when he smashed a strike at one power station by threatening to send in the troops.

The Labour Party are calling for a National Ballot and condemning violence on the picket line, they don't actually believe all the stories in the media, do they?, they are also calling for talks and negotiation. There is nothing wrong with talks taking place between the N.C.B. and the N.U.M as long as what they are discussing is the terms of the N.C.B.'s surrender. Up until that time talks are unwarranted.

Throughout the strike the media coverage has been totally biased (it will always be so when the papers are controlled by capitalists), with reports of violence by striking miners both on the picket line and in the streets. We are not saying that this violence by striking miners is not true, that would be wrong of us but what we are saying is that the striking miners are not the only culprits. Striking miners have been brutally attacked by both police and miners that are working on numerous occasions. They have been the target for mass intimidation, harassment and slander. The media have done a good job in making the miners look like some sort of barbarous animal while on the picket line and on their own streets they have suffered the mass activities of the police.

541

> **Miners being chased by police at Orgreave were confronted by *Workers Power* members and asked "do you want to buy a paper?"**

Miners on picket lines have been savaged by dogs, trampled by horses, and smashed with truncheons about their body and head, kicked and punched in frenzied attacks by police. A few months ago a policeman was shown viciously attacking a picket on the Orgreave picket line (must have been a mistake from whoever was editing the film), the picket being smashed around the head with a truncheon. The officer was finally named a few weeks later (he was from Northumberland force). He was not charged with anything; in fact they said it was all in the line of his duty as the man may have been armed with a knife. This total stupidity and naiveness shows the police for what they really are. This attitude now leaves the police with a free hand on the beating up of miners.

Photographs of police beating miners have been taken on numerous occasions but they have never been shown in the capitalist press. Striking miners and their families have received threatening phone calls and letters, been threatened with violence etc. Families have received phone calls when their sons or husbands have been out picketing saying that they have been fatedly injured or killed on the picket line. Intimidation from the police has come in many forms. The mass police presence on the picket lines is obviously the most blatant.

While on picket duty miners have had to put up with police standing in front of them waving wads of money accompanied with the words, "look what I'm getting for being here scum", this list is endless and with things such as this going on who can blame the miners for losing their tempers. In their very own villages miners have been harassed by the police. Road blocks have been set up, homes raided and physical violence. Whilst towns have been taken over in the form of an occupation, and a sort of martial law implemented with miners not being allowed to move out of their homes. The following happened in the village of Fitzwilliam; *'Riot police terrorised the local community in search of a striking miner who was wanted for suspicion, a nonexistent charge. Locals came out on the streets in support of the man and around 200 people surrounded the nearby Hemsworth Police Station demanding to know why the miner (BC) was being harassed. The people left and dispersed when an inspector assured then that BC would not be arrested if he agreed to voluntarily go to the police station the next day. Later that night around 80-90 police dressed in riot gear raided a local pub to try and capture BC. While they were in the pub they went crazy and beat up locals that were inside the pub at random. That night members of BC's family were raided.'* The following came about in the village of Blidworth; *'250 police raided the homes of striking miners. Roadblocks were set up throughout the village and it came under the state of siege for three days. Many strikers from other area's who were staying in the village were beaten up by the police. Miners tried to take sanctuary in the village hall from the violent attacks by the police. When the police found the door of the village hall locked they battered it down to get inside. The village hall is where miners support group ran a food kitchen from.*

Soldiers have been used for months during the strike though Leon Brittan[542] denies this. The fact is that miners have spoken to their sons and relations on picket lines when they are supposedly serving with the armed forces. On one occasion a miner spoke to a relative who was supposed to be in Northern Ireland at the time. Leon brushes this aside by saying, it was a case of mistaken identity, the man is crazy. A few months ago photographs were taken of a soldier driving a police van; Leon said that this was a bomb disposalunit. The state still maintains that it has not as yet intervened in the strike. This is sheer stupidity on their part, we are not that naive. From the above we can see that this suggestion is ludicrous not to mention the letters which were printed in the *Daily Mirror*."

The state sanctioning of miners benefits and 'strike pay' was looked at beforemoving onto picketing, where;

"The mass picketing of the steel plants, coking works etc has failed abysmally, with the only outcome being a few smashed heads and a few arrests. The mass pickets have turned into battlegrounds between police and miners. The mass picket in its form being used today is a thing of the past, it may have worked at Saltley in 1972 where 15,000 pickets successfully confronted 800 police and closed the coke works down but times are different now. Since 1972 the numbers in miners has diminished to around two thirds of the number in 1972, miners also have the problem this time round of not having full support for the strike and having to picket pits in Nottinghamshire. The numbers of police have greatly increased since '72 and they are also much more highly trained and experienced in riot control. There is a much greater co-operation between police forces, with odds stacked against the miners like this how do they hope to win a picket such as Orgreave. If the Saltley picket was re-enacted today 15,000 pickets would set out, half that number would arrive to picket and be faced with a police presence of equal or higher numbers. These police would be highly trained, have dogs, horses and riot gear. The aim of picketing is to halt a workplace and stop production; it is not a confrontation with the police. Mass picketing is used when requests for solidarity are not adhered to and the numbers are needed to successfully bring about the aim of the picket. Once the police are in great numbers they can easily control a picket line three times the number of themselves.

A successful picket is not where 8,000 pickets are defeated by 3,000 police but rather when 200 pickets outmanoeuvre the police and shut down a place of work. As the police are able to respond very quickly in numbers the best tactics would be to shut a place down for the day on a one off basis. This would stop production at a factory for a day and leave police tied up outside it for a few days for fear of another picket. This would leave the way open for another area of work to be picketed. With the numbers of pickets on a mass picket such as Orgreave taking this type of action hundredsof places of work could be shut down for the day. This would not only stretch the police numbers and resources but would also throw them into total confusion. Where there is a situation such as Ravenscraig and huge numbers of coal filled trucks are crossing picket lines another form of action could be used. This has already been used during the strike but for different reasons. So far motorways have been brought to a standstill when miners have abandoned their cars on them en mass. This could be used to block the trucks getting to Ravenscraig and the like. This would also tie upa large number of police while miners got on with other things. The mass picket is a thing of the past there aren't the numbers it would take to win, and even if we did get the numbers the police would stillhave the water cannon, tear gas, political volunteers and the army to use if need be. We must out think the police and use new tactics if we are to win.

Contrary to media reports concerning solidarity shown to the miners there has been massive support shown from other workers (though not enough as yet) with the seamen refusing to carry coal, dockers refusing to let it in or move it, rail drivers and lorry drivers refusing to transport it. Unions have collected a list of scabs who are moving coal who will be blacked from working after the strike. Workers throughout the country have shown their support with financial donations. When coal was moved from the docks in July by scab labour the dockers lost no time in coming out on strike. Though they returned to work a few days later the support shown was greatly needed. In future nothing will be moved from the docks by scab labour and no coal will be moved for the duration of the strike. The action of blacking must be extended to ore, oil and every other material that is keeping big business operating and so keeping the state with a full deck of cards to play. Action must be stepped up to ensure a victory and the best way to achieve this is to refuse to handle anything that may undermine the strike. The country must be tied up. Support for the miners has been shown on an international basis with financial contributions and letters of support coming from many different countries including Germany, Spain, Australia, etc etc. Since the strike began the Australian seamen have refused to move coal and gave a £10,000 donation. This is the type of solidarity that is needed in this strike by every worker in the country, for a failure in the miners' strike will surely represent the downfall of us all.

The mining industry is a way of life, communities will be obliteratedif the strike is lost, thousands will be put on the dole queues (already over 5 million) with no chance of future work. Children growing up will have no future of work, industries that supply the mining industrywill be severely affected and so on, a union which was one of the most militant will be smashed (which is what the government wants) thus leaving the way open for all other unions to come under attack. The whole of the working class will be affected if there is a failure, we cannot contemplate defeat, and everything in our power must be used to ensure a victory for the miners which will be a victory for us all. THE MINERS FIGHT IS A FIGHT FOR ALL THE WORKING

CLASS!!"[543]

Meanwhile the announcement that Japanese car manufacturer Nissan were to open a plant in the North East is met with some local celebration, and, in what is unmistakeably Albert Meltzer's writing in *Black Flag*, with reserve.

> "How is Japanese capitalism to "save" Tyne & Wear? North East England is regarded favourable territory for colonization because of its 'good labour relation'. Naturally, with the huge rate of unemployment, deliberately fostered by the government as a matter of economic policy, with enforced idleness leading to total desperation of ever working again, 'jobs' are welcomed, strikes are avoided, wages are at a minimum and 'good' labour relations prevailed." "The Japanese workers meanwhile have their livelihood threatened because no sane capitalist is going to employ them when there is a pool of colonial workers the other same side of the world where the capital is provided for the sake of turning up and taking it – unless of course they will work for considerably less, as they will have to."

The article would end with an appeal on behalf of the current Anarchist Black Cross campaign "Don't forget solidarity comrades. K. Omori the Japanese anarchist facing the death penalty and appealing against this threat to his life by the State needs support. Protest telegrams, phone calls, letters should be sent to the nearest local Japanese embassy."[544]

Local Middlesbrough Anarchists are also taking up the fight to 'Free Omori' and tell us "Omori is a Japanese anarchist under sentence by the Japanese authorities. He has been convicted of the bombing of a government building on extremely flimsy evidence; the Japanese press has contorted thus. The main evidence is that Omori possessed the items involved in the construction of a bomb...are sugar, a radio and batteries. Very dubious uncommon items indeed." After addressing other aspects of Omori's case the leaflet concludes;

"In Japan there are believed to be about 50 people under death sentence. Executions are carried out swiftly in secrecy with relatives being informed afterwards. Omori has been convicted wrongly and unless we act quickly his death is imminent. If you call yourself an anarchist do something."[545]

"Following the announcement that Nissan had chosen a site in Washington New Town for its car plant, the Tyne & Wear Council offices placarded a huge WELCOME NISSAN WE LOOK FORWARD WITH YOU TO SAVE TYNE & WEAR."[546] We also thank you for bringing us un-unionised work culture, slave shift systems and monotonous drudgery of the production line. We also thank you for giving those troublesome miners in the area the offer of segregated, dog eat dog employment to curb their proud militancy. We thank capitalism for your existence whilst your mother country executes its innocent civilians.

April 1984, and in the sheer joy of creating temporary autonomous spaces local anarcho punks would squat the old Robert Kelly Coal Merchant buildingin the centre of Gateshead at High St West, for the purposes of putting on an all day gig. "I helped to organise this gig, me & S found the empty building and checked it out, lots of people worked together to do it. Was just a fuck you sort of carry on to the government, showing we could do what we wanted, was lots of squat gigs around that time in unusual places - Barnsley one was goodn all. We could have used the Bunker or Station but just thought why not do a squat gig, nothing more to it than that really."[547] Local anarcho bands, including Reality Control, Blood Robots, and the Famous Imposters played alongside those from further afield from Yorkshire, namely, Chumbawamba and the Passion Killers. Friends remember nearly blowing up petrol generators with candles, cutting carrots by candlelight for the shared mass vegetable stew,smokey fumes, near darkness, and the visit from a lone policeman who was disinterested in the proceedings.[548]

Asked whether the gig was put on for any 'political reasons'?

> "I really can't remember other than there were the zigzag squat gig and later the Leeds squat gig (we played at , and how we got to know Chumbawamba and others ) so I think it was about doing one here - to show it can be done I guess! Went to ones in Leeds, Barnsley later that year and the following year one in Middlesbrough. I believe there was one in Whitby round then too. Temporary autonomous spaces eh, good times."[549]

Writing on the later (October 1985) Middlesbrough squat gig, local Teesside band Join Hands would give us more of an explanation;

> "Squat gigs mean freedom. Freedom from the barriers so many gigs hold these days. They are organised and set up by everybody so it's up to you to make them work. No rip-off entrance fees to make agents and manager's fat and the bands are not making vast amounts of money at your expense. No age restrictions so the doors are open to everybody, young or old. No bouncers deciding you are upholding the rules of his bosses club and who they can or can't admit. A squat gig was set up in Middlesbrough not so long ago, for quite a lot of reasons but mostly as a protest at the none existence of alternative venues for bands to play and to add a splash of colour and life to the cold, grey steel town. All went well for the first couple of hours, lots of people peacefully co-operating and making it all work, lots of food (all vegan), fanzines, records and in general an atmosphere of love and happiness. Then as usual the police found out that somebody was actually enjoying themselves on their patch and decided to put a stop to it. They came and stopped the gig by illegally entering the building, and then they proceeded to take everybody outside for searches and questioning. Flexing their muscles and flaunting their power they halted everything we had created, so much for our squatter's rights."[550]

> "The police turned up in riot gear minus any batons n shields.

> There was some resistance to keep them out but they forced entry... A bit clueless what to make of it, they ended up kicking us all out and nicking a mate for theft of a generator as he didn't have the receipt from the hire place on him! I suppose they wanted to impress their superiors with at least 1 arrest for their trouble. He was later released without charge"[551]

ML (who I believe recently moved to Esh Winning, Co Durham from Sheffield) was at this time writing the magazine *Sinews*, described as 'an independent newsletter of the Spanish Information Network, containing news and views about anarchist/syndicalist unions in Spain today.' A prolific amount of letters from ML would 'grace' the pages of most of the national anarchist press during this period,[552] especially writings and debates centred on the CNT and its various 'splits' at the time.

*Sinews* was seen as controversial, as *Black Flag* in their review of issue 1 explain;

> "Like their pamphlet *Organising an Anarchist Syndicalist Trade Union* the authors are clearly followers of the CNT-V 'Renovadas' who left the CNT-AIT after much disagreement over strategy and personalities. Instead of changing their organisations title they retained CNT (dropping the affiliation with the AIT/International Workers Association the anarcho-syndicalist International and opting for contacts with 'Independent' unions in other countries e.g. the SAC in Sweden). For reasons of 'patria' (i.e. the machinery, funds, offices, etc seized by the fascists at the end of the Civil war which amounts to some £10 million now) which the socialists will give upto the real CNT, they kept the CNT title. Further to this, the Socialist approved 'factory council elections' were used as a 'pragmatic' reason for becoming obedient and denying the 'purity' of anarchism i.e. no representation, all delegates revocable etc. The CNT-AIT has 40 members in prison who have no solidarity except from the CNT- AIT and AIT-IWA groups and sympathetic anarchists internationally. The case of

the 'Scala' (a nightclub which was firebombed and resulted in several deaths including 2 CNT-AIT waiters) which resulted in imprisonment for 5 CNT-AIT militants despite the evidence of the presence of a police provocateur, also is part of the background of the 'split'. Thus it is startling to see the smug attitude of *SINEWS* whose 'independence' is clearly weighted towards the CNT-V 'Renovada'. Quotes from *Accion Libertaria* (the CNT-V paper) abound which state their case for experimenting with elections, seeking to now reunify the 'two CNT's' etc. When the CNT-V split from the AIT they should have changed their title and then as 'syndicalists' whatever play about with elections, merging with independent (sic) Catholic and Nazis unions and so on."

A page of text or so later and the review would conclude

"While *SINEWS* proclaim both CNT's to have 'anarchist/ syndicalist goals' they very clearly have different tactics. We well know the situation, 'anarchists' whose 'action' is at best militant liberalism / permanent protest at the worst excesses of the system, a good middle class hobby (and such people are usually nicer than the Tory middle class who would hang and flog the lot of us), but hardly revolutionary. Do the CNT-V in fact reject the State as a goal as well as a practice? Only the CNT-IWA does." And more interestingly "Contrary to some illusions, the Spanish anarchist movement ismuch larger than the CNT. The anarcho-syndicalist tendency of the movement with its roots in the revolutionary section of the working class has reflected the ebb and flow of the combat against wage labour, for self-management of the industrial and community battles using direct action to bring about a quick solution to social problems. The larger anarchist movement has concerns with education/publishing, anti-militarism, prisons, ecology, women's emancipation, youth's freedom etc. Some of these groups overlap with CNT militants participating BUT there is an anarchist goalwhich the methods of getting to are not different from; that is: horizontal organisation! To participate in vertical

> elections is therefore is only an argument when methods and goals are separated for 'populism' 'expediency' 'realism' etc. To renounce anarchism, its ideas and practice would be useful only to those social climbers/trendies/bureaucrats whose pose as 'anarchists' becomes redundant as power beckons and their rowdy origins have to be refined to be acceptable to the bourgeoisie We have received letters from *SINEWS* which they wanted us to print (even though they admit they never read our paper!). We decline."[553]

This 'discussion' between ML and the Spanish Information Network and *Black Flag*, the DAM, etc would continue for a number of years, and is a long debate I won't delve into.

May Day 1984 and Middlesbrough DAM are hosting a public meeting in the centre of town with discussion on the current miners' strike, and the origins of May Day. This would also coincide with the release of their regular news sheet *Strike Back!* Number 5 being a May Day special and would state;

> "As anarchists and ordinary working people we recognise the true meaning of May Day. It is the day of INTERNATIONAL working class solidarity, where working people the world over show their class feeling. It is the day when ordinary people show their desire for a better world; a world where the capitalist, the boss, the warmonger, the politician no longer exists, but where everyone lives a communal peaceful co-existence. This is what we anarchists strive for every single day of our lives."

In a call of 'Victory to the Miners', *Strike Back!* would also emphasise;

> "We totally support the miners in their strike to save their communities & their jobs. But it is our fight as well as theirs. If this obnoxious Tory govt. Defeats the miners they will continue their attack on other weaker sections of working class. NOW IS THE TIME TO STAND UP AND STRIKE BACK. We have been on

our knees too long. Don't listen to the media or the politicians. The miners can win but it will need militant action by ALL workers. The fight needs to be spread to the power stations and the steel works. NO COAL SHOULD BE ALLOWED TO MOVE. The miners want, and need, more than sympathy. If the miners are defeated we are all defeated. Become active in their defence. Organise collections in your workplace & in your community, join the pickets, invite miners to speak at your meetings. IT IS UP TO YOU.[554]

[555]

STRIKE BACK

Issue 4. Published by Middlesborough DAM c/o Red & Black Bookshop, 120 Victoria Rd, Middlesborough, Teeside. Miners dispute, Strike Strategy, Eddie Horner and lots more!

REVOLUTIONARY UNIONISM IN ITALY.

An excellant in depth descriptio of the Italian equivelant to the CNT-AIT. from the resolutions of their recent congress. 20p plus large sae from: D.A.M., 120, Victoria road, Middlesbrough, Cleveland.

Meanwhile, back up the road in Newcastle, the formation of a new group is being announced "I would be grateful if you could include our new groups address (Bishopdale House, Sutton Estate, Benwell, Newcastle) in your contact list. We are made up of ex-members of Newcastle Anarchist Group, who, due to personality clashes, felt it better to start a new group. NAG, as you know, still exists, and we shall, of course, still be working with them. Tyneside Libertarian Group."[556]

Exiled Geordie Dave Douglass, now living in the Doncaster area and deeply entrenched within the miners' strike as co-ordinator of the Doncaster NUM Strike Committee would release '*Bores Under the Floor - a brief guide to the wave of 'left' groups and newspapers currently invading the pit villages*'. Released in June 1984, it would guide the reader through each of the parasite paper sellers of the left,

> "Such is the Will O The Wisp nature of many of these groups that few if any will ever have been seen in and around the coalfields before; if the strike finishes it is more or less certain that the vast majority of them will vanish as quickly as they came. Almost without exception they see themselves as 'Marxist' prophets, dispensing their tablets of gold, to the untutored masses, who, to their minds anyway, will flounder without their 'expert' advice and guidance." "They are political self appointed messiahs".

The last group Dave deals with is the anarchists, and states;

> "It will come as a surprise to many but the Anarchists have in fact been far more helpful than many of the self-proclaimed saviours of the working class. Since they are against people telling other people what to do, they have in fact spent what time and energy they haveto actually helping us in the ways <u>we</u> ask to be helped. Printing is often their strong point and they have often done this for free; they have also helped in food collections, etc and when WE have asked they have shown up on picket lines, without the newspapers the others on the left usually carry. You will have no problems with Anarchists moving in to try and take things over, or sell you a line; the only problem will be that many of them look funny. You might find that quite acceptable if the choice is the company of some of the groups mentioned above; in addition you will find that when push comes to 'shove' in dangerous situations on the picket lines, the 'left' are way back with an arm full of papers, whilst the Anarchist is stood with you."[557]

DM from Middlesbrough would echo similar sentiments in a lengthy letter concerning the strike;

> "...was correct to state the paramount importance of the miners' strike for the working class in this country. Considering themselves an integral part of that class it goes without saying

that class struggle anarchists up and down the country are committed to supporting the strike and aiding its victory. The article was also right to point out the various intrigues and manipulations that other groups of the revolutionary left are indulging in during the miners' strike. But then this was expected; we know from experience the parasitic way Leninists feed off workers struggles. We hope that as libertarians we take a more *principled* position in workers struggles." "This strike holds a number of lessons for the workers movement, and maybe one or two for the anarchist movement...Firstly it has shown once more the tremendous resilience and power of organised and militant workers. Secondly it has shown the ethical bankruptcyof the Leninist groups whose main priority is selling their paper behind the picket lines while people at the front are getting their heads cracked open. Thirdly it has shown yet again that reformist unionism isn't up to the job."[558]

On Tuesday 18th September, under the heading of 'Coal not Bombs',

"Ten members of the Northern Non Violent Direct Action group occupied two offices of the North Eastern Electricity Board (NEEB) headquarters in Newcastle. The action was planned to draw attention to and to oppose the siting of a nuclear power station at Druridge Bay on the Northumberland coast. They occupied the offices at 1.15pm and barricaded themselves in with filling cabinets, tables etc. Banners were hung from the windows and the protestors spoke to passers-by with a loudhailer. Outside supporters leafleted and spoke with passers-by. After about 45 minutes the filth arrived. A struggle was made to retain the offices but only as a gesture because the TV and press had already been there. The protestors were led away to the police station past supporters and pressmen. They were held for three and a half hours, questioned and photographed. Charges have not yet been pressed. I hope very much that you print at least part of this letter. *Freedom* is getting better, as has the whole of the anarchist press since the start of

> the miners' strike. M."[559]

By October *Freedom* is announcing "The Freedom office has been handed over to a group of Geordie miners for the duration of the strike. They came down of their own initiative, which is probably how come they found us."[560] Actually, the miners in question from Bates Pit, Blyth, Northumberland were told locally, once they decided to head to London to raise much needed funds and asking where was a good place to begin / stay, try asking *Freedom*, they should know. Fair play to them though for they soon were actively encouraging other anarchist groups in the capital, despite differences, to come around to *Freedom* to help and 'arrange things quickly with the miners themselves'.

*Black Flag* is also getting Geordie praise;

> "Congratulations on *Black Flag;* a serious and theoretical Anarchist Journal has been badly missed since the mid-60's. Would-be Anarchists have too readily swallowed the 'non-political' tag and took that to mean a rejection of all political processes (including Anarchist ones). Anarchism has become equivalent with apathy and fashion and a spray can. Hopefully *Black Flag* will raise the level of political consciousness on the left generally and at least stimulate a more serious discussion of the issues and nature of the beast. Your non-preaching, solidaristic, extensive coverage of the Miners Strike has been second to none. It is appreciated. Revolutionary Greetings.
> D. Douglass, Hatfield Main Branch, NUM, Doncaster."[561]

November see's a plea from a 'comrade in the North East' who is hoping to put together a booklet record and analysis of the 'current' miners' strike from an anarchist perspective. Anarchists are asked to send in contributions and reports of anarchist activities in regard to the strike to Black Flag for collation.[562] I don't think this project ever 'got off the ground'.

More zines would appear this year including *Remember who we are?*

(Co Durham), *Aural Nightmares* (Blyth, Northumberland), *Organised Confusion* (Gateshead), *Active Anarchist* (Consett, Co Durham), *What's* left (Newcastle), and No-one kills the children anymore (Newcastle), etc.[563] Numerous benefit gigs in the region were taking place as the strike continued towards Christmas, including "06/11/1984, The Redskins played Stockton Road Bunker, Sunderland as part of our ongoing support for the striking Miners and their families."[564]
December and M from Durham is writing;

> "Some news from Durham: At last we've managed to get an anarchist group of sorts going here, and there are various projects beginning to creak into motion. The problem is that Durham is so small, such a (right) Labour stronghold and commitments are widely spread (e.g. Durham Miners Family Aid, Peace Action Durham etc) that the group has often ended up comprising of a few core members only. Nevertheless, I think we've got some people thinking about anarchism's relevance to the numerous aspects of their lives."[565]

Looking back on the year, local anarcho band Reality Control, would in one oftheir hand outs, state;

> "THE NOOSE IS TIGHTENING. Ok, so now more and more people are beginning to realise that the world isn't so nice after all, and perhaps there is more than meets the eye on those sickly sweet smileTV adverts. But things are now getting a hell of a lot worse. In this country alone for example, the new white paper on experiments involving the torture of animals for "research", which will make the already hideous conditions and torture much worse. The forthcoming police bill which will make a huge step in the direction of a British police state, which is already painfully apparent in the current miners' strike. The endless capitalist competition races on supported by the unquestioning acceptance of the public, which endorses the racist, sexist, profiteering we have to live with.
>
> The distorted image of western affluence carries on and on

> and on... while the third world starves. The earth cries out to deaf ears. C.N.D. still play into the hands of the state: 250 thousand people marching into a field watched by the police changes nothing at all, we just can't afford to say "please" anymore, the noose is tightening. To stand by and hope is not enough, we must do as much as we can in whatever way we can to communicate and expose and attack their lies. So, do we finally begin to take back control of our own lives, take back and preserve our earth? Or do we sit back and watch it die? It is up to us. Reality Control. 1984."[566]

As it did in 1983 with a similar themed article, 1984 would also end with Teesside Anarchists writing;

> "First I would like you to understand that Teesside has local peace and CND groups, Animal Rights activists as well as socialist and the various ecological groups. It also has an active anarchist group which apart from the fun caused during the election has been involved in setting up an unemployed workers union and they have also been involved in strikes etc in the area. The local Poly also has a large group as well and there is a well stocked bookshop with a printing facility. The anarchists have been involved in the protests against the proposed nuclear dumping under Billingham in the old ICI mines, by carrying out fly posting etc. Most of the populace are against having the waste dumped and none are convinced by the Nirex companies lies (a full page advertisement in the local press, TV & radio) that the waste would cause no safety hazard. Especially because of the fact that a lot of the population has worked in the mines and know how dangerous they really are. Since this affair has arrived it has been revealed that ICI have been dumping on a site, nuclear waste FOR NEARLY 20 YEARS. The site is now some food factories and carries the risk of spreading the waste through the air, a recent Geiger counter reading showed that the level of radiation to be nearly twenty times more than normal (more than surrounding areas of Windscale). The waste can be felt emitting heat. The Council

also has a site (nuclear dumping) which carries the risk of spreading radiation through the water systems. There's an awful lot of mud flying (especially between Councillors) about these two issues. Local Councils here have a good track record though. Recently signs appeared on a Council built BMX (bike) course that the track was not to be used again as it was contaminated by toxic waste. The local population have shown themselves ready to act in a sticky situation (as in the 13 week steel strike of 1980) and already they are talking about direct action in this Billingham affair. The waste they plan to dump at the old ICI mines at Billingham is a lot more dangerous than the stuff they plan to dump at Elstan. Today Cruise, tomorrow Nuclear dumping; what kind of future do we offer our children?"[567]

## 4.6 1985 AND THE BATTLE TO SURVIVE

January 1985, and *Black Flag* are informing us that their paper is available to buy from Days of Hope Bookshop in Newcastle, Red & Black Books in Middlesbrough and interestingly at the Durham Co-op, Railway St, Langley Park. Despite the existence of other groups in the region, the only advertised contacts in *Freedom* are Tyneside Libertarian Group, Benwell, Newcastle, and Middlesbrough Anarchists.[568]

"Happy new year? It hasn't turned out to be for 800 workers in County Cleveland who've been told they're to be laid off... first came the announcement that 200 jobs are to go with the closure of the Teesside Bridge Foundry and engineering works in Middlesbrough, which is over 100 years old. This has been followed by the announcement that 350 jobs are to go with the closure of the Rank Hovis Mcdougal bakery in Stockton later this year, and another 250 in Hartlepool with the closure of British Steel's plate mill. Retiring steel union leader and scabbing bastard BS must be sad to see the demise of his home town – Hartlepool now has an unemployment rate of over 30%

(County Cleveland has the worst jobless figures in the UK apart from Ulster). But never mind, his coming knighthood should cheer him up. The lesson should be obvious to everyone but the masochist – keeping your head down won't save you: they'll kick you in the teeth just the same. Might as well stand and fight like the striking miners. – Teessider."[569]

DM from Middlesbrough is also writing on violence and the anarcho-syndicalist response.

"There's been a lot of nonsense talked about violence during the miners' strike. And violence, by the State or by people in opposition to it, is problematic for some people, even on the Left. Anarcho- syndicalists, on the other hand, have a very clear perspective on this. During the miners' strike, traitors like Kinnock and Willis have used picket-line violence (by the strikers, mind, not the police) as the excuse to cover their betrayal of the people they claim to be representative of. Their cowardice will have sickened many strikers and their supporters, especially those who have been on the receiving end of "law and order" as meted out by the police during the strike, while Kinnock and Willis were nowhere to be seen. Although there is much in Arthur Scargill's brand of socialism with which we anarcho-syndicalists would disagree, the man has to be respected for having steadfastly refused, despite great pressure, to condemn NUM members for defending themselves as best they can, while all about traitors sneered and cowards flinched. At the other end of bourgeois politics from Kinnock and Willis, after the Brighton bombing[570] the Government tried to use the event to criminalise all opposition. Thus Mcgregor compared the bombing to what had been happening on the picket lines.

The State is violence institutionalised; repression and containment of unrest on behalf of the ruling class. The apparatus of this domination are the police and the courts – as we've seen throughout the course of the miners' strike. When the police lines are breached the armed forces come into play, as in Ulster. And when the ruling classes of different states fall out they throw their armies at each other (at least, before they got nuclear weapons; now we are all conscripts). The result is, and has been throughout history, the slaughter of millions of poor people in the wars of their masters. When the State condemns political opponents for resorting to violence (as for instance in the case of the IRA) it talks with its hands dripping with the innocent blood of generations.

Having established, I hope, that the State is violence, what then should our response be to the violence of people who, for a variety of reasons, clash with the State? It cannot be a blanket condemnation of violence, since anarcho-syndicalists are neither pacifists nor opportunists like Kinnock. We recognise the legitimate right of people to defend themselves from oppression and injustice, and also to go on the offensive against their oppressors. However, as with our politics generally, we view violence with an ethical perspective. The indiscriminate bombings of various nationalist groups around the world for instance are indefensible – though even here we look at the disease, not the symptoms whether it be the British presence in Ireland, the disinherited Palestinians or whatever.

The killing of the taxi driver hit by a lump of concrete dropped from an overhead bridge while taking a scab to work in South Wales is a case in point. We regret the death, more sincerely than the likes of Thatcher and Kinnock. Whenever workers are set against workers it's the boss that stands to gain (and it's the boss that's set them against each other, usually). Thus we lay the responsibility for this death and the several others of strikers (which were quickly forgotten by the media) squarely at the feet of Thatcher, Mcgregor and their class. And despite all their condemnations of violence on the picket lines, traitors like Kinnock and Willis bear a responsibility too, for with their betrayal they have aided the bosses and prolonged the strike.

Long after Willis has received his thirty pieces of gold (like his mates Lord Chapple and Lord Murray), history will condemn the real violence of the last 11 months: the threatened destruction of thousands of livelihoods and entire communities, the use of legal thugs (police) to try to batter defiant workers into submission, the useof the laws and courts of the rich to try to hamstring the miners union organisation – by people who say they support free trade unions in Poland. Victory to the miners."[571]

The "official" end of the miners' strike was 3rd March 1985. 'It was a defining moment in British industrial relations, the NUM's defeat significantly weakening the trade union movement. It was a major victory for Thatcher and the Conservative Party, with the Thatcher government able to consolidate their economically liberal programme.' The North East has severely suffered the after effects ever since, not only with the destruction of the industry and the communities built around this, but more importantly, the destruction of its people.

**MINERS**

As we go to press there are a total of 152 miners with prison sentences. Out of the 7874 charged during the strike, 5528 cases have been dealt with. There were 4112 convictions.

There are still many of the serious cases, involving assault, riot, etc, to be heard. The number of dismissals to date are 718, with around 40 reinstatements. Further dismissals are possible as a result of the pending Court cases.

[572]

A comrade in West Germany comments "During this strike the anarchist movement, especially in Scotland and Northumberland, has won the trust and respect of many strikers. On the other hand, many anarchists have used the strike to step up their activities."[573]

Albert Meltzer, in *Black Flag*, informs us;

"A valued comrade wrote to us regretfully cancelling his

subscription, for "the war is over, and I'm afraid we've lost". Many miners feel equally depressed and it's no good saying we only lost a battle, not a war. One of the greatest upsurges of the workers for many years, in this country certainly, has ended with a victory for starvation tactics, with the forces of repression entrenched, with cynics smiling and those who flinched from battle feeling justified. It is true there is a positive angle: that thousands of English, Welsh and Scottish miners have learned that the heavy hand that rules in the north of Ireland can fall on them too overnight; they have relearned the techniques they pioneered in free co-operation and solidarity in which the women from the mining communities in particular have shown once again some of the mechanism that would make a free society tick.

But they have not won. Nor can it be said that they were betrayed by their 'leaders'. They have not put trust in leaders, who have been content to follow the movement rather than presume to direct it, and the politicos among them have lost all credibility as the TUC has proved itself once again useless in regard to showing solidarity, capable only of delivering votes to the Labour Party. Could they have ever won? The most that the miners were fighting for was the right to be exploited in the same way they had always been; to carry on with the same exhaustive work they had always done. They were fighting a rearguard action against a vicious enemy. All they were trying to preserve was their place in the battlefield. They did not want their communities broken up and people dispersed from productive work to become car-park attendants and door openers in the prosperous south. In going back without an agreement they have at least maintained a presence in the coalfields.

In the past, following victories and defeats, the miners have had mighty discussions on how they should proceed, on what should be the future of the industry, and on how they should prepare for a battle to take over command of their destiny. In the early part of the century, miners took an active part in establishing the Trade Union Congress, so that all workers could come to the assistance of each other. This was doomed to disaster since the growing trade union leadership sought to establish themselves, and extend to political power, rather than form a fighting union. Their idea was that if they could exert political power, they could obtain more from parliamentary than industrial action. The closed-shop principle, dear to the hearts of British trade unionism, meant that leaderships were impregnable (dare to challenge the machine and you're out, with nowhere else to go), but that nobody was ready for industrial action, everyone expecting parliament to step in or political influence to be used. Unions sought legalisation which has now resulted in the courts taking over and presuming to decide union policy – much as if during the war German Generals were enforcing British military policy.

The greatest debate of all was on NATIONALISATION OR SYNDICALISM. The decision went wholly in favour of the former. That distinguished 'Socialist' theoretician, Ramsey Macdonald, proved convincingly that state socialism was incompatible with syndicalism, and that his answer (taken from the Fabian Society) was nationalisation. It was strange that nationalisation should have become popular in Britain as a socialist measure, since in Germany it had already been adopted in the 19th century as a capitalist one by Bismark, who nationalised the railways, to benefit the landed estates and to exploit the workers. The syndicalists were attacked for various reasons, every one of which is seen now to be phoney. It was thought heavy industry could hold the country to ransom – it was held that workers control meant that there would be no place for the community – it was alleged that there would be an excess of power in the hands of key industry workers. All these Macdonaldite arguments carried the day; as a result heavy industry holds us to ransom, the communities are destroyed

> and there is an excess of power in the hands of managements.
>
> Nationalisation of the mines, originally a compromise solution, became a dream of miners throughout the '20's and '30's, and in 1945 the Labour Party came into power and it was the first promise it carried out. The national flag flew at all the pitheads. The mines became 'ours'. The National Coal Board was created and was hailed as the harbinger of the state socialist utopia. It is this same National Coal Board that is the enemy today. The old private owners could not have withstood the billions of pounds losses incurred by a yearlong strike. The NCB can.
>
> The TUC notion that it is only Mr Macgregor's wilfulness that is at fault and that if Mrs Thatcher were not Prime Minister and Mr Kinnock was, the NCB would still be 'ours', is pathetic. It is the NCB that is the enemy. It was a sad day for the miners when they decided that they would follow the path of state socialism and nationalisation, encouraged by the 'militancy' of the Communist Party integrating itself into the establishment, and rejected syndicalism. If, or rather when (as they may do) they return to the old method of struggle they would find that a greater battle might well be won."[574]

In the larger, scarier, and in no doubt unfortunately probable scheme of events, the state faced with any sense of losing the 'battle' could and would be capable of implementing atrocities to favour and instigate defeat of the opposition. "If the State can get away with the Falkland/ Malvinas War, with all its obvious incongruities, then they could easily get away with blowing up a working colliery and blaming the massacre on pickets." "The killing of scabs by provocateurs claiming to be striking miners might sound far-fetched, but it's probably nothing compared with the conspiracies they *could* hatch up. A terrorist bombing blamed on the strike movement could force a blanket repression of all forms of class anger, justifying armed raids on whole mining communities and elsewhere."[575] Frightening with its implications for future battles, but not unfeasible. This is especially true if we delve into the recent inadequacies, inconsistencies and conspiracies surrounding certain European 'Muslim terror attacks' and some of their, quite obvious, state / security forces involvement.[576] State sponsored diversionary tactics - lets create a bit of sympathetic patriotism in the populace, especially in times of rebellion.

March 1985 and MM from Durham has a letter in *Freedom* discussing economic classes under Thatcherism, and in a section discussing technology points out;

> "Despite the increasing importance of biotechnology, information technology, etc, these innovations will always be secondary to the control of capital. Whether their expertise is put to use is still up to the profiteer (State or capitalist). The conversion to the 'management of things' is not irreversible. I suspect that when under threat, economically (if the new technology gets too expensive) or politically (by upstart technocrats) these 'wealth-creators' will swiftly revert to old fashioned man-management."

"I think that the new technology is not an alternative to man-management: it compliments it. By serving to increase unemployment it terrorises the working class, pushes down wages and makes the workforce more placid. A balance between cheap new technology and cheaper, placid human beings will probably be struck. This sort of outcome necessarily limits the power of the technocrats."[577] The issue would also contain a lengthy article on 'Power & Probability' by ML (Durham).

April, and another letter from Durham is requesting contact details for a group of anarchists previously writing in *Freedom,* "Two of us here in college are desperate to make contact with such a group – we're stifled by the narrow outlets existing within the university for political expression and discussion. We're both philosophical anarchists with a bit of practical experience (Stop the City, etc...) so we think we've got something to offer the group."[578]

In another lengthy article on 'Power', MM from Durham interestingly concludes his point when talking of how power can be perceived as in some way as natural, as some are receptive and take pleasure from it, and;

> "Is it necessary to assume that this receptivity is biological? Some feminists, for instance Shulamith Firestone, reckon that authoritarianism really took off in prehistory when men, on realising that they were necessary for procreation, began oppressing women. Under conditions of scarcity the subordination of women links the exercise of power to the experience of pleasure. From these beginnings developed all the other forms of power and oppression we've seen in history. Now this might be a bit simplistic, but at least it points to the possibility that power-lust is not innate. It then becomes conceivable that we can have individuals who under the right social conditions develop (are 'constructed' to experience) a deep disgust of power whether it is exercised by others or by themselves. (And in fact Pygmies are well-known for their compulsion towards collective decision-making). Such people would be psychologically incapable of accruing power. In the same way that we are partly resistant to autonomy, such individuals would be resistant to power.
>
> All this doesn't make the exercise of power any less unacceptable. However, it does acknowledge that the anarchist abhorrence of power is largely a *moral* abhorrence, not one simply based on social, psychological or anthropological or whatever facts. These academic disciplines create/consolidate as much as 'discover' the human condition, and we should be wary about making scientific claims based on their 'discoveries'. What I've tried to do is stress the fact that we are going to have to be more active/creative in constructing anarchy; we can't afford to let it surface under the impetus of its own 'naturalness'. Hopefully this will make us all the more sensitive

to power's historical hold over us and the ways in which we might effectively combat it."[579]

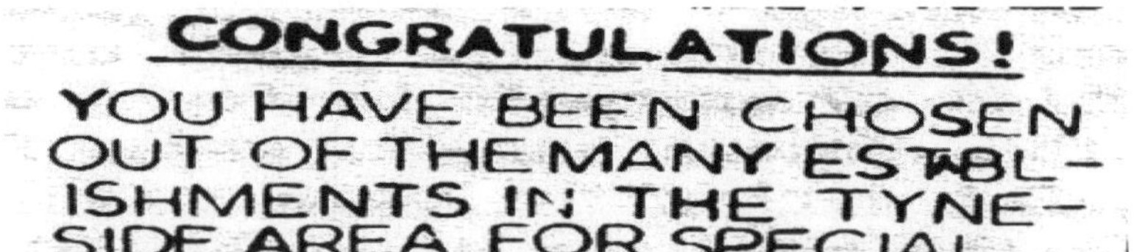
CONGRATULATIONS!
YOU HAVE BEEN CHOSEN
OUT OF THE MANY ESTABL-
ISHMENTS IN THE TYNE-
SIDE AREA FOR SPECIAL
ATTENTION. DUE TO YOUR
UNHEALTHY INVOLVEMENT
IN EXPLOITATION OF PEOPLE
ANIMALS & THE EARTH'S RE-
SOURCES. THIS ACTION IS
A SHOW OF DEEP DISGUST
& REVULSION AT YOUR OB-
SCENE ACTIVITIES.
WE SINCERELY HO-
PE THAT THIS ACTION BR-
INGS TO EVERYONES ATTE-
THE INJUSTICES PERPETR-
ATED BY YOUR 'SUPERIORS'
IN THE NAME OF 'FREE
ENTERPRISE'.....

One of the 'activists' stickers

In an international event on the 29th and 30th April, known as 'Stop Business As Usual', protests took place around the world against the arms race, big business, capitalism, from animal rights to targets of sexual and racial oppression. Newcastle was no exception, where;

> "On April 30th, at least 30 business premises were attacked. These included banks, butchers and Army buildings, many of whom had their windows smashed and were suitably graffitied. On this occasion the group got good local coverage in newspapers, and had their communiqué read out on a local ITV news broadcast. Fourpeople were arrested, but we have no news of any charges."[580]

This communiqué would emphatically state;

> "Tuesday 30th April saw a worldwide day of action against the businesses and institutions of death who are destroying our world above our heads and behind our backs. "Stop Business As Usual" sought to highlight and take direct action against those who keep us all on our knees. With the materialistic rubbish they force down our throats to give us a false sense of security and contentment, we are led to believe that everything is "ok", while they get on with the job of destruction.
>
> In their tiny, one- track minds, land, people and animals are expendables for their stinking profits...Multinational companies destroying people's homelands, cultures and lives under the wheels of "progress", power and gain. If we sit back and let them do it, we will all be crushed. "You can't feel the chains until you try to move." The media yet again used shock-horror tactics to condemn any actions, but they of course failed to explain why the actions were taken, typical of the lying twisting parliamentary fools that they are, protecting their own positions of power while we suffer."[581]

Groupings of anarchists, libertarians, anarcho-punks, and other activists throughout the entire North East were occasionally coming together for actions, individually and collectively, from Newcastle, Durham, Gateshead, Middlesbrough, South & North Shields, Ashington and Blyth in Northumberland, Consett, Sunderland, Stockton, and Darlington etc etc. Loose networks were being formed through gigs, zines, papers and magazines, as well as the pub. Many were moving from the pit villages into shared hoses and flats with like minded people in the Town centres of Newcastle, Middlesbrough and Sunderland. These houses themselves became hives of activity, meeting places, shared collective areas of activism, at times 3, 4, or 5 houses in one street alone.

One such collective of people began the publication of *Tyne and Wear Free News*, the first issue of which hit the streets in May 1985. An A3 double sided, and unmistakably anarchist, broadsheet which was distributed and fly posted throughout the region.

Issue 1, with Days of Hope Bookshop[582] as the contact address, as well as containing local news and views, would also contain an exploration of the media in the aftermath of the miners' strike entitled 'Newspaper (Dis)information' which emphasised the thousands of acts of injustice and brutality against striking miners and their families, not covered by the media, yet when one scab gets hurt, it becomes front page news.[583]

'Teessider' is also announcing during this period;

> "At the end of January the government announced that the plans to dump nuclear waste in the old ICI anhydrite mines under Billingham, on Teesside, had been abandoned." "Nuclear power holds advantages for capitalists only. It is expensive and the working class will be made to pay for it. It will require a small workforce, closely controlled under the pretext of necessary security rather than potentiality troublesome miners and power station workers. Thus the working class will lose a vital element of its power." "Their plans must be resisted. but a marginal anti-nuclear movement based on pressure group style politics will prove as ineffective as it has to date (not one nuclear missile or power station halted).It has to be realisedthat nuclear power is a class issue: it affects both the miners and the wider working class. And the only thing capable of halting both the nuclear programme and the missiles (whose materials it supplies) is an organised and militant working class. This must be the last time agovernment can sit out a year long strike by running nuclear power plants flat out regardless of safety requirements as the Tories did this time. We' must put a stop to their limitless programme of investment in this lethal and extravagant technology. NUCLEAR

POWER IS BOSSES POWER."[584]

In a full page article celebrating and delving into the historical roots of May Day, Middlesbrough's DM firstly tells us about pagan spring festivals of European peasantry, before explaining how this developed into the International Workers Day, after events in Chicago 1886 (this was covered earlier).

The article then brings us up to present times and, at length, concludes;

> "In Russia, following the decay of the revolution, May Day was turned into a State occasion, and in all the "communist" countries today it is the excuse for a display of military strength and the dictatorship of the Party. Meanwhile, in the West, May Day has been absorbed as a harmless public holiday in many countries. Thisfinally happened in Britain in 1978 with the first Monday of May becoming a Bank Holiday. The British Trade Union movement still prefers the nearest weekend. In fact we seem to have forgotten what May Day is about altogether. For us syndicalists May Day isn't simply a matter of a Saturday afternoon stroll by a handful of trade unionists thorough the town centre, to be harangued later by some Labour Party or TUC bureaucrat. For us it's a commemoration of the many martyrs who gave their lives for our class gains in the past, and an expression of determination for a better life in the future."

> "In the "free world" last May Day the British miners had entered into a bitter struggle with the full force of the State enraged against them, and most of the rest of the British workers movement left them to fight alone. In "communist" Poland workers May Day demonstrations are usually met with tear gas and baton charges... So, we syndicalists insist on a return to the roots of May Day. We'll observe it this year as best we can, and shall continue to observe it till the day May Day once again sees millions of workers all over the world streaming on to the streets to conquer their future."[585]

June 1985 and the second issue of *Tyne and Wear Free News* looks at the 'Economics of Starvation' 'housing', 'police murder', 'colliery closures', and the capitalist money made from women's "feminine" products, whilst giving us an insight into its production "This publication is aimed at bringing to light news & our views of certain topics here in Tyne & Wear and also in world affairs." "This paper is meant to try & offer a platform for alternative viewpoints & reports not normally covered or distorted by the established media."[586]

Our old friend TJ "returned to activity during the miners' strike of 1984/5, where he recalls, talking with some of the miners on the picket line, where he found his critique of the state and the union bureaucrats "*struck a chord*" with them. The reaction of some of those engaged in the dispute tends to substantiate the contention that anarchism becomes more relevant during periods of self activity. TJ recounted how;

> "*Local Labour Party members would eagerly buy*" syndicalist literature. For local (anarcho) syndicalists, it was a promising period where their ideas and methods engaged and found a level of latent support among the strikers. TJ observed that there were "*an awful lot of people who knew, who could see and feel which politics were relevant*". The massive increase of sales of *Class War* among the miners nationally, gives some validation to this assertion."[587]

The pages of *Freedom* would benefit from the return of TJ, and June sees the beginning of many letters and articles, the first of which is a reply to an earlier letter on 'Life without leaders', where after highlighting a few points, concludes;

> "To encourage "*people to see anarchism as a viable social theory*" we will have to do just what PF fails to do, that is to produce a theory that relates to people and communities actually dealing with the complexities and frustrations attendant on life (personal, social, economic and political). Utopian

generalisations and simplistic tautologies such as those expressed in the article are themselves exactly what will convince people of the irrelevance and pointlessness of anarchism."[588]

*Red on Black* (later *Red and Black*), the first of which was produced from York this year, and described itself as 'An anarchist-socialist paper of the North East' would have in its first issue an article about music collectives in the North East, and would give some illuminating insights into this little explored area of the period. MH educates us;

"The contradictions existing within 'pop' music are pretty obvious – on the one hand the "rock business" is notorious for its ruthless, cut- throat commercialism, making music just one more commodity to be reckoned in terms of profit or loss; on the other hand, many people see music not just as a product to be consumed but as their own means of self-expression.

In our society, most of us passively consume music, television, books etc as pre-packaged entertainment – a culture which we buy and behold, but don't actively create and make use of ourselves. This passivity and acceptance of what is fed to us can only be challenged if people who want to make music (or writing or whatever) on their <u>own</u> terms take it into their own hands to do so.

Music Collectives have been formed in many areas in the past few years – there are now 17 in the North East. There are considerable differences in the ways in which Collectives organise themselves, but there is a general commitment to democratic control and active participation. Collectives are an attempt to reclaim control of music by those involved in making it – offering an alternative to the domination of the record companies, radio stations and local profiteers (promoters, commercial venues, etc). In many cases, by removing the criterion of "commercial acceptability", Collectives have provided an opportunity for some radical, innovative music to reach wider audiences than would otherwise be the case.

In Sunderland, the Collective has been able to operate various venues under its own control – gigs have been run largely on trust with admission charges kept as low as possible and "with very few rules except those of common sense – such as no glue and no glass". In Middlesbrough, Collective policies are discussed at large weekly meetings and PA and recording equipment has been acquired which would normally be too expensive for most local musicians to have access too. The Middlesbrough Collective, (amongst others) has run successful benefit gigs for the miners and for Cleveland Rape Crisis Centre. It has also decided not to give gigs to any bands with racist/sexist material, following an incident where one outside band made anti-Jewish remarks. The Collective supported an Anti-Apartheid picket of Leo Sayer after his tour of South Africa.

Some Collectives are simply co-operatives organising gigs for local bands. Others run wide-ranging facilities such as poster printing, schemes for sharing equipment, and low price cassette releases of local music. It goes without saying that there are problems. There is a strong temptation for Collectives to compromise their intentions in order to scrounge money off local councils to buy equipment with. Inpractical terms, there is little choice but to seek funding from grant giving bodies, but some Collectives have become bogged down in the bureaucracy of getting grants at the expense of other work. Apart from the danger of becoming mere Arts Council – approved, conservative 'community co-ops', Music Collectives also run the risk of degenerating into inward looking cliques of would be rock stars which reflect rather than challenge the whole individualistic mentalityof the rock and roll industry.

The most important role of Music Collectives is to bring people together to learn how to take control of what has previously

> been largely beyond their control. People can be involved to whatever degree they choose: all the work is shared between members – many members aren't musicians themselves, but just interested people wanting to participate."[589]

This bringing together of people, with similar interests in music, also encouraged and inspired the coming together for many other 'activities'.

Issue 3 of *Tyne and Wear Free News* (July) contains writings on 'nuclear power, and its alternatives', 'health care', 'multi-national corporations', 'cruise', etc. It also tells us that "A man who was arrested at an anti royalist demonstration in Sunderland in May has been charged with 'Behaviour likely to cause a breach of the peace' – his alleged crime was that he shouted 'Parasites' at the royals."[590]

July also has an article in *Freedom* by TJ on 'Power'[591], which sparks much future debate. *Direct Action* has a lengthy article by DM on 'Football violence- who's to blame?' and also a long letter in reply to an earlier piece which stated "the power of the working class lies at the point of production". "A housewife is a worker. The millions of unemployed are workers whose labour is surplus to Capital's requirements at the moment. The unemployed youth who in today's climate may never have had a job is nonetheless a member of the working class. Pensioners, students, school kids etc can all be working class.""Syndicalism seeks to unite and weld together a working class constituted of men and women, young and old, white and black, wage earnersand their families, those with jobs and the unemployed. All have a part to play in revolutionary change." The letter carries on at length looking at the role of support during the miners' strike carried out by 'wives groups' etc. Support groups that supplied solidarity and practical help whilst some 'workers at their point of production' did not. The letter concludes;

> "Our task as syndicalists is to help bind together the working classas a cohesive fighting unity. The "crisis" and the Thatcher years have been all about dislocating and uprooting the

working class in the interests of restructured capitalism." And "Our task is to combat this social disintegration, (ambiguity about this will only aid the bosses), and do our bit to ensure that the working class responds in the manner we know it can and must. Coal miners, housewives, school kids, and the unemployed...all workers: if only we realised our collective power and organised it the world could be ours."[592]

*Black Flag* reports on a recent visit of Thatcher to the region entitled 'Thatcher Invades Newcastle'.

"From the media coverage of M. Thatcher's visit to Newcastle, comrades could be forgiven for thinking it was unopposed or even welcomed...this, is far from the Truth...over 5,000 people took to therain drenched streets for a NUPE sponsored, police guided tour...being kept well away from the City Hall/Civic Centre area where the old love had come. So on to a nice car park for some nice speeches off some nice union people...as, the local press reported they went down well, 'apart from a small number of hecklers', - mainly 'cos they stuck to safe ground...Y'know the big bad Maggie takes your jobs, shuts your schools and hospitals and doesn't much like the miners routine...well the heckling increased, faves of the day were 'let's go trash the City hall'; 'Amnesty for all sacked miners' and 'Kinnock is a Labour scab'...Then a member of Newcastle Anarchist Group and Tyneside Unemployed Workers Movement got up and made an impassioned speech – at the end of it said 'Let's go and tell Thatcher to FUCK OFF!' this brought loads of cheers and threw up an impromptu march on the City Hall leaving the Labour sheep speaking from the platform bleating inanely about how we were running away and that we could only fight Thatcher by stopping and listening to him and, presumably by voting Labour! Still nobody paid him much attention...

Most of the Constabulary had gone away at this point in time so they got quite a shock to find a substantial proportion of those nice people from the march had returned and now were intent on gettingto the guardian of our democratic system...but we were blocked off and in, so we turned around and walked off. We had a nice little sing-a-long rendition of a Newcastle Football Song called *Harry Roberts* which is all about a bloke who killed one or two policemen(shame) – I was quite cheered by the sight of the middle- aged housewife (sic) next to me joining in with the chorus.

Next we headed down the street that separates the City Hall from the Civic Centre complex – and yet again found the forces of Law & Order blocking our way...so at this point the march ended and the 'Stop the City' tactics began with people sitting down in the road – when eventually the police shifted the people (after about 20 minutes) everyone turned around and walked up to the round-about at the top of the street and started walking over it – again disrupting traffic – but this didn't last long due to the arrival of the cavalry. Some people being forced into the pedestrian railings by the nice new men on horseback...at this point about 200 people were gathered on the University steps (directly facing the Civic Centre) and they disappeared from police view down a back alley and into the 'Playhouse' car park which looks directly onto the Civic Centre –it was virtually a clear run across the road to the Civic Centre only a few barriers and NO cops – unfortunately due to the slowness of people getting across the car park the cops got there first...By this time the demo had dwindled to about 150 and contended itself with singing those rosy old chestnuts 'Brighton Bomb' and 'Airey Neave' at the fur coat wearing rich scum who were leaving the Conference. There were no arrests, but enough action took place to show there's life in Newcastle yet...

A good little quote on the whole event which appeared in the local press came from Sunderland Labour MP B.C. (who is at present facing a breach of the peace of the peace charge from his involvement in the miners' strike) *'I find it quite creepy and reminiscent of the miners' strike. The police are all over the City Centre. It's quite unnecessary, but perhaps the police have not got out of the habit yet of receiving massive overtime payments'"*.[593]

As was becoming the norm for many anarchists, repeated raids of offices and homes, and the constant tampering of mail, were again taking place at this time.

> "York Anarchist-Socialist Group has recently heard of several letters and parcels sent to us, which seem to have been 'borrowed' indefinitely by Post Office / Special Branch snoopers. We don't know the full extent of this, but we are certain that at least two bundles of the paper *'Direct Action'* were posted to us some months ago and never arrived – along with various other packages. Hull Direct Action Movement, who produce the paper, report that this is a widespread occurrence...in fact so few are getting through to sellers that they haven't got the revenue to bring out a September issue of *DA*."[594]

Whilst Septembers *Freedom* tells us, after a break in / raid at their premises, which left money and only took subscription lists, artwork and text for the paper, that the secret police were more than likely the culprits;

> "When they've got time off from checking out BBC personnel and other important duties they might just have read the major editorial piece in *The Daily Telegraph* on Wednesday 3rd July '85. An article by Peter Shipley (a former member of the Prime minister's policy Unit) on the upsurge of interest in anarchism ended with these words: "*In the hierarchy of political violence, the anarchists are not yet a major force. But if the movement continues to grow it will require a more considered response than just a firm smack from the authority it so despises!*" "It was

> a very *clean* raid, unlike the neurotics who are inclined to trash everything along the way."[595]

Anarchists in Sheffield were also suffering 'an unprecedented amount of police harassment' with police attempting to confiscate street sold issues of *The Sheffield Anarchist* and attempting to declare it an 'illegal publication'.[596]

The September issue of *Freedom* also contains another article by TJ, this one dealing with 'Submission to authority – the child's experience of power' and the October issue contains another on 'Evolution – Anarchy and natural selection'.[597] This month would also see riots erupt again throughout the country.

Conservative economic policies, dealing with the 'enemy within', having 'dealt' with the miners and now taking the fight again to the 'naturally and philosophically different' sections of the working class, blatant police racism, murder, not to mention Thatcher's warped plans for political, economic and ultimately world capitalistic domination would all again lead to resistance. As "master" you can only pull a dog's tail so many times before it turns around and bites back with savage and unrepentant glee.

October 1985 and issue 5 of *Tyne and Wear Free News* would give us a local analysis of events;

> "September 1985 will probably be recognised and remembered as the month of the riots, Handsworth, Toxteth, Brixton...where thepeople, who are on the bottom of the "social scale", gave vent to their anger and frustration and showed their disgust at the way things are going in the only way open to them.
>
> For years now, people in the inner city areas, particularly those with large black communities have had even worse than most of the rest of the country, high unemployment, bad housing,

more open racism etc, etc. And equally for years those who were supposed to be their "elected political representatives" ignored them, and looked after their own interests (which after all, is what politicians are all about).

So that left Handsworth, Brixton, and Toxteth in a similar position to us here in the North East: - ignored and left to rot, the only strength being in their own communities. When you add to this the unashamed harassment of those communities, especially black youth, on <u>an everyday basis</u>, then it is surprising that people were so quick to respond to yet another instance, in the only way possible?

Despite what most press reports said, the riots weren't just black against white or Afro-Caribbean vs. Asian, they were anti-police, anti-white establishment riots by the <u>whole</u> community. In Handsworth, about 2/3 of those arrested were white, in Brixton, about ½ of those arrested were <u>white</u>. In each case, the riots were sparked off by police harassment.

In Handsworth, the police had been operating a campaign against what it called "local drugs traffic" – this meant stop & search campaigns, breaking up of parties and eventually the dragging out of a car of a man which sparked off the riot. In Brixton, tension has been simmering since the last riots in '81, and then with the still unexplained shooting of Mrs Cherry Groce, everything was brought to a head. In Toxteth, trouble began after the trial of four men and then simmered until early evening when it erupted again.

So what are the conclusions to draw then? Obviously the riots did noone any good directly. The targets were indiscriminate, so that almost everything, acceptable or not got trashed and there were also several injuries to the public and of course two deaths. And no one for a minute seriously believes that all the fuss made by the politicians will lead to anything, as soon as it dies out of the media they'll be straight back to Whitehall, and it'll be as if nothing has changed, they still won't listen, they still won't care.

But there have been some really good things to come out of the riots. Most importantly, its shown that there is still some life left in those communities and that despite Government and media attempts to divide and weaken them, people have shown that the most strength lies with other people, not politicians, who've been shown up for being as out of touch as they really are. Maybe we will learn from these events that it's about time that we stood up to those who use us as pawns in their political games, and that if we stick together, then we can start to respond to the measures which are aimed at leaving us helpless."[598]

October's issue of *Tyne and Wear Free News* would also contain articles on the 'Shocking poverty in the North', 'Multinationals', 'Africa', 'Army activity', 'Combating Nazis at St James Park', and a piece looking at the situation with the women at Greenham Common and their admirable struggle and protest, which would also conclude;

"The manipulation by censorship and brainwashing does not however only extend to the Greenham women, but is in fact the insidious foundation of the Governments whole way of thinking. We are fobbed off with timely distractions, notably the Falklands episode, intended to restore flagging faith in Government, with a false sense of unity, power and glory, while cleverly and effectively obscuring the realities of the situation, namely enabling the Government to get away with this oppression by forcing us back into Victorian standards of poverty. The isolating environment of this kindof poverty divides and weakens us, causing us to blame each other instead of looking past the end of our noses we fight amongst ourselves, finding scapegoats at every corner – the unemployed, ethnic groups, young people and active resisters of government oppression (e.g. Greenham women)." [599]

By now, Anarcho-Syndicalists (Tyne & Wear), after a bit re-structure and furtherlocal recruitment would now be known as Tyneside Revolutionary Syndicalists (TRS). The groups 'Aims and Principles' would emphasise the group as 'revolutionary syndicalist', but clearly 'anarcho-syndicalist' in both theory and nature. These are worth highlighting in full.

1. "The object of revolutionary syndicalism is to destroy the state whether it be left wing, right wing or liberal democracy and to replace it with a free classless society based on the re-organisation of all economic and social life on the basis of libertarian communism. The majority of workers are held both economically and socially in shackles by the state. As revolutionary syndicalists we see that the only way in which these shackles can be removed and destroyed is by the united solidarity action of the workers both in theworkplace and the community. True economic and social freedom cannot come about through the reforms of the statist machinery or through the gradual transition to a different system but only through the mass revolutionary action of the working class culminating in the social revolution.
2. Revolutionary syndicalism is the confirmed enemy of all economic and social monopolies by any group, minority or party over the working class. Its aim is for the formation of free communes based on the workplace and social community organisations freely federating together and free from all forms of power, political parties and statist bureaucracy. The decision of what is to be produced, when the work shall be done and the conditions in which they live must be the sole decision of those workers affected themselves. The workers alone have the right to directly control the factories, offices, farms, hospitals and shops where they work and the houses and schools where they live and learn and all other social and economic institutions. Revolutionary syndicalism opposes all

governments, parties and states who would take power on behalf of the workers. Revolutionary syndicalism aims at the complete destruction of the exploitation of man by man and statist control of the workers rather than attempting to win power from them, this would only have the affect of throwing up new injustices, inequalities and new privileged classes. No-one can work for the best interests of the workers but the workers themselves.

3. Revolutionary syndicalism encourages and takes part in the day to day struggles of all workers that are not in conflict with the aims and principles of revolutionary syndicalism, both in the workplace and in the community. Revolutionary syndicalists see the fight for interim reforms such as shorter working and greater social conditions etc as being a major part in the development of the broader struggle against the state and exploitation. The ultimate aim of revolutionary syndicalism is for the working class to reach the position where it is capable of transferring to itself all the apparatus of production, distribution and organising social life and then to re-organise and manage the apparatus itself free from any direction from above by any government, state or political party. The re-organisation of society would be built up on the structure of below upwards in such a way that each factory, office, housing estate etc would be an independent unit in general widespread social and economic federation running its own particular concern and joining together with others to mutually agree on decisions and plans to improve the conditions of the entire community, region or society.

4. Revolutionary syndicalists in the day to day running of communities and workplaces encourage rank and file initiatives and actions on the shop floor and in housing estates etc. Within the workplace revolutionary syndicalists fight for the right of rank and file control within each place of work and propagate the ideas of workers control. Revolutionary syndicalists see the fight to take the trade union power out of

the hands of bureaucrats and reformists and to put it into the hands of the workers as being a major step towards the social revolution. Trade union barriers which make solidarity action almost impossible are a major stumbling block towards the revolutionary general strike and must be smashed with the formation of rank and file revolutionary unions. Within the community revolutionary syndicalists encourage and actively support action taken in the form of rent strikes etc for better housing conditions and all other areas where people's social and economic lives are affected. The revolutionary syndicalist also encourages the formation of local rank and file community groups and encourages solidarity action and support for workers when in struggle.

5. Revolutionary syndicalism believes in the voluntary and independent social structure directly controlled by all those affected, it therefore opposes all organisational tendencies towards centralism which involves a small group of people taking decisions on our behalf. The results of power being placed in the hands of the few are that the individual becomes a robot directed from above, the interests of the people are replaced by the interests of a controlling elite, varietygives way to uniformity instead of personal responsibility for our own lives and discipline is imposed and enforced from above by the states institutions, the courts, police, armed forces and educational system.
6. Revolutionary syndicalism is opposed to all parliamentary democracy and parliamentary activities. The so called democratic 'ballot box' has nothing in common with the needs and aims of the workers who are used as the cogs in the repressive state machinery by those that are elected into power. Revolutionary syndicalists maintain that no matter whoever is in power, whatever the name or political standpoint that power aligns itself to the evils and manifestations of state control remain. Revolutionary syndicalists maintain that the so called 'workers state' is a vicious lie to gain power for the elite from

the backs of the workers and that no matter how sincere members of the statist elite are the state shall not wither away but shall grow stronger and even more repressive and authoritarian as time goes by. Revolutionary syndicalists oppose the exceptional evil of the dictatorship of the proletariat in the guise of the workers state.

7. Revolutionary syndicalism rejects all arbitrarily fixed political and national frontiers and it sees in nationalism nothing more but the religion of the modern state, behind which are concealed the material interests of the possessing classes. It recognises only regional differences and demands for every group the right to self determination in harmonious solidarity with all other associations of an economic, territorial or a national order. It is for these same reasons that revolutionary syndicalism opposes militarism in all its forms and considers anti militarist propaganda one of its most important tasks in the struggle against the present system. Revolutionary syndicalists see that it is not in the best interests of the world's workers to slaughter each other. In the first instance it urges individual refusal of military service and especially organised boycotting of the manufacture of war materials. Revolutionary syndicalists see in the revolutionary general strike the only real means of preventing war and the preparations for it.
8. Revolutionary syndicalism stands on the platform of direct action, and supports all struggles which are not contradictory with its aims, i.e. the abolition of exploitation of man by man and the domination of the state. The methods of struggle are the strike, boycott, sabotage, occupation etc. Direct action finds its most pronounced expression in the general strike, which at the same time, from the viewpoint of revolutionary syndicalism, ought to be the prelude tothe social revolution.
9. Although the enemies of all forms of organised violence in the hands of any government or state, the revolutionary syndicalists do not forget that the decisive between the capitalism of today and the free communes of tomorrow will

not take place without serious collisions. They recognise violence therefore, as a means to defend against the methods of violence of the ruling classes. The struggle of the revolutionary people for expropriation cannot be commenced and carried to a successful issue except by revolutionary and social and economic organisations of working people, so also the revolution should be in the hands of these organisations.

10. Only the revolutionary economic and social organisations of the working class have the power for self-emancipation, as well as the creative energy necessary for the re-organisation and re-structure ofsociety on the basis of libertarian communism."

This internal paper would also outline the 'activities and action' of the group and a constitutional guide for meetings etc.[600]

Late 1985, would see the publication of the first issue of *The Syndicalist* an A3 'Anarcho-syndicalist paper' which included interviews and frontline reports of disputes throughout the North East. TRS would be instrumental in spreading the news and actions of the short shipyard workers strike in the region.

> "On August 28th all workers at the four Swan Hunter shipyards on the Tyne downed tools to attend a mass meeting at the Newcastle City Hall. Shipyard workers agreed unanimously that their only weapon was that of an occupation and agreed that all four Swan Hunter yards should be completely taken over by the workers at 1pm on Sunday 1st September. For the remaining days before occupation sit-in tactics were implemented, this was to enable all workers to receive wages that they were owed. Sunday 1st saw a management attempt to stop the occupation. Management, all armed with sleeping bags etc arrived at the yards 12pm to take the yards themselves and lock out the workers. Their arrival at the yards saw the tables once again turned as on hearing of this action earlier on Sunday morning the yards had already been occupied by the

workforce.

Banners proclaiming 'Now under workers control' and 'Under new management' were raised throughout the yards. All gates and entrances were either boarded up or welded shut and at the Wallsend yard a crane had been placed across the road way to prevent any vehicles from getting anywhere near the gates"

Despite workers protests, shop stewards eventually ended the occupation after their talks with management.

"The occupation was the only real weapon the workers had; this has now been given up by the stewards on the grounds that their negotiations would begin if the occupation was called off. These negotiations have obviously not come about and the stewards are now beginning to realise they have made a major mistake. 20th September saw a mass rally in support of the strikers, delegates from up and down the country. Donations shall not win the workers their dispute, industrial action must be organised by all those that work in and supply the Shipbuilding Industry. Solidarity, rank and file control and direct action are their only keys to victory."[601]

"A hopeful but inspiring graffiti on a wall in Newcastle Upon Tyne. Wallsend is one of the main shipbuilding centres in the UK. In September '85 a strike broke out there which spread to other yards belonging to the Swan Hunter group on the Tyne. It lasted for some two months and, though the pickets were mounted daily, these were scarcely needed to prevent scabbing. It began initially as an occupation of the main yards, above which there hung a banner saying 'Under Workers Control'. The strike remained unofficial throughout its duration, when, after 7 weeks, the management unexpectedly capitulated to meet the main demands in full. These included an end to on ship rest breaks & an assurance that there would be no return to the bad old days of the right of foremen to hire & fire. The victory was all the more remarkable considering the degree of demoralisation that existed amongst the working class especially of Durham & Northumberland after the defeat of the miners. There was even talk of setting up a breakaway Union. Put like this the central question of the Unions as capitalist institutionswas never posed – but there was enough self-activity and initiative tothrow a scare into the Confederation of British Shipbuilders."[602]

"Swan Hunter is now devoted to warship building"[603]

15th October, and 3,000 strikers decided unanimously at a mass meeting to return to work after peace talks between management and national union officials.

"On Tyneside the workers at the Swan Hunter yards are preparing for future action over privatisation which will result in the loss of hundreds more jobs and an erosion of their rights that they have won over the years...Lessons learnt during the September, October must be heeded well, the occupation being the only weapon, the rank and file must take complete control of any future action, power must not be allowed to slip into the hands of incompetent cowards on the Stewards committee as happened on the last action."[604]

Local zines released this year, apart from a few, were all predominantly non music related with the emphasis concentrated on articles, poetry, art, and other efforts of self expression. Some include *Face of the*

*Future* (Consett, Co Durham), Ugly *People, Ugly People, Ugly Fucking People* (Co Durham) which was a benefit booklet for Durham Women's Aid, *The troops out of Ireland issue* of *Shit* (Blackhill, Consett, Co Durham) which concentrated sorely on the then situation in the North of Ireland, and the same folk also produced both *Let there be love, Let there be life, Let there be an earth* and *The Sentient Paradox?* This was a benefit for the Imprisoned Miners Fund, whilst RM from Sunderland would release He Who Laughs Last.[605]

Some of those involved in *Tyne and Wear Free News* and/or groupings based around the anarcho-punk scene, and in particular certain bands in the region would also release a series of leaflets / handouts at gigs and other events under the title of the Flat Earth Collective. Some of these include *'The Price of Resistance'*, and *'Apartheid / South Africa'* and later 1986 leaflets include *'A Wapping great lie'* and *'To all the male* members of tonight's audience'.[606] The year concludes with the debates between TJ and others in Freedom regarding previous articles.[607]

## 4.7 1986

*The Syndicalist* No 2 in its beginning of the year editorial would emphasise the battles ahead and states;

> "1986 and what it will bring, must surely be a major concern for all workers both employed and unemployed. Over the next eleven months the working people of this country face even more cut backs in Health, Education and Social Security. The selling off of British Gas and Water Authorities will mean yet a further concentration of the wealth of this country into the hands of a minority. Plans for even more anti Trade Union legislation and the new and oppressive Police Bill will be used to ensure that any real opposition to this governments policies are made a criminal act. The hierarchy of the Trade Union and labour movement has shown itself to be completely ineffective in

> countering attacks such as these on the working class. While the Labour Party has joined in the bickering about which group of shareholders should control Westland Helicopters the unemployment figures have risen yet again and the C.B.I have this month issued a report predicting even more job losses in the manufacturing industries. Now we see hard won union rights, working conditions and wage levels being whittled away before our very eyes while bosses unions such as the E.E.P.T.U., A.U.E.W. and the U.D.M. are allowed to make sweetheart agreements and no strike deals while the trade union movement looks on in despair. It is quite clear that many of these unions have the ultimate aim of breaking away from the T.U.C. and forming their own right wing trade union body. Only by organising at both rank and file and inter union grass root levels can we mount an effective opposition. The Teachers, Building workers and Miners are now in the process of building such organisations. This must be extended throughout every industry and community. The time to organise is now."

The issue also covers further local disputes such as the 'Contracts Ltd' (Garment workers in South Shields) five month strike, articles on 'union recognition', a dispute in Glasgow, 'miners under direct management', hospital cuts, tenants under attack, etc, whilst giving support to the 20+ jailed miners throughout the country, including eight;

> "Who were sent down to Durham jail shortly before Christmas. On Christmas Eve a vigil was held outside Durham jail in solidarity with the jailed miners. AS (Durham Miners Support Group) said: *"We will never rest until these men are released and the sacked men reinstated"*, and "On Sunday 19th January, miners at Westoe Colliery in South Shields voted that if there were any more sackings or victimisation at the pit they would strike."[608]

Some anarchists in the region (Durham and Tyneside) who had been meeting for the last couple of months under the name 'Libertarian Organisation and Structure' (LOS) would issue the following statement[609] to the national anarchist press explaining themselves during this period.

> "L.O.S. was set up with the intention of understanding some of the things which prevent groups with basically anarchist intentions from achieving them. We are also open to the possibility that we might have to modify what we mean by 'anarchist forms of organisation'.
>
> We are dissatisfied with the usual anarchist ideas of that to avoid in groups. For example we feel the classical anarchist concept of authority as something a minority inflicts on an unwilling majority is only relevant in a limited number of situations. Our experience is that there are many more, subtle ways, in which authority can develop, such as people getting bored, people becoming well- intentioned experts, personal links inhibiting challenge or criticism, etc, and these can affect even the most committed anarchist.
>
> Also we believe that classical anarchist theory is not based on the way people really do think, feel and behave. For one thing it has nottaken on the vast changes in culture and economics which have occurred since its foundation. Also, it reflects an over-simplified nineteenth century concept that a group is a collection of autonomous individuals who decide everything through rational processes that they completely understand. In fact, a decision may be reached which seems rational (on first impression) but actually results from hidden motivations, such as a desire to smooth things over, the impressive way someone speaks for it, or even just because people want to go home. Such considerations may seem trivial, but they can often be a significant as what people would insist their reasons were, and allowing for them can radically alter the way we decide to act.

Starting off from these criticisms we have been looking at groups, collectives and co-ops that we have been in. For example, the County Durham network of miners support groups has shown that large numbers of people can decide to adopt our ideas, such as delegates to be mandated, although they would never dream of calling themselves anarchists. Unfortunately, these ideas often seem to get distorted or lost, even if no-one intentionally decides to set themselves up in authority. We feel it would be a good thing if the mechanisms behind this were better understood.

We'd like to work with a wider range of experiences than just our own, so if you have been in a group which came across these 'structural' problems (bearing in mind that there is often more going on in a group hi-jacked by Leninists than just their manipulations) we'd like you to send us details of what happened, why you think it turned out the way it did and how such failings might have been avoided. Any other comments would also be welcome, all letters will receive a reply and, in a few months, when we bring out a pamphleton the subject, you will get a free copy. LOS. c/o Days of Hope Bookshop."[610]

Another communiqué would follow in June which gives further insight into both the pamphlet and the group entitled "Libertarian Organisation & Structure: What next?"

1. "Since the summer of 1985 LOS has been meeting regularly to discuss aspects of libertarian theory and practice. In particular we share the concern that anarchist ideas have remained fairly static, irrespective of repeated experience of failure and defeat. A rather "holier than thou" attitude has allowed anarchists to blame the State, authoritarians and other external conditions. The possibilities that the ideas as they stand may not have some kind of inevitable, trans-historical relevance, and that having those ideas does not in itself lead to good libertarian practice, continually escape attention. We have therefore concentrated

on the details of the failure of libertarian organisation, trying to pin down what it is about anarchistprinciples and anarchists in action that may be at tault. We have been very aware of the fact that few precedents exist for this kind of criticism and self-criticism among anarchists.

2. There are several contexts in which this examination of libertarian organisation is important. Most obvious are anarchist groups or movements, and organisations whose structures have been strongly influenced by libertarian individuals or principles. But equally important are situations where ordinary people come together in groups and spontaneously choose basic anarchist structures. From the start we have tried to bring together analyses and critiques of these forms, stressing social and psychological factors rather than crude ideological rationalisations.

3. We began by focussing on specific personal experiences of libertarian groups or organisations breaking down or degenerating into authoritarian or hierarchical structures of one kind or another. These "case studies" included strike support organisations, anarchist groups, housing co-ops and educational groups. From discussions of these, several prominent areas of concern arose. We then began to concentrate on these more general aspects of political groups.

4. Our first publication, a large pamphlet, is emerging from this work so far. In it we introduce our perspective, and discuss in some detail particular factors in political groups which we feel affect their activities profoundly. These include:

- The social ecologies in which groups operate,
- How admitting the impossibility of achieving absolute goals (such asabsence of authority) affects our understanding of anarchism,
- The effects of emotion,
- The development and influence of rituals.

These parts of the pamphlet are being written individually, and as far as possible we have tried to keep them rooted in the reality of groups as we experience, perceive, think and feel about them.

5. Our immediate attention is to get the pamphlet published. Up to now we have remained a small group of 5 or so individuals. We plan to expand somewhat, and to extend our contact with other libertarians. If the pamphlet makes any impression we may try to continue in that vein and turn it into a semi-annual journal."[611]

The communiqué continues in an encouragement of communication with like minded groups and individuals for further publications, which, other than the aforementioned pamphlet, didn't occur.

Intellectual self analysis aside, the pamphlet when released in 1987 would describe itself thus;

"This pamphlet takes a careful look at anarchism as it is talked about and in practice. By exploding some myths and exploring some new viewpoints that might be useful, it aims at an anarchism which bears a closer relation to how real people and groups operate. It seeks to begin a task of reconstructing libertarian ideas so that they can be used without dogma and are instead relevant to the needs and aspirations of working people, the poor, the unemployed and oppressed."[612]

We can't propagate or ideal unless we show we can practice it in our own groups.

Encouragement of a national boycott was taking place, where in *Black Flag*;

> "A series of flash, trendy like adverts are on television screens at peak time at present, pushing the 'French Connection' clothes. The owner of Contracts Ltd, a subsidiary of French Connection said in an interview *"I believe in dictatorship"*. The 140 clothing workers who have been on strike since 17th Sept 1985 to improve their lot (for 39 hour week they get £76 without meal breaks, compulsory overtime,a disc system to use

toilets, dismissal without warning...) and to get 9 sacked workers their jobs back. National Union of Seamen have stopped imports and exports of F.C. goods the least you can do is boycott F.C. too!"[613]

*The Syndicalist* No 3 would look at the union sell-out of the 'Contracts' strike, the teachers strike and an interview with a striker, health, Northumberland mines and an analysis of the 'Wapping dispute' and the actions against Murdoch's empire, including the picketing of the Hetton-le-Hole warehouse. News of Durham Miners Support Groups donation of £415 to the sacked print workers, and the groups travel to participate in the picket at Wapping was alsocovered.[614]

Newcastle DAM, commenting on the end of the strike at Contracts Ltd, South Shields inform us "A vote of 54 to 12 on Wednesday March 19th, under pressure from union officials who, three weeks before, had withdrawn support from the strike, called for a return to work. The workers marched back into their factory, on Monday 24th, in an organised return to work, knowing that their central demand – union recognition had not been conceded by management. The union officials consider this a fair settlement." "On behalf of the strikers we express fraternal thanks for the support, in the form of picketing, leafleting and financial donations that DAM groups have given." Any further financial help was to be sent to Tyneside Revolutionary Syndicalists. Whilst at the shipyards of Wallsend, "Bosses at the privatised Swan Hunters shipyards launched the £100m HMS Coventry at 3.45am before dawn, on Tyneside, 8-4-1986 to beat a wildcat strike by 2,500 shipyard workers. While Mrs Thatcher cheered the management in the House of Commons, angry workers facing redundancy, marched through the town."[615]

March would also see the publication of an article on 'Sexuality – fantasies of freedom' by TJ which looked at the 'suppression of sexual psychology', and which concludes;

> "If social and psychological repression are so distinct it follows that lifting the former will *not* provide sexual emancipation. As

> in the sixties it may be possible for people to delude themselves that they are now sexually 'free' – the main freedom achieved was the improved access of deluded radical men to uneasy radical women. Of course it will be necessary to break social suppression of sex in many areas, maybe all, I'm not sure. But to believe that to do so would on its own produce natural human sexuality is just as naive as ignoring the personal dimension altogether, and relying on economic change alone to achieve a 'real' revolution."[616]

This was followed with a further exploration into 'Psychology' with an article by TJ on 'The separation of selves' which ends;

> "Character / personality / psychological 'health' etc are rooted in the prevailing social and political structures. In order for a society to operate at all, these structures must to some extent 'fit' the personality distributors of the population. The fit is now very bad (and it's never been much better). A useful radical psychology can show this vividly and in detail. Its aims should be to offer a coherent, comprehensive explanation of human-in-society. In combination with other levels of analysis and struggle it should be able to pinpoint new opportunities for resistance to the insanity of Capital and State."[617]

Early 1986 would also see the release of the seminal study of 'The Clousden Hill Free Communist and Co-operative Colony 1894-1902' by local labour historian Nigel Todd. The knowledge that an anarchist commune existed near Forest Hall, Newcastle was common amongst the older generation of local anarchists, but never had such an in depth historical study been known. NW, in a disappointing and inaccurate review in *Freedom* states that Clousden Hill was in the East of Newcastle, when it's in the North. Kapper and William Key were quoted as 'leaders' who had 'long local experience of left wing activity' in the North East. Kapper had only been around the region for a few years, and Key was a 'socialist' from Sunderland.

Nevertheless "Todd has produced a very detailed and sympathetic account of Clousden Hill, based mainly on primary sources. The level of accuracy is high and the whole book is very impressive. The booklet contains some excellent illustrations, though unfortunately none of the community itself, and it is a really valuable addition to the history of the anarchist movement."[618]

*The Syndicalist* No 4 would give coverage of the on-going dispute by 6000 sacked print workers at Wapping, and also highlight local actions in support of the struggle, including three major pickets at TNT distribution depot at Houghton le Spring, and other smaller pickets at other W.H. Smith warehouses, inc Gateshead to highlight the distribution of scab papers such as *The Sun* etc. Scab vans were also stoned in Gateshead. Coverage of a South African talk on rank and file unionism at Newcastle University, Colway Tyres in Durham and the workers fight for union recognition and the brick layers dispute in London were all also looked at.

Issue 4 would also highlight the work of Gateshead Unemployed Action Group.

> "Organised unemployed groups are a sheer necessity in the present climate of mass redundancies and shop and factory closures. As even the official unemployment figures rise to frightening proportions and the social security system is being slashed to the bone unemployed groups are beginning to spring up all over the country. However some of these organisations can prove to be as bureaucratic and ineffective as even the most reformist trade union structure due to the involvement of certain elements. It is quite clear that what we do not need is another body willing to take actual initiatives and control out of the hands of those that build and belong to an unemployed grouping which has happened on occasion in Tyneside.
>
> June of last year saw the formation of an active unemployed

rank and file group in the Gateshead area. The organisation is not the usual Trades Council, M.S.C. or Communist Party controlled failure but an autonomous grouping bringing together those willing to fight for the rights of those while unemployed and to join with employed workers in their fight without pushing any party political line. Due to the experiences of some members in the Tyneside Unemployed Workers Movement the Gateshead Unemployed Action Group are determined that they shall always remain a grass root unemployed controlled organisation. The aim of the G.U.A.G. is a very simple one, 'to organise together with employed workers and fight back against attacks'. The G.U.A.G. feels that an unemployed organisation must be run by the unemployed members themselves.

Since the formation of the G.U.A.G. they have been involved in many campaigns for both the rights of the unemployed and workers in employment alike. On an industrial level the Health Workers, Shipyard Workers, Miners and most recently the Contracts Strikers (where over £2,000 was collected along with other support given) have all been on the receiving end of G.U.A.G. support. The Gateshead group hope that in the near future workers all over the Tyne will take up their example of strike support groups and begin to incorporate such bodies in their day to day working in the work place as a permanent thing.

On another level the G.U.A.G. have launched many campaigns around the issues of unemployment such as fights against cuts in thesocial security system, the use of Specialist Claims Control 'Snooper Squads' etc. It is felt by the group that work must be done on the streets where benefit cuts that affect people can be explained to the public and the campaign can be built.

The last time 'Snooper Squads' were in Gateshead the group held leafleting of the DHSS building, as well as frightening the snoopersto death when they occupied the office and proceeded

> to take photographs of members of the snooper teams. The G.U.A.G. is a self-funding organisation. The message of the G.U.A.G. is that of, 'UNEMPLOYED, EMPLOYED UNITE AND FIGHT', 'OUR POWER LIES IN ORGANISATION'."[619]

Summing up the time perfectly, O.R. in a letter to *Black Flag* would say;

> "Shipyard workers, mainly in North East England and Scotland, have been designated by the state to join the ever spiralling unemployed millions who have been cast off by the uncaring capitalist exploiters. The waffle and 'cold flannel' by the present and future government spokespersons is enough to make people weep. Labour, Tory and the other windbags have never given a toss for the plight of the working class, as has been very clearly demonstrated over the last couple of years. Profits by the billion and by whatever means is the call of the capitalist class, and if that means greater intensity of exploitation through the blood, sweat and tears of fewer workers, then they will ensure that less people are allowed to work. The fight back against the state by a solid working class is being hampered by the exploitation via the media, of sectional differences, be they real or imagined. A working class free from the shackles of status, trade, profession, racism, fascism, sexism, and religion, forged in the reality of class struggle, will smash to smithereens the state and all the institutions which appear to hold it intact. The time has come to grasp the nettle of working class reality."[620]

Another nameless group was also formed in and around Gateshead whose activities encompassed the distribution of papers such as *The (Tyneside) Syndicalist, Class War, Direct Action,* and *Counter Information,* etc as well as numerous zines from around the country. The group was also instrumental in creating their own zines, collectively and individually. As well as attending numerous marches around the country, hunt sabbing activities, fly posting, leafleting, and elements of 'nocturnal art' on many a wall. Some were also involved in the direct action activities against such institutions as Barclays Bank (because of their investment in Apartheid, in South Africa), anti fur protests in Newcastle and other 'animal rights' issues. Some formed punk bands, some performed live poetry, and some did nothing. Of course this wasn't unique to Gateshead, as other groups with similar aspirations and actions were happening all over the North East in South Shields, Newcastle, Stockton, Durham, and Blyth, etc. Coming up for the sixth year of the Thatcher / Conservative regime, for many a generation coming of age during these years, survival and protest was commonplace in many lives, not to mention the permanent threat of nuclear war under the Thatcher and President Reagan relationship. Rebellion came natural.

May 1986, and *The Syndicalist* is now on for its 5th issue. Included within were reports on actions regarding sacked miners, South African unions and their struggle, events surrounding Murdoch and Wapping, and other local industrial news and disputes. Increasing reliance on trade unions and repeated let downs by their hierarchy, prompts the editorial to conclude, in an optimistic note that;

> "On the other hand, imaginative direct action can bear fruit. Energetically seeking the support of other workers, better planning of picketing, and hitting the bosses' profits where it hurts most should be the order of the day. When they are not mesmerised by the posturing of their union leaders, the rank and file employ these methods to great effect. They are the means by which the bosses' laws can be bypassed so that we stand a fighting chance of victoryin any dispute."[621]

*Tyne and Wear Free News* No 8 is also hitting the streets in June, and includes writings on the hypocrisy of Newcastle City Council giving the imprisoned African National Congress leader Nelson Mandella the freedom of the city andnaming a University building after him whilst, at the same time, giving permission for the National Front to hold a public meeting in a City School, amongst other listed hypocrisy's. A report was also given on the attempt of the aforementioned National Front and their opposed and disrupted try at havinga local meeting. Other pieces included 'the right to work', 'local travel structure', and 'social contracts'."[622]

*The Syndicalist* No 6 is also picking up on the National Fronts attempt to hold their meeting, and reports how the janitor of the school in question, when seeing the build up of anti fascists outside the school prior to the NF turning up, phoned his union for advice (the G & M) only to be told "no comment", after which the janitor was 'forced to open the gates of the school'.

> "The major question arises on the G&M attitude towards the fascists meeting. In our opinion the janitor should have been informed by the union that he could keep the gates locked and go home for the evening. The whole question of union involvement in the anti-fascist movement is obviously crucial. The power to stop the fascists from holding meetings such as the one reported above is in the hands of the organised union movement. With a real anti-fascist policy from the unions, and not a piece of rhetoric that never gets implemented, there would be no reason why the fascists should be allowed to organise on Tyneside, let alone even exist. Our power to stop ale supplies to pubs that refuse to stop allowing the fascists to meet, our power to keep rooms locked, and to single out and isolate fascists is a weapon that the unions hold. Street battles and physical confrontation are grounds chosen by the fascists – we should only use them when there is no alternative. It is up to us to make sure that our unions have anti-racist and anti-fascist policies. If the union already has the policies we must make sure that it is not just lip- service but an actual measure being taken against racists and fascists on Tyneside."

Other articles in issue 6 include reporting on the Silentnight strike and efforts to get the Co-op to refuse Silentnight timber, a listing of the huge amount of job cuts and losses throughout the region, Contracts Ltd organising, etc. The issue also interviewed RC and his involvement during the miners' strike and looked at the closure of the Bates Colliery at Blyth.[623]

The merging of those involved in the Anarchist Communist Discussion Group (previously the Libertarian Communist Discussion Group), the Syndicalist Fight group, those involved in the production of *Virus*, and others led to the formation of the Anarchist Communist Federation (ACF) in March 1986.[624] As well as continuing the magazine *Virus*, the ACF also produced a paper called *Liberation*. *Virus*, which would eventually change its name to *Organise* in early 1989 was at first produced by an exile from the North East, namely CP from Crook, Co Durham, then residing in the London area.[625] Further local participation was cemented by July with announcements that there was now a group / contact in the Newcastle area.[626]

July 1986 was a busy commemorative month with it being the 50th anniversary of the Spanish revolution. The release of numerous pamphlets nationally was coupled with many of the movement's newspapers and magazines having special supplements highlighting the events of 1936. *The Syndicalist* No 7 would have a large four page supplement entitled 'The Spanish Revolution 1936-1986, The Struggle Continues', which looked at events in detail of the collectives and public services of the time. The paper was also unique in its interview with a CNT militant and participant of the period (see the 1936 section of this history). The editorial would also look at length at the apartheid situation in South Africa whilst drawing conclusions of worldwide support needed as in given to the, in aspects similar, anti fascist struggle of 1936. Other local disputes were given coverage, particularly those of the Health workers.[627]

This month also saw the closure of Days of Hope bookshop after financial worries and eventual eviction by the Theatre next door who owned the property and wanted to re-develop the site. Tyneside Revolutionary Syndicalists, publishers of *The Syndicalist* were now contactable through Tyneside Free Press, Charlotte Sq, Newcastle.[628]

In a previous letter 'deriding teachers and saying they are all "soft cops" who reinforce social control in children' John form Newcastle DAM would respond;

> "I found the articles on education very worrying. They argue that teachers by nature are middle class and therefore imply that they cannot be revolutionaries. The first article says teachers are instruments of social control like the gutter press. In this case why is the writer supporting the printers? The other point is that the "upwardly mobile image" prevents "revolutionary consciousness". Is s/he really arguing that if you work in a "profession" you are not really working class? To artificially protect children from capitalism and repression strikes me as a defeatist, cop-out argument; aren't they going to enter just as much a social control mechanism when /if they get a job anyway? Is it right to expect parents to educate at home? Who pays for all the books? What about the handicapped child? Should parents give up their lives, and pay for all the recourses as well? I find it anti-syndicalist to suggest that being onthe dole is "not so bad because we can spend time with the kids"."[629]

Meanwhile, *Tyne and Wear Free News* No 9 would cover events surrounding the proposed building of a nuclear power station at Druridge Bay in Northumberland, the dodgy dealings of 'politicians' such as Derek Hatton, local protests against Newcastle's 'adult/porn' bookshop, and local transport issues surrounding 'de-regulation'.[630]

August and *The Syndicalist* No 8 encompasses within its editorial a scathing attack on the situation in both Spain and at home;

> "The political climate in Spain at the moment shows the degree of contempt felt by the so called "socialist" government towards true working class organisation. The Spanish government has tacitly and materially supported a completely dishonest attack on a rank and file union which wouldn't succumb to the needs of big business. In a similar vein the working class in Britain has

on many occasions been on the receiving end of "socialist" policies. Ever since the first Labour government in 1924 which sent in troops to smash a long-running transport dispute (some strikers had actually canvassed for the "party of the workers") right up until the last, which saw troops being used to break up the fireman's strike, police attacking workers at Grunwick and the "Social Contract" to keep wages down, workers have been betrayed by their (sic) party.

The criminalisation of workers in rank and file organisations in Spain is not a far step from our own social democratic Thatcher government, with its anti-union legislation making almost all union opposition to redundancies and cuts a criminal act. But would a Labour government be all that different? After all, most of the current waves of anti-union laws were devised by labour policy planners during the 1975-9 government. In previous Labour campaigns workers were at least given to believe that everything would be alright so long as enough seats were won. This time around nobody believes that except the right wing and a few confused "radicals". Canvassers are now even instructed not to discuss "politics" on the doorstep! Plans are already afoot to revamp the Thatcher union legislation. Labour intend to take away the right of trade unions to tax relief, if they do not hold secret ballots before taking industrial action, an idea Tories would congratulate them on.

The reactionary and anti working-class nature of Labour in power is not restricted to seeking to render unions impotent. As people in Spain are currently discovering, socialist ministers seem to delight in passing the most repressive laws. Labour brought in the Official Secrets Act, internment in Northern Ireland and the Prevention of Terrorism Act. They did absolutely <u>nothing</u> to restrict the activity of intelligence agencies like MI5, who continue to harass and interfere in the lives of people as unthreatening as trade union officials and CND members. Labour commissioned nuclear weapons testing and the British Bomb and joined NATO. They consistently accepted updated

> nuclear weapons technology and American bases. Labour in opposition talk a lot about "freedom of information". Would they do more than the Americans, who made sure that security was advanced enough to cope with apparent openness before allowing access to low-grade official information?
>
> Look at how the Tories are rolling back the Welfare State. People are being punished at every available opportunity for suffering the effects of government policy and the movements of Capital. But in power a Labour government would not restore the losses. As always it would do as little as it could get away with, while trying to keep its false image of protector of the poor. In the past Labour stopped married women from claiming benefits, withdrew free milk in secondary schools, set the ball rolling for YTS schemes, and presided over massive cuts in health and education and the "winter of discontent" in their last term of office."

The editorial concludes with an emphatic statement of;

> "Socialist government means political leaders helping the bosses increase their profits, trade union leaders making sure that workers don't get what they want, and the whole system working to ensure that ordinary people don't rock the boat or cost too much. This sounds rather similar to Conservative government!"[631]

By September, the newly formed Newcastle ACF are reporting that they now have a core of four members who are also in DAM, LOS and TRS. No separate ACF activities were reported due to the majority of activity being TRS syndicalist based with its 20+ activists / members and more popular events given the current political situation.[632] *Virus* No 8 also contains a letter from MT of Newcastle ACF discussing 'scientific' approaches to anarchism.

*The Syndicalist* No 9 is reporting on the strike by 90 workers at

Newcastle's Freeman Hospital, news from Wapping, South African unions, justice for sacked miners, and news and participation of local pickets of Co-op stores because of their refusal to not stock Silentnight beds, made by scab workforce during their current strike. The editorial looks at unemployment, the social needs of workers and fights with employers for 'rights', before concluding;

> "Whatever we achieve in the area of wages, hours, conditions and unemployment we must not lose sight of our ultimate objectives. Short-term reforms are too susceptible to being taken away at any time. They are no replacement for the complete destruction of capitalism and the state, and the building of a libertarian society which is structured around social need and mutual aid, not power and profit."

Interestingly this month's issue also lists eight pamphlets for sale, including the 'Spanish Revolution' supplement from the July issue being sold as a separate entity.[633]

Nationally the DAM were organising a 'Plastic Bullets Video Tour' showing the devastating effects of the use and implementation of plastic bullets, which were introduced into Northern Ireland by a Labour government, by the way[634]. The 'tour' stopped off at Newcastle on the 21st September for a showing.[635]

This year would also see the formation of the Northern Anarchist Network (NAN) which brought together groups from Manchester, Newcastle, Durham, Rochdale, Preston, Leeds, Huddersfield, Bradford, Hull, Doncaster, Sheffield, Liverpool, Bolton, Edinburgh and Macclesfield. After a successful march, conference and social in Leeds, September 20th NAN is announcing that future conference meetings would be bi-monthly and the next was scheduled to be hosted in Newcastle on December 6th by Newcastle Anarchists, contactable through *Tyne and Wear Free News*.[636]

The first NAN bulletin includes a letter from RM of Newcastle and highlighted concerns that needed implemented immediately;

> "Last month's short & hectic discussion of racism at the launch of the NAN, showed in graphic detail, the ignorance of most anarchists on the subject, their unwillingness to listen and take racism seriously, and how complacent they are about it. It was left to the only black person there to raise it as a problem seriously...Faced with such a reaction, and being in a minority of one, I left disgusted at the attitude of some of those there. But racism as an issue and aproblem will not go away quite as easily. Racism in Britain is on the increase, both in terms of organised groups & on an individual level and as living conditions fall further, we can expect racism to get worse. Yet anarchist groups have consistently refused to take racism seriously. The activities and actions of black groups throughout the country are ignored and discounted by almost all of the anarchist groups and anarchists media, or interpreted by anarchists for their own benefit (e.g. almost all of the coverage of the riots in '85 was from a white anarchist viewpoint, the views of the black people who were involved & who it affected was largely ignored). The racism of anarchist groups is never looked at, British imperialism and its relation to the 3rd world is never considered seriously and the question of anarchists combating racism is barely raised, never mindtaken seriously. The list goes on & on. Certainly racism must be taken seriously by anarchists, if they expect to be taken seriously, particularly by black people. So I hope that at future NAN meetings, consideration of this will be made, and that we don't get a repetitionof the last meeting."[637]

Certainly this was not an issue in the North East, as RM was a frequent participant and activist within local anarchist groups on Tyneside.

Naturally this letter caused a bit of a well aimed stir and kick up the proverbial arse of those complacent enough that is wasn't a problem that needed addressed, and the debates surrounding the issue would continue in future Bulletins by Leeds, Durham anarchists, and RO of Newcastle, amongst others.[638]

Meanwhile, Octobers issue of *The Syndicalist* has a large section commemorating the events of Hungary 1956, disputes at Swan Hunters Shipyards, refuse collectors dispute, repression and resistance in South Africa, Spanish workers land occupation, the actions of various mines and their industrial disputes in the region, and other local news. The list of pamphlets available has increased to 19, whilst the editorial would take an in depth look at the exploitative role and actions of multi-national corporations and the perpetuation of cannibalistic capitalism it purports.[639]

Newcastle ACF are now becoming more active within the Federation with many internal articles discussing, for example, the wording of proposed pamphlets i.e. the future *'Anarchism as we see it'* publication, attending delegate conferences and national conferences throughout the country. Membership was also slowly growing with interested parties getting in touch.[640]

The slow growth was hampered slightly by the group's activities in other areas, as one member states "Newcastle ACF is composed of 4 individuals (all members of LOS) and there is a chance that several other interested people will join. The 4 of us formed the group because we saw the advantages of a national libertarian communist organisation and felt we should be part of it. But on our own we have neither the time nor resources (due to our involvementin other groups) to engage in the kinds and extent of activity that would be appropriate for the core of a new, growing Tyneside branch of the ACF." "A more useful strategy would be to attract people we came across through our work in other groups (e.g. LOS, Tyneside Revolutionary Syndicalists, unemployed groups, anarchist groups, etc) and when the time was ripe announce widely and publicly an ACF branch on Tyneside."[641] Fear of 'burning out' was also prevalent amongst the group because of jobs, political activity, and union involvement, and so on.

*The Syndicalist* in its November / December issue celebrates the victory of North East Garment workers and their victory for pay increases after a series ofwildcat strikes, trade union restriction at the Nissan car plant in Washington, Tyne & Wear, apartheid, the opening of the Metro Centre in Gateshead, DHSS fraud, etc. As ever the editorial would interestingly give us an excellent analysis of current events, and this month's I quote in full for this reason.

> "Capitalism in its modern form exploits workers twice, once at the point of production where profit is squeezed out of the labour process, and again at the point of consumption, where workers buy the produce they themselves and others have produced at grossly- inflated prices. The interests of workers are further harmed twice, through unhealthy and dangerous conditions at work and by the effects on people of consumer goods that are produced without any consideration for the needs or well being of the consumer. So modern capitalism entails a many faceted and systematic process which operates to the detriment of the mass of the people in every way. Materially workers are paid far less than the profit to be gained from the production of their labour to secure 'super profits' for the employer. People are deceitfully persuaded to pay over the actual worth (in production terms) for the fulfilment of their needs as dictated by the voracious appetite for profit of the capitalist. Conditions at work, or even when unemployed due to the inability to 'purchase' a healthy existence, mean bad health and severe psychological damage. Consumption is equally unhealthy, firstly because the goods themselves are dangerous to health in many different ways (such as the use of additives and colourings in food on sale etc) but also because we are beguiled by advertising, fashion and the glossy packaging to ignore real needs and instead to buy what the capitalists want to – our interests are not part of theirmotives.
>
> At present capitalists are consolidating their capacity to maximise profits through the use of the state. The increasing use of computers and other means of efficient surveillance and

control are combined with tools such as an expanded police force (expanded both in numbers, national co-ordination and areas of responsibility) an the Police and Public Order Bills, try to ensure that resistance is fragmented and unable to grow or achieve anything lasting. Reliance on changing public opinion and superficial passive opposition is a fashion that fits well with the psychology of consumerism. We choose among an array of consumer goods (paid for on many occasions through plastic cards and credit) that are more or less the same and equally worthless or unhealthy. Likewise we select issues to be angry about (but not do anything about) from a range of fads presented by experts in the media. In the workplace the same trend is apparent – union bureaucrats protect their position through diverting real issues of the workforce into non-existent causes and through making sure that the boat is not rocked. None of these tactics make any difference, and in fact fit our rulers' interests perfectly.

To reverse this trend there is a need to convince people of the utter sterility and pointlessness of the consumer society and its illusory attractions. More than this we need to explain how damaging it is to ordinary people from all points of view – physical and mental health, the waste of our lives in the pursuit of fashion, and the progressive erosion of the conditions of our existence. Moreover the entrenchment of consumer society can make the possibility to change things more remote. Partly this is because the real forces controlling society have become more invisible to us as we focus our attention on the surface level of things, on superficial appearances. Once this spell is broken the system can be seen for what it is – an edifice designed to promote the material interests of the rich and the power interests of politicians and bureaucrats. Collective direct action to effect change makes all the difference – by workers in rank and file control of disputes in their workplace and by communities' pressure groups not relinquishing control of their struggles to experts, local government, charity workers or other outsiders. This makes the difference to people involved in small scale struggles and holds out the hope that links will be made between struggles so that rank and file and mass control of social revolution can be worked towards.

Those resisting all over the world, can show us the way forward. For example, striking miners realise that their previous existence paying HP (hire-purchase) for the video etc was not what life was about. Collective action, mutual aid and solidarity made life meaningful for them, not the fantasy fodder of Metro Centres or American soaps. By using positive aspects of human social life, rather than emphasising money, we can begin to challenge the system that denies us our basic material and social dignity."[642]

*Tyne and Wear Free News* No 11 is also hitting the streets and appearing on the regions walls and bus stops, and amongst its pages looks at racism and the local immigration service, a look at Eldon Square shopping centre, local policing, and an exposure of what was to become known as gentrification and the proposed re-development of Newcastle & Gateshead's Quayside area with luxury hotels and expensive 'yuppie' flats.[643]

As stated previously, the national criticism centred on the Spanish Information Network and the individual ML and the supporting of the 'wrong CNT' is a subject I haven't delved into. Nevertheless, the production of (as far as I am aware) the last issue of *Sinews* in the region deserves a minor place in this history. Thus issue 5 was released in the winter of 1986 from Co Durham, and describes itself as 'annual report on the CNT-U and other Spanish unions with anarchist forms of organisation'. Articles inside include, 'Spain – 50 years on from 1936', a discussion on the two CNT's, Rebirth of village assemblies, and Solidaridad Obrera newspaper, etc. They also produced a short booklet 'What is the CNT?' during this period.[644]

The Northern Anarchist Network Conference in Newcastle on December 6th didn't get off to the best of starts, as 'Disgusted' from Huddersfield reports;

> "Okay, so Newcastle might not be quite as close as Leeds for many groups. Granted it was the start of the Xmas shopping season. Agreed the weather wasn't as warm as the day of the Leeds launch meeting. But what's your excuse? Personally I didn't expect half as many people to be at the last NAN meeting in Newcastle (no it's not way up on the Scottish border) as attended the grand spectacular launch day at Leeds. But I expected a few more than the six who were, SIX!!. Not counting the twelve from Newcastle itself, one person from South Shields or the half dozen plus from nearby Durham. Come on!"

Several points were raised and debated during the conference, one of which concluded;

> "The movement is right to put an emphasis on the personal as political, but this is not enough in itself. Challenging people's prejudices is part of the struggle and a change of lifestyle may help us to see the alternatives to today's society. But so long as there are capitalist / state institutions then these institutions will determine the attitudes of those who live and work in them. We have to destroy the institutions which reinforce racist, authoritarian and sexist attitudes everyday and not just struggle for personal change. Otherwise we are in danger of being concerned with personal perfection rather than revolution – becoming yet another mutual appreciation society for the right on – and getting nowhere as a result."

Another decision was paper selling to spread our ideas to those not normally reached with anarchist and libertarian propaganda. "Just because the Trots do it badly doesn't mean we shouldn't do it at all."[645] Although not a new idea or practice in itself, public paper selling of such publications as *Class War* and *Organise!* would become quite prevalent in the coming years on Tyneside.

The year ends with an open invitation / letter to both the newly formed (as a national grouping) Class War Federation and the Direct Action Movement from the ACF;

> "At the moment in Britain, reformism and Leninism still dominate the working class movement. Action from libertarian groups and organisations has been on a fragmented and uncoordinated basis. There has been little sharing of experiences among libertarians in various campaigns and struggles. Even on something as basic as a demonstration, libertarians have marched separately and in different parts of the demonstration.
>
> The Anarchist Communist federation realises that while there are differences of approach between the class struggle libertarian organisations in Britain, the possibility exists for co-operation on a practical level. Through co-operation, we could become a more effective force, with the possibility of spreading our ideas more widely throughout society. Co-operation could be in terms of joint contingents on demonstrations, notifying each other of meetings, pickets, etc, and possibly co-operation in campaigns or particular industries. If the ACF receives positive responses from the CWF and the DAM, it is prepared to arrange a venue for an initial co- ordination meeting."[646]

These meetings and requests for joint participation didn't really affect the situation in the North East, not to mention the whole of Northern England and even Scotland, where anarchist groups such as the earlier North Eastern Anarchist Federation and the current Northern Anarchist Network regularly met and worked together. This theme was also consistent on Tyneside where joint co-operation was not only actively encouraged, but was also a naturally carried out normal endeavour.

## 4.8 1987

Despite this large increase in local anarchist activity in the region, *Freedom* only lists LOS, and the Spanish Information Network, both addressed in Durham, as contacts. Future academic historians would no doubt write the North East off as inactive, if the reliance upon *Freedom* as a primary source is to be counted. The relationship between the paper and anarchists in the local area would take a further turn for the worse when what was deemed as a racist article in the January 1987 issue sparked insult and outrage.

The article in question was a badly written piece by Tony Gibson with the abhorrent title of 'The day I became a nigger'.[647] The article is trying to showthe links of discrimination of black people to that of aged people. Fair enough,but to litter the article with words such as 'nigger' and 'coon' reeks of old school colonial racism written by pompous upper class academics, and *Freedom* should have known better. But then again, the paper was used to pampering to these fools (accepting a Knighthood from the monarchy anyone?) in order to keep the donations rolling in.

Of course the article incited disgust, especially from those, who having been on the receiving end of veiled racism for the majority of their lives, felt that the last place they would encounter it again was within the anarchist movement. And none more so than a local anarchist who happened to be black. Many letters of protest were sent to *Freedom* from local anarchists regarding this issue, some got published, and some didn't. Perhaps the relationship between *Freedom* and the North East was personal after previous denouncements of anarchism in the pages of the paper, i.e. Will Lawther or MS in decades past. Perhaps the current editor didn't particularly like those from the region (losing contact details and failing to put others in the contacts section). Perhaps the editors were upset that the Northumberland miners left the building a £250 phone bill on their departure after the strike? Or perhaps it was a class issue?A North / South divide? Or the wrong colour socks?[648] Locally, not many were concerned with any reasoning behind any perceived reasons of dispute with *Freedom* (the paper for many at this time was way above anybody's heads in both comprehension, and understanding etc) as long as the issue wasn't because of the colour of another's skin, then that WOULD become a problem.

The first letter of protest was published in the following issue. The editor of *Freedom*, I believe, deliberately misspelt the wording in order to belittle the writer, as how dare anyone criticise the paper or its upper class authorship andreadership. I firmly believe this to be the case as I have personally known or met those involved in Tyneside Libertarian Books, and through this study have witnessed the handwriting / spelling (i.e. handwritten minutes) of those involved. I quote the letter in full, in the spelling that *Freedom* published it in order to show how ridiculous they made it to be;

> *"Tyneside libertarien Books received 5 copies of Freedom vol. 48 no. 1 Jan '87 as part of are usual order of your magizine. We found the Article entitled 'The day I begame a nigger' extremely offenceive in several respects, particularly it's Unbelievable racism (not least the title). We were going to write down a list of specific phrases, sentances etc. that we pound especially offencive, only to relise such a list would be far longer than 500 words. We hereby cancel our order and would only concider ordering Freedom again if we were satisfied that your editorial policy had changed so that it would be impossible for such articles to be printed. Yours TLB"*

This was then followed with the patronising comment from *Freedom* as follows "This letter is set exactly as written, We interpreted the article as meaning that victims of ageism have similar experiences to victims of racism. Is it possible our correspondent got no further than the title?"[649]

Three further letters reflecting disgust would follow (all of which with correct spelling!) and are worth quoting in full;

> "Re 'The Day I Became a Nigger': throughout my life I have

heard white people insulting black people and then qualifying it with 'no offence mate, but . . .' or 'Don't take it so seriously', etc, etc, - an insult is an insult and no amount of apologising, rationalising or back sliding can change- that. The title of that article was an insult, a pathetic racist comment (which was further aggravated by some more racist statements further in the article), for which there are no excuses. It merely reflects the short-sightedness and stupidity of the editorial group that no rider or disclaimer was produced with the article. It reflects the author's and the editorial group's blatant racism that it was written and published at all. Is this what freedom of speech means to you? Licence to promote racism (or even more often sexism) under the 'respectability' of intellectualism? Or on an 'anti-censorship' ticket? If that headline had been in the *Sun* or the *Star* I can imagine *Freedom* readers being disgusted and outraged by it, but if it's in *Freedom* then its okay — well it certainly isn't by me. It has just confirmed what I had been told by others –*Freedom* is written by and reflects the views of middle-class, white, male intellectuals . . . Well no thanks, you can keep it. RM."

"Not being a regular reader of Freedom, mainly because I do not wish to support a paper which propagates and promotes such reactionary attitudes on sexism and porn, it comes as no surprise to me to read your article 'The Day I Became a Nigger', which is highly offensive and racist in the extreme. To print such shit under the guise of anarchist theory is despicable — but comes as no surprise from a magazine whose interpretation of anarchism is clearly rooted in the white male revolutionary stance of 19th century radical politics. Your reactionary stance on racism, sexism and pornography, your nonexistent support of the printers, your non-existent support of the miners, and your attempt to intellectualise, mystify and distance revolutionary anarchist theory from ordinary working-class people are as out of date, out of touch and offensive as your paper - I'd suggest you extract your heads from your collective arse, or piss off back to your cheese and wine parties with the vicar, and your consciousness-raising seminars with the libertarian right, and leave anarchism to those of us who at least have some idea of what it is. Yours in disgust. MM."[650]

And finally, some five months later;

"I am not one of the group of people involved in Tyneside Libertarian Books (who sent you angry letters-concerning Tony Gibson's article on ageism), and I'm not going to presume to speak for them. But statements of Gibson's such as 'if your skin is black it is unlikely that you will often be called a "coon" to your face in modern Britain...' are pretty astonishing. That this kind of unconscious racism (I don't know what else can explain it) provoked no more readers' remarks perhaps reflects the lack of black people among the readership. Black people the length and breadth of Britain get called 'nigger', 'coon' and worse very frequently, and often with menaces. Gibson obviously doesn't know this, but *assumes* that he does know about such things because of some antiracist sentiments. Or so it seems. But one doesn't magically become *non*-racist as a simple corollary of *stated* anti-racism. Further, one can't challenge one's own unconscious racism by showing a ridiculing, sneering contempt to people who try to point it out (however clumsy the attempt). It's a shame that TLB wouldn't enter into a correspondence so as to be able to explain how they feel in this particular case. But given your response it's not really very surprising. I have to say' I'm rather disappointed by the whole episode. TJ"[651]

That aside, *Freedom* had more important things than the episode of racism within its pages to debate about, as the following letter and proceeding debateshowed.

"*Freedom's* policy of not including poetry creates an artificial barrier between political and artistic expression, and in doing so mirrors the actions of the State. Should we not be making the effort to bring inspired creative work into every aspect of our daily lives; to be seeking new ground through which art may be liberated from its present elitist form'? Our earliest literary foundations are poetical stories handed down as the product of entire societies; the Teutonic sagas, the Greek epics and the Old Sanscrit narrative poems. As products of the societies, these works could not fall to the claim of single authors - the bardic tradition produced work that was held dearly as a common possession. The institution of art which confronts us today is, like that of politics, an institution of privilege and elitism. As anarchists, we should be working to invert this situation, and is not the publication of poetry alongside political work not a step in the right direction'? Patrick. Durham."[652]

The now released Libertarian Organisation & Structure pamphlet *'The Future in the Present No 1: Critical Anarchy'* is also getting an independent review in *Freedom*, and after delving into each section, concludes;

> "I found this pamphlet a challenging one, sometimes difficult to follow, often sociological, in places a little Marxist. I have reviewed it hastily and sketchily, and I hope the contributors will forgive me if I have misinterpreted them, but my purpose in outlining it at length is because it is an honest document which deserves to be brought to the attention of all anarchists and libertarians who are concerned with the question of organisation, not as providing answers but as providing a platform for open discussion; and because LOS may become a significant new presence on the British libertarian scene; but this will depend on the response it gets, so finally, it should be noted that LOS welcomes criticism, contributions and correspondence from all its readers."[653]

In what would be its final year of publication, *The Syndicalist* has changed its name to *The Tyneside Syndicalist* and February's issue 12 would contain writings on the anniversary of the Wapping dispute, transport 'deregulation' in the North East, South Africa, privatisation in Spain, low pay, and Telecom engineers strikes. The editorial this month would look at trade union officials, where it was stated;

> "Full time, highly paid appointed officials have interests fundamentally different to those workers they supposedly "represent". The union official's idea of what is good and what is bad for workers is built up from self preservation in their positions." And "this shows quite clearly that they are no more "friends" of workers than are bosses."[654]

Both *The Tyneside Syndicalist* (No 13) and *Direct Action* are bringing to our attention the ongoing rank and file disputes and growing militancy at 'Contracts Ltd' South Shields where more actions were taken place, without union involvement and "The North East garment workers have no interest in such organisations as the "Broad Left" which spend most of their time trying to get "left wing" members elected into union positions. Garment workers in the area have experienced full well the bureaucratisation of union officials once elected." Including those that went on to sell out the workers during their earlier 1985-1986 dispute. "It is hoped that in the long term an active rank and file union will in the end enable workers to smash management tactics of control and gain workers better wages, conditions and other practices."

"This development in the North East may turn out to be one of the most important tasks undertaken in the working class movement for a very long time."[655]

This was also picked up by the Anarchist Communist Federation in their editorial which comments;

> "Recent events have shown a series of defeats for more militant sections of the working class. The predictable sell-outs by the Unions at Wapping, Silentnight and others show only too clearly that if we want to fight the boss class effectively, then rank and file solidarity and direct action is the only way. But there are

> initiatives. According to *Tyneside Syndicalist*, NUTGW rag trade workers are making moves to form a rank and file garment workers movement in the North East. It indicates a new mood developing in some sections of the working class which can only give us new hope for the future."[656]

The local fight against fascism during this period deserves an entire history of its own, suffice to say, issue 13 of *The Tyneside Syndicalist* also informs that a meeting in February of Gateshead Trades Council delegates was disrupted during a talk by a Tyneside and District Anti Fascist Association member by seven members of the fascist British National Party who unfurled a union jack and shouted slogans, "scuffles then followed before police arrived resulting in arrests".

The latest Northern Anarchist Network bulletin would contain an article by RM on the structure of NAN and how to improve it for everyone's benefit, especially after the recently attended conference in Manchester. M from Newcastle is also writing;

> "It has struck me that many anarchists are prepared to sit back on their 'revolutionary' laurels, in the hope that people will all of a sudden become anarchists and everything will become hunky dory. Things are made all the more difficult by a subconscious anarchist snobbery, where people are looked down on and dismissed becausethey say the wrong word, do or eat the wrong thing etc...So instead of appealing to real people we find ourselves stuck in an anarchist ghetto with its own unwritten rules and regulations, which has completely lost touch with what is going on in day to day life. For a movement to divorce itself from the working class and behave at times like a blinkered middle class brat is giving itself no chance.
>
> Another thing is our willingness to take a backseat in any campaigns, demo's etc, which as anarchists we should be supporting, and letting people know we are around. Even in leftists groups we still have the image of caped 18$^{th}$ century

bomb chucker's who don't actually appear to have any politics. In the past anarchists have withdrawn support and been reluctant to get involved in particular issues and campaigns, simply because they are spearheaded by lefty groups. We all know that these groups can be trying at the best of times but I feel we have got to make the effort. A prime example being the Viraj Mendis[657] Defence Campaign conference in Manchester in April (87); granted it has a large Revolutionary Communist Group involvement, but the anarchist presence there was fairly minimal, even after the latest NAN conference was held at his sanctuary in Manchester!

> Even though our ultimate goals are fundamentally different to lefty groups, I think our presence and involvement, both physical and visual in campaigns such as the above can help to change the attitude that we are a joke not to be taken seriously, and we support people in realistic fashion instead of looking for more opportunities to sell papers."[658]

Another insightful report of the situation on Tyneside is also published in the summer under the title of 'Tyneside – A personal view' by MT.

> "Class-conscious anarchism / syndicalism on Tyneside has undergone a dramatic growth over the past 18 months or two years. TRS (Tyneside Revolutionary Syndicalists) were formed in late 1985, in an attempt to get together the most class-conscious elements in the area. Since then it has been successful in producing a local paper, which has helped it gain many local, national and international contacts.

> One of the main features of TRS activity has been its concentration on grass-roots activism, especially on the picket line and in support groups. At present it is still the largest single group in its area, though not the only one. Others include a Direct Action Movement branch, an Anarchist Communist Federation branch, a libertarian bookstall group and a group

based around the Northern Anarchist Network.

There is a good deal of co-operation between all the various "parties". Partly this is due to a large degree of membership overlap between them; also there is a general recognition that there are too few anarchists to afford splits over definitions of "anarchist/syndicalist/anarchist-communist etc". And there is a genuine feeling of having common aims and interests.

This is exemplified most in a local strike at "HFW Plastics" in Gateshead. We are seen by others as "the Anarchists", and are a recognised force. We were instrumental in helping to form a support group for the strikers which is non-hierarchical in form. Delegates from the (mainly female) workforce attend each meeting and get involved in the activities and decision-making process.

One of the Gateshead's Workers' Support Group's major projects is the calling-for and organisation of the SUPPORT Conference in Manchester on July 25th. Hopefully, this will result in the formation ofa national organisation capable of effectively helping workers fight back, instead of the present tardy, confused way of doing this.

There has been some discussion of a regroupment locally. We "unofficially" co-operate anyway, and there is not enough money around for so many separate groups. But in the short term this is not a likely development. In a year, perhaps it may be possible – bit it will require a lot of patient discussion to overcome the inevitable difficulties. Many, including myself, see this avenue as a very useful one in the long term.

Relations between "the Anarchists" and other left-wing groups are variable. The WRP locally are very easy to work with, notably in the Gateshead Support Group. This is because they are genuinely non- sectarian in this area. Conversely, the RCP's

> new non-sectarian approach is seen for what it is – another twist if the Central Committees policy. The RCP have been taking a close interest in anarchist activity, apparently on a national scale. So watch out! The other major grouping, the SWP, seems to be in decline. Their foiled attempts to subsume Militant seem to have led to some confusion and demoralisation. Their leading militants appear burnt out and will use any excuse to avoid practical action such as attending pickets. All they do is "build" (sic) the Party. Turnover of members is high.
>
> All in all, the situation for rank and file libertarians here is very positive. We now have visibility on the streets, due to the bookstall and selling the *Tyneside Syndicalist*. And we are now seen as a forcein local struggles, not just bystanders. The key to all this has been close co-operation, regardless of shades of disagreement or membership of particular groups. Our future tasks include extendingour activities to those areas which in the past have been ignored or by-passed due to lack of re-sources (people and money), that way permanent roots can be established, and we'll not be a passing phase, as is so often, unfortunately, the case."[659]

Quite an optimistic write up from MT, but perhaps unbeknown to the author, there was, as already mentioned earlier, un-named groups appearing and combining for actions, events and the distribution of literature. Admittedly, the majority of these were from the anarchist / libertarian sections of the 'punk' scene, but still, a lot weren't. *Class War* barely gets a mention prior to Tyneside Class War's soon to come formation, yet some individuals in the region had been selling the paper, or taking part in 'class war confrontational style' actions for years. For example, some individuals would regularly participate in the act of hunt sabbing in the region, not necessarily for any particular passion to save a hunted fox, although admirable as that may be, but to continually harass, abuse, and confront pompous rich bastards from Hexham and surrounding areas who thought it was their 'eternal heritage and right' to perpetuate such a thing, and to then call it a 'sport'! No thank you.

There was also an increase again in the output of zines, many of which were benefits for various causes, the musician's collectives were still active, benefit gigs were happening at places like The Bunker. In order to openly defy the new Public Order Bill, the grouping in Gateshead was already organising Newcastle's first 'punk picnic' at Leazes Park 25th July. The Gateshead 'group', with friends in Durham, was also instrumental in the creation of 'Newcastle / Durham Bust Fund' which was set up with the intention of covering fines, particularly for "those taking part in animal rights / Animal Liberation Front direct actions, since heavier fines are being imposed on those arrested for taking part in direct action for the animal rights campaign."[660] The punk picnic 'after party' gig at The Bunker was also a benefit for the Bust Fund.

Tyneside Libertarian Books was a collective of 10+ people, initiated by members of both NAN and TRS and would regularly attend events such as the local May Day rally (quite a sight with the borrowed Tyneside Revolutionary Syndicalists huge red/black banner as a backdrop), the Durham Miners Gala, and 'anarcho-punk' gigs with their table of literature. Other events in and around this period included the forthcoming 'History Workshop', the National Trades Council conference, an anti-strip search march and rally in Durham (held June 13th) etc. Most importantly they were a regular presence in the City Centre of Newcastle on a Saturday morning where such pamphlets as '*Quiet Rumours – An Anarchist-Feminist Anthology*' would repeatedly 'sell out'.[661] After the closure of Days of Hope book shop, the group felt there was a need for an outlet of anarchist literature and a contact point for interested people onTyneside.

Mays issue of *The Tyneside Syndicalist* is giving extra coverage (and participation) in the ongoing battle at H.F.W. Plastics in Gateshead. The dispute began in March when after the sacking of 8 workers, a further 47 workers were sacked after supportive strike action. "There have been 45 arrests, 7 pickets injured needing hospital treatment, picket lines broken up and moved on by police, scabs herded into buses and convoys of cars to get management into work and scab lorries bringing supplies into the factory. Since March 1987 these 47 victimised workers have stood solid against the combined forces of the police, scabs, bosses and Tory government laws." "Due to anti-union legislation and public order acts the government have effectively paralysed the trade unions, making them almost impotent. This fact makes it clear that to fight employers who are intent on using such measures we must stand and fight together, for it may be HFW PLASTICS workers today but it maybe your place of work tomorrow."[662] Pickets (40-50+ people) were also heldGateshead police station to regularly protest at arrests after skirmishes with 60+ police at the factory to enable scab access.

The paper also had a 4 page May Day special in which "we look at the past events that surround May Day, the losing of the original demands and tactics and the political manipulation that is now inherent throughout the world on this occasion. May Day 1987, and for many years prior, has become just another event. In the West politicians and bureaucrats continuously mouth off about a 'socialism' that has very little, if anything at all, to with the rights of the working class. In the Eastern bloc May Day has become a show of the Dictatorships military strength. We hope in this special May Day section to recapture the 'real meaning of May Day' and hopefully generate discussion to enable us to confront the problems that the working class are faced with today."

May Day advertising literature for this year was an encouragement of "smash the public order act – smash the anti union laws – stop the police state – support HFW sacked workers" and the Gateshead end of the march held their rally at the factory gates.

TRS had a high level of involvement in not only a regular presence on the picket line, but also in the production of the support bulletin, and along with further involvement with Gateshead Workers Support Group and Gateshead Unemployed Action Group were involved in the calling for the SUPPORT conference (25th July in Manchester). The conference was called by "both workers and supporters presently engaged in disputes. The sponsors hope to unite those workers in struggle on an active level and hope that a body of supporters can be built to give solidarity to those in dispute."[663]

June 87 and during the NAN delegates meeting in Huddersfield, the group report for Newcastle says that they are "involved in HFW Plastics dispute / Picketing Laura Ashley's[664] / Run a regular bookstall – Tyneside Libertarian Bookstall / Organising a trip to picket line at Ardbride / Involved in Viraj Mendis campaign." The Leeds group were planning a demonstration at the Nissan factory, Washington, Tyne & Wear in protest at the ongoing (previously mentioned) Japanese Omori case.[665]

The summer also saw the beginning of a much needed initiative, especially for those seeking a postal address to use, called Common Ground, who shared a Newcastle city centre office space with Tyneside Anti-Nuclear Campaign. The group was a "voluntary organisation set up to support local community and campaigning groups." And to "publicise the existence of such groups and to promote their ideas, activities and events." Of course this included local anarchist and libertarian groupings in and around Tyneside, as their first newsletter would emphasise, with a full page dedicated to listing libertarian groups, and a brief write up of who and what they are.[666]

Meanwhile, Newcastle ACF is having a slow start in activities. This was due to beginning as a relatively small group, active in many other areas, and the continual drain and expense of attending regular delegate meetings and national conferences throughout the country.[667] This was also coupled with the accepted motion of becoming editors for the national magazine *Virus*, and the large amount of work this entailed, and where the group emphasises "We need articles now. We are editors, not writers, so unless we receive enough material, there simply won't be another issue."[668] Nevertheless, issues 11, 12, & 13 of *Virus* were produced in Newcastle and would be the last, as by issue 14 the magazine would undergo a change of name to *Organise!*. The group, in early June, would begin local activities with a discussion meeting for interested parties at the Quaker Meeting House at Jesmond, Newcastle.

The penultimate issue of *The Tyneside Syndicalist* is again covering the HFW Plastics dispute and other local news. Women and class struggle at work was also looked at. The editorial this month exposes the whole parliamentary system and the democracy it purports to implement. It is an evocative writing on the whole fiasco of elections, and which I quote in full for its historical interest.

> "As we approach another General Election the media circus is regurgitating the usual sickening clichés and nonsense about the difference it will all make. We are not going to go along with this by criticising the parties, policies or manifestoes. Instead we prefer to question the whole idea of parliamentary democracy, and to broaden the argument by talking about the underlying issues of authority, power and control.
>
> Our system of government is geared to fitting in with the needs of capitalism. The small differences there are between the major parties concern how best to accommodate to the quest for profit of the multinationals and financial institutions. As voters we are presented with apparent choices of style, but we have no realistic opportunity to reject the whole sordid assumptions and practices of capitalism. So our power to wield our votes to change things is mainly an illusion.
>
> But that's not all. The structure of any political party means that we are made even more passive by supporting or joining it. Parties consist of massive overbearing hierarchies where even straight- forward and sensible change is virtually impossible to achieve unless the leadership already desire it. Changes that would imply removing control from the top obviously get nowhere.
>
> Some people enter the party hierarchy with the intention of improving things from within. They very quickly get swallowed up by the dead weight of bureaucracy and neutralised by the

control of those at the top, and it's irrelevant how much support from the base they have.

The only other alternative is to get to the top themselves, but by the time they've managed it, the distortions and perverting effects of the hierarchy have inevitably taken their toll – so that the old status quo is now accepted. We can see this very clearly in one-time radical labour politicians or broad-left trade union officials who become more and more reactionary as they climb the ladder and leave the base behind. Meanwhile those at the bottom are left passive and powerless, and maybe worse off because of the time and effort wasted on keeping the faith in a "better leadership".

Clearly this type of analysis applies to supposedly revolutionary parties and to trade unions just as much as to the big parties. If decision making isn't placed squarely at the base, then the mass of ordinary member's maybe active, but only in doing what they are told, what is permissible, and they are in no position at all to challenge the status quo. These days most organisations involving politics make a big show of internal democracy, but when it comes down to it those at the top have to agree before anything gets done.

But we have to take the analysis a bit further than this. Most people seem fully aware that they have no control, but still manage to muster up enough motivation to support the big parties and to make no effort to challenge bureaucratic and authoritarian control. We can present alternatives to hierarchies and powerless membership – in this paper we consistently offer ideas and examples of rank and file control, assembly – based decision making, mandated and re- callable delegates and so on. Such ideas are acceptable; people agree that they would be better. But there's a tendency to say "it won't work" (even when given cast iron evidence of it working), and to not really want or be able to apply the ideas in their own real lives. It looks as though people feel more comfortable being passive, don't want the bother of being responsible, in fact desire to be dominated. Why is this?

'The desire to be dominated'

People aren't completely logical; we all behave irrationally quite alot of the time. So while working class people want freedom, struggle to make our lives better and recognise the injustices of society, other parts of us also desire to be controlled to let others make our decisions for us. That is why it is possible for Thatcher to attract so many of our votes. All of the other parties have massive blind spots to the problems of power and authority too, and can't afford to examine these areas because it would expose their own (equally large) shortcomings.

In this society virtually all of our lives are lived under the shadow of forms of authority that are completely out of our control. It is built into us to be subservient. It's a difficult pattern to break down, but the best path is in active struggle. Real lived experience of battling against authority begins to give us confidence in our own collective power.

Experience of the double-dealing, betrayal and manipulation of politicians and trade union officials clinging onto their positions in the hierarchy tests our faith in their influence, whilst we know we can trust one another.

So rank and file control is not enough – we need also to be conscious of why we need it. Because otherwise we will find ourselves trusting the next plausible dominator who comes along, and the gains of our experience of collective self-control will be lost."[669]

NAN Newcastle activities were being reported as involvement in HFW dispute, travelling to other towns for demos, the book stall, Viraj

Mendis campaign (including organising local public meeting), and a "public meeting was also organised, with Harry K*** a Longshore Workers Union activist from San Francisco. He spoke on workers sanctions to fight against Apartheid, and described the history of the action taken by San Franciscan Dockers over the last 10 years. On Men's anti-porn day (July 23rd) there was a picket of the SVEN porn shop for approx 45 min's until moved on by the feds. The press turned up but nothing was printed."[670]

The Direct Action Movement organised a national tour with a documentary video showing of "de Toda la Vida" ("All Our Lives") which was a series of interviews with 4 of the founders of Mujeres Libres (Free Women) and events surrounding the role and participation of women in the Spanish Revolution. Newcastle DAM arranged a local showing on August 1st.[671]

In an echo of distant visits to The Clousden Hill Free Communist and Co- operative Colony in 1897, some 90 years later and Marie from Middlesbrough is writing in *Freedom* of their groups visit to a similar endeavour, the Lifespan Collective near Sheffield, which not anarchist in name, certainly was by its described nature.[672]

NAN national meeting in Leeds, 17th October and Newcastle are reporting their activities;

> "Gateshead Workers Support Group set up to support sacked workers. HFW Strike now officially over, SOGAT withdrew support after 20 weeks. Compensation was negligible and holidays pay still unpaid. Young scab workforce now employed at £30 per week. Many accidents such as 17 year old losing two fingers in machine. GWSG produce bulletin to keep support going. Involved in Viraj Mendis campaign, but find it difficult to get on with other groups / individuals involved. Bookstall going well. Tyneside Anarchist Federation set up to unite local anarchists. Public meeting organised. Small attendance at DAM video but well received. Council voluntary

> sector – in last two years three sacked for opposition to racism – series of campaigns but only six turned up for one meeting."[673]

The 22nd of October was still 'Stop South African Business Day' worldwide. Locally, the day was encouraged with;

> "The idea of SSAB is simple - A national day of havoc for all those who make money from the misery of Apartheid. Our anger cannot be expressed through traditional organisations. Only sustained autonomous attacks on the profits of those who operate in South Africa will bring about change. From leafleting, pickets, phone blockades, trolley actions...to glueing, redecorations. Just get up anduse your imagination. The black workers of South Africa keep up their pressure...we must support them to bring an end to Apartheid, every day. Large organisations involved in S.A. include Shell, B.P., Dunlop, ICI, Barclays, and Del Monte. South African fruit is a popular target."[674]

Newcastle ACF is by now adding the odd new member locally and the main area of activity is the production of *Virus*, even more so since the ACF nationally had decided to no longer produce *Liberation* and move all focus to and concentrate, as a federation, on *Virus* as the sole national production.[675] The local group also mention that;

> "We have initiated a strategy of alternate workshops and actions which may contain the potential for a flourishing ACF presence here. We have held a discussion meeting on 'Patterns of Racism' at which the victim of a complex and long-standing saga of local institutional and personal racism explained her experiences. From this we have begun to discuss how to combat racism and how to participate in black peoples struggles without ignoring the desires of black people themselves (i.e. what anarchists and white radicals generally do). We will be following this up in the near future, and attempting to demonstrate our seriousness and commitment to an area of

> struggle disastrously neglected by anarchists. We have been responsible for beginning to organise a public meeting on 'Anarchism Today', to be publicised extensively (e.g. at the "History Workshop" in Newcastle in November). We hope and expect that this event can draw local anarchists and newcomers to anarchism to the ACF (since although it will, touch wood, be organised jointly with other class struggle anarchists, the impetus and driving force, not to mention only coherent strand, will be Newcastle ACF)."[676]

The formation of Tyneside Anarchist Federation (TAF) occurred as it was felt that a 'broad based class struggle anarchist group' on Tyneside to initiate campaigns around issues rather than just reacting to situations as they arise, sometimes weeks / months afterwards, was needed. Some also felt that with the 'History Workshop' fast approaching and national anarchist attention and presence focused on the North East as a result of the Workshop weekend, that a united front of all anarchists on Tyneside was required.

An initial meeting was held early October, at which the idea of the formation of TAF was discussed, who to invite, aims, constitution, and proposed activities.This meeting was attended by members of Newcastle ACF, Newcastle DAM, TRS, LOS, TLB, and NAN. Along with other non-aligned individuals the meeting occurred 3rd November and agreements were made for closer cooperation between all with the groups aim of 'to encourage working class self organisation'. Despite renewed local optimism and enthusiasm with this coming together, some in the ACF expressed reservations "especially whether ACF activity and involvement would decrease because of it".[677]

TAF activity was already making its mark locally as already by the 14th November 'there was a large TAF presence outside St James Park in an anti- National Front leafleting session' at Newcastle United's home game. This was done in response to local fascists who would regularly attempt to leaflet the home fans with their filth. Things were beginning to appear on the up for TAF, but unfortunately this wasn't to be for the

Tyneside Revolutionary Syndicalists and their paper.

At a meeting 13th October it was decided to put TRS 'on ice' and invite interested parties to a readers meeting 15th November to discuss it's, and in particular the papers, future.

> "A brief introduction was given as to how and why the TRS has been put on ice and the editorial collective opened up to those who wish to participate in the production. Each issue has been put together by 3-5 people and the time has come when we can no longer continue with the present set up. Each issue often consuming a week of someone's life." The last issue of the paper was at the printers, it was going to cost £70 and the group only had £35.[678]

Nevertheless, despite time and financial constraints the final issue 16 of *The Tyneside Syndicalist* (Winter 1987) was published. The 'illusive' issue[679] contained reports on recent SUPPORT conferences, the end of the HFW Plasticsdispute, South Africa, international attacks on Dockers, as well as other snippets of local and international news. More admiral was its special 4 page supplement commemorating the 70th anniversary of the 1917 Russian Revolution, the amount of writing included in which, was enough to compile a full pamphlet. Again this was obviously a lot of work for so few people and inevitably 'burn out' had set in.

Despite the editorial group's encouragement and hope that the paper would continue ("it was stressed that we have an advantage over other papers as ours is Tyneside based") with a new editorial team, and a proposed production meeting for early 1988, unfortunately the paper didn't appear again.

The aforementioned 'History Workshop 21' was held this year at Newcastle Polytechnic on the weekend commencing Friday 20th— Sunday 22nd November.

> "History Workshop is a movement of socialists and feminists who publish a journal and run workshops every year. The theme this yearis "speaking for ourselves?" and aims to look at how working class people – particularly women, and oppressed minorities – have (and do) express themselves through literature, culture and history. History Workshop 21 is organised by people who believe in recording working class history as opposed to "kings and bishops". The theme is that history is happening now, and has more relevance than is usually portrayed by schools, the media and historians. Yet it is not an academic affair. This year people from the mining communities, the 'Contracts' workers, among others will be presenting workshops. The various titles include; Approaches to teaching history, community publishing, the women's voice, technology and the workforce, anarchism, gay history and writing and working class experience."[680]

The anarchism table of events, which stresses it "is concerned not only with the history of anarchism, it will also examine aspects of anarchist theory and of anarchist practice, past and present." The programme listed 'Dan Chatterton and the Atheistic Communistic Scorcher',' 'Clousden Hill', 'Bakunin on revolutionary organisations', 'Bakunin and the problem of power', 'Children against the state', 'Libertarian communities and collectivisation', 'Non elective democracy in early labour and self-help organisations', 'The control of space; planning for anarchy', 'The social democratic outrages in London 1909-1911'[681], etc.

Novembers issue of *Sinews* (No 8) is only a 4 page stapled A4 affair with minor bits of news from Spain, whilst *Freedom* has a small column from the same author. The Newcastle / Durham Bust Fund are advertising that they are now in urgent need of donations and Tyneside Anarchist Federation and Newcastle ACF are still regularly meeting for the remainder of the year.[682]

Some of the zines released this year include *No Restrictions* No 1

(Gateshead/Durham) which was a benefit for Newcastle/Durham Bust Fund, *Hope* No 1 (Gateshead) also a benefit for Bust Fund and local Hunt Sabs, *Adrem* No's 1 + 2 + 3 (Blyth), *HAGL* No's 14 + 15, *10 Years On/11 Years On* No's 8 + 9 (Durham), *Guernica* No 1 (Newcastle), and *Lambs to the slaughter* No 2 (Middlesbrough).

December's *Freedom* also has an obituary of Daryl Hepple, who passed away 24th September 1987 at 68 years old.

> "Daryl was a life-long pacifist and socialist who supported and subscribed to Freedom Press for many years. He was also an active trade unionist, and as much a thorn in the side of union officialdom as that of management. Always maintaining that workers' struggles must be organised by the workers themselves." "Working with the Black Star Collective he was involved with the reproduction of material produced by the United Socialist Movement, the Anti parliamentary Communist Federation and the works of Guy Aldred, a fellow revolutionary Daryl had great admiration and respect for."[683]

1987 would end with local and national anarchists and other activists beginning to come together within their communities to begin the fight against the recently announced upcoming Poll Tax. The Poll Tax was to be a replacement rates system. The Community Charge ("Poll Tax") was a new system of taxation and was to be introduced in Scotland in 1989 and England and Wales in 1990 by the then Conservative government. The Community Charge replaced the "Rates," a system of tax where a certain amount was charged by the local council depending on the rental value of a house - with a flat rate charge paid by every adult, earning the nickname "Poll Tax" as a result.

"The only winners under the tax will be the rich. Only households with an income of £558 a week will benefit, according to Scottish research. Shared households will be worse off, inner city households will be worse off, the unwaged will be worse off, as will pensioners. Student nurses, YTS "trainees" and apprentices will be liable for 100% of the tax. Even the homeless will be made to pay. As Age Concern put it "The government will be soaking the poor to pay the rich.""[684] People living in the same 'government district' will have to pay the same tax, whether they are a millionaire in a mansion or a factory employee living in a council high rise flat.

Already (November 14th) Scottish libertarians, including the DAM etc were holding constructive conferences in Glasgow on how to combat and practically fight the tax with encouragement of collective refusal, non-payment and non- registering.

Newcastle ACF were receiving reports and minutes from Edinburgh Unemployed Workers from the conference and "suggested ideas were originally information and publicity, and to get involved with Tenants Associations etc" as well as to form anti poll tax groups in their own areas.

Newcastle ACF at this time were still the then editors of the national *Virus* magazine, and like the rest of the national anarchist press, moves were already being established to include articles on the tax within its pages.[685]

The Northern Anarchist Network meeting / conference of December 13th at Bradford, had as its main agenda items, discussing the poll tax and ways to fight it, as well as future anarchist coordination of regional anti fascist activities and the spreading of anarchist propaganda.[686]

Thus a shared common enemy, common cause, and common incentive to refuse and resist within our own communities, whilst creating national networksand groups enthused with non-hierarchal methods of struggle, gave local anarchists the impetus to take the fight into the next couple of years.

## 4.9 1988

Tyneside Anarchist Federation were busy throughout January with organising a counter offensive and national mobilisation against a planned National Front march through Newcastle on the 31st. The fascists had been busy fly posting and leafleting their filth in Benwell inciting a march against the "Irish Freedom Movement, propaganda pushers for the IRA". The anarchists were "ready with a physical presence...but they (NF) changed plans."[687]

Newcastle ACF's time and energy is taken up with the production of *Virus* and attending delegate meetings and national conferences throughout the country for the first couple of months of the year. This, coupled with local meetings, created a situation where "meetings are all business at present – danger of us becoming a small clique doing *Virus* etc", with this in mind it was agreed to begin a series of public discussion meetings. These were to be held at what had become a regular meeting place and ideal venue for public meetings, in the form of 'Gingerbread' on Westgate Rd, Newcastle.[688]

The first of these meetings, titled 'Union Resurgence?' held 14th march described itself thus "After a period in which the trade union movement has widely been proclaimed to be dead, workers in the NHS, Dockers, at Ford, NACODS etc, are hinting otherwise in mass, solid industrial action. What does all this mean? Is it a "fight back"? How does it relate to government strategy? ... and to the requirements of the trade union bureaucracies?" The meeting was poorly attended but "we will press on undeterred". It was then decided to 'reach out' to more local interested parties from the mailing list and "It was pointed out that we don't need to keep any lower profile than necessary, after all we have been in existence for over 2 years in Newcastle. Now that no other group seems able to be consistently active on Tyneside we should continue to develop into more than a contact point for the national ACF. A vital part of this is to keep in touch with people who may already sympathise with our politics."[689]

The ongoing dispute over support for the real and phoney CNT in Spain is now becoming serious as reports were coming through of knife fights etc between the different factions. *Black Flag* would emphasise

> "*Freedom* could do themselves a favour in future by checking the accuracy of their international 'news' or at least asking the CNT-AIT for their version of events before going to print. Instead they preferto rely on ML and his 'Spanish Information Network', which is where this particularly nasty piece of 'information' originated. ML, it should be remembered, is a past master of deception, not above doctoring photos of CNT-AIT demos (a la Stalin) and claiming them to be 'CNT-U' demos in his publication *Sinews*. Portraying CNT-AIT militants as mindless thugs and terrorists or CIA controlled morons, may be funny to the likes of *Freedom* and ML but in a country where not so long ago membership of the CNT-AIT meant the death penalty it's about as funny as a kick in the teeth."[690]

This would be the last of the link between ML & Sinews and the North East as I believe he moved back 'down South' during this period.

Anti poll tax groups were starting to appear in Elswick, Cowgate, Fenham and Benwell etc, some of these were run by local Labour Party branches. These were a show of tokenistic opposition, as Scotland was to show. To begin with the Labour party promoted the 'Axe the Tax' campaign and organised the first marches. However, a Scottish Labour Party Special Conference held in March 1988 in Glasgow, refused to back non-payment and non registration. This marked the end of official Labour opposition; they couldn't be seen to support civil disobedience.

In order for local anarchists to continue meeting at 'Gingerbread', especially inthe case of advertised public meetings, the venue requested a written statementfrom 'Newcastle Direct Action Group' (this was the name given for venue booking), and accordingly an interesting statement was produced, as follows;

"The Newcastle Direct Action Group was formed in September 1985 and it at present made up of six active members and a dozen or so less regular attendees.

Our guiding principles are those of direct democracy, which is the notion that struggles should be controlled by those who are oppressed, not by elites purporting to speak for them, nor by bureaucracies or committees of experts and the famous, nor by paid officials who develop their other motivations and allegiances. In practice this means mass meeting – or assembly – led organisations, with decisions made by all of those concerned and delegated officials subject to recall and rotation.

Our ideas and actions are focussed on participating in the struggles around us with the aim of helping other ordinary working class people to defend and further their interests against those of capitalism, the state (local and national) and their institutions and against racism and patriarchy. We believe these interests are better served by libertarian means; therefore we propose and argue for direct democracy against hierarchical and bureaucratic alternatives. Likewise we believe that direct action holds out more hope foradvancing struggles; and that even when "going through channels" has to be done, that no illusions should be held as to its effectiveness or significance. For example, all other things being equal we would argue for occupations rather than picketing, alternative structures being built rather than begging for reforms, and direct, physical, collective action being taken against oppressors rather than set-piece, image-conscious, publicity-seeking passive opposition.

The Newcastle Direct Action Group has links with the Anarchist Communist Federation (ACF), a national network of like-minded groups. The ACF share our emphasis on grass-roots autonomous organisation and the tactics of direct action, and we participate in the communication and support network that the ACF offers on a free, equal and autonomous basis.

In recent years there has been a considerable upsurge of interest in libertarian ideas and practice, but no stable and coherent framework has existed on Tyneside within which this interest could develop into action. Activity has tended to be spasmodic and disorganised. We are providing a reliable forum for discussion, anda consistent base for action. We wish to continue this process through our programme of discussion and public meetings. We are also developing a strategy for local action which we hope will provide a stark contrast to the opportunism, manipulation and sectarianism of many other political tendencies.

Our support for local struggles is based upon the expressed needs and desires of those in struggle. We constantly question our involvement, will not attempt to provide any leadership of ideas, and do not promote ourselves in the name of other people's struggles. We will foster the emergence of direct democracy and fight the onset of hierarchy, hijack by bureaucrats or dominance by experts from a grass-roots involvement, humility and, we hope, integrity."[691]

Justification of name and principles was perhaps necessary to the 'Gingerbread' committee as the next advertised public meeting was entitled 'Fighting Legislation' and was described;

"The Poll Tax, the Alton Bill, Clause 28, the Education Bill and many others are being fought by narrowly-defined single-issue campaigns. By and large these campaigns do not manage to link with other issues, and seem to stick to conventional lobbying tactics. Is this enough? What else can be done? How can "single issues" be widened?"

Leeds Direct Action Movement provided the speaker for the next public meeting 9th May under the title of 'Paris, May 1967'. "On the 20th anniversary of French uprisings which saw workers occupying factories, students taking over their colleges and De Gaulle fleeing the country we review and discuss the limits and possibilities of a period which shattered the lefts pessimistic view that revolution in "advanced" Western liberal democracies was impossible." Reported attendance at this meeting was 'quite good'.[692]

The public meeting On June 13th was on 'Grass-Roots Organisation'. "How relevant is libertarian democracy in real life? How do we, and how should we, apply the principles of accountability and participation? How do we envisage mass grass-roots organisation in practice, and how do we contribute to it? How do we counter Leninist claims for the efficiency of "democratic centralism", and the persistent charge that "anarchy" is "chaos"?" A 'long and lively discussion on the inns and outs of small group activity, focussing on what we could and should do to develop our strategy and action' occurred.[693]

This summer would also see, not so much the foundation of, but the emergence into more of a public face, of Tyneside Class War. Individuals had for years been reading and selling copies of the *Class War* newspaper locally with basic knowledge of each other. The time was now ripe for the coming together as a group, as this was happening with the formation of the Class War Federation throughout the country and new groups appearing everywhere.

The group was slow to fully merge, and when it did it encompassed those from Tyneside Anarchist Federation, Tyneside Revolutionary Syndicalists, Tyneside Libertarian Books, Newcastle ACF, Tyne & Wear Free News people, the unnamed Gateshead grouping, and those from the 'punk' community amongst others. Newcastle ACF were soon reporting "A Class War group is being set up on Tyneside. One of us is involved in the project, which has been very successful so far."[694]

The Heavy Stuff Number 1, which appeared December 1987, was Class War'stheoretical journal and pretty much 'sold out' quickly when displayed locally, therefore a cheaper pirated version was produced by Tyneside Class War to sell at the cheaper price of 'ten bob' (slang for 50p).

This year's Durham Miners Gala (July 16th) were charging a £6 fee to do a stall, and Tyneside Libertarian Books were to take up the offer. "A good day out. The stall drew lots of interest from the public and also a journalist from the"Independent" took notice which resulted in an article in the paper."[695]

Meanwhile, Common Ground is reporting;

> "Five members of the Snowball anti nuclear campaign who were arrested and charged with criminal damage at Albermarle Barracks, 10 miles from Newcastle have had the charges against them dropped in letters from the Ministry of 'Defence'. No reason for the decision to drop the charges is given, but a spokesperson for the campaign said it was in line with the military's policy of trying to playdown the occasional presence of nuclear weapons at the base.
>
> The base has in the past been used as a stopover point for convoys of Polaris warheads on their way between Faslane submarine base, north of Glasgow and Burghfield in Berkshire, where the warheads are 'refurbished'. The five who all live in the area, were arrested for spray painting the word 'Peace' (and an anarchist symbol) on a Ministry of 'Defence' sign on an approach road to the base. They were then taken and held for four hours at Hexham police station before being released.
>
> The Snowball campaign is an open non-violent campaign of civil disobedience which calls for a freeze or reduction in the testing, production and deployment of nuclear weapons, a call which is supported by 79% of the population. The protestors were hoping to use the process of the courts to give voice to

> their case."[696]

Newcastle ACF were to suffer a further set back with the resignation of RM from the ACF after concerns over the state of the national organisation, and more predominantly the fact that the organisation was in the process of writinga pamphlet on racism, without consultation, advice, or participation from the only black member in the organisation, that being RM. The local group fully supported his reasons for departure and all signed a statement emphasising RM's points and concerns.[697] Despite losing one of its most active members, the group would persevere and complete the final (locally produced) issue of *Virus*, issue 13. Public paper sales of *Virus*, soon to become joint efforts with Tyneside Class War selling issues of *Class War*, were now also taking place at Grey's Monument in Newcastle City centre, on Friday and Saturdays.

The group still felt as though they could be doing more in encouraging supportand activity for the national organisation and in an open and honest look at themselves the Newcastle group would announce to the rest of the federation;

> "Our position is, as always, precarious. All of us do many things in addition to doing ACF work. Combined with our continual bankruptcy, this means we're often unable to do things like writing, conferences, setting things up locally, keeping anything like a high profile. It's very demoralising when you can't do much, and it makesus more isolated than just geographically – and the two feed into each other. Some groups we've been in before tried to make up for these kinds of problems with manic, almost heroic activity. And some very good work got done (e.g. in Tyneside Revolutionary Syndicalists, Gateshead Workers Support Group) before mass burn- outs left class struggle anarchism on Tyneside set back years. So were not about to repeat those mistakes, and are fumbling around for alternatives – a reliable presence, regular meetings, the opportunity for serious discussion, involvement in local struggles

up to our capacities; but not so that any of us feel that the ACF is taking over our lives (as it could easily do). We're not too good at it yet, but we're learning."[698]

The self analysis would continue throughout the federation, and in October the Newcastle group would proclaim;

> "We need to sort out our position and activity <u>in</u> and outside the ACFon racism. All white people are privileged and we have to tackle that. Need to develop our awareness of racist oppression (though we don't have that experience) Anti-Racism must be a priority in our theory and action (praxis) because we haven't developed our ideas enough. Anti-racism must be linked into what goes in our propaganda, not tacked on the end. We should not get stuck in guilt, which is counterproductive. Need to take <u>responsibility</u> instead, for combating racism in ourselves, the ACF and outside."[699]

Towards the end of the year, local community anti poll tax groups were appearing throughout the region, and on 10th December a 'national conference' on the poll tax was held in Newcastle. "Organised by Socialist Action (i.e. Trotskyites etc, in the Labour Party). This might well be bureaucratic,talk-only, trendy left, and manipulated outrageously, but it's still important that some of us go for genuine contacts etc."[700]

> "There were various workshops of interest to us; I decided not to go to the trade's unions one, as it is fairly obvious what local government workers should do about the Poll Tax. So I went to the 'Civil Disobedience' one to try to meet some activists. The workshop was really interesting – the lead in was about not trusting notable individuals to take action on your behalf, but working towards building mass action. The speakers particularly talked about the effectiveness of the Glasgow rent strikes. I pointed out that the ACF distrusted initiatives like the poll tax 'Committees of 100' because they encouraged people to be passive and took power away from them – and are

> tactically ineffective anyway. Also, the reason that all the Trots present were denouncing community action was that they hadn't got a structure that could contain it, so they denied its potential. What is needed is community action, which is also in support of local government workers taking action."[701]

It wouldn't be until December 1988 that Tyneside became an established contact in the issue No 31 of *Class War* newspaper. By this time Class War had developed from a small group of people producing the paper to a full blown national federation. The paper had moved from an attack against the middle class pacifist lifestyle-ism of many liberal sections of the early 1980's anarchist movement, and to some degree the ghetto-isation of much of the 'anarcho-punk' scene.

> "The apparent pre-occupation with violence, the forthright use of language and the no-compromise attacks on the rich and the royal family were, to a large extent, a reaction to the complacency and arm-chair intellectualism that characterised the movement then and now. However, in retrospect, the paper was still aimed at other 'anarchists', and was populated with articles urging them to drop their pacifist ideas and join the class struggle. Despite this the paper still appealed to many non-anarchists, particularly certain groups of 'disaffected' youth, who would otherwise have been unlikely to give a political paper a second glance. It also became immensely popular amongst certain groups of workers, namely striking miners, who eagerly read any copies they could lay their hands on."[702]

One of the most favoured features was the 'page 3' hospitalised copper picture and caption. *Class War* was predominantly an encouragement to fight back against the state and its oppressive institutions of control. It showed you are not powerless; you don't have to accept the copper trying to smash your head in with a truncheon because you are on strike, you don't have to repeatedly be the victim, fear is an element of control – fight back is possible and rightly acceptable against injustice.

Pictures of hospitalised police emphasised this point, authority is not invincible. As much as an attractive idea the history of the thought, theory, and history of the Class War Federation is to delve into, this is not the space and we must concentrate on local developments.

*Tyne and Wear Free News* has by now become 'The Newssheet of Tyneside Class War'. Continuing where *Tyne and Wear Free News* left off, it would become an agitational broadsheet which was given out with street sales of *Class War*, and the ACF's newly named *Organise!* (formerly *Virus*) as well as being fly posted weekly around the region. The first issue contained news and analysis on the then P&O Shipping company dispute with the National Union of Seamen, and the role of the state in events. Union bureaucracy, and care for the elderly were also written about. The newssheet would just have the title 'Tyneside Class War' with the next issue.

## 4.10 1989

The year begins with the announcement, despite local protest, of the closure of the last ship yard in Sunderland with a loss of 2,200 jobs from the yard itself, and a further couple of thousand who were dependent on the yard.[703]

Newcastle ACF, with some activists from Tyneside Class War are meeting early this year to discuss 'Anarchist activity on Tyneside', with a view of how to 'keep things going'. It was discussed and agreed to continue joint fly posting of literature, joint paper sales in Newcastle city centre two days a week. The Tyneside Libertarian Book stall now had a permanent shelf within the Polytechnic Students Union book shop, and was still in attendance at larger regional events, like the yearly 'Green Fair'. Further 'public meetings' were encouraged as they were "a long term thing to attract people, and discussion meetings also allow us to 'educate ourselves'". Another "good suggestion that would not entail a vast amount of work and might reap good rewards was to try and recruit a few students next September. A few paper sales might be all it takes."[704]

Two of us did try this during the year to no avail, interest was shown and University 'Anarchist Societies' mentioned, but when communication details were given, nothing ever transpired. The same can be said for the 'contacts section' in the paper *Freedom* during the latter years of this decade, where the only contact listed for the North East was 'Durham Anarchists' contactable through Durham Students Union. Despite attempted communication, we never saw these people and were not even sure they existed, and if they did, then they never ventured out of their pompous little university debating society ghetto's to speak to real people like ourselves.

The next *'Tyneside Class War'* sheet was full of practical information on the poll tax, what it was, who benefits, how it was to be implemented and how to avoid payment and registration. Under the title of 'Yuppies Out' the sheet also looked at the development of gentrification beginning in the region.

> "All over Tyneside new housing developments are springing up, where small flats and houses are given fashionable interiors, landscaped exteriors, huge prices and the promise of posh amenities and facilities for the yuppie bastards who move in. The centre of Newcastle is being colonised, and taken over, by the rich. As in London and other cities, people who spend the wealth we create at work are having our working class communities, culture and areas re-built to suit their disgusting, selfish, show-off lifestyle. None of it will benefit us at all. The yuppie infection is taking hold of Tyneside, having reservations of the rich out of Ponteland and Darras Hall was one thing, now we can't avoid them. We're not going to take it lying down. The reason this gentrification is so popular now in inner cities is not just the immense profits to be made by the developers, or the profits the rootless yuppies make when they move onto somewhere bigger after a couple of years. No, the inner city riots earlier in the 1980's have caused a big re- think by

government policy makers and planners. To make the cities less vulnerable to working class action and anger, our communities needed to be broken up and stuck in ghettos away from the city centres, where they can be policed and controlled that much more easily. Of course they couldn't come out with this as their aim, so they found another justification that tied in with the housing needs of the new rich. They call it "inner city re-generation" – and what it means for us is to have our cities virtually closed to us in the long run, through everything being made to suit rich people only – houses, shops and all."

Now if the stupid yuppies want to spend £50,000 on something the size of the smallest Tyneside flat, that's their problem – but their making it <u>our</u> problem because we're being pushed out to make way for them. And not just for them, but for the wine bars, posh restaurants and other "classy" shops that we couldn't afford to use even if we were dumb enough to want to. And if our houses aren't knocked down or done up and sold off for them to live, whole estates may be demolished to improve their view! Meanwhile at their "work" they dream up new schemes to plague us, like the Metro centre, which may be all very nice for those with plenty of spare cash, but is often <u>hellish</u> to work in.

Local councils, Tory and Labour alike, welcome these developments– trendy lefties as usual identifying much more with middle class values than with working class people. Newcastle Council decided long ago that the only thing they can do for us is to invite the developments that can only make our lives more and more intolerable – and they're now preparing to administer the Poll Tax which will be used to help pay for them. Soon we'll have a fucking marina in Byker. Old warehouses all over the Quayside are being bought up for yuppie flats – yet another piece of central Newcastle which could have been used to the benefit of the working class but which will now be exclusively for the rich. One warehouse there is owned by the tiny Trotskyist sect the Workers Revolutionary Party – they're going to build and sell part of it as expensive, chic little flats. These so-called revolutionaries are about as socialist as the Labour council if socialism to them means inflicting this on us. Mind you, Newcastle Council have just set up a "Poverty Working Group" – they must have some inkling in the backs of their minds that all is not well – we wonder if to them poverty means not being able to afford the car phone to go along with the BMW?"[705]

The article would then take a look at housing associations, and propertydevelopers, before concluding;

> "But it's no use just kicking the yuppies out – this has to be combined with encouraging and initiating all manner of resistance to yuppies, bosses, bureaucrats, police and government – so that eventually the working class can keep them all out. But for a start its worth knowing that it is not all inevitable, it can be fought. Let's havea go in the City while we still can."

Newcastle ACF are advertising a list of discussion and public meetings for the forthcoming months, including 'Capitalism in the Near Future', 'After the Revolution', 'The Death of the Labour Party: The Anarchist Alternative', and 'Prisoner Support', and are soon reporting nationally that;

> "People are active in Anti-Poll Tax groups, in anti-fascist pickets of NF paper sellers outside the football ground, and in producing a local newssheet inserted in *Class War* and fly posted. Not a great deal else happening so we do a fair amount of fly posting etc, and street sell *Class War;* and upon making a sale offer *Virus / Organise!*, with some success. We do a bookstall when possible which makes some money and helps with establishing a presence."[706]

The next *'Tyneside Class War'* sheet highlights the case of Martin Foran after his move to Frankland Prison in Durham. In a nationally well publicised case, Foran was serving an 8 year sentence for robbery of a Birmingham pub, where the publican described the robbers as young black men with Birmingham accents, whereas Foran is white and has an Irish accent. Free Martin Foran graffiti was prevalent down and around the Newcastle Quayside,and Tyneside anarchists were to leaflet Durham City Centre publicising the case. An article exposing local fascists, snippets of news on poll tax resistance and a look at the potential of a national Dockers strike were all covered.

An article 'Attack on working class protest' tells us;

> "Everyone should now be aware of the 1986 Public Order Act which replaced the 1936 Act. But unless you have been involved in any sort of struggle it may come as a surprise how it affects your rights, especially section '5 (1) a' of the Act. Take the example of the recent trial at Hexham of 24 Hunt Saboteurs from up and down the country. The magistrates agreed that the defence won in terms ofthe evidence presented, but still convicted the 24 because he decided that the Saboteurs had turned up to stop the hunt. Even just being there caused distress to the hunt and their supporters. Under the new Act they were guilty. Who really cares whether some middle class idiots are upset that someone is trying to stop them killing hares or foxes? Apply this to pickets during a strike shouting "scab", they could be said to be causing distress to scabs and therefore convicted and fined.
>
> The new Public Order Act came about after things like the miners' strike and the "hippy convoy". The police have still been wary about how they can use the Act, but with the help of "head in the sky" judges and magistrates they are being handed what few rights we still have on a plate. So any protest will have to be at the discretion of the police, such as the recent protest at Caphaton in Northumberland over the

closure of the Post Office – really militant, that was.

We're not talking about improving the law system, it isn't there for us, it's there to protect the wealthy and powerful. Why else do the police go to the trouble of stopping strikers, saboteurs or other protestors? On the other hand maybe we should get Thatcher arrested for upsetting us when she comes up this way. No, it wouldn't work that way round, would it?

Work against the Public Order Act, and in the meantime you can expect to get arrested, convicted and fined up to £400 any time you disagree with something politically and try to do something active about it. NB – Four people from Tyneside were convicted at Hexham and fined £75 + £25 costs each, so any sympathetic people out there, donations via Tyneside Class War would be much appreciated. After all it is your countryside and hunts destroy it (except when hunt saboteurs turn up)."[707]

April 1st, was usually a day for practical jokes against family and friends, fun stunts for a laugh, yet this year was no laughing matter for the vast majority of Scotland's population as it was the day the Poll Tax was introduced as a testing ground before proposed implementation in England and Wales a year later. The day was marked with many protests, including a march of up to a reported '25,000' people through the streets of Edinburgh. Activists from the unnamed Gateshead grouping of 'class warriors' were quite prevalent on the march with their bright orange (old curtain) of a banner which proclaimed 'pay no poll tax – they can't imprison us all' and which also appeared on that evenings brief national news broadcast.

*Strike!* Teesside Anarchist Newssheet, paper of Teesside Direct Action Movement number 7 is hitting the streets and folds out into a large window poster of 'Pay No Poll Tax – we're not friggin paying!' and gives us the news that;

"The Poll Tax registration forms are being sent out now, and they'll try to register every adult over the next few months. The government hopes that the fear of fines for non-compliance will keep any resistance minimal. But the news from Scotland is more than hopeful. Despite the attempt by government sources and the media to cover up the full extent of the resistance, it is emerging that over 100,000 Scots have managed to avoid being registered. Furthermore only a few of the refuses' have been fined...Take heart from this. The Poll Tax can be resisted, if people stand firm and stand together. Can't pay won't pay."

Another interesting piece entitled 'Here comes the summer' gives us asnapshot of the period;

> "This summer is likely to see the biggest upsurge in working class militancy in many years, mostly over pay. This spring has already seen strikes in the docks, London Transport, London Underground, the BBC, on North Sea oil rigs, and amongst building workers (someof them Teessider's) working in London. Disputes are ongoing on the railways and in local government.
>
> We welcome this rebirth of militancy, and the confidence that it shows exists amongst the rank & file. And we don't want to see it wasted by useless bureaucrats sat in union head offices. Take for example the situation in the docks. After the government announced its intention to scrap the National Dock Labour Scheme dockers were ready to strike, but the TGWU leadership put things on hold until after negotiations had been held with the employers. In accordance with the law they held a strike ballot. There was a 3 to 1 vote in favour of strike action, and still nothing has happened. Union bureaucrats are totally paralysed with fear of the Tory anti- strike legislation. To save their union funds from sequestration union bosses will delay action so long that people will lose heart for a struggle. This is "new realism" in practice.
>
> The unofficial strikes on the tube in London show that it is still possible to strike effectively, despite the anti-strike laws (which

> make legal strike action virtually impossible). The Tories are so worried about wildcat strikes that they intend to introduce legislation in the autumn to outlaw unofficial strikes and make the unions liable for them. We must build a different kind of unionism, one that fights instead of retreating all the time. We must break down artificial barriers between different firms, trades and unions. We must ditch the bureaucrats, not elect new ones. We must create structures which are accountable to us, giving us control over our officers, our funds, our solidarity and our politics."[708]

May 1989 and Newcastle ACF's next public meeting is 'The Death of the Labour Party' and an evocative poster advertising the advent, would proclaim;

> "The Labour Party 'left' is in retreat. Defeated in the leadership contest, brushed aside in Policy Review, it has no strategy for stopping Kinnock's onslaught. As the leadership promises to 'manage capitalism better than the capitalist', the tired old myth of reforming the Labour Party from within is exposed as increasingly absurd.
>
> "The Labour Party is incapable of acting in the interests of the working class. It is an obstacle in our struggle for liberation and must be smashed along with the system it wants to manage"

As much as a temptation it is to reproduce the locally written and rather excellent text of the public meeting on 'The Death of the Labour Party' it is some six A4 pages of type long. The rest of the national Federation thought likewise and after a bit minor re-writing in places, and added introduction, it was eventually released as an official Anarchist Communist Federation pamphlet under the new name of 'The Myth of Labour's Socialism'.[709]

News was filtering through of the British National Party's national mobilisation and proposed rally to be held in Darlington Town centre,

Saturday June 10th. Anti fascists from throughout the north, including Tyneside etc would physically prevent them, and the next *'Tyneside Class War'* sheet gives an in depth storyof the day[710]. Also covered are events emerging in the Scottish resistance against the poll tax where mass non-payment was now a reality and an estimated one million people were not paying, and an expose of who exactly was involved in the 're-generation' of Newcastle's Quayside. This was a consortium of the ruling class on Tyneside, managing directors and so forth under the name of 'The Newcastle Initiative (TNI)'.

An 'expose' pamphlet was produced this year highlighting exactly the reasons behind the 'Initiative' and would conclude;

> "Ever since the Quayside developments were announced, the local media has been trumpeting about the benefits which will be brought to the residents of Newcastle, but who will really benefit from The Newcastle Initiative. Certainly those involved will and already have gained considerably from the developments proposed. Some have benefited directly, John Hall's building firm has the contract to build flats on the Quayside, others own some of the wasteland to be developed in the St Peters Basin project, whilst all have benefited in terms of prestige. There is no doubt too, that all the other companies who own land around the Quayside areas or the proposed Theatre Village will benefit, as the value of their property rockets. The various schemes will also provide good, centrally situated housing...for those who can afford it.
>
> However what the proposed developments fail to address is the current homelessness problem in Newcastle Council. Rent arrears are now in the millions, the recent interest rate increases have put many families in jeopardy of having their houses repossessed by the bank or building society and the Social Security Act of 1985 means that payments to those claiming Social Security in temporary Bed and Breakfast accommodation stop after a maximum of four weeks. Instead

of addressing this, the current developments try to paint a veneer over the problem by providing luxury housing and top price facilities and then claiming how well the region is doing. Of what real value are top class restaurants to a city where the unemployment rate is still running at about 15% (and that's just the official rate). In fact the only attention T.N.I. has paid to the unemployed is as a potential source of cheap labour. Its proposed that local unemployed people be recruited to Employment Training Schemes and then contracted out to do the labouring work, ensuring even more profits for the developers. What chance will any of those who build these developments have of buying the houses, or using the facilities?

It must be concluded that The Newcastle Initiative is purely and simply a cosmetic exercise, intended to divert attention from the real problems of the inner city, whilst those who already have most, the *nouvea riche,* the property developers and speculators, make a fortune with the help of public money."[711]

Of course any local small business's who resisted 're-generation' were either 'Compulsory Purchased' by the local Council or 'mysteriously' burnt down.

The usual activity of fly posting, paper sales, marches and demos (local and national) would take place for the remainder of the year. Nationally, Class War had arranged a tour of the UK with Joe Strummer of The Clash under the banner of 'Rock against the Rich'. The Newcastle 10th August gig was at the expensive Mayfair venue (complete with restrictive doormen / bouncers) and no procedures were in place for free inclusion or participation in the event of local Class War activists. With this in mind and finances short, Tyneside Class War organised their own, at the Bridge Hotel, 24th November, with the evening being quite a success.[712]

Despite this, the relationship between Tyneside and the rest of the Class War Federation would gradually develop and grow stronger over the next couple of years, even though some local activists were to retain their fierce independent streak and would often proclaim, 'No not a member but an activist' (especially when asked to pay subs!).

Over in the ACF camp, the wording and content of the 'Aims & Principles' is continuing to instigate much debate, especially after the resignation of more members.

> "Newcastle agrees that the ACF desperately needs a coherent political analysis – the lack of, which largely explains the historical failure of anarchism as a political force. Instead, anarchism has been based on "gut feelings" – never really progressing into an analysis which can seriously challenge other influential political ideologies. However, the development of our political analysis should not be at the expense of what motivates us, and has always motivated anarchists, and what sets us apart from Marxists and socialists. Our sensitivity to power and oppression, our emotional and human response to struggle, should not be subordinated to the demands of rapidly achieving an integrated analysis."[713]

This analysis is further explored in relation to questioning ourselves, capitalism, and society within the framework of 'class struggle anarchism' by TJ and is reproduced in APPENDIX A.

The Class War Federation were now sending out, in batches of 500—1000, large posters of each issues cover of *Class War* for the purposes of fly posting and advertisement of local paper sales which were now taking place Fridays at the Haymarket Metro area, Saturdays at the Monument, and Sundays at the Newcastle Quayside Market. On the sale of a paper, the buyer was then offered a copy of *Organise!* or *'The Poll Tax & How to fight it'* pamphlet. Tyneside Class War was also present and forging links at the National conference in Manchester in September of this year.[714]

1989 concludes with the latest *Strike!* Issue 9 which concentrates on the

Poll Tax and council disruptions in the area, and asks;

> "We are sick and tired of hearing how Labour members of Middlesbrough Council are against the Poll Tax. Why don't they do something? All they've done so far is give the people of Middlesbrough platitudes. Why was Middlesbrough Council the first in the North to move fines against people who haven't registered? Is this how they mean to "minimise its impact"? Councillor Carr and his like don't support the non-payment campaign because they are frauds and parlour socialists. Any excuse is used to avoid making a stand. In the meantime some of the poor people of this town aren't going to wait until Councillor Carr and friends win the next General Erection. The Tory flagship is in deep water now. We're going to do our bit to help sink it. We'll be back Councillor Carr!"[715]

## 4.11 THE NAUGHTY 90s? 1990-1992

Efforts early in the year to re-launch a 'Bust Fund' in the region were short lived with lack of funds, and pretty soon wider events were to play a larger focus and demand further attention for those involved in the attempt.

The weekend of 10th-11th of February and Tyneside Class War were attending the national Class War conference in Bristol where the central debate of the whole weekend was about the clarification of the Federations politics, and moving forward with them into the new decade.

The Tyneside Class War (TCW) group report for February / March illuminates how busy the times were.

> "PAPER SALES – We sell the paper through seven newsagents, record and bookshops etc in the centre of Newcastle. We are planning to get more shops to stock them. We street sell the

paper regularly for an hour in the city centre of Newcastle (on a Friday during the dinner hour rush, and on a Sunday at the Quayside market). On an average we sell 8-10 papers a day. We also sell it at other events, demos, gigs, & the occasional pub sale. FLYPOSTING – We fly post one night every week, mainly concentrating on the city centre and Newcastle Quayside (where re- developments are taking place). Occasionally we fly post on the outskirts of Newcastle, at working class estates etc. We also fly post our newssheet. FUNDRAISING – We organised a local "Rock against the rich" gig, which went very well and raised £70 towards a pamphlet we are working on, as we are in debt we will be putting on more benefit gigs in the future. PAMPHLET – We are at the moment working on a pamphlet in conjunction with Newcastle Anarchist Communist Federation on gentrification on Tyneside. The pamphlet will show who benefits from the redevelopments (the ruling class), how they were allowed to redevelop in the first place, plans for what's in store for Tyneside, possible and practical alternatives to redevelopment, what's happening, how, why, and why it should be stopped, also a critique of local Labour council and show local resistance to gentrification etc. The pamphlet should hopefully be out sometime during this year if all goes well. NEWS SHEET – We produce a free news sheet mainly concentrating on local events and issues. We give this away with the paper as well as fly posting it. Leaflets and possibly a weekly class war revue are planned for the future. MEETINGS – We have weekly meetings at the moment (with people from another local group, more on which later). At these meetings we discuss our politics and opinions on certain subjects for an hour, and then discuss business. We also have meetings on a monthly basis with Newcastle ACF as well as our socials down the pub. ANTI-FASCIST ACTIVITIES – We have been actively involved in stopping BNP scum rally's at both Darlington and York, as well as occasionally picketing Newcastle football ground. POLL TAX – We are individually involved with local anti Poll Tax groups, one of which is a grassroots set up. *Militant* free and is getting more local working class people involved all the time. GRAFFITI – Loads of graffiti has appeared all over Newcastle, ranging from anti-Poll Tax, anti-yuppie / rich, to anti-fascist etc. Hundreds of Class War stickers have been stuck everywhere. OTHER LOCAL GROUPS – We are in contact with a group from South Shields, who have also been active lately...fly posting, paper selling etc. We are getting in touch with other contacts on Tyneside to maybe get involved. GENTRIFICATION – Gentrification is still a big issue in the North, at a recent Council meeting Class War was discussed because of the fly posting / graffiti, because they see it as the first sign of local unrest and resistance. MARTIN FORAN – We had a successful day recently paper selling and leafleting in Durham (where Martin Foran is currently being held). Another similar day is planned soon. LATE ITEM – After the Bristol conference we started meeting in our own right...previously we had shared meeting time with the ACF. We have now geared up our activities as described earlier, and are now in the process of helping people on South Tyneside set up their own group, we are also actively chasing up our contacts in the Blyth valley, Northumberland area."[716]

*Strike!* Number 10, released in February is covering news on the ongoing ambulance dispute, revolution or reform? South Africa, the Poll Tax, police state, and shoot to kill. On the ambulance dispute "Everyone supports the ambulance workers fight for better pay. Even *'Sun'* readers who were vehemently against the miners, printers or dockers when they were on strike see the ambulance workers differently."[717]

"So, after six months of a hard-fought dispute starting in September 1989 with a rejection of a 6.5 per cent pay offer amid an overtime ban and a work to rule; with police and the army on the streets doing ambulance work; Christmas and New Year without pay; marching and demonstrating in London's Trafalgar Square with40,000 others; collecting money in buckets from a very generous and supportive public; being locked out of ambulance stations; breaking back into ambulance stations for "sit ins"; being called "van drivers" by the then Health Secretary, Ken Clarke; taking 999 calls straight from the public at stations in a kind of Soviet/commune atmosphere; presenting a 4 million plus signature petition, which at the time broke the British record for the largest ever collected (and may well still be the largest for an industrial dispute); having thousands and thousands of other workers stop work in support on one lunchtime: after six long bitter months...At 07.00 on the 16 March 1990 ambulance workers across the country went defiantly and proudly back to work."[718]

*Class War* No 38 with its cover in support of the ambulance workers, was one of the most popular sold papers at Newcastle's Monument during this period, not only with a sympathetic public, but also with the ambulance drivers themselves who stood alongside Tyneside Class War collecting money. Large posters of the cover, when given to the drivers, were adorning many a drivers workplace canteen we were assured.

Tyneside Class War was soon attracting media (& later State[719]) attention when their fly posted posters of the cover (Run down Kenneth Clarke – not the health service) were upsetting some people in high places. The local *Sunday Sun* are writing to the Federation's Bristol address;

"Dear Sir, I would be grateful if you could telephone me as soon as possible. We will be running a story in the *Sunday Sun* this weekend on Class War posters which have appeared in Newcastle showing health Secretary, Kenneth Clarke run down by an ambulance. Can anyone justify what the Department of Health, COHSE officials and the local chief ambulance officer all regard as a "sick joke?"[720]

Perhaps if they asked the drivers themselves, they could have easily justified it. The aforementioned Sunday Sun article when it appeared would report;

"A cartoon poster which shows Health Secretary Kenneth Clarke

> being run down by an ambulance has been branded as "distasteful" by both sides in the dispute. The offending publicity, fly posted in the North, is printed for the militant Class War organisation based in Bristol", and so forth before concluding "A spokesman for the Department of Health said the poster campaign was a typical approach by Class War."[721]

Newcastle ACF is by this time losing half of their group as they join the growing ranks of Tyneside Class War, but the working together would of course continue unabated. They are also commenting;

> "Street selling *Class War* and then offering 'customers' *Organise!* Is very successful up here – a few just buy *Organise!* Instead of both! Class War's appeal is much more immediate at a street and gut level to working class people (of all ages as far as the paper goes) who have so far shunned conventional politics. They are attracting some excellent people that no other British anarchist organisation I've ever heard of could have. They're now facing the dilemma of how to develop politically without alienating instantly their new support. To some extent they'll have to carry on the momentum – politics as we know it will have to wait. But anyway, wherever theygo in the long term, we should work with them <u>now</u>. Street selling jointly, and other compatible activity, means that we can complement each other, I reckon, and not just our politics with their gut appeal. Both are just as valid politically, and always have been, for working class people, and we're often guilty of forgetting that. I don't agree with a lot that's in their paper, intellectually, but my heart is warmed by it. I agree with rather more of *Organise!* But it sometimes leaves me cold. We'll grow by combining, in practice with those we've enough in common with – and its getting clearer that a lot of Class War people respect us (and say so) while still seeing our differences clearly."[722]

The weekend of March 10th and;

"Early March 1990, two of us hitch-hiked down to the Class War Federations regional delegates meeting at a house in Moss side, Manchester. After much discussion on various things, it was decided to do a sticker for the forthcoming anti poll tax march (which turned into the 'poll tax riot'). Getting bored of the meeting by this stage and wanting to get to the local pub ( the Whalley I think) the discussion on what to put on sticker was going around and around the room, at which point, and having not said much else at the meeting, I piped up in a loud broad Geordie accent... 'hear man..FUCK THE POLL TAX'... ha ha it was like them cartoons when you see the light bulb above the heads light up in a communal YES!"[723]

Whilst 'hitching' back the duo also visited Teesside Direct Action Movement in Middlesbrough, keeping communication links and co-operative endeavours open.

Over in Sunderland;

"Poll Tax resistance has recently taking a significant step forward in Sunderland, long regarded as a 'moderate town'. The Northern Region Anti-Poll Tax Federation helped to organise a demo and rallyin the town on Saturday 24th March" to an estimated attendance of 2000. "In the main these people were "ordinary folk", but as one might expect the SWP and Militant were out in force, hence it was pleasing to recognise a solitary anarchist flag fluttering in the breeze. There are currently eleven anti-Poll Tax groups in Sunderland with the possibility of more appearing in the near future.The key to such development undoubtedly lies in the twin pillars of commitment and solidarity. It remains to be seen, of course, how serious present dissension will prove to be in the future."[724]

Saturday 31st March and an anti Poll Tax march in London was attended by some 200,000 people opposed to the tax. Coach loads from the North East were also present, including a contingent of Tyneside Class

War. In what became the infamous 'Poll Tax Riot', the aftermath of which included 500 police injured and 60 hospitalised, 400+ arrests, 394 shops and businesses attacked and looted. Much of which was in defence of, and from, attacks from the police against demonstrators.

> "The day after, the capitalist media came down like a ton of bricks in an attempt to reimpose their reality, portraying the rioter's violence as sheer mindless lunacy and trying to hide the much wider support it had amongst the working class."

All newspapers, media commentators, all politicians (left and right), and the 'leading lights' of such groups as *Militant* and the *Socialist Workers Party* were "united in utter condemnation." Self styled 'leaders' of the anti working class left groups such as the aforementioned *Militant* and the *SWP* were openly saying that they would be conducting their own inquiries and any evidence found was to be passed onto the police. Some socialism! Indeed, but then again, not unexpected.

The capitalist media and state suppression of facts could no longer cover up mass resistance.

> "Remember the Glasgow demonstration against the Poll Tax in April 1989? Over 20,000 people were on it, a massive display of defiance that was quietly censored. But the riot was too big to be ignored – and they hoped to smear the anti-Poll Tax movement as well. So the demonstration and subsequent riot were spread across all front pages, on all news bulletins: nobody could now say that they did not know that there was enormous and powerful opposition to the Poll Tax. And this of course, can only help to build mass non- payment of the Poll Tax."[725]

The media exposure (and blame) threw many anarchist groupings into the 'limelight' so to speak, and much interest was sparked in anarchist groups, particularly Class War. Tyneside Class War would also 'benefit' from the 'media speculation' with a visit from *'The Independent*

*Magazine'* reporter later in the year and sales of the *Class War* paper went through the roof.

Local paper sales were now becoming highly boisterous affairs with amusing and to the point shouted slogans coupled with *Class War* covers on display. This naturally attracted lots of attention in the centre of Newcastle, including the National Front who came to confront / attack two sellers at the Monument as both *Militant* and the *SWP* ran away back to their 'nice middle class bosoms of respectability' and leaving two of us to defend ourselves. 'Kick the Tories out? – we say kick them in, get your copy of Class War, only 40p' was a regular loud chant in and around the Monument area, perhaps in a mimicand to defiantly annoy the left who also regularly sold their papers with a mumble of 'kick the Tories out' (pretty please), or perhaps as a nod back to a letter in *Freedom* in 1983 that declared, on the founding of the paper that "The Class War anarchists don't just want to kick the Tories out, they 'just want to kick them' in a literal sense."[726] Either way, the response was enthusiastic and thus militant anarchist propaganda (*Class War*) coupled with theoretical anarchist - communist analysis (*Organise!*), and locally produced broad sheets and leaflets were regularly, openly, and receptively being distributed and read throughout the region.

Not everyone would agree though...

> "You are plainly not aware that this is Environment Week in the Borough of Darlington. School children, council workers and voluntary organisations are busy clearing graffiti and rubbish to make our streets look better. Your contribution has been to post hideous fly posters on letter boxes and hoardings. In particular you have had the impertinence to use the window of a shop, for which I am responsible, as a site. Kindly let me have your assurance that this nuisance will not be repeated. If you have any difficulty in apprehending this letter and the likely consequences I suggest you take the letter to the office of the Citizens Advice Bureau."[727]

Building on the momentum and the fast approaching May Day march in Newcastle, and the attendance of events with us of a journalist from the *Independent*, Tyneside Class War are soon announcing that 'May Day is no Poll Tax day' and a leaflet for the event states;

> "WE'VE GOT THEM BY THE BALLS...NOW LET'S SQUEEZE.
>
> The Poll Tax, unfair, undemocratic, of course it's unfair. The world we live inis unfair. The price of a pint, the crappy wages we are paid, aren't fair. The list is endless. The Poll Tax is an ambitious attack by the rich bastards on the working class. But in attempting to squeeze a little bit more out of us, the Tories and the ruling class have put their future in our hands.
>
> The word on the streets in Scotland is that they've got it sewn up. Coupled with one million non payers and effective anti bailiff patrols, this has meant that not one warrant sale has been possible, and now more and more people are joining in as they see their friends and families get away with not paying. Better than giving it tothe rich Tory bastards.
>
> Now we reach a new phase which has made us stronger. The rest of the UK has been billed with this hated tax (except the North of Ireland – we ask ourselves why?!). Spring saw the biggest outbreak of anti government violence in England and Wales since the hot summer of the 1981 riots. Town halls the length and breadth of the country were mobbed and attacked by angry crowds. The nowfamous London anti Poll Tax riot was the biggest outbreak of civil unrest in the capital for half a century. If the Tories are shitting themselves now, just think what they'll be like when we really get stuck in.
>
> Scrapping with the police may not stop the Poll Tax but then voting Labour won't, or taking advice from the loony left with their crap strategies won't either. Resisting collection will, so now is the time to have a word with your friends, neighbours,

family and workmates. We have to make it impossible to collect one person's Poll Tax.

For Class War a victory against the Poll Tax could lead to the creation of stronger, safer and more friendly communities (this is what scares the ruling class) and could give us the opportunity to start changing some of the shit we have to put up with under this lunatic economic system. Bollocks to the roof tax the only alternative to the Poll Tax is revolution. Down with the Poll Tax, down with the government, down with the ruling class."[728]

After the Poll Tax riot in London and the subsequent barrage of publicity surrounding it, the 'involvement and praise of the rioters' by, in particular London Class War, instigated numerous requests for interviews. When the *Independent* Newspaper and its weekend Magazine asked for an interview, many in London, tired by now of the media, rang around the rest of the Federation requesting help and only Tyneside responded yes.

"There might have been some trouble at Newcastle's Cattle Market, where the May Day marchers assembled. The question, it seems, was raised: would you please march further towards the back, somewhere between, say, the Christian Young Workers of England(A new world through a new youth) and the Ryton Woodcraft Folk (span the world with friendship)? No, we won't, said Class War, and the point was not pressed; this was a great day, a day of Solidarity and Strength, Tyneside's centenary May Day, the last thing you want is argy-bargy at the outset.

So that was how it came about: the march set off through the streets of Newcastle, a banner reading 'Tyneside May Day – Health Jobs Peace Homes' carried by a line of women at the front, Tony Benn ina suit behind, a silver band in blue jackets, the ornate, archaic banners of the United Society of

> Boilermakers, Shipbuilders and Structural Workers, the Confederation of Health Service Employees, the National Union of Railwaymen. And Class War, their banner adorned with a skull and crossbones, immediately followed by Nalgo.
>
> They trundled through the middle of town, men with matted hair and patched jeans alternately swigging ale and handing out leaflets, L (she sewed the banner) with her shaved head and rings, F with his two big dogs, T & P & M & A and the rest, a dozen or so in all: a little band of the dispossessed, an angry little blister on the respectable face of organised labour. I had met them by arrangement the previous night in a pub in the middle of Newcastle. I wasn't sure what sort of folk I was looking for: decaying hippies? Punks? Steely-eyed politicos in leather jackets? They turned out to be a bit of each.

About 30, not a 'dozen or so' supporters gathered around the Class War banner on the day. Patronising descriptions then followed of a few present before;

> These were not middle-class students slumming it; most were local and solidly proletarian, the exception being T, southern and genteelly bred, whose years in the ranks of the army had left him with a powerful handshake and a strong aversion to authority. Women were thin on the ground, a fact for which the aggressive posturing of the *Class War* paper might have prepared one. Apart from L, the seamstress, there was only Jo, with stark make-up and long swoops of peroxide-blonde hair, who was mute and mostly wrapped in the arms of T***y.
>
> Class War leapt into the public eye after London's poll-tax riot. The Deputy Assistant Commissioner of the Metropolitan Police, David Meynell, announced that the violence was the work of "anarchists and fringe elements" who were identifiable by their black flags. Class War, while denying that they had organized it, announced their view that the violence was justified. The

result was instant notoriety.

Class War is not as insignificant a phenomenon as their tabloid fame might lead one to suspect. They no longer call themselves anarchists – not because of any anathema the word attracts but because the only people in the country who describe themselves thus, they have discovered, are ineffectual middle-aged men in woolly hats.

But Class War are certainly anarchists, with all the radicalism and naivety and rowdy sloganeering that implies. "Violence is a necessary part of class war," they declare, "...the law is merely a weapon of the ruling class... Real change can only come about through working class people organizing themselves to deal with the problems they experience, using direct action against the individuals and institutions responsible for them." Their venom is divided roughly in equal parts between Mrs Thatcher – images of her being stabbed or hanged are favoured – the rich, the police, and Trotskyite groups, such as the Socialist Workers Party or the Militant Tendency, with which they vie for the attention of the disaffected.

Their paper, also called *Class War*, deliberately tries to out-Sun *The Sun*, and sells far more than other extremist publications – 20,000 copies a month, they claim. The cover of issue number 39 shows a surly youth with two fingers in the air, alongside the caption, 'You can count on two fingers how much poll tax to pay!' It is extremely rude and silly, and without question the liveliest political paper in thecountry. It also makes money.

Class War started in London in 1983. Now they have 18 branches around the country and their claim to have 'several hundred activists and supporters in the thousands' is not improbable. They also boast of branches in Helsinki, West Germany and the USA, and fledgling groups as far apart as Australia, Sweden, Poland and the Philippines.

After the poll tax riot and the subsequent volleys of flak, however, the only ones willing to raise their heads above the parapet were the Tyneside group. In some ways they are different from their comradesin the metropolis. London's Class War has its roots in the city's squats; in Newcastle squatting is practically unheard of. Here they all have homes to go to. They have parents and uncles and aunts around the city. Their dislocation is local, recent, perhaps only temporary.

Take F, for example: he looks the wildest of the lot, with his fearsome Alsatians, his breeches and his crazy hair. But at lunchtimeon Sunday he would only drink lemonade because he was driving over to see his mum and dad in the afternoon. "*We talk about politics,*" he said, "*but it always ends in a shouting match.*" His parents are stalwart socialists from the Tyneside working class bedrock. Dad works in a local factory making heavy machinery, Mum is a cleaner – and, now that they've bought their council house, she has to work seven days a week so that they can keep up with the mortgage payments.

F is unemployed. "*I'm looking for work – I'd work if I could find the right job.*" His last experience was shovelling mud in the hold of a ship on the docks. He boils with indignation as he describes the painof it, and the rotten money. Most of the group are going through themotions necessary these days to extract money from the state, half- heartedly clocking on at training schemes, applying for grants, pretending to play their part in the enterprise culture.

Anti poll tax agitation is what keeps them all busiest at present; several were present in Trafalgar Square, and described those who attacked the police as "heroes". Groups around the country fighting the poll tax have been scooped up by the Trotskyite Militant Tendency which runs the Anti-Poll Tax federation, and Class War has become a haven for tax-resisters who resent being manipulated by Marxists for their ulterior goals. They also talk a lot about solidarity with strikers and working class communities.

But it was L the seamstress who, in the pub on the first night, raised the theme which was to crop up over and over again in conversation during the following days: "hunt sabbing". T, the ex-army man, reminisced about his days breaking up fox hunts and hare coursing. L had the bruises to show from the time she was bowled over by the police while trying to disrupt a hunt. They spoke of the occasion they managed to grab a fugitive hare and throw it in the back of their van – whereupon the enraged coursers jumped in after it and threw the hare to the baying dogs.

It seemed a bizarrely marginal occupation for dedicated anarchists. Yet it was clear that it was the one which many of them threw themselves into most eagerly. When I mentioned this impression, they told me it signified nothing.

On this I disagree. The new British anarchists have a curious mishmash of prejudices and preoccupations, and breaking up hunts is a form of action which satisfies most of them. They are sentimental about animals – most I met were vegetarians, for example. They cultivate their class hatred sedulously, and spoiling the sport of the gentry is second only to intimidating yuppies as a way of getting it out of their system. They have a powerful sense of hostility to the police – instead of topless bimbo, *Class War's* page three usually has a photo of a 'hospitalised copper' – and 'hunt sabbing' guarantees a punch-up with the law."[729]

The article concludes with the author's perception and pre-conceived fallacy of how Class War are mere followers and hero worshipers of the early 1980's anarcho-punk band Crass, after the song 'Do they owe us a living' was overheard by the reporter at a party, held by a supporter on the fringes of the group, during the Saturday evening. This gave the angle the reporter had already pre-empted in his head, nevertheless, it was another outlet gladly accepted by the group to spread the ideas, and promotion of Class War.[730]

Having dealt with the pre-conceived notions from ambitious reporters and the media aftermath from the 'Poll Tax Riot', it was soon 'back to hard work' for Tyneside Class War.

The summer would see the release of a 16 page pamphlet in conjunction with Newcastle ACF entitled 'Non Payers Guide to the Poll Tax' and which described itself thus;

> "This pamphlet explains why the law has to be broken in order to defeat the Poll Tax. Many of us cannot afford the luxury of a moral stance where the Poll Tax is concerned – we can't pay and we won't pay. There is nothing wrong with breaking the Poll Tax law- just like we break the law on numerous occasions in many areas of our lives – the law is not there for our benefit.
>
> Break the law not the poor. This pamphlet analyses and expands on the March Poll Tax Riot and reactions to it. It also sets out what legal powers councils have in trying to get the Poll Tax out of us; explaining why we need not fear these powers. Local councils will try to collect the Poll Tax in slightly different ways, so keep in touch with your local anti-Poll Tax group to be up-to-date on the situation in your area. But remember, we can successfully avoid paying – and we can defeat the Tory flagship. SO DON'T PAY."[731]

Hundreds of the pamphlets were sent to be sold by Class War and ACF groups throughout the country and street sold locally, for a mere 20p. The *Class War* paper would also have a prominent advert for them.[732]

Another group report would state;

> "Still selling lots of papers in Newcastle. Have branched out and done paper sales in Wallsend, South Shields and Hexham. We are going to the Miners Gala in Durham Sat 14th July, so as usual should sell loads of papers there. We now have regular discussion meetings which have been attended well with our influx of new members / supporters. We've been actively involved in stopping NF meetings in Newcastle lately as well as having to defend ourselves atpaper sales from them. Have just released a pamphlet entitled *'Non payers guide to the Poll Tax'* it's a split project with Newcastle ACF. On the subject of the Poll Tax, we're still involved with local grassroots groups and have been actively supporting non-payers at their court cases in South Shields, and we have just received an invitation from North Shields anti poll Tax groups to attend a march they are having. We have just set up a library, so local people interested can lend books etc. We hit the papers again about "Anarchists City Centre base"...Tyneside Free Press, which we used as a mailing address; it may have to close down if the council get their own way. We have just had a 'Northern Regional Conference' which was really good and more are planned for the future. We are now taking over *The Heavy Stuff*."[733]

The national *Class War* paper is also commenting on the achievements of the group;

> "A year of hard graft on the part of Tyneside Class War is now beginning to show results, with a well established group in Newcastle and new groups forming in North Tyneside, Gateshead and South Shields. They are very active in the local anti poll tax campaign, and have recently produced the excellent pamphlet; *'A Non Payers Guide to the Poll Tax'*. Some seriously vigorous agitation by local activists, backed up by paper sales, lively discussions and livelier socials, has produced an ever increasing network of supporters in the area."[734]

Anarchist friends over in Sunderland are also producing an a3 broadsheetwhich gives us a glimpse into their anti-poll tax work;

> "Sunderland Central Anti Poll Tax Group was formed March 1990 as an integral part of the Sunderland Anti Poll Tax Union in order to foster and support local resistance to the Poll Tax. After contributing to the Sunderland demonstration of 24th March '90 in which 2000+ marched through the streets to a mass rally at Wearmouth hall. Most of the group attended the London rally of 31st March '90, unfortunately suffering one arrest after clashes with representativesof the 'neo fascist' state apparatus in the vicinity of Trafalgar Square. 24th April saw a successful turn out from the central area to lobby Sunderland Borough Council demanding that no legal action should be taken against non payers.
>
> The official consequences of non-payment were investigated and a leaflet produced, which is available on request. With the advent of May Day the group attended celebrations in Newcastle where we joined up with comrades from 'Tyneside Class War' to protest at oneMay Day speaker, Tommy Sheridan, chair of the Anti Poll Tax Federation for his willingness to pursue witch hunts within the movement following the Trafalgar Square riot a month earlier.
>
> Sunderland Central Anti Poll Tax Group meets every Monday 7.30 upstairs in the Bunker, Stockton Road. Meetings are run on social rather than political lines without the need for the formalities of elected officials etc. All welcome, come along for a natter and help smash the tax!"[735]

It was also during this period that proposals were being put forward, from within both camps, for an organisational merger between the Class War Federation and the Anarchist Communist Federation. Observers from both federations were attending each other's conferences and meetings, swapping national internal bulletins, and having shared discussions.[736]

Locally this impacted little, as both naturally worked together, as shown previously, anyway. One memo from Tyneside CW would state;

> "We feel that until Class War has defined its politics, direction, stance and organisational structure then it is in no position to merge with the ACF or any other similar organisation. To explain the last point a little, we feel that if Class War at present did enter into any political union with the ACF then because of our lack of formalised ideas we would inevitably be a junior partner in such a relationship. We don't think it is enough to inject the ACF's politics into our organisation and present them in Class War's distinctive style. We must develop our own! If the ACF's political line is right we will arrive at it eventually and in our own way and hopefully will not as the ACF has done loose all our members into the bargain."[737]

Without delving into long drawn out eventual reasons, the merger didn't occur, but this didn't detract from the 'working together' ethos that had been established and which would continue. An ex local ACF member, reflecting on events some 29 years later would emphasise;

> "At the time I was enthusiastic about possible joint organisation of all the class struggle anarchist groups – according to the principle that it would make us stronger. Others, especially in the DAM but also many in the ACF, perhaps weren't so keen – mostly due to worries about ideological "purity" and all that precious nonsense as well as suspecting some in Class War just wanted publicity for its own sake. In effect, though, I think a lot of Class War people tended to think people in the other groups would interfere with their "image", and would be too boring for them, etc, as much as any political reasons. In hindsight, I suppose, it was a non-starter – nobody was into thinking that ambitiously. But I still think that was a shame (or even a tragic missed opportunity ...). Having said that, maybe it would have been a disaster.

Who knows?"

Whereas a rather naive ex Tyneside Class War activist would conclude;

> "The Class War Federation and the Anarchist Communist federation had been having a series of talks, nationally, about an organisation merger. A lot of people in both camps were both for and against, whilst us here on Tyneside didn't particularly care because we had been working together closely for years anyway. For years we had joint paper sales on the streets of Newcastle etc...If someone came up to us to buy a copy of *Class War*, we would then also offer them a copy of *Organise!*, and vice versa. I didn't particularly care what was sold as long as the message was getting spread"[738]

July 1990 was particularly interesting with regards to the North East of England after the release of the anarchist quarterly journal *The Raven* Number 11 The Freedom Press publication, in book format, would have its theme this issue centred on 'Class'. Firstly it contained an educational short essay by GP entitled 'Anarchist Influences in the Durham Coalfield before 1914', and perhaps more importantly for the period, an essay by our TJ; 'Politics and Class Struggle in the 1990's: Libertarian Theory'. Prior to publication, TJ's essay had been passed around, read and commented on locally, with much approval.

The introduction would give insight as follows;

> "From the mid-1970's to the present we have witnessed the most dramatic ever erosions of income, welfare provision, housing conditions, rights, workplace protection, hopes and expectations of ordinary British people. Yet it is possible for the idea that 'class' no longer exists, or is no longer significant, to gain ground and approval. Eruptions of working class anger and action all over Britain during this time are perceived as irrelevant or even reactionary, not just by the apostles of the New Right, but within the Communist Party, wider sections of the trendy left, trade union bureaucrats and welfare state

> professionals, and in the pages of many alternative political journals. Meanwhile, working class, and class-conscious, anarchism is undergoing rapid growth and diversification across England, Scotland, Wales and Ireland. The causes and consequences of this apparent contradiction are one thing, but what is certain is that class struggle anarchism is generating many agendas, priorities, debates, organisational experiments and above all, *action*. This essay isn't intended to be representative of these developments, nor to justify or explain them. It does illustrate some theoretical preoccupations of some of the people involved, as well as perhaps offering original, modern perspectives on politics, society and anarchism to set against the image of class theory offered by its opponents."

The essay would continue looking at developments within anti-capitalism, 'Class, Race and Gender', and 'Class, Identity and Action', before concluding;

> "The significance of 'class' is what effects it has on our political theory and practice. We can say that the probability of groups of people moving in libertarian, collective directions is greater if their backgrounds, present position and consciousness enables them readily to employ the discourses appropriate to those directions. And the purpose of our action as class struggle anarchists is not to be 'right', but to express our ideas in ways that increase the likelihood of movement in those directions. I would say that that this is the common thread of current class-conscious libertarian thought and activity in Britain – and personally I find it a great relief that in my political activity I no longer have to expend vast quantities of time and energy pandering to the sensitivities of middle class people who, in any case, only ever seemed to view me and my kind with patronising condescension, or, at worst, contempt."[739]

The October 'Tyneside regional round-up' from Tyneside Class War wouldinform us;

"Signs that the ruling class are on the run were evident by a recent visit to Tyneside by Margaret Thatcher. The visit to Newcastle College and the Gateshead Garden Festival was kept secret with only top City officials being informed and it only becoming public knowledge once the visit was over. Indeed the last time Thatcher paid us a visit the City centre came to a virtual standstill and thatwas before the hated Poll Tax.

Non-payment in some areas of the North East far exceeds the national average and demonstrations outside courts remain healthy as Labour councils display their true feelings towards the common people. However the anti-Poll Tax Federation is dominated by leftie groups, with Militant being the most prominent. These groups play a major part in stifling genuine working class activity. This was evident at a recent Newcastle City centre march as genuine activists were notable by their absence, although one local anti-Poll Tax group's banner did declare "Not Militant, not SWP, not paying". Later on in the day a Militant meeting with guest speaker Tommy Sheridan was disrupted by local Class War supporters (regular readers of *Class War* will be acquainted with his traitorous tendencies – e.g. a willingness to act as a coppers nark). Tyneside Class War's pamphlet *"Non Payers Guide to the Poll Tax"* sets out to explain why more generalised action is both urgent and essential in order to make sure that the biggest working class movement in Britain for years this century turns into a truly creative movement that does not restrict itself to the agendas of the ruling class but instead creates our own.

Recently Poll-capped North Tyneside Labour Council took no time in implementing cuts with sackings and redundancies the order of the day. One in three of the workforce is one figure suggested by ex- NALGO branch secretary and now £30,000 per year council leader John F. Two advice centres have been marked for immediate closure, which has created even more

> hostility towards the council. These centres have for years provided meeting space and back-up for local tenants groups and anti-Poll Tax groups. Councillors are being run off estates as locals see their actions as "a cynical attempt to silence working class communities". Ironically increased funding has been granted to the official council Peoples Centre. Throughout the area demand for *"Non Payers Guide to the Poll Tax"* has outstripped supply."[740]

October saw another national anti Poll Tax gathering in London, also attended by Tyneside Class War. A large picket and protest of Brixton Prison was held by the Trafalgar Square Defendants Campaign and led to some clashes with police, whilst the 'infamous' large Tyneside Class War banners metal poles were apparently 'flung like javelins' and the red and black banner itself was later 'lost in a pub back in Newcastle after a 'No Gulf War' march'.

A large official march and rally was also held with up to 35,000 people in attendance, dominated as ever by Militant and their 'grassing leaders!' Class War members in attendance, after heckling various speakers – particularly those who incited shopping 'rioters' to the police after the March riot – were again pointed out to police after Militant stewards "had to move in to deal with the disrupters". The *Militant* newspaper would later describe those present as 'fascists' and / or 'agent provocateurs' as;

> "On all demonstrations now, in London especially, many young people gather who are totally alienated from everything. They are the victims of Thatcherism. Some are homeless and totally destitute. Others have opted out of society and have no class roots whatever. If they are pulled behind the banners of groups like *Class War* on marches it is because the labour movement's leaders have totally failed to show them that the working-class movement is the vehicle for organised protest and social change."

After crying that these 'young people etc' should be recruited to follow the 'socialist programme and class outlook that *Militant* is based upon', and saying 'Totally' another 27 times, the drivel concludes; "all demonstrations must be well stewarded and disciplined. Deliberately provocative actions must be kept in check and attempts to disrupt meetings prevented."[741] Otherwise we will tell the police on you on our way back to our nice middle class lifestyles. *Militant*, in my eyes, were and shall always be beyond contemptible.

Even *Freedom* would come to Class War's defence, where they write;

> "Following the national anti-poll tax demo of 20th October, the Militant Tendency leadership of the All Britain Anti Poll Tax Federation have attacked the Trafalgar Square Defendants Campaign for being associated with anarchist groups such as Class War. They strongly criticise the TSDC's apparent lack of organisationand stewarding of the march and picket of Brixton prison. It seemsto me that Militant, with their statist aspirations, regard 'good stewarding' as success in *controlling* a crowd; in other words, a 'good steward' acts as a would-be policeman, attempting to contain crowd anger and stifle crowd action. I expect much of Militant's irritation stems from the hostile reception given to Steve 'coppers nark' Nally at the Brockwell Park rally, particularly by comrades from Class War.
>
> In a letter to the TSDC, Militant claim that those who are critical of them are either fascists or agents provocateurs! Such absurd smears are surely signs of desperation as the anti-poll tax movement becomes increasingly disillusioned with Militant's tactics. Further evidence for this is an over the top attack on Class War specifically, which Militant have accused of racism and anti-semitism. This may be an attempt to capitalise on the (deliberate) misunderstandings in the Tory press, who reported that European 'Nazis' were present at the October demo because journalists saw youth with armbands with the word 'Nazis' on. (In fact the armbands said 'Gegen Nazis' – *against*

> Nazis!) Anyone who has read *Class War* will know that accusations of racism are simply nonsensical; in the past Class War have been completely cleared by anti-fascist organisations of any involvement with fascists."[742]

Meanwhile TJ and Newcastle Anarchist Communist Federation are having a long debate with DR in the pages of *Freedom* after the review of *'The Role of the Revolutionary Organisation'* pamphlet, which was released by the ACF. The debate would carry on for five months and defended as such;

> "Not all people who come across *Freedom* magazine, and who continue to read it, should be written of as hopeless 'liberals'. Also, among the ephemera of anarchism, *'Freedom'* persists. So although such publications are not the main focus for convincing people of our ideas, it is worth using them to publicise ourselves and our literature, and from time to time entering into debate – it's free space for us, after all. Sometimes, worth while material seeps into the pages of 'Freedom' and 'The Raven'."[743]

In November 1990, Thatcher failed to receive a majority in the Conservative Party's annual vote for selection of a 'leader'. She then withdrew her nomination, and John Major, the Chancellor of the Exchequer since 1989, was chosen as the next Conservative 'leader'. On November 22nd, to the joy of many, including many in her own Party she announced her resignation and six days later was succeeded by the aforementioned Major. Tyneside Class War in their 'Kick the Tories out? We say kick them in' leaflet released at the time would emphasise that;

> "After twelve long years of Tory rule, and pathetic slogans of "Maggie, Maggie, Maggie, Out, Our, Out," Thatcher has finally gone down the plug hole of history, only to be replaced by the pathetic John 'Pratt Face' Major. The 90s have so far seen a massive resurgence of working class anger aimed at the Poll

Tax and oppression in general. With the looming General Election the Tories are shitting themselves, having already ditched Thatcher they've now ditched the Poll Tax (the Tory Flagship has finally sunk) and are making any last-ditch attempt to regain popularity. We know its crap, you know its crap.

So what's the answer? Vote Labour? Bollocks. Neil Pillocks crew are looking so much like the Tories you'd need a microscope to spot the difference. Even the Labour Party's policy document has the same name as the Tories: 'Opportunity Britain'. How many times have we heard this crap before? Thatcher and the Poll Tax were not defeated by kind-hearted politicians who wanted to help us. It was defeated by the working class who united and refused to pay the same Poll tax as some rich scumbag in St Peter's Basin or Darras Hall.

Whoever wins at the next General Election, nothing will change. All it does is con people into thinking that they have some control over their lives. We have no time for parliamentary democracy; the only time we get anything is when we take it for ourselves.

We've won the battle against the poll Tax but we still have to win the war against poverty, unemployment, the rising cost of living and oppression in general. This is why we say: "Don't kick the Tories out – Kick them in". Let's give them a taste of their own medicine. Class War, neither left nor right, but ahead."[744]

The rest of 1990 was taken up with regular discussion meetings (some with Newcastle ACF), *Class War / Organise!* street sales and the regular stocking of local newsagents, meeting new supporters and establishing new groups in the region, attending anti fascist 'get together' events / call outs in both York and Glasgow, as well as local St James Park pickets, attending national delegate meetings, and the usual fly posting, leafleting, etc. It was agreed nationally that Tyneside would take over the production of *'The Heavy Stuff'*, Class War's theoretical journal, beginning with issue 4. Fundraising events and gigs were already taking place for this purpose, as wellas the collecting of writings for inclusion.

Concluding 1990 with a touch of optimism for 1991, the then secretary for Tyneside Class War would state;

> "Here it is, the December newsletter and who would have thought we would outlive Thatcher! Does this mean no more yuppies, Poll Tax, or even Class War? We don't think so! Since our last newsletter we've been well busy, to be honest we've never stopped. Loads of paper sales and meetings, we've been on loads of marches, we've been rioting, we had the excellent Northern Class War Conference followed by our rave where we raised £100 and had a fucking brilliant time, the *Heavy Stuff* will soon be out again after being silent for too long, we've been accused of being fascists by *Militant*, we've been on TV again and we've also attracted two new members and we've suffered no arrests. We won't be fooled by Thatcher's resignation and promises of a classless, multiracial society by John Major PM, at our last meeting of the year we will discuss our plans for 1991. Only cynics, liberals and leftists doubt the strength and influence of Class War. The future is ours, 1991 belongs to us!"[745]

1991 begins the same for Tyneside Class War with regular paper sales and further recruitment in areas like Sunderland and Darlington.

> "We did not participate in any of the ad-hoc anti Gulf-war groups that were set up by local students, leftists and liberals. The demands of these groups were a mixture of broad demands for peace and apologists for Saddam Hussein. These no-hopers are isolated from daily Tyneside life and are regarded as the loony left and rightfully so. Our activities were limited to loud graffiti, selling papers, and distributing an excellent leaflet that we produced, that was pro (class) war,

> and anti-Saddam, Bush and Major. We attended only one of the anti-Gulf war marches, we were determined not to be dismissed along with CND and the loony left. Our chants included: "Kill the rich, not the poor", "Bomb Darras Hall (local rich area) – not Baghdad", etc. Over the past financial year most local anti-Poll Tax groups on Tyneside have either collapsed or been taken over by the Militant Tendency (with their usual tactics). This week Newcastle City Council is setting their Poll Tax rate and a big demonstration is expected. We will be attending in full force."[746]

Class War and friends were defiantly in attendance as the local *Evening Chronicle* as well as that evenings TV news mentions;

> "Police were called in to eject poll tax protestors amid angry scenes at Newcastle Civic Centre. Lord Mayor Coun T.C. ordered the packed public gallery to be cleared as heckling broke out (including a remark about his robes) at the start of the city council's budget meeting to set a poll tax of £390.60. Some demonstrators had to be dragged out of the building to join an angry crowd of about 600 gathered outside".[747]

Much organising was taken place for the forthcoming National Class War conference to be held in Newcastle, whilst *The Heavy Stuff* No 4 was eventually finished and sent off to the printers. A valiant achievement encompassed without any financial support from the rest of the federation.

The Class War conference commenced over the weekend beginning 19th April at West End leisure and learning, Elswick Road, under the auspices of 'Tyneside Care Workers'. The agenda was set, and was predominantly focusedon future publication of Class War's politics.[748]

In the spirit of being un-biased towards the events of the weekend, I quote an outside the area report.

"On Saturday 20th and Sunday 21st April, I attended my first Class War national conference, held at the West End leisure centre near the centre of Newcastle.

As a newcomer to Class War (though not a member at the time of writing), I didn't quite know what to expect or what kind of people I would meet. After all, if you pick up a paper like *Class War* and see it plastered with cross-headings like "bollocks", "shit" and "crap" you could be forgiven for having a few misgivings. Mind you, you only have to read *"The Heavy Stuff"*, Class War's theoretical journal, to realise that these people are thoughtful, serious and mean business. There were between forty and fifty delegates in all (though only members were allowed to vote). They came from Bristol, Manchester, Liverpool, Luton, London, and various other places. Although most of them were in their twenties there was a fair representation of older people in their forties (like myself). I looked in vain for a green – or purple – haired punk with the arse hanging out of his/her jeans.

There was a mood of determination to get on with the business in hand. What impressed me, as a Class War supporter but not a member, was that non-members had an equal say in any of the debates. Having been a member of two lefty parties – the Communist Party and New Communist Party – and having just left the Labour Party, I noticed a distinct absence of the normal atmosphere that fills such conferences. You know the kind of thing I mean – the experts on the platform showering us with the droppings of their great minds, other self appointed "experts" or cadres in the body of the meeting making long, balls-aching speeches, showing off their knowledge to any-one who will listen.

The main business of the conference was the discussion and amendment of a pamphlet outlining Class War's politics to replace the previous pamphlet, *"This is Class War"*. It is a criticism frequently levelled at Class War that they offer no real alternative to the status quo, other than a mindless rebellion against it. The new pamphlet, when it is ratified by the next national conference and printed for distribution, should dispel the image of Class War as a bunch of directionless piss artists who revel in violence for its own sake. Class War does, of course, recognise that any change to a better society must involve violence, both as a defence against the violence of the capitalist state and in recognition of the fact that the rich will not voluntarily give up their opulent lifestyles.

The pamphlet deals with capitalism, the state, class and the class system, class struggle, revolution, revolutionary organisations, the new world, and appendices on several subjects, including Northern Ireland. What it amounts to is a sober clear-headed appraisal of where we are now, how we got here, and what we need to do to get us where we want to be. There is none of the simplistic sloganising and plain wishful thinking you find in much of the left parties' propaganda. Class War is obviously prepared to learn from the pastwithout being hampered by it.

The pamphlet deals at length on how to get our politics out to the working-class, and how to rebuild a working-class culture and identity, after the erosion of the values of community and solidarity by the syphilitic ravings of "greed – and – self" Thatcherism. It did not underestimate the problems posed by revolutionary change, or promise some kind of "nice" liberal utopia. It did point out that a world shorn of capitalist greed and envy, a world where people have enough to eat and live in peace with their neighbours, is only going to be built with a lot of hard slog and self discipline.

The Newcastle conference confirmed everything that I have long suspected – that people can find a coherent political direction and organise themselves without power–hungry leaders. Such efforts do, however, need to be co-ordinated and presided over by someone to keep a little order and we were very fortunate in having a brilliant chairperson for the part of the conference involving the pamphlet. He did a job that would certainly have scrambled my brains.

All in all, it was a weekend I wouldn't have missed. We congratulated the Tyneside comrades on a well-organised conference, with a good social on the Saturday night and excellent food on both days.

Although only a young organisation, Class War is growing in numbers and influence. Its progress towards a more organised, "together" approach to its activities can only be a cause of anxiety to the wealthy scum who have profited vastly from the previous decade of human misery. (Will they ever forget Trafalgar Square 1990?) The class enemy might very well tremble in his favourite night-club or massage parlour. Our time has come."[749]

The locally produced Heavy Stuff No 4 was released in time for distribution at the conference and contained articles on 'Questioning Marx', 'The war in Ireland', 'Language and Power' which interestingly explored the way the political and social power of the ruling class is reinforced by their control of language, 'Mutual aid and community care', 'the Poll Tax', and for the first time contained reviews and a letters page, which incidentally contained a massively cut-short letter from our TJ on the middle class.[750]

After a proposal from Tyneside at the national Class War conference, it was agreed to have a 'National Day of Action against the Bailiffs' 1st July, and locally at a bailiff's office in Gateshead.

"The object of this action is to take the fight against the poll tax on the offensive. We aim to confront the bailiffs as an angry, organised mass of people rather than sitting at home waiting for these state bully boys to call on us."[751]

When, in September, the death of two 'joy riders' after a high speed police chase through North Tyneside, riots broke out in the region. This was just one of many incitements nationally as between 1991-1992;

> "Riots have taken place in cities like Cardiff, Oxford, Newcastle, Sunderland, Leeds, Coventry, and Bristol and in towns such as Burnley, North Shields, Blackburn, Salford, Carlisle, Huddersfield, Stockton and Middlesbrough, Luton and Dunfermline, and county towns in leafy Shropshire such as Wellington and Telford. During the first seven months of '92, there've been, almost everywhere, countless heavy incidents involving brick and bottle throwing aimed at the cops, which, except locally, are hardly reported."[752]

Without delving into the sociological aspects and political narrative of the how and why the riots occurred, as others have[753], Tyneside Class War was soon giving a straightforward explanation of events in their newly fly posted broadsheet.

> "*Police are murderers, Dale 'n' Colin we won't let them get away with it* – graffiti plastered on walls during September's riots. Sparked off by the murder of these two local ram raiders it came as no surprise when the Meadow Well estate kicked off on Monday night with parts of Newcastle, mainly the West End, continuing in the week.
>
> Labour Councils blamed high unemployment, Tory policies etc which of course is true, but it was the police who were singled out. Even locals who condemned the riots blamed the police for provoking more than they could handle. *"They don't treat you like human, they walk around like they're gods"* – Meadow Well youth on TV's 'Northern Life' describing the police. The media has tried to make out that it's only the joy-riders or ram raiders who are rioting, but with a combination of police harassment, unemployment, boredom, and decaying estates, it's obviously

more than that. Even Stanley Bailey, chief Northumbria pig got it right when he said *"there aren't that many ram raiders."* In any case many of the buildings burnt were derelict houses, closed down youth clubs and community centres, showing that the youth's anger was directed at the state of the places they have to live in. Riots have been happening all over the country but the media picks out a couple of areas and blames it on local influences. This stops us realising how widespread dissatisfaction and frustration are. It all totally pisses on John Major's "classless Britain". People do have to turn to crime to survive, but it's daft when people start robbing off their own. Major stated the riots were unacceptable, but it's his government with its sick policies and police which are totally unacceptable."[754]

Another interesting note would emphasise;

"Immediately after the deaths of the two joy-riders killed in a high speed cop car race and which sparked the violence on the Meadow Well estate in North Shields in September 91, there was a call from some of the area's youth for a work stay away as a mark of respect. North Shields is right at the centre of what's left of the engineering and ship building industries on the river Tyne. Whether individual workers heeded the call or not, it's difficult to say.

In some ways it wasn't such an unrealistic thing to call for. A lot of the youth, remember, have no money at all. In many ways they are forced into activities like the Newcastle invention of ram raiding vansinto security shutters across store fronts, then doing a hit and run with the goodies – merely in order to survive. Tyneside has never come out of the recession which started in the early 70s, and off- the-cards "scrounge" work whilst signing on the dole has got more and more difficult to find. Ram raiding has consequently become dammed hard work, a substitute for grafting[755] in heavy industry which the area not-so-long-ago was noted for. The more playful aspects of joy-riding tend to go by the board; it has to be put within the context of the work-a-day world. A police chase. A car crash. Several injured. A death – it's viewed more as an industrial accident in an engineering plant like close-by Reyrolles, or a pit disaster at Easington colliery. To call for a sympathy strike in such a situation is perfectly logical – even if it did fall on deaf ears."[756]

Pretty soon the West End of Newcastle is rioting, as *Class War* takes up the narrative;

"Tory bigwigs, John Major and Home Secretary Ken Baker did a hatchet job on playing down the events of a whole week, throughoutthe whole of Newcastle upon Tyne's West End. In the press, Major burbled on about "copycat rioting" and "handfuls of youth's" how "unacceptable" recent uprisings were – what the prime minister was doing was putting down publicly something he and his cabinet of deadheads were shitting themselves over. So what's really happened? – Class War's been in touch with contacts in Newcastle and the story is NOT of an isolated, copycat thoughtless riot, resulting in little more than a few outraged locals and the Dodd's Arms pub being burnt down – what happened was a week-long riotous uprising! Organised T.W.O.C (taking without owners consent) ram raider teams have been down Meadow Well estate in September, cleverly sussing out how to outmanoeuvre the cops, and how to organise against them. Ram raiding has been established in Newcastle for two years, and the TWOC squads know what they're doing: using hand-held radios to communicate with each other, avoiding cop cars and police roadblocks. The squads have been able to confound the cops by broad-daylight 'riding' in such posh motors as convertible BMW's.

The events of mid-September were expertly organised and widespread through the Elswick, Scotswood, Benwell and

Cruddas Park areas. Local paper ads were substituted by poster invites to riot! Tyneside cops tried to persuade the press that all that happened was *"not above the normal level of violence for the area"* – absolute crap! Two housing offices were burnt out and all 'social services' departments in the West End had to close by 2pm throughout the week. While whole shopping centres were covered with messages of solidarity with the two men who died in Meadow Well: *"Dale and Colin we'll avenge your death"*, other graffiti plastered theregistration numbers of unmarked police cars over the walls with a message to the cops: *"We're gonna get you!"* Cops were so scared that attempts to take over the city centre were met with the forced closure of restaurants, bars and pubs from 8pm. Police barricades were thrown up all around the city centre with cops swamping the area to prevent people from taking it for themselves." "The anti-cop organisation was interconnected[757] throughout more than four areas and fires and scuffles lasted well after the high point of Tuesday to Friday. Cops were being attacked well after this; two of them were petrol bombed.

The local media were instructed to institute a huge cover-up. Local radio stated that "no disturbances" were going on at the same time that uprisings were plainly in evidence not only in Newcastle, but in Sunderland, Gateshead and all over Tyneside and Wearside. To keep a lid on 'disorder', the state's media simply did not report mostevents.

There are many important lessons to be learned: When we are in violent struggle, we must organise, communicate; control events so that the right targets are dealt with in the right way; we must act in solidarity against the cops and make sure that when the state TV and newspapers carry out news blackouts, we are able to get the truth out – by our own newsletters, or even taking over local radio and TV broadcasts: it may sound far-fetched, but it's been done before and we can do it again. Quite clearly such blackouts are done to prevent thousands

> more coming to join the uprising and beat the cops. This is why they put so much time and energy into telling us all's well now, that they were "copycat" incidents, that it was "*tattooed yobbos and crackpots...an anti-social minority*" We all know that this is complete lies designed to set the working class against itself – let's let them know the TRUTH."[758]

Basically the North East, just like previous decades, is left to rot. We've built your warships, with the steel we've made for you, heated with the coal we've dug for you. Now no longer needed and generations of given labour cast aside as imports are now cheaper, and we can't disrupt the fatal flow of the worldwide capitalist markets now can we.

> *"All the hatred and bitterness that ever was now had the chance to be released. The boil had burst forth all sorts of ill feeling that was translated into mass destruction. This was the last chance they would get to exit with a bang that would leave a trail like a comet to be seen long after it had burnt out but on a bigger scale than when Dale R and Colin A had self-destructed in a fire*ball that sent ripples of burning embers into the hearts of the authorities."[759]

Oppressive 'gang mentality' instigating and inciting daily confrontation from Northumbria police with their 'bully boy' tactics and attempts of control and domination of the local 'downtrodden and displaced' populace would inevitably lead to a fight. The bully only continues until the 'victim' naturally comes to a point where they have had enough and retaliates with venom morebitter than the authoritarian bully can muster, and a fight back more extreme. What was perceived as the 'murder' of two young lads was the catalyst, the ignition, the lit fuse that had been lying dormant for generations waiting to explode, and it came as no surprise that it did, and no doubt shall again. Our hatred for them is eternal.

See APPENDIX B: 'Riotous Responses: Media Balance & its uses.' For further excellent local analysis of these events and their regional aftermath.

23rd to 28th September, Class War held an International Conference in London and of which some from Tyneside would attend events. The event was also advertised in a locally, Newcastle produced zine during this period called *'DNR'*. Written from an 'anarchist-feminist' slant, the issue included articles on 'Female circumcision', 'Lesbian and gay Class War', 'Biotechnology', and 'Woman's football'.

Early 1992, and the Anarchist Communist Federation is welcoming new members from both Chester Le Street and Middlesbrough. The latter are soon reporting;

> "An anarchist meeting is held each week in Middlesbrough with members of the Direct Action Movement. Involved in local anti-Poll Tax and anti-fascist activity; producing and distributing leaflets and posters. 22nd February attended the mobilization against the British National Party in Sunderland. About 30 BNP, protected by police, were moved from where they had been selling papers regularly."[760]

70-80 copies of *Organise!* were being sold by Newcastle ACF every issue, coupled with the 300+ copies of *Class War* each issue (and unknown quantities of *Direct Action* and *Black Flag*) which equated to quite a large amount of 'class struggle' anarchist literature being sold and read monthly within the region.

By July the next issue of *The Heavy Stuff*, number 5 is being released. Edited byTyneside, this issue was produced by members of the recently formed Edinburgh Class War and contained articles and debate on 'Oxford – the Blackbird Leys riots', 'United Europe in 1992', 'Green / environment issues', 'The left, working class trade unionism and the experience of the miners', letters on Northern Ireland, and 'some thoughts on the role of the Class War Federation'.

This was soon followed with the last ever issue of *The Heavy Stuff* with the release of an unnumbered special edition in pamphlet format entitled 'Coal communities in conflict' and authored by DD. The pamphlet was a call to action in light of government announcements of the closure of a further 31 pitsnationally. The forward would bombast;

> "Events are changing rapidly, but whatever 'Me Tarzan U-Turns' appear to be announced, pits have been shut already. Death by a thousand cuts, a repeat of the strategy that's been employed since 1985. As Britain's mining communities face what NUM boss, Arthur Scargill calls 'industrial genocide', carved up by our politicians and ruling class as they stumble from one economic cock-up to another – capitalism has never smelt so rotten or looked so twisted and anti- working class. If we don't take the bastards on, head on, the miners, their families and communities and other support industries will end up with isolated devastated communities, in poverty, with an increase in national unemployment well over the poxy national press' estimate of 3 million. As though 3 million wasn't criminal enough in itself. During the last two great coal strikes, the miners, their families, their communities and all the national networks of support and solidarity showed how well and tightly, fight back could happen. How imaginative we could all be, how out tactics could outwit the cops, the Tories and their boss scum masters."

Despite the national mobilisations of marches in London, despite the protests, the fight back against pit closures, the struggle was in vain against the pre- planned, years in advance agenda of destroying these communities, and destroy and devastate them they certainly did.

The pamphlet ended on a slightly optimistic note, with its declaration of...

> "We might yet learn the lesson. That the pit communities are more resilient than the pit. Our traditions are too deep, too red, too etched in struggle for them to die with the colliery. Our struggles will continue. In other forms. In other ways, in every way. The visions of freedom first raised by the miners 152 years

ago will live on, to fight on."[761]

Further zines released 1992/early 1993 include *'All Talk No Action'*, *'Fuck Off'*, *'Beermat'*, *'Haddaway And Shite'*, *'Punk Shocker'*, and *'All the Rage'*, and the rather excellent one-off issue of *'Newcastle Anarchist'*.

By autumn 1992, as is common for 'anarchist groups', people 'move on' to pastures anew, groups regularly disintegrate and re-grow. Our struggles take different directions. New generations take up the mantle. Most of Tyneside Class War had moved out of the area (still continuing the struggle though), the 'main participants' from Newcastle Anarchist Communist Federation have resigned from the national Federation, after minor internal disagreements.[762]

As this history draws to a close, so another begins. The newly formed Tyneside Anarchist Group would become the dominant voice of anarchism in the North East for the remainder of the 90's.[763] This was begun with the release of the 'Danger! Anarchists on Tyneside!' leaflet which announces;

> "Autumn 1992 in Newcastle. Weather getting colder and here weare in the worst recession since the Thirties. Mind you, some aren't doing so bad. British Telecom makes £97 per second but even they have to make 30,000 people redundant. But you see, management has got to have the right to manage we're told. It's what put Britain where it is they say! Shame the likes of you and me at this end of the corporate ladder don't have similar 'rights'. Like the right to a job and a decent standard of living. But, they answer us, 'let market forces decide', 'unemployment is a price worth paying', 'let profit rule', blah, blah, blah...!
>
> Once upon a time... Then they talk of the 'right' not to be dominated by Europe / Germany (which has achieved a much higher standard of living for its people than any government here has), while Westminster dominates the North East. Was it

local people who decided to shut Horden Colliery, Sunderland Shipyards or Consett Ironworks? As anarchists we don't call for nationalism, but feel local control should be exactly that. We should decide what happens in our streets, our estates and our towns, rather than every few years putting an 'X' next to the name of someone we've never met and probably never will. How can such faceless people know our opinions and feelings? What makes them any cleverer or better than us?

Mines a pint! As anarchists we believe that the State and this system that puts profit before people is fundamentally wrong. We intend to change it, but we're not here to tell anyone what to do. We only ask that you question the things you're told (including this) and have faith in the abilities or yourself and our community, rather than some unknown in Town Hall or Westminster.

If you're not happy about the situation then you have the ability to change it. We've already seen with the Poll Tax, through widespread opposition and practical non-cooperation (i.e. not paying it!), that if we stick together WE can change things ourselves and improve our own lives, whether they like it or not! Tyneside Anarchist Group. Newcastle."[764]

Afterword? ... No ! Conclusion? ... Never !

The end? ... Is only ever the beginning anew.

## THE STRUGGLE CONTINUES

# ABOUT THE ARCHIVE

Tyneside Anarchist Archive exists to preserve and showcase the collection of literature preserved over the last 40—50 years by anarchists on Tyneside. All too often our history is ignored and disregarded by academic middle-class historians only interested in self-righteous self-promotion. We hope to remedy this. We believe the badly photocopied anti-war leaflet produced by Newcastle Anarchist Group in 1983 is just as important, if not more so, than a copy of 'Chomsky on Anarchism'. We are not intellectuals and have no aspirations to be so., we only seek to share our propaganda from the streets of Tyneside to our friends in countries worldwide...

OUR HISTORY....OUR CULTURE....OUR FUTURE....

Get in touch:

(Web) https://tynesideanarchistarchive.wordpress.com

(Email) tynesideanarchistarchive@riseup.net

(Facebook) https://www.facebook.com/Tyneside-Anarchist-Archive

# APPENDICIES

## A: WHY WE NEED A NEW ANALYSIS.
## By TJ, Newcastle ACF. August 1989.

The use of concepts like 'patriarchy' and 'institutional racism' have, I think, been used by many of us for a long time as descriptions of other faces of the state/capitalist network of power – and their use has been uncritical to some extent. It's a shame that we are forced to try to deliver completely–formed expressions of ideas that are really still only incubating. It's also sad to have to justify the inclusion in our Aims & Principles of proper statements of our commitment to fighting fascism and sexism. Having said that, it's only right to question parts of our expressed beliefs that seem at odds with each other.

### QUESTIONING OURSELVES

Put crudely, why are we 'class struggle anarchists' rather than 'anti-racist, anti- sexist class struggle anarchists'? If we say that we prioritise equally struggles of race, gender and class, then how is it that our conception of the revolution over-throwing class society is the single most important element of our analysis – with no clear-cut role for the fights against sexism and racism?

### THE QUESTION

More specifically, and quoting (sort of) an ACF member at the April 1989 National Conference, *"if racism and sexism are institutional (and that's the main problem with them) then how come the revolution which abolishes class (by abolishing the institutions of class society) won't also abolish sexism and racism?"*

## SEEKING INTEGRATION

I think we can find integration of our apparently different positions – a constructive solution that isn't a wishy-washy compromise. I think we can go beyond both the 'bald' old-fashioned class struggle theory we seem stuck at now and the warmed-over new-left catalogue of oppressions that we're sometimes in danger of falling into. Here are a few areas that might be worth looking at.

## WHO'S INTERESTS?

Firstly, we are class struggle anarchists because the working class struggle against capitalism is the only force capable of dismantling the structure of capitalist society. It is also in the interests of working class women and working class black people to fight and defeat capitalism. But, that is not to say that the interests of working class women are the same as those of working class men; or that those of working class black people are the same as those of working class white people. All working class people may share certain important long- term interests (whether they know it or not), but that's not all there is to it.

## ANALYSING INSTITUTIONS

We need to look more closely at what it is about society that will be changedby doing away with capitalism. To say 'capitalism' is not to say 'society' – in other words the institutions of society are not exactly the same as the institutions of capitalism. Furthermore, an institution does not just consist of the overt, structural, codified relationships that reflect its operation (ie not just the positive power exerted by the agents of the institution); it consists also of the acquiescence, passivity and activity of the institutions 'objects' as well as the behaviour of its 'subjects'. For example, the institution of the police consists of the law-abidingness of citizens and their anti-police behaviour as well as the strategies and actions of the police themselves. Or, the welfare state would bea very different institution if it wasn't for the sheep-like behaviour often to be observed in its objects (myself included!).

## PRODUCING RESISTANCE

The picture of individuals and collectivities that emerges from this view of institutions is that we are, to an extent, made up of our relationships with institutions (...the bit relating to the mother + the bit relating to the family + the bit relating to school + the bit relating to economic power + all the other bits + their interactions etc. etc). Now the point of this is that institutional power relationships produce not only the desired conduct (from the rulers' point of view) but also, crucially, produce resistance – so that capitalism's social relations themselves generate working class opposition. Our struggle does not emerge magically from ideas – but from the interaction between capitalism's effect on people and what we call, for want of a better word, human nature. And this may or may not be mediated by consciousness or ideology.

## THE REVOLUTION

So, the revolution we envisage will destroy the institutions of capitalism – in the old sense of the term 'institution'. What I am saying is that this is only partly true. The revolution will suspend, temporarily at least (we hope permanently) only one side of the institutions of capitalism – that is the structural manifestations of those institutions – the laws, the agencies and the positive power of capitalism. The subjects of capitalism (those who 'do' capitalism) will be out of action. And nothing is possible unless this happens. But, the objects of capitalism (those who capitalism is 'done to') remain – made up as they are partly out of capitalism's social relations.

## THE MATERIAL OF POWER

Now, no power relation can work unless there are at least two parties to it – basically a subject (in control, with the power to achieve private goals at the other's expense) and an object (lacking control, having to move within constraints set by the subject). And what happens when one side of a power relation is absent is that the other tries to create a counterpart – a subject looks for an object (ever seen a bureaucrat in search of lackeys, or an entrepreneur after consumers to exploit?) But also there is a strong tendency that the objectof a power relationship, being made up partly out of the experiences of being an object, will search for a subject when one is not present. In other words, in looking for certainty in an uncertain world people can produce from among themselves whatever fits their previous experience – even when an appropriate outside agency is not available. And since we are unavoidably and deeply formed and influenced by the social relations of capitalism (and sexism and racism) – what will stop the working class from re-creating capitalism, or some other form of hierarchical and exploitative society after the revolution?

## ANARCHIST COMMUNISM

One reason we differ from the anarcho-marxists is that we do believe that something has to be put in the place of the positive power of capitalism, once the latter is broken. This is where our organisational theory, our (embryonic) analysis of power, comes in. This is why we need to encourage the tradition, the ideas and practice of libertarian relations. Of course it has always been part of the working class (and of communities long before capitalism) but given the ideas sketched above we cannot rely upon this particular part of our human heritage coming single-mindedly and consistently to the fore in the revolutionary and post-revolutionary periods, unless there is some damn good reason for things to go in that direction. And part of the reason why a strong, influential anarchist communist organisation is necessary is to try to increase the chances that the institutions produced after the revolution exert their power by and upon everyone. A situation where the subjects of institutions are the very same people as the objects of those institutions is only possible in an anarchist communist society. In any other structure hierarchies and bureaucracies would inevitably form, so that different groups of people would be placed once again in different relationships with the institutions – meaning the return of class or caste structure of some kind.

## IMPLICATIONS

So, the growth in influence of libertarian ideas and practices before the revolution and the libertarian content of social organisation after the revolution will hinder the direct return of exploitative economic and social relations. Likewise, the strength of the voices and action of the working class movements of women and black people will determine how quickly racist and sexist patterns die out – a death similarly prepared for before the revolution, and potentially achievable afterwards.

## THE ORIGINS OF CAPITALISM

But studying the emergence and growth of capitalism tells us that things are more complex still. As a particularly vigorous and vicious set of power relations, capitalism was built from a productive combination of eighteenth century religion, state power, racism and sexism, welded together with the new instrumental ideologies of bourgeois individualism and science. One implication of this is that racist and sexist patterns and the process of objectification at the heart of capitalist social relations are much more thoroughly woven together than we might think. It certainly isn't the case that capitalism simply invaded ground previously held by other forms of domination, then used them to further its own interests, and finally absorbed them into itself. That could only be true if capitalism was ever separate, in practice, from sexism and racism – and it never was. No, the social relations and domination of capitalism always depended upon, right from the start, the prevailing power relations within and between societies. And if racist, sexist and other objectifying social practices could help generate capitalism once, how can we be sure they couldn't again facilitate our enslavement? The answer, of course, is by tackling the power relationships inherent in the social relations and practices – the institutions of sexism and racism – that are as strong now, if not stronger, than they have ever been before (even if they've never been independent from economic and State power). They form us as individuals and groups just as thoroughly as ever, and they could quite easily emerge from our darker sides again – even if the material conditions presently maintaining and producing them were to be disposed of.

We don't need to get into discussions of just how separate sexism and racism are from capitalism, or the implications of which came first, because the inter- relationships are so deep that nothing constructive could come out of it – even if we were able to find any answers.

## OUR TASK

We have to change both terms of all power relationships – subject hood <u>and</u> object hood. And we have to do it both in terms of the social structure of power <u>and</u> the productive capacity of working class people – the capacity to produce power relationships that diverge from or simply re-create the preceding ones.

The revolution deals with existing structure; and the depth of preparation for full libertarian practice can hope to achieve a society where subject hood and object hood are not arbitrary, fixed and unequal, as they are in our society.

Our political analysis, tactics and strategy need to take both sides of the problem of power into account. And this makes it necessary to find a new solution to the question of the relationships between class, race and gender.

## CONCLUSION

So we are class struggle anarchists because we can envisage and work towards the specific event(s) of social revolution as a political goal. But we are anti-racist and anti-sexist because we realise that racist and sexist patterns ruin all movement towards libertarian practice, and would be particularly dangerous after the social revolution. Racism and sexism could sabotage the revolution 'from within' in the same way they oppress and divide us now. Sincethere is no specific timescale or events which will abolish sexism and racism wehave to do all in our power to participate in and encourage the working class movements of women and black people, so before, during and after the revolution those movements are strong enough to prevent the return of the exploitative, authoritarian power relations which were crucially implicated in the rise of capitalism in the first place, and which the wider working class movement may not be in the best position to deal with.

That is why, as class struggle anarchists, we should prioritise equally struggles of class, race and gender. And it is why we need to work towards an analysis which does not parachute racism and sexism into capitalism; but which also doesn't merely add them to it.

Working class women's struggles <u>as</u> working class women (not simply as working class people or as women) and working class black people's struggles <u>as</u> working class black people (not simply as working class people or as black people) are where we can gain the inspiration and understanding to develop our analysis accordingly.[765]

## B: RIOTOUS RESPONSES:
## Media balance & its uses
### By T.J. & S.B.

Riots in urban centres in 1991 again showed working class youth refusing to accept their lot. We were told local problems led to isolated disturbances – fouling our own nests in orgies of destruction. Liberals squabble over the real causes, the Right know we are dirty animals – all unite in calling for more, better policing. The 80s idea of outside influences helped the police mobilise nationally in time for the Miners Strike. Now they emphasise local factors. But 1991 was more characterised by youth travelling from nearby areas to have a go, knowing the crack without help from the media. They ignored the growth of a culture aware of the malign realities of modern policing, and prepared collectively to fight back. Riots followed intensified police harassment purporting to fight drugs, armed robbery, joyriding and ram raiding. Regional forces went to expand 'community' policing – helicopters, personnel, neighbourhood narks – the run up to a General Election is always the time to play the law and order card. The media and other professionals agree – after all, they may be targets, and riots hit the material basis of their power. Local voices are heard only if they fit discourses and solutions on offer.

Coverage of Tyneside showed dramatic night-time war-zones – buildings ablaze; police, reporters, fire engines attacked; hordes of malevolent youth; a narrative of criminality and random violence. It only counted as rioting if cameras were there, so Meadow Well (North Shields), and West Newcastle got the headlines. A pattern across the region was downgraded to 'isolated' incidents elsewhere. Crime was set against amoral evil values, with small doses of welfare charitability. On TV, with various Ministers (government / shadow / religious), and in more mundane debates in council chambers and newspaper letter pages, the issues resolved into beating car crime and brow – and breast

– beating about the state of society and the need for more intervention and punishment. This led away from the experience of millions, in thousands of decaying council estates and run-down land lorded neighbourhoods. Once characterised as vulnerable, they are now seen as the source of evil itself.

In fact these events are going on all the time – except not all at once, not with most of Northern England's riot squads in attendance, and not on camera. Most destruction is down to local authorities and developers, and we're always aware of an enthusiastically hostile police presence. If it wasn't for violence turned inward – to the family, burglary, habitual white racism – it might actually feel safer in the zones where the police are reluctant to go. But they get their revenge, coming in force after riots lifting kids, youths, anyone local narks finger, those with priors: fabricating evidence to turn gossip into jail, 'sus' into fact. It's not bias, it's a different world. The media speak to those concerned that their cars don't get nicked, building a 'them and us' worldview.

## THE GOOD, THE BAD, AND THE UGLY

Residents of 'problem' estates are stereotyped: The good – respectable victims, to be patronised / recruited; the bad – parentally-deprived, uncooperative, alienated, needing heavy handed discipline / training schemes; and the ugly – no hope, anti-social, violent criminals, to be stamped on. Sir Stanley Bailey, Northumbria Police Chief, philosophically analysed the situation, stressing that it wasn't just ram raiders and joy riders (they're just the worst of a bad lot). On Channel 4's 'Right to Reply' (Sept 28 1991) he cheerfully counter posed young rioting vandals with school kids altruistically clearing rubbish – so easy to overlook the latter.

The underclass myth is handy for projection of society's ills. Nurtured in rank and file police ideology, it is always subject to slippage of categories – young working class and black people can be seen as 'animals'. Certain 'men and women in the street' add hating, vengeful rantings on TV, making experts and leaders sound positively benign. It becomes unthinkable that Bailey's daytime primary school ecological volunteers and the miniature Molotov cocktail waiters after dark are one and the same, as on Tyneside. Does this represent the end of all hope? Is it worth encouraging the 'good' in the lower reaches of our 'classless society'? It seems not. Ghettoisation is extending further into working class areas, now that our inherently evil nature is accepted – cut off, starved, hammered, taunted by images of surrounding affluence. Councils show their indifference to the locals – who can't generate capital, afford to buy yuppie flats, or even pay their Poll Tax.

## ALTERNATIVE TV?

Where might we look for less hysteria? TV current affairs slots purport to go beyond tabloid headlines. 'Serious' documentaries construct arguments using policy-makers, academics and other 'experts' to give an interpretive framework, then data are chosen to fit. BBC's 'Panorama' (Nov 4 1991) started from the theory of the criminal underclass. This concept appears attractive, but can be questioned by looking closely at the sheer diversity of life in poor communities. But no, the conclusions were dictated by the theory.

Minority programmes portray specific real-lives, but find it hard to tackle widespread common interests and experiences. Regional TV fragments and isolates issues otherwise recognisable universally. The head of BBC North described with pride a short programme about Meadow Well as *"the people talking to themselves"* with no hint of irony – given that people do this anyway without his help ('Right to Reply', Sept 28). In the haste to examine purely local factors, nothing of significance is learnt. Old-fashioned social history documentary realists are declining. But their heroic working class myths mesh with imagery of the respectable poor in sitcom, crime drama, soap opera and most other television outlets. They're no great loss, seeing riots as totally retrogressive, signalling the need for a resurgence of middle class moral leadership – as in the conventional wisdom.

What about the youth-orientated pop gang? They use montages of styles – snappy editing, reportage, 'amateur' hour, across-sofa interviews and cynicism a la mode, cut with radio jingles, sharp editing and virtual reality graphics. They are infiltrating all 'informational' slots, hard news to chat shows, minority to general audiences, but so far mainly for the fashionable youth market. Channel 4 is catching up, e.g. in their access flagship: 'Right to Reply'.

## FEEDBACK TV

Competing with BBC's awful 'Points of View' and the sneering superiority of 'What the Papers Say', 'Right to Reply' is 'accessible'. Ordinary folk come inoff the street to tackle programme makers; public video boxes give space to 'disgusted of X'. To reduce the honouring of experts, discussions are held between media bigwigs and unknowns with axes to grind, umpired by a presenter. Most punters are at a big disadvantage in this environment. Some groups thrive, such as professionals and those with college education – in effect anyone prepared and able to conduct civilised debate without effing and blinding or allowing open passion to complicate things. C4 bosses haveordered more populism – the yuppie intelligentsia is not a sufficient market. A quiz show presenter replaces the sincere leftie, more popular subjects are featured and the diversity of styles increased. The first of the new series (Sept 28th 1991) changed its emphasis in content, with reports on boxing on TV and Tyneside's riots. Next we need to discuss the making and editing of the latter.

## 'RIGHT TO REPLY'?

The viewer's participation was much vaunted. In the presenter's words: "If you, like Sue B, want to make your own report, or if you have anything to say about television...write to us at Channel 4 at (address)." I introduced myself as follows:

*"I used to live on the meadow Well estate. When I saw it on the news, I was disgusted at the way everybody here was portrayed as troublemakers. The media was not interested in the real reasons behind*

*the riots. In fact I was so disgusted, I rang Channel 4 up to complain. 'Right to Reply' has asked me to come down to the estate to get a good idea of what the real people think."*

I did not make this report. The schedule, agenda and editing were completely out of my control. Local coppers and politicians maybe, but why talk to Chief Constables or local vicars? They were sent a list of questions, but I didn't get a copy until filming – my questions were disallowed. Most material from talking to residents was cut, the crew were told where to film, the editors crammed in as much sensational footage as they could, plus BBC News extracts such as:

*"Local politicians learning that car theft in the North East had leapt by 64% in two years, agree...the region faces massive problems;"* and *"2 or 3 hundred youths were roaming (the) streets, waging what many saw as a reprisal against the police (after) the deaths...of two friends, Dale Robson and Colin Atkins in a stolen car pursued by police. The vehicle burst into flames engulfing the occupants, bringing accusations that the police had rammed it."*

Residents criticised news coverage for showing no sensitivity to the bereaved:

*"This has been brewing up for a while – they just used the two lads death as an excuse for this riot;"* and *"I think the television coverage glamorised the car theft and ram raids. I think it's all been blown out of proportion totally."*

All the head of BBC North could say was:

*"We avoided predicting violence to come, because that can be a self-fulfilling prophecy. We avoided showing weapons, petrol bombs or anything of that nature...We are aware that, on occasion, the use of violence...sorry, the use of language can inflame a situation."*

'Right to Reply's' editors inserted BBC1 Nine O'clock News footage of night time riot scenes with smoke and flames in the background, and latter a banner on a wall ("This is for Dale 'n Colin") in front of a burning building, plus a pointless shot of a smashed-up car and shop security video of a ram raid –time which could have represented what residents had to say much more thoroughly.

## COMMUNITY CULTURE

The energetic, vibrant community and its diverse activity would have been easy to depict. But residents knew exactly what to expect from the media:

*"The estate's been here for years, they've never wanted to know. Now because of the riots it's the centre of attraction. They've never come...to see the good people on the estate, the good things what's happening."*

In community centres, the report showed fleeting glimpses of silent residents. But larger numbers were present, in and out, discussing events. Close-ups and splitting up points made gave an impression of isolated individuals responding to outsiders questions. Voices sounded depressed rather than angry – due to the media's constant pestering: *"They're vultures, like flies round shite"* (this was cut). Worse still:

*"Some of the reporters have interviewed little kids. I mean, what do little kids know? They're getting all the bad things – I seen one little kid even talking about his own brother that does ram raiding – it's ridiculous."*

Residents described many self-organised local initiatives – food co-ops, credit unions, clearing rubbish for kids playgrounds, mending fences, mutual aid gardening. A women's writing group for developing literacy has published a book – now the group's work is the basis of a locally-made feature film, 'Dream On', taken up by the Odeon for nationwide screening. A resident who set up a kid's judo club described the kids' sense of self-discipline and confidence – hundreds will be devastated if new premises and equipment can'tbe found, new council funding may be axed. None of this reached the screen in the report. No effort was made to show the results of the community's concerted efforts to make up for its environment. Instead we saw a burnt-out shop and the most boarded-up road in the area.

Council workers were told they'd be sacked if they spoke to the media – so the cuts to local amenities (before being were torched) were not mentioned. Politicians may have 'poured cash' into these estates, but it goes to the developers, planners and bureaucrats career-building. After yuppiefication, remaining funds go on schemes controlled by council workers, taking away residents autonomy. Amenities have been lost when council workers are cut after monopolising co-ordination and organisation of initiatives that locals felt the need for, and had begun to set up their own.

The programme makers' agenda was pursued by ignoring most of the interviews and editing-in unnecessary footage. The vicar's conclusions stood as the report's main findings: *"Society is spiritually and morally sick, at 6s and 7s with ourselves and each other"* – evil, squalor and lack of hope, by omitting contrary evidence. Many of his pathetic utterances, proving his failure to understand life in his parish, were cut, but the editing couldn't conceal the crazed look in his eyes.

## NO RIGHT TO REPLY

My opening remarks were screened last – made to sound superfluous, since allmaterial showing that there was anything to be "fair" about was cut.

*"The impression given by national news programmes means that now if you say you're from Meadow Well, you're labelled a troublemaker. Somehow television has got to find a way of portraying communities like this more fairly."*

The report did its best to contradict my conclusions, placed at the beginning:

*"Sensationalised fragments of real life are presented as best-sellers...It gets forgotten that on countless council estates people are struggling everyday... not evil, not ignorant, not mindless, and sadly, not represented."*

If this was for dramatic effect, only some methods were allowed – not residents statements. Editing links had to be checked to make sure that they were safe and fitted the artificial overall plan. Experts and leaders were given space at the expense of residents – who had much more to say. All the Head of BBC North's comments were included, as were those of the Chief constable that made any sense amongst his drivel. These people's points were either made more effectively by residents, or were contradicted. This couldn't be reflected without showing that 'Big Noises' had no place in the report – echoing, not criticising mainstream coverage.

None of us had a 'right to reply'. Compare the Video Box offering earlier in the programme on the faking of live action by programme makers, putting 'Right to Reply's' dishonesty squarely into focus. Of course anyone knowing thesituation had ample warning. The presenter introduced the report with a lie:

*"riots broke out after two local youths, joy riding in a stolen car, were killed following a chase by police."* Even the mainstream news had replaced this lie with another – that it was something to do with ram raiding. In effect all crime is conflated to produce a one-dimensional view of the community based on theidiots who burgle from their own or single out black people to attack. Images of idle squalor add insult to injury:

*"It was terrible the way they portrayed people on the estate – made to look like hoboes, hanging around on street corners, doing nothing, wasting their time;"* and *"let's face it, we're people we've got feelings. To hear outsiders calling us scum is beyond us. I've lived here all my life, and I'm no scum."*

The problem is said to be insoluble because the honest, respectable victims are portrayed as powerless. Not because of the institutions and economy that structure the environment, but by neighbours. Sightseers proposed a 'final' solution:

*"We were standing down at the youth club on the morning after. People were driving past in their cars...shouting "burn, burn the lot,"...people that didn't even know – just driving through to see what had gone on."*

The community's huge range of beliefs, attitudes, energy, intelligence, potential and activity has contradictory passions co-existing inside families, peer groups and individuals. Instead we were shown feeble good and overwhelming bad behaviour hermetically sealed in, ruled by malignant Robin Hood – style Mafiosi. But organised crime has been a feature of poor communities since the Middle Ages – the new underclass is not new or a 'class'. Pay attention instead to the community's rich complexity, the active struggles produced running contrary to powerful interests. The media manufacture consent, about world events and localised conflict. The alternative media play devil's advocate, scorning other views, and propagandadising the position of intellectuals within benevolent government, calling it 'balance'!

## TIPPING THE BALANCE

Many refuse to be fooled. Tempted to see the media as a monolithic enslaving 'spectacle', we echo its own grandiose pretensions. We can interpret the treatment of riots as the unease of the middle classes, faced with a challenge to the cosy hegemony that they nurture, as the monitors and operators of welfare liberalism. But Meadow Well folk watched the box with a mixture of anger and disbelief in September 1991. Some may despair – one intention of the form and content of news coverage of all conflict. Some turn to hatred of their own people, becoming part of the problem. Others will find fresh determination to carry on, even consciously to begin struggle, feeling a deep sense of outrage at the images of themselves on the telly. The riots may have made life even harder in the short term. But the capacity to feel, desire and act – against 'legitimate' authority, or in positive direct action for a better life – canreceive impetus from the distaste and disgust broadcast into our living rooms. Knowing what this is about, we can draw together and use parts of ourselves found vulgar, dirty and inconvenient to those who try to control us. Compared to images of rich sterile suburbs, there are real problems here. All the anguish and anger can't be administered away, hidden inside four walls, or sold back to us. Technology can't abolish it, without taking the entire planet with it.

Television reflects ways others wish to see us, for the purposes of vested interests. It's not a question of bias. The images fulfil their task – reassuring all those charged with the job of classifying, educating, and disciplining us. They want us to see ourselves like that. If we don't play the game, seeing through media-speak, refusing to wear 'well-adjusted' bourgeois Straitjacket, then we'll impose fewer obstacles on ourselves when it comes to doing what's needsto be done. Just as in Meadow Well, the youth didn't wait for police permission to express their fury. People don't just beg for the charity of the local council to get things organised, or the objectivity of the media to tell them who they are or what the worlds like. The autonomy of community life needn't require the whole apparatus of officialdom to be parachuted in to take charge. We have seen, in many 'riot-torn' areas in the 1980's, that communities are capable of policing their own anti-social elements. The success of this is patchy, to be sure, and is never allowed to flourish. On Tyneside, black people, for example, suffer greatly – the community not yet being organised in its own defence – but as in other areas, the idea that the police or local council can play a part in this is known to be absurd. The community itself has to define 'anti-social', and will, given the chance, unerringly include police, bureaucrats, and local and national politicians in with the rest. The media walk a tightrope, keeping a shaky grip on reality, trying to please buyers, sellers and bosses, while not losing their mass audiences. It's a precarious balance. No wonder their responses are so riotous.

# Notes

[1] Agustin Guillamon. *'The Friends of Durruti Group: 1937-1939'* AK Press. 1996.

[2] Albert Meltzer, quoted in *Personal Recollections of the Anarchist Past.* George Cores. Kate Sharpley Library. Pamphlet. 1992.
I have searched for decades looking for these memoirs, to no avail, and I now believe that only some handwritten notes for a projected autobiography were written by Tom, but uncompleted. These were held by the North East Labour History Society and / or the late Raymond Challinor 1929-2011. As to the whereabouts to these now, I have no idea. After Ray's death, his 'garage full'of literature was distributed to various libraries throughout the country. Tom brown visited London 15th May 1972, two years before his death; he made no comment regarding any memoirs to comrades at the time, and certainly no mention of an American woman / students (It is believed the student who borrowed the notes was American).

[3] With the emergence of publishing archives like that of the Kate Sharpley Library during the last 30+ years or so, this has reversed this situation, with many a fine pamphlet / book etc of 'history from below' and fascinating untold 'stories' becoming available.

[4] *Anarchism.* G. Woodcock. Pelican. 1983.

[5] *Anarchy.* Errico Malatesta. Freedom Press. 1974.

[6] *Red Emma Speaks.* The selected speeches & writings of the anarchist & feminist Emma Goldman. Ed A.K. Shulman. Wildwood House. 1979.

[7] Quoted in *The Essential Works of Anarchism.* Bantam. *1971.* Ed. Marshall S Shatz.

[8] *The secret anarchist history of Newcastle.* Mike. Self published pamphlet.

[9] After meeting Sergei Kravchinskii (1851-1895), a Russian revolutionary who had killed the head of the Russian secret police in 1878 before leaving Russia for Europe, where he became known by his pseudonym Stepniak (meaning 'man of the steppes'). Spence Watson, having first met Stepniak in person when he invited the latter to speak at the Sunday Lecture Society in January 1890, was intensely interested in the Russian revolutionary cause from a humanitarian perspective. His support, both financial and otherwise, was crucial in founding the Society of Friends of Russian Freedom and its press organ, Free Russia. Robert Spence Watson (1837-1911), a lawyer, businessman, and civic figure in Newcastle-upon-Tyne. Spence Watson was President both of the Literary and Philosophical Society, and of the Society of Friends of Russian Freedom, founded in 1890.

10 *The Anarchist Prince*. G. Woodcock & I Avakumovic. New York. 1971.

11 *Memoirs of a Revolutionist.* Peter Kropotkin. Black Rose Books. 1989.

12 Newcastle Daily Chronicle. 3rd July 1882. Also G. Pattison – anarchist influences in the Durham coalfield before 1914. The Raven 11. Freedom Press.Vol 3 No 3. July / sept 1990

13 *The Durham Miners' Gala: From History to Heritage*. David Hopper. NorthEast History. Vol 43. 2012.

14 *The Durham Miners' Gala: From History to Heritage*. David Hopper. NorthEast History. Vol 43.

15 Newcastle Daily Chronicle. 3rd July 1882.

16 G. Pattison – anarchist influences in the Durham coalfield before 1914. The Raven 11. Freedom Press.Vol 3 No 3. July / sept 1990

17 Sunderland Daily Echo. Tuesday, July 4. 1882.

18 *The Anarchist Prince*. G. Woodcock & I Avakumovic. New York. 1971.

19 G. Pattison

20 Newcastle Weekly Chronicle 8.7.1882. Also *The secret anarchist history of Newcastle*. Mike.

21 The Durham County Advertiser. Friday July 7th. 1882

22 G. Pattison

23 *The Anarchist Prince*. G. Woodcock & I Avakumovic. New York. 1971.

24 The Tyne Theatre & Opera House originally opened in 1867 and wasdesigned by William B Parnell for Joseph Cowen (1829-1900)

25 Freedom. Vol 1 No 3. December 1886.

26 *The Anarchist Prince*. G. Woodcock & I Avakumovic. New York. 1971.

27 The Shields Daily Gazette. Monday, November 1st. 1886.

28 The Shields Daily Gazette & Shipping Telegraph, Thursday, November 11th. 1886.

29 Sunderland Daily Echo. Monday, November 15th. 1886. The local lecturesof this period are similar in content to *The Place of Anarchism in Socialistic Evolution – An address delivered in Paris* by Pierre Kropotkin (1887). Reprint by Practical Parasite Publications. Pamphlet. Cymru. 1990.

30 *The Anarchist Prince*. G. Woodcock & I Avakumovic. New York. 1971 &

*Memoirs of a Revolutionist*. Peter Kropotkin. Black Rose Books. 1989.

31 *Reasons for Pardoning the Haymarket Anarchists, 1893*.

32 *Tom Mann's Memoirs*. Kindle edition!

33 The Newcastle Courant. Friday, November 18, 1887.

34 Northern Daily Mail. Tuesday, November 29th. 1887.

35 The Shields Daily Gazette & Shipping Telegraph. Monday, April 23rd.1888.

36 *The Anarchist Prince*. G. Woodcock & I Avakumovic. New York. 1971.

37 The Evening Chronicle, Monday, Dec 2nd. 1889.[38] The Evening Chronicle, Monday, Dec 2nd. 1889.[39] The Evening Chronicle, Monday, Dec 2nd. 1889.[40] The Evening Chronicle, Monday, Dec 2nd. 1889.[41] Freedom. Vol. 4.--No. 41. April, 1890.

42 The Northern Echo. Friday, March 7th. 1890.

43 The Northern Echo. Monday, March 10th. 1890.

44 *The Anarchist Prince*. G. Woodcock & I Avakumovic. New York. 1971.

45 Johann Joseph "Hans" Most (born February 5, 1846 in Augsburg, Bavaria – died March 17, 1906 in Cincinnati, Ohio) Anarchist who "fervently promoted propaganda by the deed as well as by the word..(who) preached violent revolution." Demanding the Impossible. A History of Anarchism. PeterMarshall. Fontana press. 1993. P 416.

46 *Northern Anarchist Lives* – No. 5. Christopher Draper.

47 Todd says this was 1893, Draper says 1890. We have opted 1890 as it fitsin with other corresponding events

48 *Northern Anarchist Lives* – No. 5. Christopher Draper.

49 *Northern Anarchist Lives* – No. 5. Christopher Draper. And *Chesterfield's anarchist of the abyss. Northern Anarchist Lives – 4*. Christopher Draper

50 *Roses & Revolutionists*. Nigel Todd. Peoples Publications. 1986.

51 *Northern Anarchist Lives* – No. 5. Christopher Draper.

52 Freedom. Vol. 5.--No. 43. April, 1891.

53 *Northern Anarchist Lives* – No. 5. Christopher Draper. And Freedom, quotedin Draper.

54 *Personal Recollections of the Anarchist Past*. George Cores. KSL Library.1992.

55 *Northern Anarchist Lives* – No. 5. Christopher Draper. And Freedom, quoted in Draper.

56 Sunderland Daily Echo. Friday, January 29. 1892.

57 Histories state that the ILP was formed 1893, yet I have a news clipping dated Nov 28 1892 which states details of a meeting of an ILP in Newcastle. The Evening Chronicle. Monday, November 28th. 1892.

58 Background reading..*The Slow Burning Fuse. The Lost History of the British Anarchists.* J. Quail. Paladin. 1978.

59 The Evening Chronicle. Monday, November 28th. 1892.

60 Agnes Henry (1850-1915) For further information see https://irishanarchisthistory.wordpress.com/2018/03/02/agnes-henry-an-anarchist-from-tipperary-1850-1915/

61 Many reports of this tour fail to mention this fact, and concentrate more on the Scottish aspect of the tour, see for instance "A short biography of Agnes Henry, active in the British anarchist movement in the 1880s-1890s" Nick Heath. Libcom website.

62 Freedom. 13th October. 1893.

63 A concept that individual instances of political action, particularly aimed at members of the ruling class i.e. bombs and assassinations – would inspire the masses and lead to revolution

64 *The Slow Burning Fuse. The Lost History of the British Anarchists.* John Quail. Paladin. 1978.

65 *A Beautiful Idea – History of the Freedom Press Anarchists.* Rob Ray.Freedom Press. 2018.

66 *A Beautiful Idea – History of the Freedom Press Anarchists.* Rob Ray.Freedom Press. 2018.

67 Errico Malatesta: Violence as a Social Factor (1895). From *Anarchism: A Documentary History of Libertarian Ideas, Volume One.* Robert Graham. 2005.

68 The Shields Daily Gazette & Shipping Telegraph. Wed, December 20. 1893.

69 *Le Temps*, 29th Sept. 1897. Quoted in *Roses & Revolutionists.* Nigel Todd. Peoples Publications.

70 Freedom. April. 1894. Quoted in *Roses & Revolutionists.* Nigel Todd. Peoples Publications. 1986.

71 The Shields Daily News. Saturday, February 17. 1894.

72 I have only given a brief outline of Clousden Hill. We recommend you get Nigel

Todd's book for more of an in depth study and historical background. After discussion with Nigel Todd, and his reading part of this before release, I emphasise, Roses & Revolutionists has been fully updated and re-released with corrected dates and more information by Five Leaves Books. This text remains the same, as I only own the original 1986 version, and as I have only gave a brief overview of Clousden Hill, I feel it is unnecessary to change my text. NOTE...Sadly whilst we were editing the final stages of this book, Nigel Todd passed away during the last week of March 2021. RIP.

73 *Roses & Revolutionists*. Nigel Todd. Peoples Publications. 1986.

74 *Liberty*. April. 1894. Quoted in *Roses & Revolutionists*. Nigel Todd. Peoples Publications. 1986.

75 *The Slow Burning Fuse. The Lost History of the British Anarchists*. John Quail. Paladin. 1978. See also *Fields, Factories & Workshops Tomorrow*. Peter Kropotkin. George Allen & Unwin Ltd. 1974. *Kropotkin – Selected Writings*. Freedom Press. 1942. *The Conquest of Bread*. Peter Kropotkin. Penguin Classics. 2015. *Selected Writings on Anarchism & Revolution*. P.A. Kropotkin. MIT Press. 1970. *Kropotkins Revolutionary Pamphlets*. Ed R.N. Baldwin. Dover Publications. New York. 1970. *Words of a Rebel*. Peter Kropotkin. Black Rose Books. 1992. *Fugitive Writings*. Peter Kropotkin. Black Rose Books. Quebec / New York. 1993. *Act For Yourselves. Articles from Freedom 1886-1907*. Peter Kropotkin. Freedom Press. 1998.

76 *Northern Anarchist Lives* – No. 5. Christopher Draper.

77 On A Proposed Communist Settlement A New Colony for Tyneside orWearside. Peter Kropotkin. Feb. 16, 1895. Bastard Press. 2005.

78 On A Proposed Communist Settlement A New Colony for Tyneside orWearside. Peter Kropotkin. Feb. 16, 1895. Bastard Press. 2005.

79 The Evening Chronicle. Wed Feb 12th. 1896, The Northern Echo.7th and.11th Aug. 1896.

80 Jacques Élisée Reclus (15 March 1830 – 4 July 1905) French geographer,writer and anarchist.

81 The Northern Echo. Tues. Aug 11th 1896.

82 Draper.

83 The Evening Chronicle. Jan 13th. 1896.

84 *The secret anarchist history of Newcastle*. Mike. Self published pamphlet.And Draper.

85 The Northern Echo. Tues. Aug 11th 1896.

86 *Anarchism in North East England (1886-1990)*. D. Morrow. Unpublished

dissertation. University of Sunderland. May 1996.

[87] Review of Todds *Roses & Revolutionists*. Freedom online. Oct. 2018?

[88] The 1901 census revealed that inhabited houses had grown by 15%—to 6,260,852—although population had grown by only 12%. The average number of persons per house also fell slightly, from 5.32 in 1891 to 5.2 in 1901. Population densities were higher in the towns, where there was an average of 5.4 persons per house, than in the rural areas, which had an average of 4.6. Devonport, South Shields, Newcastle-upon-Tyne and Gateshead showed the greatest degree of overcrowding (that is, more than eight persons per house). A friend of mine, researching her family tree, discovered that her family, living in a semi-rural mining village, had 14 members in one household (a small 2 bed terraced house).

[89] The mystery of Garibaldi's heed. Tyneside Anarchist Archive website. https://tynesideanarchistarchive.wordpress.com/2018/06/07/the-mystery-of-garibaldis-heed/

[90] The Shields Daily Gazette & Shipping Telegraph. Tues, August 7. 1900.

[91] The Shields Daily Gazette. Thursday, September 12th. 1901.

[92] Freedom. Vol . X X .— No. 207. June. 1906.

[93] Freedom. Vol. X X .—No. 208. July. 1906.

[94] Freedom. Vol. X X .—No. 209. Aug. 1906.

[95] Of course this group could have formed much earlier.

[96] Whilst not concentrating on any race or religion, this snippet of information confirms my preconception of an anarchist presence within Newcastle's, and particularly Gateshead's, large 'Jewish' community's. During the International Anarchist Congress in Amsterdam (1907), Rudolf Rocker, whilst giving a report, stated there was 17 groups of Jewish anarchists throughout the UK, including Newcastle, see *The International Anarchist Congress in Amsterdam (1907)* Ed M. Antonioli. Black Cat Press, Canada.2009. Also the Jewish anarchist conference, held at Leeds in 1912, also gives mention to a Bessie Ward from Newcastle.

[97] Freedom. Vol. X X I. No 217. May. 1907.

[98] Freedom. Vol. X X I. No 219. July. 1907.

[99] Freedom. Vol. X X I. No 224. Dec. 1907.

[100] Freedom. Vol. X X II. No 225. Jan. 1908.

[101] Freedom. Vol. X X II. No 225. Jan. 1908.

[102] Freedom. Vol. X X II. No 226. Feb. 1908.

[103] Freedom. Vol. X X II. No 227. March. 1908.

104 *The Slow Burning Fuse. The Lost History of the British Anarchists*. John Quail. Paladin. 1978.

105 Freedom. Vol. X X II. No 228. April. 1908.

106 Strangely, Peter Kropotkin very rarely mentions Sophie, and in his *Memoirs of a Revolutionist* does not even name her, despite her own writings, lectures, and participation in shared ventures, her lifelong commitment and helping (and her work with the Kropotkin Museum in Moscow long after his death). Perhaps someday someone will remedy this situation with a publication of Sophia's story. As a further footnote, Peter Kropotkin also presented an album of press cuttings on the 'emancipation of women in Russia' to the British Museum before he left London permanently for Russia. Perhaps he should have put this into practice much closer to his own home !

107 Northern Daily Mail. Friday, March 6th. 1908.

108 Northern Daily Mail. Jan 11th, Feb 26th, March 2nd, March 6th. 1908. And Bexhill On Sea Observer Oct 16th 1909, Glasgow Daily Record, Feb 13th 1915.

109 Justice. June 6th. 1908

110 Freedom. Vol. X X III. No 240. April. 1909. 111 Freedom. Vol. X X III. No 240. April. 1909. 112 Freedom. Vol. X X III. No 241. May. 1909. 113 Freedom. Vol. X X III. No 242. June. 1909. 114 Freedom. Vol. X X III. No 243. July. 1909. 115 Freedom. Vol. X X III. No 243. July. 1909.

116 *First Flight. The origins of Anarcho-Syndicalism in Britain*. Albert Meltzer. KSL Library.

117 Freedom. Vol. X X III. No 245. Sept. 1909. 118 Freedom. Vol. X X III. No 247. Nov. 1909. 119 Freedom. Vol. X X III. No 248. Dec. 1909.

120 *The Slow Burning Fuse. The Lost History of the British Anarchists*. John Quail. Paladin. 1978.

121 Freedom. Vol. X X IV. No 259. Nov. 1910

122 Northern Daily Mail. Wed, January 11th. 1911

123 Freedom. Vol. X X V. No 270. Oct. 1911

124 Freedom. Vol. X X V. No 271. Nov. 1911, and No's 272,273,274,275 etc.

125 Freedom. Vol. X X VII. No 288. April. 1913.

126 Some of this section is coined from my earlier unpublished essay *Fanning the flames of discontent. A brief look at the ideas & history of anarcho- syndicalism in*

*Britain.*(with particular reference to the North East) 1996.

127 E.J.B. Allen, *The Syndicalist*. No 9. 1912.

128 *Syndicalism*. E.C. Ford & W.Z. Foster. Charles H Kerr. 1990.

129 Background reading..E.P.Thompson. *The making of the English working class*. Pelican. 1980.

130 *The Birth of the Strike*. Dermot Feenan. Online.

131 *Anarcho-Syndicalism*. Rudolf Rocker. Phoenix Press.

132 *A History of Anarcho-syndicalism*. Selfed Education Collective. Unit 2. Solidarity Federation.

133 *The Slow Burning Fuse. The Lost History of the British Anarchists*. John Quail. Paladin. 1978.

134 *The Slow Burning Fuse. The Lost History of the British Anarchists*. John Quail. Paladin. 1978.

135 *British Syndicalism 1900-1914*. Bob Holton. Pluto Press. 1976.

136 *The Syndicalist Challenge in the Durham Coalfield before 1914*. Lewis H Mates. This is a 'print off' of an essay I used separately as a source. The essayis encompassed within the full book *The Great Labour Unrest – Rank and file movements and political change in the Durham coalfield.* Lewis H Mates.Manchester University Press. 2016. Kindly given to myself by the author.

137 *The Slow Burning Fuse. The Lost History of the British Anarchists*. John Quail. Paladin. 1978.

138 *Anarcho-Syndicalism*. Rudolf Rocker. Phoenix Press.

139 Quail.

140 Quail.

141 Geoff Brown. Introduction to *The Industrial Syndicalist*. Spokesman Books.1974.

142 *The Syndicalist Challenge in the Durham Coalfield before 1914*. Lewis H Mates.

143 George Harvey *Industrial Unionism and the Mining Industry* (Pelaw on Tyne 1917) P191. Quoted in Geoff Brown *Sabotage* Spokesman books. 1977. P25.

144 Northern Daily Mail. Thursday. October 9th. 1913.

145 I have only touched upon the vast historical data and importance of the 'syndicalist revolt'. I can't recommend enough '*British Syndicalism 1900-1914*. Bob Holton. Pluto Press. 1976.' Or for anarchist related build up to events '*TheSlow*

*Burning Fuse. The Lost History of the British Anarchists*. John Quail. Paladin. 1978.' I also recommend *Threads Through Time*, writings on history and autobiography by Sheila Rowbotham which touches on a few areas of emerging feminism.

146 In 1974 Chopwell became part of the metropolitan county of Tyne & Wear and of the Metropolitan Borough of Gateshead after previously being part of the Administrative County of Durham.

147 Quail. Mates. Holton. Pattison. Etc. Will Lawther, later accepted a knighthood and became somewhat of a 'right-wing' union bureaucrat.

148 Freedom. Vol. X X VII. No 289. May. 1913.

149 Freedom. Vol. X X VII. No 290. June. 1913.

150 Whilst the priest has their pulpit, the professor their podium, and the parliamentary socialist their self important pedestal, at factory gate and street level the anarchists used a hastily constructed or requisitioned wooden box to stand upon and agitate, not in order to look down upon the 'audience' like thepriest, but in order to be heard more clearly at street level. This was done anyplace crowds could be found in and around Newcastle..the Bigg Market, the Quayside, the Haymarket, the Town Moor at race week (the Hopping's as its known today) and mine / factory gates.

151 Freedom. Vol. X X VII. No 291. July. 1913.

152 William Lewcock was the husband of the infamous suffragette Connie Lewcock, who it was said, after she burned down the wooden Waterhouses train station in Esh Winning in March 1914, was to burn down / blow up Durham Cathedral with explosives apparently supplied by Will Lawther. The 'mission' was aborted as she couldn't work out how to use said explosives.

153 Freedom. Vol. X X VII. No 293. Sept. 1913.

154 Colin Osman. Biography of George Davison. Online.

155 *The Syndicalist Challenge in the Durham Coalfield before 1914*. Lewis H Mates.

156 Freedom. Vol. X X VIII. No 298. Feb. 1914.

157 Freedom. Vol. X X VIII. No 298. Feb. 1914.

158 Freedom. Vol. X X VIII. No 299. March. 1914.

159 Sunderland Daily Echo. Monday. April 13. 1914. And Newcastle Daily Journal. Monday. April 13. 1914. Daily Herald. Sat April 11$^{th}$.1914. The Evening Chronicle. Monday April 13. 1914. The Nottingham Daily Express, Tues. April 14. 1914. Daily Mirror front page spread Tues, April 14. 1914. Etc etc.

160 Freedom. Vol. X X VIII. No 301. May. 1914.

161 Sunderland Daily Echo. Monday. April 13. 1914. And Newcastle Daily Journal. Monday. April 13. 1914.

162 Freedom. Vol. X X VIII. No 301. May. 1914.

163 It may just be my viewpoint, but after reading over a hundred years worth of *Freedom*, I often pick up elements of 'patronising' undercurrents and elements of the fact that anarchism, and anarchists are not 'important' enoughor prevalent enough outside of the London Freedom Press bubble, we are mere 'paupers from the provinces' so to speak. This fact was brought to the fore during the mid 1980's when a deemed racist article in the paper sparked much protest, in particular that of a 'black' member of the local Newcastle group, and the patronising responses from *Freedom* in their letters pages, evencriticising the spelling in some of the protest letters, a fact that personally infuriates. Many of the older generation of anarchists on Tyneside actively avoided and boycotted *Freedom* after this debacle. This will be looked at and referenced later. (See 1987)

164 Freedom. Vol. X X VIII. No 301. May. 1914.

165 Freedom. Vol. X X VIII. No 301. May. 1914.

166 Sunderland Daily Echo. Monday. April 13. 1914.

167 The Evening Chronicle. Monday April 13. 1914.

168 Newcastle Daily Journal. Monday. April 13. 1914. And Sunderland Daily Echo. Monday. April 13.

169 Newcastle Daily Journal. Monday. April 13. 1914. And Sunderland Daily Echo. Monday. April 13. 1914.

170 Newcastle Daily Journal. Monday. April 13. 1914.

171 Freedom. Vol. X X VIII. No 301. May. 1914.

172 I refuse to label WW1 as the 'Great War' as there is nothing great about an estimated nine million combatants and seven million civilian deaths as a result of this monstrosity.

173 G. Pattison – anarchist influences in the Durham coalfield before 1914. The Raven 11. Freedom Press.Vol 3 No 3. July / sept 1990

174 G. Pattison.

175 Newcastle Daily Journal. Friday. October 2. 1914.

176 *Anarchists, Syndicalists, and the First World War.* Vadim Damier. Black Cat Press. 2017.

177 *First Flight. The origins of Anarcho-Syndicalism in Britain.* Albert Meltzer. KSL Library.

[178] Quoted in *The Industrial Syndicalist*. Spokesman Books. 1974. Geoff Brown.

[179] *Against His-story, Against Leviathan!*. Fredy Perlman. 2016 edition. Active Publishing. P206.

[180] *A Short History of political Violence in Britain.* Martyn Everett. Undated pamphlet. 1991?

[181] *First Flight. The origins of Anarcho-Syndicalism in Britain.* Albert Meltzer. KSL Library.

[182] Freedom. Vol. X X IX. No 309. Jan. 1915. [183] Freedom. Vol. X X IX. No 310. Feb. 1915. [184] Freedom. Vol. X X IX. No 313. May. 1915.

[185] Sunderland Daily Echo. Tuesday. January 18. 1916.

[186] Freedom. Vol. X X IX. No 313. May. 1915.

[187] Quoted in *The Rise of Professional Society – England since 1880.* Harold Perkin. Routledge.1999.

[188] *Critique of Syndicalist Methods, Trade Unionism to Anarcho-Syndicalism.* A.M. Bonanno. Bratach Dubh pamphlets. 1979.

[189] *Black Star.* No 7. Sunderland. 1982.

[190] Yvetot, Quoted in *Anarchism*. David Miller. J.M. Dent & Sons. 1984.

[191] Not many records of the tribunals have survived – 'many were destroyed in the years immediately after the War upon the orders of the Government' (I wonder why!!!). However, some of the conclusions and businesses of the tribunals were reported in local newspapers.

[192] The Newcastle Journal. Tuesday. March 28. 1916.

[193] *Dont be a Soldier – The Radical Anti-War Movement in North London 1914-1918*. Ken Weller. 1985.

[194] *Dont be a Soldier – The Radical Anti-War Movement in North London 1914-1918*. Ken Weller.

[195] *Anarcho-Syndicalism. History and action.* Direct Action Movement.Pamphlet. 198?

[196] *First Flight. The origins of Anarcho-Syndicalism in Britain.* Albert Meltzer. KSL Library.

[197] *A Beautiful Idea – History of the Freedom Press Anarchists.* Rob Ray.Freedom Press. 2018.

[198] *God and the State*. Michael Bakunin. Dover Publications. New York. 1970. [199]

Background reading..*The Kingdom of God is Within You*. Leo Tolstoy. In *TheEssential Works of Anarchism*. Bantam. *1971*. Ed. Marshall S Shatz. & *Powerand Liberty*. Leo Tolstoy. Simian Pamphlet. Jan 1975.

200 Religious Worship, England and Wales, Report and Tables, Volume LXXXIX. Online.

201 Bebbington, David (1992) *Victorian Nonconformity* (Bangor, UK: Headstart) online.

202 Of course instances of this happened during the Spanish Revolution of 1936, but the Catholic Church in Spain, had for generations been an extremely oppressive and brutal perpetuator of coercion and violence, and understandably in moments of revolutionary fervour, targets of oppression were rightly destroyed. Although, most churches during this period became places for the distribution of food etc.

203 Northern Daily Mail. Friday. January 31. 1919.

204 Northern Daily Mail. Monday. September 29. 1919.

205 *The Common People 1746-1946*. G.D.H. Cole & Raymond Postgate. Methuen. 1946.

206 *Black Friday 1921*. Patrick Renshaw. History Today. Vol 21. Issue 6. June 1971.

207 As well as coming to the North East seeking employment, the eventual erosion of local industry, mines, shipyards, steelworks etc, would curtail this in the following decades.

208 Whilst many of these 'horrors' became apparent quite some time afterwards, the anarchist press of the period was quick to point them out. Some of the better later descriptions include *The Guillotine at Work. Vol 1: TheLeninist counter-revolution.* G P Maximoff. Cienfuegos Press. 1979. *The Unknown Revolution 1917-1921* Voline. PM Press / Jura Books. 2019. *The Bolshevik Myth*. Alexander Berkman. Virus Pamphlet. Undated. *An anarchist introduction to the Russian Revolution*. Alexander Berkman. Virus Pamphlet.
Undated.

209 And of course, I know from experience, that many anarchists don't join anarchist groups or advertise their existence or activities, many just 'get on withit' working in their local community etc.

210 Freedom. Vol. X X XV. No 384. June. 1921.

211 *Organise*. Magazine of the Anarchist Communist federation. No 42. Spring. 1996

212 Northern Daily Mail. Saturday, June 18. 1921.

213 The Berwick Advertiser. July 31. 1924.

214 The Shields Daily News. Saturday. October 10th. 1925.

215 *The secret anarchist history of Newcastle*. Mike. Self published pamphlet.

216 *A History of Anarcho-syndicalism*. Selfed Education Collective. Unit 14. Solidarity Federation.

217 *A History of Anarcho-syndicalism*. Selfed Education Collective. Unit 14. Solidarity Federation.

218 Newcastle Evening Chronicle - Thursday 23 May 1940.

219 *Tom Browns Syndicalism*. Phoenix Press. July. 1990.

220 Newcastle Evening Chronicle - Monday 03 May 1976.

221 Newcastle Evening Chronicle - Thursday 27 December 1979.

222 G. Pattison – anarchist influences in the Durham coalfield before 1914. The Raven 11. Freedom Press.Vol 3 No 3. July / sept 1990.

223 The Berwick Advertiser - Thursday 13 May 1926.

224 I.e., Dave Douglass in *Geordies Wa Mental,* and in a written piece in *The Heavy Stuff* (1992) wrongly states that this was the Chopwell miners.

225 Wor story. Self published booklet. Autumn 1998.

226 *The Rise of Professional Society – England since 1880*. Harold Perkin. Routledge.1999.

227 *Tom Browns Syndicalism*. Phoenix Press. July. 1990.

228 *Anarchism in North East England (1886-1990)*. D. Morrow. Unpublished dissertation. University of Sunderland. May 1996.

229 *Tom Browns Syndicalism*. Phoenix Press. July. 1990. And A *Beautiful Idea – History of the Freedom Press Anarchists*. Rob Ray. Freedom Press. 2018.

230 Two of these huts remain in Birtley to this day, I personally worked in one for a number of years when it was converted into a garage, and it is said, and felt, on the odd occasion, to be 'haunted'!!!

231 Tom Brown. *Direct Action* vol.4 no.7 (25) July 1963.

232 The Shields Daily News. Monday, October 17th. 1927.

233 *The Common People 1746-1946*. G.D.H. Cole & Raymond Postgate. Methuen. 1946.

234 *The Common People 1746-1946*. G.D.H. Cole & Raymond Postgate. Methuen.

1946.

235 *No Justice Without a Struggle – The National Unemployed Workers Movement in the North East of England 1920 – 1940.* Don Watson. Merlin Press. 2014.

236 *In Exited Times. The People Against the Blackshirts.* Nigel Todd. Bewick Press. 1995.

237 *The Common People 1746-1946.* G.D.H. Cole & Raymond Postgate. Methuen. 1946.

238 *No Justice Without a Struggle – The National Unemployed Workers Movement in the North East of England 1920 – 1940.* Don Watson. Merlin Press. 2014.

239 *In Exited Times. The People Against the Blackshirts.* Nigel Todd. Bewick Press. 1995.

240 *In Exited Times. The People Against the Blackshirts.* Nigel Todd. Bewick Press. 1995.

241 This is a heavily edited version of events, for full transcribe see David Walsh. *The Battle of Stockton*. republic-of-teesside.blogspot. And Libcom website.

242 Sunderland Daily Echo and Shipping Gazette - Friday 22 June 1934.

243 *Anarchism in North East England (1886-1990).* D. Morrow. Unpublished dissertation. University of Sunderland. May 1996.

244 Gateshead's "speaker's corner" of the time.

245 Tom Brown – *Telling it as it was. The Struggle Against Fascism in the Thirties.* North East Labour History Bulletin. Number 18. 1984. These notes for a projected autobiography by Tom Brown were found after his death in 'rudimentary form' and carefully edited as "as a result of his final illness, he was losing his memory." These particular ones were re-written and updated by Albert Meltzer along with Tom and appeared in "Direct Action - World Labour News Vol. 3 no. 1, 1962 - "Pages of Labour History" series" under the signature of Geordie. They also re-appeared as "*Newcastle Fights the Fascists*"in the Kate Sharpley library Bulletin, Number 2. 1991.

246 Tom Brown. Direct Action - World Labour News Vol. 3 no. 1, 1962 - "Pages of Labour History" / Kate Sharpley library Bulletin, Number 2. 1991.

247 *1936 The Spanish revolution.* Tyneside Anarchist Group. 'Pamphlet'. 1996.

248 *1936 The Spanish revolution.* Tyneside Anarchist Group. 'Pamphlet'. 1996.

249 FAI – Federacion Anarquista Iberica. (Iberian Anarchist Federation)

250 *Spain and the World.* Vol 1. No 17. August 11th. 1937

251 *I Couldn't Paint Golden Angels, Sixty Years of Commonplace Life and Anarchist Agitation.* Albert Meltzer. AK Press. 1996. *The Spanish Revolution – Anarchism in*

*Action*. Tower Hamlets DAM-IWA. ASP. 1986. *The Spanish Civil War - Anarchism in Action*. Eddie Conlon. WSM. 1986. *The Tragedy of Spain*. Rudolf Rocker. ASP. 1986. *Red Years Black Years. A Political History of Spanish Anarchism, 1911-1937*. Robert W. Kern. ISHI. 1978.

252 *First Flight. The origins of Anarcho-Syndicalism in Britain*. Albert Meltzer. KSL Library.

253 From Newcastle but then living in County Durham.

254 *I Couldn't Paint Golden Angels, Sixty Years of Commonplace Life and Anarchist Agitation*. Albert Meltzer. AK Press. 1996.

255 *The Anarchists in London 1935-1955*. Albert Meltzer. Cienfuegos Press. Orkney. 1976.

256 *Spain and the World*. Vol 1. No 10. April 16th. 1937.

257 *I Couldn't Paint Golden Angels, Sixty Years of Commonplace Life and Anarchist Agitation*. Albert Meltzer. AK Press. 1996.

258 *The Syndicalist*. (Tyneside) No 7. July 1986. Special supplement on theSpanish Revolution.

259 *The Tragedy of Spain*. Rudolf Rocker. ASP. 1986.

260 Revolt ! , Vol III. No 1 (48). 11th Feb. 1939. And *A Beautiful Idea – Historyof the Freedom Press Anarchists*. Rob Ray. Freedom Press. 2018.

261 Revolt ! , Vol III. No 1 (48). 11th Feb. 1939.

262 Revolt ! , Vol III. No 2 (49). 25th Feb. 1939.

263 Revolt ! , Vol III. No 3 (50). 25th March. 1939.

264 Revolt ! , Vol III. No 4 (51). 15th April. 1939.

265 Revolt ! , Vol III. No 5 (52). 1st May. 1939.

266 Revolt ! , Vol III. No 6 (53). 3rd June. 1939.

267 This is not the place to delve into splits / arguments at this time within the London groups over 'ownership' of *War Commentary* and/or *Freedom*. Nevertheless, the following claim/quote, in its mention of Tom Brown at the time may be of interest. "The feeling among the anarcho-syndicalists was that they had been victims of a shameless asset grab by pacifists and intellectuals who were out to sideline the class-struggle orientated anarchists and shift Freedom Press towards a more literary, artistic and academic focus. Four men, reportedly including Tom Brown, visited (Vernon) Richards and (ML) Berneri at their flat. The tales about what happened next are varied, but David Goodway managed to track down a definite member of the four, Cliff Holden, who recounted that he was the one who put a pistol to the

back of Berneri's head and marched her to the bank, acquiring £25 (about six weeks wages) to start anew anarcho-syndicalist paper, *Direct Action*." From *A Beautiful Idea – History of the Freedom Press Anarchists*. Rob Ray. Freedom Press. 2018. The old adage of check / question your sources springs to mind, this has none other than a name. As a further personal observation, this was said to happen during a period of high war alert and the monitoring of the Freedom Group by Special Branch police, where militants were being jailed and raided for simply selling literature, yet others were allowed to walk a woman to a bank with a gun to her head, unmolested or arrested and / or monitored during the act. But, this is just an observation; I haven't researched the facts surrounding the issue.

268 *War Commentary*. Vol 2. No 4. February. 1941.

269 *War Commentary*. Vol. 3 No. 7. March, 1942.

270 The Morpeth Herald and Reporter. Friday, March 19th. 1943.

271 *War Commentary*. Vol. 6 No. 1. November, 1944.

272 *War Commentary*. Vol. 6 No. 2. November, 11th. 1944.

273 *War Commentary*. Vol. 6 No. 3. November, 25th. 1944.

274 *The Word*. Vol III. No 1. August 1941 has a full page on John Morley, and his two sons, their imprisonment and writing against the war (and photo of thefamily).

275 Mapping radical Tyneside. Website.

276 *War Commentary*. Vol. 6 No. 4. December, 9th. 1944.

277 *War Commentary*. Vol. 6 No. 6. January, 13th. 1945.

278 *War Commentary*. Vol. 6 No. 16. June, 10th. 1945.

279 The Evening News. Saturday, July 13th. 1946.

280 Direct Action. July. 1945.

281 The Morpeth Herald and Reporter. Friday, Feb 18th. 1949.

282 Direct Action. Vol 4, No 5 (No 37). October 15th. 1949.

283 Direct Action. Vol 4, No 7 (No 39). December 9th. 1949.

284 Of 1948.

285 *A History of Anarcho-syndicalism*. Selfed Education Collective. Unit 19. Solidarity Federation.

286 Direct Action. Vol 5. No 5 (No 44) September 1950.

287 Direct Action. Vol 5, No 7 (No 46).November. 1950. + Vol.5 no.9 (no.47) December 1950. And *Tom Browns Syndicalism*. Phoenix Press. July. 1990.

288 Freedom. Vol 13, No. 13. March 29th, 1952 to May 1952.

289 Freedom. Vol 14, No. 43. October 24th, 1953.

290 Evening Chronicle. Wed, March 16th. 1955. And Newcastle Journal. Thurs, March 17th. 1955.

291 A minor personal example. When the 'lads' on the estate etc that I grew up on found out I was a vegetarian (in the days before it was 'trendy' to be so) themajority of them couldn't understand, or comprehend why. They said it was strange, and as a result, for decades I was on the receiving end of countless 'jokes' and 'banter' about it. Hence at times, especially where I lived, I kept my'anarchism' to myself.

292 Freedom. Vol 19 – Vol 20. 1958-1959.

293 *The Anarchists in London 1935-1955.* Albert Meltzer. Cienfuegos Press. Orkney. 1976.

294 *Don't You Hear the H-Bomb's Thunder?* Youth & Politics on Tyneside in theLate 'Fifties and Early 'Sixties. John Charlton. Merlin Press. 2009.

295 J Creaby to J Charlton. *Don't You Hear the H-Bomb's Thunder?*

296 J Charlton. *Don't You Hear the H-Bomb's Thunder?*

297 Brief online questions bring up - "In the United Kingdom baby boom has occurred in two waves. After a short first wave of the baby boom during the war and immediately after it peaking in 1946." "Couples were eager to have babies after the war ended because they knew that the world would be a safer place to start a family".

298 Freedom. Vol 22, No. 8. March 4th, 1961.

299 Freedom. Vol 21, No. 9. Feb 27th, 1960 to Freedom. Vol 29, No. 31. Oct 12th, 1968.

300 Ray Challinor obituary - . John Charlton. North East Labour History Society website.

301 Freedom. Vol 22, No. 32. Oct 7th, 1961.

302 Direct Action. Vol 2. No 3. March. 1962.

303 Freedom. Vol 24, No. 16. May 18th, 1963.

304 Evening Chronicle. Monday, June 24th. 1963.

305 Freedom. Vol 24, No. 25. Aug 10th, 1963.

306 Direct Action. Vol.4, No 12. (30) December, 1963.

307 Conversation with Dave Douglass, in *Anarchism in North East England (1886-1990)*. D. Morrow. Unpublished dissertation. University of Sunderland. May 1996. See also *Geordies – Wa Mental*. Dave Douglass. TUPS Books, Newcastle. 2000.

308 *Don't You Hear the H-Bomb's Thunder?* Youth & Politics on Tyneside in the Late 'Fifties and Early 'Sixties. John Charlton. Merlin Press. 2009.

309 *Geordies – Wa Mental*. Dave Douglass. TUPS Books, Newcastle. 2000.

310 Direct Action. July, Aug, Sept & Oct. 1964. And Freedom May, June, July, Aug, Sept. Dave Douglass - Nov & Dec 1964.

311 *Anarchism in North East England (1886-1990)*. D. Morrow. Unpublished dissertation. University of Sunderland. May 1996.

312 PR. I believe this letter is from Peter, as only initials are supplied, not area.

313 Freedom. Vol 24, No. 32. Oct 12th, 1963.

314 Direct Action. Vol 5, No 1 (31). January 1964.

315 *Nationalisation and the new boss class* - Tom Brown. Direct ActionPamphlets. No 3. 1958

316 Freedom. Vol 25, No 3, Jan 1964 To Freedom. Vol 25, May 1964.

317 Freedom. Vol 25, No 4, 5, and 6, 8th Feb – 22nd Feb. 1964.

318 Direct Action. Vol 5, No 2 (32). February, 1964.

319 Direct Action. Vol 5, No 3, 4, 5, & 6. March, April, May, & June. 1964. And Tom Brown *Lenin and Workers Control*. Direct Action pamphlets, Number 8.

320 Freedom. Vol 25, No. 11. April 11th, 1964.

321 Direct Action. Vol 5, No 4 (34). April, 1964.

322 The name of a cruel slave driver in Harriet Beecher Stowe's *Uncle Tom's Cabin*. KSL note.

323 The article in question - '*Anarchism and Trade Unionism*' by Gaston Gerard. KSL note.

324 Direct Action. Vol 5, No 8 (38). August, 1964.

325 Direct Action. Vol 5, No 9 (39). Sept, 1964. & *The Christie File*. Stuart Christie. Partisan press / Cienfuegos Press. 1980. & *Granny Made me an Anarchist. General Franco, The Angry Brigade and Me*. Stuart Christie.Scribner.2004. & *Geordies – Wa Mental*. Dave Douglass. TUPS Books, Newcastle.

326 The Journal. Thursday, September 3rd, 1964.

327 *Geordies – Wa Mental*. Dave Douglass. TUPS Books, Newcastle. 2000.

328 Direct Action. Vol 6, No 2 (44). February .1965.

329 Direct Action. Vol 6, No 3 (45). March .1965.

330 Direct Action. Vol 6, No's 4 + 5 + 6 (46, 47, 48). April, May, June .1965.

331 Freedom. Vol 26, No. 15. May . 1965 To October. 1965.

332 Direct Action. Vol 6, No's 6, 7, & 8 (48,49,50). June – Aug. 1965.

333 Direct Action. Vol 6, No 10 (52). October .1965.

334 Direct Action. Vol 6, No 12 (54). December.1965. and see Freedom. Vol26, No. 36. Nov 20. 1965.

335 Direct Action. Vol 6, No 11 (53). November .1965.

336 Conversation with Dave Douglass, in *Anarchism in North East England (1886-1990)*. D. Morrow. Unpublished dissertation. University of Sunderland. May 1996.

337 Direct Action. Vol 6, No 12 (54). Dec.1965. And Direct Action. Vol 7, No 1 (55). Jan.1966.

338 Direct Action. Vol 7, No 2 (56). Feburary.1966.

339 Direct Action. Vol 7, No 3 (57). March.1966.

340 Direct Action. Vol 7, No 3 (57). March.1966.

341 Direct Action. Vol 7, No 4 (58). April.1966.

342 Direct Action. Vol 7, No 5 (59). May. 1966.

343 Freedom. Vol 27, No. 18. June . 1966 To Sept. 1966. & Direct Action. Vol7, No 6 (60). June. 1966.

344 Mick Renwick obituary. Dave Douglass. North East Labour History website.

345 Direct Action. Vol 7, No 6 (60). June. 1966.

346 Freedom. Vol 27, No. 22. July . 1966.

347 Freedom. Vol 27, No. 2. Jan . 1966.

348 Direct Action. Vol 7, No 8 (62). August. 1966.

349 Direct Action. Vol 7, No 11 & 12 (65 & 66). November + December. 1966.

350 The far right these days target to murder their opponents, for example Labour politician Jo Cox in June 2016. The state's political police are also known locally to

visit people's places of work to inform employers that xxxx is a"Domestic Extremist" – a harsh sounding label for someone who may only be something as simple as an organiser of counter-fascist demonstrations etc.
The rise in uncovered cases of exposed 'spy cops' (undercover police who infiltrate political groups) coming to light has also created (a state intended?) level of paranoia amongst the 'libertarian left'. So many of these cases have come to light, that as a precaution, because of similar patterns of behaviourthe undercover police use, that activists have been able to build up a picture of these 'behaviours' to look out for, (the biggest behavioural pattern I can see is the state creating divide and rule tactics against its opposition, probably straight from some dodgy CIA manual somewhere) again this raises suspicion and paranoia, sometimes in places, at times it shouldn't happen.
A minor personal example, I once attended an anarchist meeting of a 'well established by the time of my attendance' group. One respected member of the group and myself go back nearly 30 years together, so I was obviously 'vouched' for. After the meeting, I overheard a younger member of the group talking of how he had to get a bus etc on his long journey home, when I said I was passing that way on my way home do you want a lift.. his face was a picture of veiled unease / suspicion and my offer refused to leave him trudgingthrough the pissing rain to get a bus. It wasn't until later, after discovering that this was a regular tactic used by 'spy cops' to gain possible information / address etc that I realised that my simple act of kindness was perceived as a method of suspicious state snooping !

[351] Direct Action. Vol 7, No's 8, 9, 10, 11, & 12. (62—66). August - December. 1966.

[352] Direct Action. Vol 8, No 2. (68) Feb.1967.

[353] Direct Action. Vol 8, No 3. (69) March.1967.

[354] Direct Action. Vol 8, No's 4 + 5 + 6 (70 + 71 + 72) April + May + June 1967.

[355] Direct Action. Vol 8, No 6. (72) June.1967.

[356] Freedom. Vol 28, No.19. 24th June . 1967.

[357] Direct Action. Vol 8, No 7. (73) July. 1967.

[358] Direct Action. Vol 8, No 12. (78) Dec. 1967.

[359] Direct Action. Vol 9, No 1. (79) Jan. 1968.

[360] Direct Action. Vol 9, No's 2—9. (80—84) Feb—June. 1968. Unfortunately, after June 1968 access to further copies of Direct Action from this period have not been available to consult until issues from 1981, by which time, the paper was produced by the Direct Action Movement as opposed to the Syndicalist Workers Federation. The name and organisation change occurred in Manchester during March 1979.

361 The Journal. Monday, November 18th. 1968.

362 The Journal. Monday, December 16th. 1968.

363 Not covered in this history are the actions / events of the 'Situationist inspired' occurrences of the King Mob grouping of students based in Newcastle before relocation to London. For coverage of this I recommend *KingMob: A Critical Hidden History*. David Wise with Stuart Wise & Nick Brandt. Bread and Circuses Publishing. 2014.

364 The Evening Chronicle. Thursday, January 16th, 1969.

365 The Evening Chronicle. Tuesday, January 28th, 1969.

366 Freedom. Vol 30. No's 7 (March 1969) to No 36 (22nd Nov 1969).

367 The Journal. Monday, November 23rd. 1970. 368 The Journal. Wednesday, December 2nd. 1970. 369 The Journal. Wednesday, December 9th. 1970.

370 Freedom. Vol 31. No's 1 (10th Jan 1970) to No 39 (12th Dec 1970).

371 Freedom. Vol 32, No.31. 9th October, 1971.

372 I include Mikes full name as it is plastered all over the press at the time along with poses for photographs (Evening Chronicle – Sat, March 6th 1971. – large photo ...+ even larger hair !!!)

373 Freedom. Vol 31, No.38. 5th December. 1970.

374 The Evening Chronicle, Sat, March 6th 1971.

375 Libertarian Struggle. No 9. November. 1973.

376 Unlike some other recent books, I have refrained from the unnecessary naming of Tom Browns two daughters, where they lived, and who they marriedetc – facts like these should never be divulged in our literature, especially when they were / are nothing to do with the 'movement'.

377 *Tom Browns Syndicalism*. Phoenix Press. July. 1990.

378 During the course of this writing, I was given a copy (CD) of the interview that Ray Challinor did with Tom Brown, and his local radio programmes. These I intend giving to the Kate Sharpley Library for possible audio release on-line. On a personal note, it was strange eventually hearing the voice of someone I had previously searched for information about for so long. The 'booming' voice of the Tyneside shipyards, now kind of sadly, sounded old and frail.

379 *Anarchism in North East England (1886-1990)*. D. Morrow. Unpublished dissertation. University of Sunderland. May 1996.

380 Working Together: recording and preserving the heritage of the workers' co-operative movement – interview with Martin Spence by Philippa Lewis. 29/01/2018. Holyoake House, Manchester.

381 Black Jakes Occasional Organ. No 2. Newcastle Anarchist Group. 1977.

382 The Evening Chronicle, Thursday, August 26th 1976.

383 Freedom. Vol 37, No.24. 4th December. 1976.

384 Black Jakes Occasional Organ. No 1. Newcastle Anarchist Group. early 1977 .

385 Because people are still alive and no longer involved, I stick by my decision to not now mention names, although, in the case of MS, I am afraid it becomes quite obvious who it is due to certain pamphlets written, which in hindsight, should have been written as a group or at least anonymously.

386 The Journal. Saturday, January 29th. 1977.

387 The Evening Chronicle, Saturday, January 29th 1977.

388 Black Jakes Occasional Organ. No 1. Newcastle Anarchist Group. early 1977 .

389 The Evening Chronicle, Saturday, February 19th 1977.

390 Newcastle University Courier - Wednesday, 23 rd February, 1977.

391 Newcastle University Courier - Wednesday, 9 th February, 1977.

392 "Even prior to the emergence of anarcho-punk and other punk scenes explicitly engaged with anarchism, anarchistic currents are apparent in early punk. Once again, this is not to say that early punk was uniformly anarchist, but that even where early punk seems most removed from concurrent anarchistgroups and the canon of anarchist political philosophy, anarchistic practices and rhetoric can *still* be identified. The presence of anarchist rhetoric *and practice* in punk's earliest manifestations is clear – this emerging anarchist strand has been the prime political companion for punk over the last 40+ years, and remains the core principle of contemporary punk organisation, networking and production." *Bakunin Brand Vodka – Anarchism in Early Punk 1976-1980*. D. Bidge. Active. 2019.

393 Black Jakes Occasional Organ. No 2. Newcastle Anarchist Group. 1977. Article by MS.

394 TJ told me that when he 'got involved' in 1976 with local anarchists, there was a few 'old timers' who were around for a bit, he didn't get to know their names as they kept themselves to themselves.

395 Black Jakes Occasional Organ. No 2. Newcastle Anarchist Group. 1977. Article by MS.

396 *A History of Anarcho-syndicalism*. Selfed Education Collective. Unit 20. Solidarity Federation.

397 Working Together: recording and preserving the heritage of the workers' co-operative movement – interview with Martin Spence by Philippa Lewis. 29/01/2018. Holyoake House, Manchester.

398 Freedom. Vol 39, No.13. 8th July. 1978. To Vol 39, No.22. November 1978. Etc.

399 *National Liberation and State Power – An Anarchist Critique of the MPLA in Angola* by MS. Black Jake Collective Pamphlet. 1978 / 1979 ?

400 *Region 1*. Black Jake Collective Pamphlet. Newcastle. May 1978.

401 These were happening around various groups and individuals throughout the country as a result of the 'Persons Unknown' charges / trial/ conspiracy of conspiring to cause explosions. The case was variously dubbed the Persons Unknown trial or the Anarchists trial – "we were all voluble if unsophisticated young enemies of the state, all states. We also had absolutely nothing to do with any explosions. After several months in custody, this charge was dropped and a different conspiracy charge preferred. Opening the Crown's case at the Old Bailey a year later, the prosecutor said we had conspired 'to overthrow society'. The jury acquitted us on all counts." Ronan Bennett (One of the accused). "It's been widely suspected that England's Anti-Terrorist Squad framed an entire case around the 'anarchist terrorist conspiracy' in order to justify their existence as a time when they were coming under fire because of their lack of activity. The police have since manipulated the press, slandered activists as bombers and terrorists and harassed their supporters in an attempt to isolate anarchists and anti-authoritarians from any potential sympathisers. If the prosecution succeeds and anarchism is seen as a criminal political activity, the anarchist movement could be forced underground for the first time in the U.K." *Open Road* .Vancouver, Special Issue, Fall/Winter 1979.

402 Freedom. Vol 39, No.14. 22nd July. 1978 + Freedom. Vol 39, No.15. 5th Aug. 1978.

403 The site of a proposed nuclear power station.

404 This was part of a national speaking 'tour'.

405 Freedom. Vol 39, No.24. 9th December. 1978.

406 NEAF Bulletin No 3. Quoted in Freedom. Vol 40, No.1. 20th January. 1979.

407 After a ban on the record. Many of us still bought it 'under the counter' in brown paper bags to disguise the cover, from sympathetic record shops.

408 Killing no murder. A report by the Liddle Towers Committee. Tyneside Free Press. June 1977.

409 'Ban lifted on anarchist rock group' press cutting from Evening Chronicle. May 23rd. 1985.

410 Freedom. Vol 39, No.20. 14th October 1978. This issue also contains a large article by MS on 'Racism and Fascism today' in which "This analysis by MS is, we feel, an important contribution to the subject, going on to suggest how anarchists can constructively help in the formation of a street
culture resistance."

411 Freedom. Vol 40, No.2. 10th February. 1979. Unfortunately my copy of this paper has a couple of pages missing, so only the second half of the article by John is readable.

412 Freedom. Vol 40, No.4. 10th March. 1979.

413 Freedom. Vol 40, No.6. 7th April. 1979.

414 Freedom. Vol 40, No.2. 10th February. 1979.

415 Freedom. Vol 40, No.7. 21st April. 1979.

416 Freedom. Vol 40, No. 8 & 9. 19th May. 1979.

417 Freedom. Vol 41, No.4. 1st March. 1980.

418 It is worth remembering that during the 70s, 80s and most of the 90s that the internet / computers / mobile phones etc didn't exist for most people. Anarchist publications were often brought out on a monthly basis, so to those wanting to disagree or discuss points made by others, this would involve having to write and post a letter (after purchasing, which for most, was an expensive stamp), which may make the deadline for the next issue and may not. Hence some discussions would take up the letters pages of publications for months on end, as opposed to today's instant online discussions.

419 NEAF Bulletin No 8 (May 1979). Quoted in Freedom. Vol 40, No.10. 2nd June. 1979.

420 Freedom. Vol 40, No.10. 2nd June. 1979.

421 Freedom. Vol 40, No.12. 30th June. 1979.

422 Black Flag. Vol V. No 9. July 1979.

423 Freedom. Vol 40, No.14. 28th July. 1979.

424 Black Flag. Vol V. No 9. July 1979.

425 *Burning Britain. The History of UK Punk. 1980-1984*. Ian Glasper. CherryRed Books. 2004. And on-line conversation with ex members of Total Chaos. 426 IQ 32. No 2. 1983. (Liverpool Zine.)

427 Hate And War. No 2. November 1982. (South Shields, Tyneside. Zine.)

428 *Burning Britain. The History of UK Punk. 1980-1984*. Ian Glasper. CherryRed Books. 2004.

429 Freedom. Vol 40, No.19. 20th October. 1979. 430 The Journal. Thursday, November 29th. 1979. 431 Freedom. Vol 41, No.1. 19th January. 1980.

432 Charles Malato (1857–1938) was a French anarchist and writer.

433 Freedom. Vol 41, No.1. 19th January. 1980.

434 Freedom. Vol 41, No.2. 2nd February. 1980.

435 Freedom. Vol 41, No's 5, 10, 15, 19, & 21. March – October. 1980.

436 Freedom. Vol 41, No.8. 26th April. 1980.

437 Freedom. Vol 41, No.10. 24th May. 1980.

438 Freedom. Vol 41, No's 12, 13, and 14. 21st June to 19th July. 1980.

439 Freedom. Vol 41, No.4. 1st March. 1980.

440 Freedom. Vol 41, No.10. 24th May. 1980.

441 Freedom. Vol 41, No.21. 25th October. 1980.

442 'The hippies now wear black' Crass and the anarcho-punk movement, 1977-1984. Richard Cross.

443 'The hippies now wear black' Crass and the anarcho-punk movement, 1977-1984. Richard Cross.

444 I believe the correct terminology these days is 'zine' as opposed to 'fanzine'. Take away the fan and become a participant rather than just a casual observer.

445 Thatcher's battle against inflation raised the exchange rate, resulting in the closure of many factories, shipyards and coal pits because imports were cheaper. Unemployment reached 3 million, or 12.5% of the workforce, by January 1982, a level that had not been seen for some 50 years. The unemployment figures did not include benefit claimants who were placed on Employment Training schemes, an adult variant of the controversial Youth Training Scheme, who were paid the same rate of benefit for working full-time hours. The unemployment levels would remain roughly the same until about 1986ish.

446 Treason. No 1. November 1981. Sunderland. For contact details of group, see also Freedom. Vol 42 No 3. 13th Feb 1981 and further issues throughout the year.

447 *Uprising. The police, the people and the riots in Britain's cities*. Martin Kettle &

Lucy Hodges. Pan Books. London. 1982.

448 *Miner Conflicts – Major Contradictions*. Pamphlet. B.M. Combustion.London. July 1984.

449 *Like A Summer with a Thousand Julys*...and other seasons. B.M. Blob. London. 1982.

450 *Bigger Cages Longer Chains*. Spectacular Times, pocketbook series No 14. Larry Law.1987.

451 Treason. No 1. November 1981. Sunderland.

452 Freedom. Vol 42, No.12. 20th June. 1981.

453 Big Toot, a lovable human being taken from us too early, was instrumental in the continuation of the local punk scene throughout most of the 1980's, andwas known and loved by everyone even remotely involved within the 'punk movement' far and wide during this period. After the Garage closed it was Toot that organised most of the gigs at its successor, The Station. These were followed at Bensham and Saltwell Social Clubs in Gateshead, and eventually the Riverside in Newcastle. His address would also feature as a contact for many a Newcastle Anarchist Group leaflet during this time. RIP Toot.

454 No Comment. No 1. Late 1981. Gateshead Zine.

455 *Proletarian Aspirations. Black Star; the story of an anarchist paper 1981-1987*. Photocopy of introduction and brief history.

456 Freedom. Vol 42, No.14. 18th July. 1981.

457 Direct Action. No 4. 1981. And Freedom. Vol 42, No.15. 1st August. 1981.

458 *Proletarian Aspirations. Black Star; the story of an anarchist paper 1981-1987*.

459 Treason. No 1. November 1981. Sunderland.

460 "No Glue, No Glass Bottles" – The Bunker remembered. Rich Cross.Online. And conversation with a founding participant.

461 No Comment. No 5. December 1981. Gateshead Zine.

462 *Burning Britain. The History of UK Punk. 1980-1984*. Ian Glasper. CherryRed Books. 2004.

463 "No Glue, No Glass Bottles" – The Bunker remembered. Rich Cross.Online.

464 "No Glue, No Glass Bottles" – The Bunker remembered. Rich Cross.Online.

465 I have left Stuarts name in full as it is well documented and known via hisown books etc.

466 The Evening Chronicle, Friday, July 10th. 1981.
The book *Towards a Citizens Militia – Anarchist Alternatives to NATO & the Warsaw Pact* is actually an A4 pamphlet of 28 pages. By IRSM / First of May Group. Cienfuegos Press. 1980

467 The Journal. Saturday, July 11th. 1981.

468 Black Flag. Vol VI. No 4. September. 1980.

469 Black Flag. Vol VI. No 6. January. 1981.

470 The Evening Chronicle, Thursday, July 23rd. 1981.

471 Freedom. Vol 42, No.22. 7th November. 1981.

472 Freedom. Vol 42, No.24. 5th December. 1981.

473 "Dear Comrades, I was most surprised to pick up your paper in aNewcastle bookshop. It's about time someone took the incentive to get a'working class'anarchist paper on the streets again. Regretfully retired fromactive politics now, I shall cast my mind back to the days prior to the Great War. Syndicalism was widespread in the yards, factories and pit. Anarchy wasmost certainly in the air. The fresh clean air of freedom. My father was anardent anarchist. An anarchist of the French school, but that's a different story.His great friends Billy Lawther and Geordie Harvey often goaded him abouthis Puritanism. Once my father brought Tom Mann, who was visiting the area,home for supper. Mr Mann, although a revolutionary syndicalist, was by no means an anarchist. They argued all night. I was an apprentice blacksmith at the time and couldn't understand life without wages although I called myself an anarchist! Enough of history, the message to the workers is still the same. Revolution and not reform. There is no compromise for revolution. Keep up thegood work comrades. Yours fraternally, JF. Co Durham". Letter from Direct Action. No 3. 1981.

474 Black Flag. Vol VI. No 11. April / May 1982. & Freedom Vol 43, No.6. 4th April. 1982.

475 *Proletarian Aspirations. Black Star; the story of an anarchist paper 1981-1987.*

476 John Nott, Minister of Defence, in the House of Commons, the day after the Argentinian occupation. Quoted in *Miner Conflicts – Major Contradictions.*

477 *Miner Conflicts – Major Contradictions.* Pamphlet. B.M. Combustion.London. July 1984.

478 Freedom Vol 43, No.7. 17th April. 1982.

479 Freedom Vol 43, No.8. 1st May. 1982.

480 Freedom Vol 43, No.1. Jan. 1982. To No 22. Nov 1982.

481 Freedom Vol 43, No.9. 22nd May. 1982.

482 Self Determination For The People of The World. A4 leaflet – original typedsheet prior to copy.

483 Tsurkov – a Leningrad student, and member of the anarchist-communist "New Left Opposition", was arrested by the KGB on Oct 31st 1978 and charged with anti-soviet agitation and propaganda etc, for this he received a sentence of 5 years in a labour colony and 2 years internal exile.

484 Direct Action Movement. Internal Bulletin. June 1982.

485 Freedom Vol 43, No.12. 26th June. 1982.

486 Freedom Vol 43, No.13. 10th July. 1982.

487 Direct Action. No 10. 1982.

488 *Proletarian Aspirations. Black Star; the story of an anarchist paper 1981-1987.*

489 Freedom Vol 43, No.16. 21st August. 1982.

490 Freedom Vol 43, No.22. 13th November. 1982.

491 *Proletarian Aspirations. Black Star; the story of an anarchist paper 1981-1987.*

492 *Black Star.* No 7. Sunderland. 1982.

493 Black Flag News Bulletin. Vol VII. No 2b. March 1983.

494 A participant.

495 Black Flag News Bulletin. Vol VII. No 2b. March 1983.

496 Michael Foot (23 July 1913 – 3 March 2010) the then Labour Party'leader'.

497 Freedom Vol 44, No.6. 26th March. 1983.

498 Freedom Vol 44, No.6. 26th March. 1983.

499 Freedom Vol 44, No.8. 23rd April. 1983.

500 Freedom Vol 44, No.12. 18th June. 1983.

501 Black Flag News Bulletin. Vol VII. No 2F. 6th May. 1983.

502 *Black Star.* No 8. Sunderland. 1983.

503 Freedom Vol 44, No.17. 27th August. 1983. And *Proletarian Aspirations. Black Star; the story of an anarchist paper 1981-1987.*

504 Black Flag News Bulletin. Vol VII. No 3A. 3rd June. 1983. (opened by the Princess of Wales)

505 Freedom Vol 44, No.14. 16th July. 1983.

506 Black Flag News Bulletin. Vol VII. No 3C. 1st July. 1983.

507 IE- contact details stamped on rear of Direct Action. No 11. 1982/1983.

508 Syndicalist Alliance Bulletin. No 2. Summer 1983. Newcastle.

509 Giz a job not a bomb – a Syndicalist Perspective. A4 leaflet. Syndicalist Alliance. Newcastle.

510 A brief and dated explanation I know, and again, mostly taken from my earlier writing *Fanning the flames of discontent. A brief look at the ideas & history of anarcho-syndicalism in Britain.*(with particular reference to the North East) 1996. Unpublished essay.

511 *The IWA Today*. A short account of the International Workers Association and its sections. C. Longmore. South London DAM-IWA. 1985.

512 *The IWA Today*. C. Longmore. South London DAM-IWA. 1985.

513 Giz a job not a bomb – a Syndicalist Perspective. A4 leaflet. Syndicalist Alliance. Newcastle.

514 *First Flight. The origins of Anarcho-Syndicalism in Britain*. Albert Meltzer. KSL Library.

515 *Anarcho-Syndicalism history and action*. DAM/IWA. Pamphlet. Manchester.

516 *Anarcho-Syndicalism*. Rudolf Rocker. Phoenix Press.

517 *The Methods of Anarcho-Syndicalism*. Rudolf Rocker. Monty Miller Press. Sydney. 1981. / *Anarcho-Syndicalism*. Rudolf Rocker. Phoenix Press. / *Anarchism & Anarcho-Syndicalism*. Rudolf Rocker. Freedom Press. 1973.

518 Black Flag News Bulletin. Vol VII. No 3G. 26th August. 1983.

519 Newcastle Anarchist Group leaflets. 'Why Vote?' / 'The real meaning of May Day'/ 'You and the Law – Watch out there's a police bill about' / 'Act Now, protest & survive – CND and the State' / 'Still Dying & Work towards disarmament work towards survival' /'War: The crime against humanity' /'We will never forget Hiroshima!' booklet. All 1983.

520 The Journal. Wednesday August 10th. 1983.

521 Freedom Vol 44, No.17. 27th August. 1983. And other original 'London Greenpeace' leaflets announcing / proposing event. Etc.

522 Black Flag News Bulletin. Vol VII. No 4A. 7th? October. 1983.

523 Black Flag News Bulletin. Vol VII. No 4b. 21st October. 1983. Coincidently this is also the address for the Syndicalist Alliance.

524 Newcastle Anarchist Group documents- 'What anarchists believe', 'NAG library', 'Librarians duties', 'list of literature in NAG library', 'a list of a few well known anarchists or libertarians', 'Newcastle Central Library section on books under anarchism'. 1983.

525 Groups handwritten meeting minutes; 17th September 1983 + 1st October 1983. + draft letter.

526 Groups handwritten meeting minutes; 8th October + 29th October + 5th November 1983.

527 Groups handwritten meeting minutes; 3rd December + 17th December. 1983.

528 *Hate And War*. No 2. November 1982. / *B41984*. Sunderland. 1983. / *Would you like an enema?* No 1. Darlington. 1983. / *Protest*. No 3. Newcastle. 1983. / *Stepping out*. No 5. Newcastle. 1983. / 2nd *Edition*. Newcastle. 1983. / *Acts of Defiance*. No's 3, 5, 6, 7, 8. Sunderland.1983. etc,etc.

529 *Having a Laugh & Having a Say*. Another bloody punk rock autobiography. Trev Hagl. 2013.

530 Acts of Defiance. No 7. Sunderland. 1983.

531 Black Flag News Bulletin. Vol VII. No 4E. 2nd December. 1983.

532 Conflict. Increase The Pressure. Motorhate records. 1984.

533 I am not sure if this is our old friend Peter Ridley of Whitley Bay, Tynemouth(see the 1960's).

534 Anarchy Magazine (2nd series) No 37. Winter 1983/4. London.

535 Black Flag Extra. Jan 1984 sheet enclosed within Black Flag News Bulletin.Vol VII. No 5B. 13th February. 1984.

536 Acts of Defiance. No 8. Sunderland. 1984.

537 'The Anarcho-Hopefuls, North of England', A4 leaflet - 'Are Anarchist Groups Self Defeatist?'

538 Freedom Vol 45, No.4. 24th March. 1984.

539 Earthworks. No 2. Forest Hall, Newcastle. 1984.

540 Margaret Thatcher - Speech to '1922 Committee'. 19 July 1984.

541 Black Flag News Bulletin. Vol VII. No 6C. No 114. 1984.

542 The then Home Secretary.

543 Earthworks. No 2. Forest Hall, Newcastle. 1984.

544 Black Flag News Bulletin. Vol VII. No 5F. 9th April. 1984. 545 Free Omori - a5 leaflet. Middlesbrough Anarchists. 1984. 546 Black Flag News Bulletin. Vol VII. No 5F. 9th April. 1984.

547 A participant.

548 Other participants !

549 Another participant.

550 Join Hands. A4 leaflet / handout. Middlesbrough. 1985.

551 A participant.

552 I.E, Freedom Vol 45, No.5. 24th May. 1984. & Vol 45, No.7. July. 1984. & Vol 45, No.9. Sept 1984. & Suspension from DAM - Vol 45, No.11. November. 1984. & On criticism of Scargill etc and ballot for expulsion from DAM, and further letters see Vol 45, No.12. December. 1984. & more letters - Freedom Vol 46, No.1. Jan. 1985. NH now mentioning he a member of Spanish Information Network - Freedom Vol 46, No.2. Feb. 1985. Letter & article in Freedom Vol 46, No.3. March. 1985. Letter - Freedom Vol 46, No.4. April. 1985. Letter - Freedom Vol 46, No.6. June. 1985. Letter - Freedom Vol 46, No.9. September. 1985. ML CNT letter in Freedom Vol 47 No 6 July 1986. Letter in Freedom Vol 48, No 2. February 1987. & Freedom Vol 48, No 12. December. 1987.

553 Black Flag Quarterly. Vol VII No 6. Spring 1984.

554 Strike Back No 5. May 1984. Middlesbrough.

555 Strike Back No 4 advert from Black Flag News Bulletin. Vol VII. No 6A. 11th June. 1984. *'Revolutionary Unionism in Italy'* advert from Sinews. No 2. Summer + Autumn 1984.

556 Freedom Vol 45, No.9. September. 1984. And contact details appear in earlier Vol 45, No.8 Aug.

557 *Bores Under the Floor* - a brief guide to the wave of 'left' groups and newspapers currently invading the pit villages. David Douglass. Doncaster. June 1984. See also Black Flag News Bulletin. Vol VII. No 6F. No 117. 20th August. 1984. For further exploration of the left see *Pit Sense Versus the State – A history of militant miners in the Doncaster area*. David Douglass. PhoenixPress. November 1993.

558 Black Flag News Bulletin. Vol VII. No 6G. No 118. 3rd September. 1984.

559 Freedom Vol 45, No.11. November. 1984.

560 Freedom Vol 45, No.10. October. 1984.

561 Black Flag. Vol VII. No 7C. No 121. 13th November. 1984.

562 Black Flag. Vol VII. No 7D. No 122. 27th November. 1984.

563 *Remember who we are?* No 2. 1984./ *Aural Nightmares* No 1 + 2. 1984+5 / *What's Left* No 1. 1984 / *No-one kills the children anymore*. 1984. / *Organised Confusion* No 1 + 2. 1984.

564 An organiser of the event.

565 Freedom Vol 45, No.12. December. 1984.

566 'Can we afford to sit back and watch?' Reality Control - leaflet / handout. 1984.

567 Black Flag Quarterly. Vol VII No 5. Winter 1984.

568 Black Flag. Vol VII. No 125. 28th January. 1985. & Freedom Vol 46,No.1. Jan. 1985.

569 Direct Action. No 22. Feb 1985.

570 The Brighton hotel bombing was a Provisional Irish Republican Army assassination attempt against the top tier of the British government that occurred on 12 October 1984.

571 Direct Action. No 22. Feb 1985.

572 Black Flag. No 128. 18th March. 1985.

573 Freedom Vol 46, No.3. March. 1985.

574 Black Flag. No 131. 29th April. 1985.

575 *Miner Conflicts – Major Contradictions*. Pamphlet. B.M. Combustion. London. July 1984.

576 IE, the spate of terror attacks in Europe where the 'perpetrators' (or more likely victims of state manipulation) conveniently all left their passports on the passenger seat of the vehicle used. Etc.

577 Freedom Vol 46, No.3. March. 1985.

578 Freedom Vol 46, No.4. April. 1985. The 'then Freedom editor' admitted that contact details for the mentioned Durham Group were foolishly lost whilst out getting drunk in Hackney with Class War!!!

579 Freedom Vol 46, No.4. April. 1985.

580 Crowbar. No 43. London. 1985.

581 Tyne and Wear Free News. No 1. Newcastle. May 1985.

582 The shop would allow many to use the premises as a postal address.

583 Tyne and Wear Free News. No 1. Newcastle. May 1985.

584 Direct Action. No 24. April. 1985.

585 Direct Action. No 25. May/June. 1985.

586 Tyne and Wear Free News. No 2. Newcastle. June 1985.

587 *Anarchism in North East England (1886-1990).* D. Morrow. Unpublished dissertation. University of Sunderland. May 1996. (Interview with TJ, February 1996).

588 Freedom Vol 46, No.6. June. 1985.

589 Red on Black. No 1. York. 1985.

590 Tyne and Wear Free News. No 3. Newcastle. July 1985.

591 Freedom Vol 46, No.7. July. 1985.

592 Direct Action. No 26. July. 1985.

593 Black Flag. No 135. 1st July. 1985.

594 Red and Black. No 2. York. 1985. When I used to go 'collect mail' from the city centre location I had it delivered it to, on more than one occasion the same two men in suits loitering in the same doorway would watch my entrance/exits. Most people's mail at the time looked tampered with / missing...especially regular deliveries of zines, papers, magazines etc. The state wasn't exactly secretively cautious about their mail analysis!!!

595 Freedom Vol 46, No.9. September. 1985.

596 I.e. see The Sheffield Anarchist. Vol 3. Issues 8,9, & 10. 1985. & Freedom Vol 46, No.9. Sept. 1985.

597 Freedom Vol 46, No's 9 & 10. September & October. 1985.

598 Tyne and Wear Free News. No 5. Newcastle. October 1985. See also *Through a Riot Shield, The 1985 Brixton Riot.* Past Tense. Pamphlet. 2014. For further analysis.

599 Tyne and Wear Free News. No 5. Newcastle. October 1985.

600 Aims and Principles / Constitution. Tyneside Revolutionary Syndicalists.Internal documents.

601 Black Flag. No 142. 21st October. 1985. And The Syndicalist. No 1.Tyneside. 1985.

602 *Rebel Violence V. Hierarchical Violence – A chronology of anti-state violence on the UK mainland July 1985 – May 1986.* A4 pamphlet. London. May 19th 1986.

603 Black Flag. No 142. 21st October. 1985.

604 The Syndicalist. No 1. Tyneside. 1985.

605 *The troops out of Ireland issue of Shit.* No 2. / *Face of the Future.* No 1 /*Let there be love, let there be life, let there be an earth.* / *The sentient paradox?* / *Ugly people, ugly people, ugly fucking people* / *He who laughs last.* All 1985.

606 *'The price of resistance'* / *'Apartheid –South Africa'* . Flat Earth / G*****c Collective leaflets. Newcastle. 1985. *'A Wapping great lie'* and *'To all the malemembers of tonight's audience'*. 1986.

607 Freedom Vol 46, No's 11 & 12. November & December. 1985.

608 The Syndicalist. No 2. Tyneside. 1986. Write up / advert promoting the publication of The Syndicalist also appears in Direct Action, No 27 , January 1986. Black Flag, No 150, 24th Feb 1986 also mentions the vigil outside Durham jail, and also an advert for the same issue (No 2).

609 Originally as 'LOS communiqué, December 1985'.

610 Original 'LOS communiqué, December 1985'. This also appeared in (amongst others) Virus No 6. 1986 & Freedom Vol 47, No 1. Jan – Feb 1986. & *'The Future in the Present – Critical Anarchy No 1'* Libertarian Organisation& Structure. Pamphlet. Durham / Newcastle. 1987.

611 'LOS communiqué, June 1986.' Quoted in *'The Future in the Present – Critical Anarchy No 1'* Libertarian Organisation & Structure. Pamphlet. Durham / Newcastle. 1987. This also appeared in Freedom Vol 47 No 7 August 1986. Anarchist Communist Federation (ACF) pre conference internal bulletin No 2 (undated – mid to late 1986.) also contains a letter from LOS asking for advance payments for pamphlet in order to help with the cost of production of an initial print run of 500. Signed by TJ (acting secretary of LOS)

612 *The Future in the Present – Critical Anarchy No 1.* Libertarian Organisation & Structure. Pamphlet. Durham / Newcastle. 1987.

613 Black Flag. No 152. 24th March. 1986.

614 The Syndicalist. No 3. Tyneside. 1986.

615 Black Flag. No 153. 14th April. 1986. & see Direct Action No 30. April 1986.

616 Freedom Vol 47, No 2. March 1986.

617 Freedom Vol 47, No 3. April 1986.

618 Freedom Vol 47, No 3. April 1986. & *Roses & Revolutionists.* Nigel Todd. Peoples Publications. 1986. *Roses & Revolutionists* has been fully updated and re-released by Five Leaves Books.

619 The Syndicalist. No 4. Tyneside. April 1986.

620 Black Flag. No 155. 26th May. 1986.

621 The Syndicalist. No 5. Tyneside. May 1986.

622 Tyne and Wear Free News. No 8. Newcastle. June 1986.

623 The Syndicalist. No 6. Tyneside. June 1986.

624 Minutes of Anarchist Communist Discussion Group meeting 22nd March 1986, which announces the Anarchist Communist Federation, now exists witha membership and that a public announcement would commence when next literature magazine / paper produced in a matter of months. This was *Liberation* No 1 (June 1986). See also ACF meeting minutes, June 7th 1986, which includes a letter from the treasurer stating the ACF is now a functioning group. Minor mention of formation also in *Rebel Alliances. The means and ends of contemporary British anarchism's*. B Franks. AK Press / Dark Star. 2006.

625 Virus, numbers 1 (1984) to No 13 (1988) and Liberation, No 1 June 1986 to No 5 Jul/Aug.1987.

626 ACF internal bulletin No 1 July 1986. And Liberation No 2 1986. Coincidently the ACF internal bulletin No 1 would also contain a contribution from ML of the Spanish Information Network, Co Durham.

627 The Syndicalist. No 7. Tyneside. July 1986.

628 Working Together: recording and preserving the heritage of the workers' co-operative movement – interview with Martin Spence by Philippa Lewis. 29/01/2018. Holyoake House, Manchester. And The Syndicalist. No 7. Tyneside. July 1986.

629 Direct Action. No 32. July. 1986. This issue would also advertise The Syndicalist No 6, rather lately, as No 7 was out at this time. This edition of DA would also be known as the 'bogus edition' produced by a separate group (I won't go into this). The series of DA continues nationally with another issue 32 in September 1986.

630 Tyne and Wear Free News. No 9. Newcastle. July / August 1986.

631 The Syndicalist. No 8. Tyneside. August 1986.

632 ACF delegates meeting minutes. Held 13th September, 1986. Coventry.

633 The Syndicalist. No 9. Tyneside. September 1986.

634 I once heckled Tony Benn at a Newcastle May Day rally, late 1980's pointing out this fact, only to be roughly 'man-handled' away by 3 or 4 burly Labour party heavies!!!!

635 Direct Action. No 32. September. 1986.

636 Northern Anarchist Network. Internal bulletin No 1. October 1986. And Black Flag No 162, 13th October 1986.

637 Northern Anarchist Network. Internal bulletin No 1. October 1986.

638 Northern Anarchist Network. Internal bulletin No 3. January 1987 (This issue was produced in Newcastle). Unfortunately No 2 of the bulletin is not in my possession and therefore unavailable to consult.

639 The Syndicalist. No 10. Tyneside. October 1986.

640 Anarchist Communist Federation (ACF) pre conference internal bulletin No 2 (undated – mid to late 1986.) And ACF Internal bulletin, No 3. October 1986. And minutes of ACF National conference 4th October. 1986. And minutes of ACF delegates meeting, 8th November 1986.

641 ACF Internal bulletin, No 4. December 1986.

642 The Syndicalist. No 11. Tyneside. November / December 1986.

643 Tyne and Wear Free News. No 11. Newcastle. November 1986.

644 Sinews. No 5. Winter 1986 / 87. And *What is the CNT?* A5 pamphlet. Co Durham. 1986.

645 Northern Anarchist Network. Internal bulletin No 3. January 1987

646 From its formation in early 1986, the ACF was in constant contact with Class War groups, whilst letters to and from the DAM went back and forth. Talk of working together began as far back as the Minutes of Anarchist Communist Discussion Group meeting 22nd March 1986. See also draft of open letter to CWF & DAM in ACF Internal bulletin, No 3. October 1986 etc. the open letter also appeared in Freedom, Vol 47 No 10 November / December 1986. & Virus No 9 late 86, early 87. See also return letters from DAM 29/12/86 and CWF 9/12/86 who both agreed to joint working together as long as it was in accordance of each groups aims and principles in ACF National delegates meeting minutes, 10th January 1987.

647 Freedom Vol 48, No 1. January 1987. At the time of writing this particular section ( Christmas eve 2019) this volume of Freedom(Vol 48) is not included in their online archive, nor is any of this mentioned in their recent history *A Beautiful*

*Idea – History of the Freedom Press Anarchists.* Rob Ray. Freedom Press. 2018. Tyneside Anarchist Archive have made it known to members of the current Freedom press team, on a couple of occasions, that they have virtually every issue of *Freedom* from 1977 onwards after a large donation from an old comrade. No requests have ever been made or even hinted at to copy any for their archive. Too ashamed of their pompous racist past I wonder?
I am not re-creating buried divisions (such as those between the groupings around *Black Flag* and *Freedom* in the past), but highlighting the fact that in generations to come, or history's to follow, the writings of papers such as *Freedom* will be seen as representing the entire UK anarchist movement, of which they clearly are not.

648 Or perhaps the editors were still reeling after the recent publication by *Black Flag* of their 'Liars and Liberals' supplement and its '7000 word exposure' of Freedom Press and those associated with it, including the author of the racist article in question Tony Gibson. "Gibson is an admirer of the racialist psychologist (and former colleague) Professor Eysenck, whom he has defended in the pages of freedom". "We say that those who consider it libertarian to extol Professor Eysenck, with his racial superiority notions, or defend the National Fronts right of speech, or who consider it absurd to take action against Franco, or a libellous accusation if one said they were involvedin such an attempt, or who think the miners are 'thick thickies', or that we mustn't be beastly to the intellectuals, are nothing to do with us and our movement, but constitute something separate, apart and hostile." "We spit them out as contemptible". Black Flag. 'Liars and Liberals' supplement. 1987. "Some of Eysenck's later work was funded by the Pioneer Fund, an organization which promoted scientific racism."wikipedia.org/wiki/Hans_Eysenck. The response from Gibson to Tyneside letters, of which I will not give space to, is briefly looked at in Freedom Vol 48 No 4. April 1987. To this day (December 2019 at time of writing) the Freedom book catalogue 2019 still lists'*Love, sex & power in later life*' by Tony Gibson.

649 Freedom Vol 48, No 2. February 1987.

650 Freedom Vol 48, No 3. March 1987.

651 Freedom Vol 48, No 5. May 1987.

652 Freedom Vol 48, No 1. January 1987.

653 Freedom Vol 48, No 2. February 1987.

654 The Tyneside Syndicalist. No 12. February 1987.

655 The Tyneside Syndicalist. No 13. March 1987. & Direct Action. No 38. April. 1987.

656 Liberation No 4. April/May 1987.

657 Viraj Mendis was a Sri Lankan 'national' who claimed the right of sanctuary at

the Church of the Ascension in Hulme, Manchester, late 1986 after 'overstaying his visa' and it was said would face the death penalty if returned to Sri Lanka. He was eventually 'deported' 1989. The Sri Lankan authorities dared not 'harm him' because of worldwide interest. He later moved to Germany.

658 Northern Anarchist Network. Internal bulletin No 5. April 1987.

659 Syndicalist Bulletin. No 1. Hull. Summer 1987.

660 *No Restrictions*. No 1. Gateshead / Durham zine. 1987. Ironically the Bust Fund itself went bust after paying a large fine of someone who smashed some windows in the Durham area, and who would later become a BNP fascist!!!! What a waste of money. Bust Fund also advertised in Common Ground. Newsletter No 3. October 1987. And *Hope*. No 1. Gateshead / Newcastle. 1987. *Guernica* No 1. 1987.

661 Tyneside Libertarian Books. Minutes of meeting. Newcastle. 26th April 1987.

662 Picket HFW. H.F.W. Plastics strike bulletin. No 2. Summer 1987.

663 The Tyneside Syndicalist. No 14. May 1987. The SUPPORT conference was also advertised in H.F.W. Plastics strike bulletin. No 2. Summer 1987. Syndicalist Bulletin. No 1. Hull. Summer 1987. Northern Anarchist Network. Internal bulletin No 6. Summer 1987. ACF internal bulletin No 8. July 1987. Etc. After the conference, a debate ensured following a report in Black Flag
which was deemed unacceptable and biased, and of which, because of length,I haven't delved into within this history. For the Black Flag correspondent reportof the conference see Black Flag No 174. 11/8/1987. And for M from Newcastle's response and protest at report see Black Flag No 175. 01/9/1987. For further report on conference by Newcastle ACF, see ACF internal bulletin No 9. September 1987.

664 Sept 1986 21 women were sacked from Ardbride Products in Ardrossan, Scotland. The workers made lampshades for sale at Laura Ashley shops.

665 Minutes of NAN meeting, Huddersfield. 6th June.1987. in Northern Anarchist Network. Internal bulletin No 6. Summer 1987.

666 Common Ground. Newsletter No 1. June 1987.

667 Minutes, national delegates meeting Jan 10th 1987. Minutes of delegates meeting 28th Feb. 1987. Minutes of ACF national conference 11th/12th April 1987.

668 ACF internal bulletin's No 7 (May 87) & No 8 (July 87) It is also worth considering that, again, this was in the days before computers, and not many people owned a typewriter. The work in producing a magazine was a time consuming endeavour. I have an A4 envelope full of original hand written articles etc for inclusion in *Virus*, most of which are barely readable scrawled affairs which then needed deciphered and edited / typed into becoming collectively agreed articles for

magazine, not to mention the lay out, inclusion of graphics, headlines, etc. An all consuming task for a few busy activists to also fit in with their personal lives. Even the simple task of collecting the mail involved the long journey on the bus, or long walk into the centre of Newcastle, up two flights of stairs to Common Ground office, collect mail, back down and out the building whilst trying to avoid the scrutiny of the two Special Branch loitering with intent in a nearby doorway watching you, then repeat journey home.

669 The Tyneside Syndicalist. No 15. June / July 1987.

670 Northern Anarchist Network. Internal bulletin No 8. September. 1987.

671 Direct Action No 41 July/Aug 1987. & Black Flag. No 173. 13th July. 1987.

672 Freedom Vol 48, No 9. September. 1987.

673 Minutes of NAN meeting. Leeds, 17th October 1987 from Northern Anarchist Network. Internal bulletin No 10. October / November. 1987.

674 Common Ground. Newsletter No 3. October 1987.

675 Newcastle ACF minutes of meeting's – 20th August / 16th September / 30th September / 8th October / 24th October all 1987. And on combining *Virus* & *Liberation* see ACF internal bulletin No 10. November 1987.

676 ACF internal bulletin No 10. November 1987.

677 Minutes of meeting 8/10/87. / Invitation letter to meeting / minutes of TAF meeting 3/11/87. / Newcastle ACF minutes of meeting 30/9/87 and minutes 24/10/87.

678 Tyneside Revolutionary Syndicalists proposals from meeting 13/10/87. &Minutes of The Tyneside Syndicalist readers meeting. Sun 15th November. 1987.

679 The Tyneside Syndicalist. No 16. Winter. 1987. 'Illusive' as I have a letter addressed to Tyneside Revolutionary Syndicalists from Newcastle Central Library requesting and asking if there was an issue 16 as No 15 was last issue received. A friend of mine, some 30+ years later, also thought he had the full collection of the paper with 15 issues, not knowing there was a 16th.

680 Advert for event in Common Ground. Newsletter No 1. June 1987. Anarchism section of timetable advertised in Freedom Vol 48 No 10 + No 11 Oct + Nov. 1987. And mentioned in Black Flag. No 177. 8th November 1987.[681] History Workshop 21. 44 page Programme for event. 1987.

682 Sinews. No 8. Durham, November 1987. / Freedom Vol 48, No 12. December. 1987. / Bust fund plea in Common Ground. Newsletter No 4. Winter. 1987. / Tyneside Anarchist Federation, minutes of meetings 13/12/87 & 18/12/87.

Newcastle ACF minutes of meetings 18/11/87 & 2/12/87.

683 Freedom Vol 48, No 12. December. 1987.

684 Common Ground. Newsletter No 6. Summer 1988.

685 Newcastle ACF minutes of meeting 2/12/87. Poll Tax conference see Direct Action No 45 Dec/Jan 1987/88. Announcement of conference in Direct Action No 43 October 1987. Minutes of conference meeting in ACF Internal Conference Bulletin April 1988.

686 Freedom Vol 49, No 1. January. 1988.

687 Tyneside Anarchist Federation, minutes of meeting, including copy of NF leaflet pushed through doors. 15th January 1988. & Tyneside Anarchist Federation news & invitation letter to next meeting.

688 Newcastle ACF minutes of meetings Jan 24th 1988 & 14th February 1988 & 6th March 1988 & Virus editorial group report, April 1988.

689 Newcastle ACF. Discussion meetings a4 leaflet / list. & Minutes of meeting 20th March 1988.

690 Black Flag. No 180. 21st March. 1988. See also ACF Internal Conference Bulletin. October 1988 which is full of letters back and forth between BlackFlag and ML.

691 Internal copy of proposed letter from Newcastle Direct Action Group to 'Gingerbread' committee.

692 ACF Internal Bulletin. No 14. August 1988 & Newcastle ACF. Discussion meetings a4 leaflet / list.

693 Newcastle ACF minutes of meeting 13th June. 1988 & Discussion meetings a4 leaflet / list.

694 ACF Internal Bulletin. No 14. August 1988.

695 Newcastle ACF minutes of meetings 13th June & 11th July & 25th July all 1988.

696 Common Ground. Newsletter / magazine No 8. 28th September 1988.

697 Copy of RM's resignation letter and responses in Minutes of ACF delegates meeting, Coventry 20/8/88. Letter from Newcastle ACF to delegates meeting and national IB, 8th August 88. & Newcastle ACF minutes of meetings 8th Aug 88 / 22nd Aug 88 / 12th Sept 88.

698 ACF Internal Conference Bulletin. October 1988.

699 Minutes of ACF conference. Sheffield 22nd + 23rd October. 1988. See also letter to national IB 25th Oct 88 from Newcastle. ACF Internal Bulletin No 15. December 1988.

700 Newcastle ACF minutes of meeting 28th November. 1988.

701 'Report back from 'Socialist Conference' Anti-Poll Tax meeting. Nottingham ACF member in ACF Internal Bulletin. No 16. February 1989.

702 The Heavy Stuff. Class War. No 1. December 1987. Class War newspaper issues (un-numbered) from 'Miners have the right idea' to No 31 which mentions Tyneside Class War as a contact. Some previous and forthcoming issues contained letters from the North East – but I know for a fact that a lot of letters were actually 'made-up'. See also *Rebel Alliances. The means and ends of contemporary British anarchism's*. B Franks. AK Press / Dark Star. 2006. *Thisis Class War*. Pamphlet. CW Fed 1986. *Bash The Rich*. Ian Bone. Tangent Books. 2006.

703 Direct Action. No 55. February 1989.

704 Newcastle ACF minutes of meeting 28th November. 1988. & ACF meeting; Organisation and activity on Tyneside, 12th February. 1989.

705 Tyneside Class War. Broadsheet. Early 1989.

706 Newcastle ACF meetings list Feb-June 1989. & ACF Internal Conference Bulletin. April 1989.

707 Tyneside Class War. Broadsheet. Early—mid 1989.

708 Strike! No 7. Teesside DAM. Spring 1989.

709 Text of speech, at public meeting of Newcastle ACF. May 8th 1989 in ACF Internal Bulletin No 17 June 1989. & Original poster advertising public meeting. & *The Myth of Labour's Socialism*. ACF pamphlet. 1990. For further 'expose' of Labours failings, see also *How Labour Governed 1945-1951*. Syndicalist Workers Federation. Direct Action Pamphlet No 5. & *Vote Labour and Still Die Horribly.* Thames Valley Anarchists. Pamphlet. 1986.

710 Tyneside Class War. Broadsheet. mid 1989. And the local paper *The Sunday Sun* (which was the Sunday version of the *Evening Chronicle*) had a front page spread on the day under the heading of 'Thugs on rampage' with apicture of masked anti-fascist. Sunday Sun. June 11th 1989. The cover was reproduced within the Tyneside Class War. Broadsheet. See also letter (24th May) from Newcastle ACF to national Bulletin No 17 June 1989 informing of BNP rally.

711 *Housing, Development and Newcastle...Who's Initiative?* Pamphlet. Elephant Touch Productions. Newcastle. 1989.

712 Original poster for Newcastle 'Rock against the rich' gig. & A4 leaflet giving out at event. See also Tyneside Class War / Newcastle ACF minutes of joint general meeting 9th October 1989.

713 ACF Internal Bulletin No 18. August 1989.

714 Class War Federation. Internal Bulletin No 14. Late 1989.

715 Strike! No 9. Teesside DAM. November / December 1989.

716 Tyneside Class War group report, in Class War Federation Internal Bulletin.No 17. 1990.

717 Strike! No 10. Teesside DAM. February 1990.

718 http://www.workers.org.uk/features/feat_1010/ambulance.html

719 Unbeknown to us at the time... "Now, given I had never attended a meeting of TWAFA (Tyne & Wear Anti Fascist Association), I do not regard suchan expulsion as *personal* either. They were simply acting in the interests of *Searchlight* / MI5, for whom they are a nice little training-ground. They were not to know at that point that I was fully aware of the TWAFA practice of photographing sellers of the anarchist paper *Class War* on Tyneside in early 1993. Again though, giving that photographing anarchists is something that an anti-*fascist* organisation should have no part of, and seems highly likely to have been carried out in the interests of local Special Branch at least (if not MI5)". *Turning up the Heat – MI5 after the Cold War.* Larry O' Hara. Phoenix Press. London. 1994.

720 Ian R, reporter – Sunday Sun letter to Class War Federation, Bristol. (photocopy of..)

721 Undated copied press cutting from The Sunday Sun. 'Clarke poster fury'.

722 Newcastle ACF group report for National Bulletin. March 1990.

723 A participant (ex Tyneside Class War activist). See also 'minutes of the regions meeting 10th march' in Class War Federation National Internal Bulletin No 17. 1990.

724 Freedom Vol 51, No 8. 21st April. 1990. Letter from DM.

725 *Poll Tax Riot – 10 hours that shook Trafalgar Square*. ACAB Press. June 1990.

726 Freedom Vol 44, No 15. 30th July. 1983.

727 Letter from BN of Darlington to Class War Federation, Manchester address (on poster), and included in Class War Federation National Internal Bulletin No 19. Mid to late 1990.

728 Tyneside Class War. Poll Tax leaflet. May 1990.

[729] The Independent Magazine. 26th May 1990.

[730] For further, and in my personal opinion, an inadequate look at the relationship of Class War and punk see *The Punk Anarchisms of Class War & Crimethinc*. Sheena P. Rocker & Rudolf Ramon. Active Distribution. 2018. A great pamphlet, but the Class War section relies on information gleaned from some who were around the formative years of CW and not the Federation years of this particular period. And of course, not a single mention of Tyneside.

[731] *Non Payers Guide to the Poll Tax*. Tyneside Class War & Newcastle ACF. Pamphlet. 1990.

[732] E.g. – see Class War. No 42. 1990. Page 4. And many issues after this.

[733] Class War Federation National Internal Bulletin No 19. Mid to late 1990. For Tyneside Class War library – see internal library list's No's 1 + 2. Thislibrary would, after 30+ years eventually become Tyneside Anarchist Archive.

[734] Class War. No 42. 1990.

[735] Not the Socialist Workers Anti-Poll Tax News. Sunderland. 1990.

[736] See – Summary of discussions, ACF national conference May 1990, which includes proposal put forward from London Class War on a merger and discussion surrounding idea. & Class War Federation National Internal Bulletin No 19. Mid to late 1990. & Notes for the ACF delegates meeting 7th July 1990. & Minutes of meeting held between CWF/ACF in Nottingham 15th July 1990. & ACF Internal Bulletin No 23 July 1990. & ACF Internal Bulletin September 1990. & ACF conference minutes 27th October 1990 which mentions that two letters from Class War had been received which stated "the possibility of a merger had been a good 'kick up the arse' for Class War's development – but their development had to take priority."

[737] Tyneside Class War statement regarding merger, distributed at Manchester Weekend School, 1990 and included in Class War Federation National Internal Bulletin No 19. Mid to late 1990. A 'theory group', with Luton Class War as co-ordinators was set up within the Federation to further explore and establish the 'theory & politics' of the Fed, the result being the eventual release of *Unfinished Business...The Politics of Class War*. AK Press. May 1992.

[738] Ex Newcastle Anarchist Communist Federation member & ex Tyneside Class War activist ( not member ) from https://tynesideanarchistarchive.wordpress.com/2018/03/31/poll-tax/

[739] The Raven No 11. Freedom Press. Vol 3 No 3. July / Sept 1990.

[740] Tyneside Class War Members & Supporters Internal bulletin. October / November.1990.

741 *Militant* newspaper, Oct / Nov 1990? article reprinted in Class War Internal Bulletin No 21. See also letter from All Britain Anti poll Tax Federation to Trafalgar Square Defendants Campaign regarding events of the day and complaints of 'unruly' behaviour etc in Class War IB No 22. 1991.

742 Freedom Vol 52, No 1. 12th January. 1991.

743 ACF Internal Bulletin. January 1991. And see Freedom Vol 51 No 18 September 1990 / No 20 October / No 21 November / No 24 December / and Vol 52 No 1 January 1991. & *The Role of the Revolutionary Organisation* ACF pamphlet. 1990.

744 Tyneside Class War – *'Kick the Tories out? We say kick them in'* leaflet. November 1990.

745 Tyneside Class War Members & Supporters Internal bulletin. No 3.December. 1990.

746 Tyneside Class War Members & Supporters Internal bulletin. No 6.March/April. 1991.

747 Evening Chronicle. March 1991. (Undated original news clipping).

748 Tyneside Class War - welcome letter / agenda / map / conference guide.

749 Merseyside Anarchist Newsletter. Number 27. May 1991.

750 The Heavy Stuff No 4. Newcastle. April. 1991. For the full letter andthoughts on its editing by TJ, see ACF Internal Bulletin. August 1991.

751 Tyneside Class War – 20th June. 1991. Internal handout / diary of events.

752 Hot Time: Summer on the estates. Riots in the UK, 1991-92. BM Blob. Computer text print off.

753 *Goliath. Britain's Dangerous Places*. Beatrix Campbell. Methuen. 1993.

754 The Hockler. Tyneside and the North East. No 1. Autumn. 1991.

755 All in a nights 'work'! The act of stealing a car to go ram raiding was actually called 'Grafting' by Gateshead (& other local) 'youths', who seen it as , admittedly an exciting and dangerous, 'chore', 'work', or 'graft' – something that had to be done to survive. For example see *Ramraiders*. Stephen Richards. Mirage Publishing. Gateshead. 2000.

756 Hot Time: Summer on the estates. Riots in the UK, 1991-92. BM Blob.

757 Regular mini-busses full of rioters (and gallons of petrol) were travelling back and forth between the West End of Newcastle and North Tyneside to partake in events. "The West End of Newcastle, Scotswood and Elswick were sending reinforcements by mini-bus and these were not police reinforcements either believe it

or not! They were reinforcement rioters bringing up the rearguard action. We are actually talking about rioters getting together to organise this in a professional manner what with transport laid on you would have thought that they would have even had a mobile catering unit like film crews have laid on for them. "Egg and chips twice, oh, and a Molotov please"." *Viv 'Simply the best'*. Stephen Richards. Mirage Publishing.Gateshead. 1998.

758 Class War. No 50. Late 1991.

759 *Viv 'Simply the best'*. Stephen Richards. Mirage Publishing. Gateshead. 1998.

760 ACF Internal Bulletin. March 1992. & see ACF IB Jan 1992 ref new members.

761 The Heavy Stuff. Special Edition. Tyneside / Edinburgh.1992. & see alsoThe Heavy Stuff. No 5.

762 Resignation letter (4/1/93) from TJ, Newcastle ACF to ACF Internal Bulletin Jan 1993.

763 Various mail outs and minutes of group meetings of Tyneside Anarchist Group - November 1995 to 1997. /1993 Xmas social leaflet./draft of a worldto win leaflet / draft of anti election alliance leaflet / lock out benefit night leaflets / out of the ghetto meeting agenda & leaflet / Orwell + anarchism leaflet./ anti election day 1st of May leaflet / criminal injustice act – leaflet / this is TAG. Leaflet / reclaim / roots of Mayday leaflet. / May day social leaflet. / uniting our struggles - roots of mayday. Leaflet. / A4 4-page leaflet - what is anarchism etc. /constitution of TAG + aims + principles.

764 'Danger! Anarchists on Tyneside!' leaflet. Tyneside Anarchist Group. Newcastle. 1992.

765 Internal Newcastle ACF discussion paper prior to, and for, inclusion in national ACF Internal Bulletin No 18. August 1989. Further discussion / writing on this subject by TJ also appeared in ACF Internal Bulletin No 20. December 1989.